Anima

Also by Kapka Kassabova

Anima

A Wild Pastoral

KAPKA KASSABOVA

Graywolf Press

First published in 2024 by Jonathan Cape, an imprint of Vintage and part of Penguin Random House UK, London.

Quotation from *Goatwalking* by Jim Corbett reproduced by permission of Pat Corbett.

This publication is made possible, in part, by the voters of Minnesota through a Minnesota State Arts Board Operating Support grant, thanks to a legislative appropriation from the arts and cultural heritage fund. Significant support has also been provided by other generous contributions from foundations, corporations, and individuals. To these organizations and individuals we offer our heartfelt thanks.

MINNESOTA
STATE ARTS BOARD

CLEAN
WATER
LAND &
LEGACY
AMENDMENT

Published by Graywolf Press
212 Third Avenue North, Suite 485
Minneapolis, Minnesota 55401

www.graywolfpress.org

Published in the United States of America

ISBN 978-1-64445-300-1 (paperback)
ISBN 978-1-64445-301-8 (ebook)

2 4 6 8 9 7 5 3 1
First Graywolf Printing, 2024

Library of Congress Control Number: 2023950735

Cover design and art: Kimberly Glyder

Gods as well as animals once spoke to us. Now each self talks to itself. Maybe the subject of self is unobservable because it really isn't there at all . . . To learn why you feel compelled to remake and consume the world, live alone in the wilderness for at least a week. Don't plan things to do when the week is over. Do nothing but celebrate the goodness of the Creation – if you can.

Jim Corbett, *Goatwalking*

You sleep badly, dear, bad dreams you dream.
'I sleep badly, bad dreams I dream when I lie behind the rug.'
Tell me your dreams, I'll read them for you.
'My horse was muddy, my saddle broken.'
The horse is farewell, dear, the broken saddle is the road.

Karakachan wedding song

This book is inspired by the humans and canines still dedicated to pastoralism. These brave and loyal ones walk through the world unseen.

Pastoralism is the movement of humans and grazing animals in search of pasture. This way of life can range from daily outings in the hills to seasonal transhumance, to full-scale nomadism. The synchronic movement of ruminants, dogs and humans is key. In the past 100 years, pastoralism in all its forms has been pushed to the brink by hard borders, urbanisation and industrialisation, mechanised farming, monoculture, the ideology of endless growth and the breakdown of humanity's relationship with the organic world.

Moving pastoralism is ancient. One of its first homelands was the Balkans where flocks moved along south–north trails until the second half of the twentieth century. Since then, there are no more nomads in Europe. However, pastoralism is retained as a way of life by a handful of embattled people. This is the story of the time I spent with one such community on the western flanks of the Pirin Mountains.

Contents

Anima is soul in Latin. It is the root of the word animal – one with breath, soul and life. The Karakachan nomads called it psyche (*pshi-hi*). It appeared to them as breath, mist or wind.

BLACK WATER, SUMMER

From the edge of the dwarf-pine grove, Black Water is laid out like a drawing. The river's bone-white bed hasn't yet dried up. The two waterfalls are lively, then the water thins when it hits the floor of our valley. In late summer, it goes completely underground and you hear it but can't see it. That's why it's called Black Water, the old shepherds said. The old shepherds are gone and what's left of them are the names they gave to every spring and creek. Little Horseback, Orelek Lakes, Horse Plaza, Borovan, Zagaza, Etip – all of them named after vanished animals, humans, plants and events remembered by the mountain.

Black Water is a river that begins at the glacial lakes below Thunder Peak and passes through our steepish marble valley. The river makes a perfect vulva-shaped loop out of its own bed, then continues as a single stream down the terraces of the mountain until it joins the river known since forever as Strymon, Strymonas or Struma. The god of the river Strymon was born of Tethys and Oceanus, and on coins his hair is crazy like a tangle of snakes or a web of tributaries. And up here, we literally live inside the head of the mountain gods.

When the sun declines over the other mountain to the west – a mountain with a different character and shape from ours – then our little valley is plunged into a shadow so cold, you reach for a log to put in the stove. If you haven't gathered enough dry wood and it rains, you are in trouble. But you are in trouble no matter what.

After some weeks here, I can't tell the inside from the outside. I am wrestling with a force that feels daimonic. Whether it first appeared inside me or outside of me, I don't know, but now it is everywhere. I can't see the other hut from here, only their smoke. They are not bothering me, they're just sitting there drinking. Again. The only sober one is the child.

I count the dogs by our hut, all there. It's a habit now, to check who's here and who's not: Topi, Gashta the pants mother and daughter, Kasho, Kito, Balkán, Redhead. Only Muna the Monkey can't be seen because she is under the bed, digging a hole in the earth.

The dogs are my only true friends in this valley of quick sunsets and rock stacks shaped like things older than anything the mind can grasp, this valley where heaven turns to hell as quickly as breath turns to wind. I sit on a flat stone and battle with anger, not for the first time. How quickly everything comes and goes. The mountain is vast. You are small and so are your animals who are not yours, you are just their caretaker and they – yours. Sásho said it: 'You live if the animals live, and you die if they die. In the lower world you fool yourself that you're top of the heap, but here it's fifty-fifty in your favour. Or less.'

Just a few weeks ago, I couldn't wait to come here. The high pastures are where you come to be free and contemplate every flower, I was told, like on some yoga retreat. But only a few people actually spend the whole summer here – the shepherds.

The glacier above is in the shape of an angel with its wings spread over Black Water. We look at it every day and wonder if it's shrinking. Above it is the sphinx of Thunder Peak, a round-headed hammer at 2,914 metres, poised to smite us without notice. Everything here happens without notice, and this landslide of the mind happens every second day like clockwork. It's psycho-geological. The stones slip under your feet. The riverbank slips and the mare slipped into the gorge with Vasko the drunk cowherd.

'Life here is a game of roulette,' I'd said to Sásho, 'I can't take it anymore.'

'Russian roulette,' he said. 'It's not for you. I try my best but it's the nature of it.'

The nature of it is, they are drinking again. I understand them – it's a way out. Any day now, Kámen will come up with provisions and then I'll leave. I don't know what day of the week it is. We keep our phones turned off to save battery. Night closes in. I stumble down the scree to our empty hut where the fire has gone out and my pot with the last vegetables is half-cooked. I will rekindle it and wait.

I don't like being a woman who waits. But this is what you do here: you wait and endure.

The dogs will come and put their heads on my lap, one by one: Muna the Monkey, Topi, Redhead, Gashta the pants mother and daughter, the two toughies Kito and Kasho, even Balkán who has never put his head anywhere near me.

I stop to look at the dead ram. The eyes were pecked by crows within an hour of him dying in a lethal headbutt with another ram. It's mating season, 'a madhouse' the shepherds say, a favourite word.

'Fighting to the death for love,' Sásho said. 'Nothing we can do.'

The empty sockets confirm it: nothing we can do.

PART ONE
ORELEK

ENTERING THE CIRCLE

This story begins with a picture. A man stands inside a circle of goats. Their black-and-white coats touch the ground. They have horns like sabres and hermit faces. He does not look at the camera but at the goats. Consumed, I thought, he is consumed by his animals. Immediately, I knew that a way of life that stretched back to some unknown time was contained in this moment. The picture began to move before my eyes. I saw a fanning out of human and animal flocks across mountains and river flats, like black-and-white rugs being aired in the wind. And I felt an urge to follow them.

Outside the frame was the whole of the Pirin Mountains. I'd spent several seasons along the Mesta River that defines eastern Pirin. That became *Elixir*. It was an old mountaineer from Mesta who gave me the album with this moving picture and by doing this, he opened a new gateway – through the centre of the mountains to their western side. That side was unknown to me. At home in Scotland, I'd open the album of Pirin and turn the pages of its seasons: granite peaks, millennial pines, edelweiss like cosmic velvet, golden eagles, lone people in remote villages and – the man with the long-coated goats.

This is what I found out: his name was Kámen, and he and his brother Achilles were experts in a legendary breed of dog called Karakachan. The Kará-kachán is an ancient dog, one of the few remaining ones. I'd come across them in earlier visits with mountain shepherds. Their eyes were human. They walked with the loose gait of wolves and the puppies were like bear cubs, with expressions so knowing they stopped you in your tracks and made you stare as if into the eyes of an old friend. They were aloof and conscious of it: we don't need you, you need us and here we are because love is different from need. Superior, in fact.

These dogs had followed the pastoral trail across mountains and centuries. No – they had *made* it. Dogs, humans, horses and grazing animals, together. Any paths that are there on the map, or off the map are there thanks to these dogs.

Just thirty years ago, Karakachan dogs were in danger of disappearing. To think that these dogs that were more than dogs and at the same time the epitome of dog, would be extinct by now, had it not been for these two brothers was unthinkable. The reason why these dogs were disappearing was because the pastoral ways were disappearing. They still are, thirty years on.

Moving pastoralism emerged in Central Asia, the Balkans and the Mediterranean several thousand years ago. It began with the domestication of sheep and goats, and it was in its European heartland that nomadic shepherding lasted the longest – until the middle of the twentieth century. Even the word nomad hints that wandering and grazing go together: the Greek *nomas* means 'wandering shepherd' or 'wandering in search of pasture'.

There were four cataclysms in the last 100 years that led to the extinguishment of the nomad hearth. These convulsions affected first the nomads and eventually, everyone in the pastoral world. With them came the end or near-end of breeds of animals, humans and ways of being.

The first was the drawing of new national borders between Greece, Bulgaria and Turkey in the wake of the First World War. This made the movement of caravans exorbitant and dangerous.

The second was the complete closure of these same borders after the Second World War when the Cold War froze relations and the Iron Curtain put an end to all movement of animals, people and people with animals from the Aegean and Thracian lowlands of the Balkans to their mountainous interior. The old transhumance trail was severed but nomads endured in each country for a bit longer. The last nomads were the Karakachans.

The third cataclysm came in 1957: collectivisation. It meant the wholesale theft and sometimes the slaughter of animals belonging to transhumant shepherds and to all livestock owners in Bulgaria. That was almost everyone outside the cities, and the cities were still small in an economy driven by the very thing that the communist state most coveted – large-scale sheep breeding and agriculture. The Karakachans had more animals than most. It's all they had and they lost it.

The fourth cataclysm came forty years later: privatisation. Communism collapsed and the state cooperatives politically engineered at the cost of so much human and animal suffering were expediently dismantled. In a free-for-all, animals were slaughtered en masse or sold and shipped abroad, and vast infrastructures were left to decay. With that came the quick decline of the guardian dog.

In the late 1990s, a group of penniless animal lovers took out a loan and moved into the crumbling village of Orelek in western Pirin. The mission was to establish a haven for endangered breeds of dogs, sheep and horses. Over the centuries, those breeds were preserved by the Karakachans with religious devotion. It all comes back to them.

The Balkan Karakachans are one of the oldest nomadic peoples to have entered modernity with their animals. They are Greek speakers of mysterious origin, probably descended from pre-historic Thracian-Illyrian pastoralists Romanised and Hellenised over time. It is impossible to know the homeland of the Karakachans. They came from several different places but in recent centuries it has been, symbolically at least, the Pindus Mountain. Though most of them never set foot there because they were scattered over so many other mountains across the southern Balkans. It's the nature of the nomad.

Nobody knows for sure why the Karakachans are called this, but *kara-kachan* means 'black fugitive' in Turkish. True, they wore clothes spun from the wool of their black sheep, but it was the way they were seen by others too: quick-moving wanderers who could cross any terrain with their ancient-looking animals often at night, without leaving a trace. The Greek is Sarakatsani, which is simply a Hellenised form of Karakachani, but some fancy that it might derive from their mooted homeland of Sirako in the Pindus and Sirako means 'sad' in Albanian, 'poor' in Romanian and 'orphan' in Bulgarian – yet another tale of how nomads were perceived by the settled ones. But the settled ones were not always settled.

Pastoralists have criss-crossed the Balkans for thousands of years and with time, the difference between nomads and settled pastoralists became more marked. Although everyone with grazing animals walked an established trail, there was a difference in scale and social set-up. The nomads travelled as communities and covered hundreds of kilometres between winter and summer pastures and lived in seasonal huts. Settled pastoralists, like the highlanders of Pirin, also covered large distances between lowland and highland pasture, but only the men went off with the animals, while their families remained to keep the village fires burning.

The Karakachans lived the nomadic life to the end. Nobody knows when the beginning was. Their language is a northern Greek dialect with words that go back to the time of Homer and with Balkan words woven in – Albanian, Bulgarian, Turkish. They were Greek Orthodox practising a blend of stiff Abrahamic patriarchy and worship of the Virgin Mary and Saint George, protector of shepherds. Their own identifier was *Vlachi*. That's an umbrella term for moving mountain shepherds. There was another big group under that umbrella, the Aromanian Vlachs, but the two groups kept themselves apart and spoke, dressed and treated animals differently. The Karakachans saw themselves as exceptional. And, like all the nomads, they were indeed the exception to the rule; the rule being settled living.

There's a vocabulary that goes with nomadism. For centuries, all Balkan nomads were called one of two things: Vlachi or the more disparaging *chergari* – rug people, ones whose homes are made of rugs. Rugs carried by horses, then horse carts, then trains and finally, not at all. The chergari included the Gypsies and in some sense, all nomads were seen as Gypsies. Gypsy is synonymous with the eternal traveller.

The earliest written evidence of Vlachs is from an early eleventh-century Byzantine writer. He talks to a group of Vlach men in Thessaly who are about to join an armed revolt against the imperial authorities (a recurring theme for shepherds, that). He asks them: 'and where are your women and children?' 'In the highlands of Bulgaria,' they answer, 'with our flocks.' In the fifteenth and sixteenth centuries there came another lot of shepherd nomads – the Yuruks,

Turkic wanderers sent by the Ottoman state as settlers. Unsettled settlers, that is. The word Yuruk means 'walker' or 'one who got away'.
Inconveniently mobile in their Anatolian homeland, they were more
useful to the empire in the Balkans. They stayed for a few centuries
and made their mark but the others were here before them and stayed
after them, until they too were dispersed and settled.

Only their animals remained in the hills – just.

The mountain sheep was the first grazing animal to be domesticated by humans. It happened around 11,000 years ago in Central
Asia and south-east Europe. The Vlachs called their mountain sheep
'the oldest sheep in the world' and studies show that they were probably right. It is the same with their mountain horses, donkeys and
guard dogs who all evolved but remained genetically stable over time
thanks to the – oddly enough – conservative nature of nomadic life.
These breeds of animals have all come to be known by a single word:
Karakachan.

And miraculously, some of them were still around. I found
Kámen's email and asked if I could visit.

'If you must,' he replied.

It was the hottest August in memory. I was renting a flat in a spa
town along the Struma River. The town was flanked by two mountains and both of them were ablaze with forest fires. Ash fell on my
balcony. People stood outside and watched the turbid sky. I wondered if they would run or stay. I packed my bag just in case.

In a sense, I was already running. I had spent part of two seasons
criss-crossing eastern Pirin with a rather odd villager called Emin,
tracking his twenty wild horses. They moved across large distances
and we walked for days through autumnal beech forests, creeks that
never saw the sun and waist-deep snow, risking injury and exposure.
Emin didn't care for his life and cared only slightly more about mine.
But he gave his all for the horses. He carried an axe and nothing else,
not even socks under his Wellington boots. Gripped by fascination
and affection, I stayed too long in his inhospitable terrain. It was a
beautiful terrain. The horses were Karakachan horses – thin, agile,
muscular, brown-black, made for roaming the mountains. They

could survive on pine needles in winter. Emin could have taken enough subsidies to live on but he didn't have the wits or patience to do the paperwork, so he kept the horses out of attachment and broke his back in menial jobs. He could not bear to sell a single one, knowing they would end up as sausages or beasts of burden for the last of the forest loggers. He too had been a logger, of the pre-industrial variety. For twenty-five years, he and his father transported logs on horseback across the Pirin-Rila-Rhodope highlands, some of Europe's most inaccessible terrain. Then his father died and the horses went wild. They roamed above his highland village in winter and in the pre-alpine belt in summer. He slept with them, took them salt and bread, walked uncountable miles for them and loved and hated them for making him a prisoner of the mountain. And I walked some of those miles with him, loving and hating it with him. Quickly, the enchantment turned to exhaustion. His moods were like mountain weather – electrical and extreme. He could not switch off. A human misfit, wired for the wild, his one relationship was with his horse family.

Emin was my age, and the last of the wildmen. His isolation was crushing, a Stone-Age loneliness in a digital era. After him, there would be no horses, no story, no places-as-faces, just tourists in search of the last man and his horse. I couldn't bear that knowledge. I wanted to record our walks, his memories and the way he spoke and saw things, even when it became clear that it was unsafe to dwell in those weather swings. I kept going back. And here I was that burning summer.

'If you leave now, I'll hang myself and you'll have to feast at my wake,' Emin said, lying on the bare floor of a guesthouse room, not letting me sleep for two nights.

'Because my life is a dog's life,' he said.

I had carried logs in the mud with him, wet beech heavy as iron and he was paid 20 euros at the end of the day. I had waded with him in the snow and returned without feeling in my feet, having not found the horses and fearing them dead under the snow. I had entered his world but couldn't stay there, it was too animistic. He couldn't enter my world at all, it was too humanistic.

In those last days together, communication between us broken down, we just walked. It's what we always did. We hiked with an old cowboy called Kosta, up the terraced peaks, past the ruined stone houses and sheep pens of vanished shepherds, to a remote plateau called The Stable. Kosta had several hundred free-grazing cows and the largest herd of Karakachan horses in Pirin, and it took a four-hour hike to see them where they grazed in summer, where there had never been a man-made stable, just the open stable of the mountain.

After that, I just ran. We were always saying goodbyes on high roads. I would drive on and Emin would climb into the cliffs, both of us in tears, like in an old western. But that last goodbye was cold and furious.

'You've deprived me of sleep for two nights. That's torture. They do that to people in dictatorships. I was your friend all this time, but you're not my friend. Get out of my car.'

He wouldn't, so I pushed him out. He didn't protest. Physically gentle, verbally unhinged, that was his way. A big child with tantrums. A dog that barks does not bite, they say, but I didn't want to test that theory anymore.

'Don't ever step on my territory again or I won't answer for my actions!' he spat, and walked away fast, flinging his fringe like his Haflinger.

It would have been devastating had I not been at the end of my tether, like the stallions when you tie them up. I just needed to go somewhere peaceful and sleep.

We parted at a mountain pass by a ruin called Vlahinska Chapel. The nomads had bivouacked here with their herds for so many generations, they'd built a church next to their huts and next to the church had been a dervish monastery, gone now, without a trace. Today, there were hotels that all looked the same. The gravestones from both temples had long been recycled.

So this story also begins with Emin and his horses.

My need to live inside this mountain was more acute than ever. Walking over the horizon with Emin had created a momentum. I'd lost my guide but not the momentum. I had to recover my strength, accept the predicted parting of ways and stay on the road. I drove westwards.

After the pass, the light softened, the air became fragrant. The smell of rosemary, fig and grapes. Sandy soil, shimmering heat. Vineyards everywhere, and birds. An old, old world. The road followed the basin of the Struma which ran parallel to the Mesta. Struma-Strymonas was once a trade artery 415 kilometres long, well known to the ancients. Aristotle tracked the progress of birds migrating between the Danube and Africa and shadowing the Strymonas some of the way, and the route in the sky was named after him – Via Aristoteles. There are no birds when there are wild fires, though.

From my rented flat, I watched the horizon grow a murky yellow. A young Russian sat on the stairs singing a sad song to her baby. Two builders joined in from their scaffolding. People of various nationalities bought flats here because of the Mediterranean climate and the curative waters, but many of them lay empty. A Roma couple trained their dog in the grove of figs between apartment buildings in silence. The whole world felt the way I felt – post-traumatic. Or perhaps pre-traumatic.

'Can we come with you if the fire spreads?' asked my landlady who lived next door with her small grandson. They had no car. 'Of course.' We stood on our balconies.

'Are we going to die?' asked the boy, who had packed a rucksack too.

'Don't say stupid things,' his grandmother said.

This is what it's like now – watching the horizon with your bag packed, an imminent refugee and even an eight-year-old knows it.

Every evening, I went to a luxury spa hotel up the hill and sat in the outside pool with a mountain view. Pampered Europeans chattered in their languages and soaked their designer swimsuits, cocktails in hand, while I thought of Emin pacing inside the labyrinth of his mountain emptied of animals and people, wearing his patched trousers, talking to himself, then the horses, ranting at this mad world, then at me for abandoning him, then at himself, then at this mad world where there is no place for him and his beasts, and he might as well shoot them all.

The soul, like the earth, does not like extremes. With Emin, I nearly froze to death at the glacial lakes, and by sharing his incurable sorrow for a time, I did not alleviate it. Yet neither did I want to sit in the pool of the pampered people at the foot of the burning mountain. Is there a middle path – for me, for anyone, anymore? Perhaps that is what's needed – the forgotten middle path.

To get to Orelek, I drove up the Struma. An international road follows the river, busy with lorries with number plates from Romania, Germany, Holland, Poland, Greece and Ukraine. There is a trainline. River, railway, road. The river is all but forgotten. The railway is unkempt though it still takes people from north to south and back. The road is narrow, lorries and holidaymakers crash every year.

This is a confluence. I smell it before I understand it. On one side is the soft Maleshevo Mountain. On the other is Pirin with its vertical terraces and climates. The Pirin massif is a continuation of the Alps, they were formed at the same time. Its lower flanks are sandy ridges. The next floor is blue-green with pine and beech forests, then the sub-alpine belt and finally, a row of peaks crowned by the deathly white sphinx with a round head: Thunder Peak.

The little town of Kresna lies at the foot of a sand ridge called Melo. Two black storks circle above a burned-out factory. I took a turn-off to a forgotten place: Orelek, meaning eagle brae.

Orelek was ten kilometres uphill, there were big holes in the tarmac, then the tarmac ended. Columns of sand trailed my old Subaru, bought for this journey. A canyon opened to one side. The River Orelek springs below Thunder Peak and joins Struma in the scenic Kresna Gorge. At a roadside fountain dubbed Warm Spout was a fork. One leg went to Orelek. The other went higher and had a faded sign for hikers: THUNDER PEAK 12HRS, SINANITSA 19HRS. Goats rested in the shade. I glimpsed a round man with a stick, but not his face – the goatherd. His three dogs chased my car. Dark wooded hills rose on all sides like obstacles.

The road became hostile, as if someone had taken a sledgehammer to it to bar access to Orelek. It took dedication to keep going. The village, perched above the canyon, was long, scattered and empty.

Kámen didn't answer his phone and I had no idea where to look
for him. In the square, a weeping willow stroked a lopsided wooden
table with benches. Handsome buildings with broken windows lined
the square whose centrepiece was two monuments. One to a fanatical
revolutionary from the early twentieth century who had committed
many crimes against civilians and run a merciless state-within-a-state
in these mountains. And another, to the local highlanders who
resisted the theft of their livestock during collectivisation half a century later. The two were not directly related but a common thread
ran through both: terror.

A few houses looked as if they had been spruced up and there was
an old church, vegetable gardens and other patchy habitation. Stone
stacks in amphibian shapes reminded you of the basin of a pre-historic
ocean. The place was muted and apart from the world.

A gated house next to the willow might be Kámen's. I opened the
gate: a tiled courtyard, a pen with goat kids who munched and looked
at me critically under their curly fringes and fluffy Karakachan
puppies who tumbled towards me with happy yelps.

Two doors down, I knocked on a house with a fig tree. A sign said
it was once the village school. It had been rebuilt by volunteers. Cats
hissed from the balcony above. Among them appeared a small man
with a wizened face.

'I have nothing to do with Kámen,' he shouted irritably. There
were sounds of drips in the house and I thought I glimpsed a small
figure inside, like a child with a white head.

'He'll be at the sheep house.'

'Where is the sheep house?'

'You could stand on a rock and shout his name.'

'What about this house?' I shouted.

'This house is a nature centre. Or was before the pandemic. Good
luck. You'll need it.'

And he and the cats vanished from the balcony.

The air was like an oven. I left the car by the willow and walked
the dirt road that climbed out of the village, crossing a river called
Kosovska. A logging truck stacked with pines roared past. A stately
new building dominated the village from a hilltop. This was a visitor

centre for large predators, built by Kámen's family with international help. Everything here signalled their ambitious mission, set up twenty years ago: to safeguard indigenous breeds of guardian dog, horse, sheep and goats, plus rescued bears and wolves in open-air enclosures. The visitor centre was built to showcase the history, heritage, and habits of bears and wolves. And to show people that domesticated grazing animals and predators can, and should, exist side-by-side.

What made this coexistence possible was the guardian dog.

So this ghost village was kept going by a small handful of animal-lovers. They had come down the Struma River from the North in the last twenty-five years, while the last of the actual villagers left and died out.

But all was not well here. It was in the air, like a silent 'No'. Should I light a candle? But the church was locked.

At the top of the village, among the creature-like stone stacks and ruined houses stood a small farmhouse with a wooden balcony from which a sturdy bearded man watched me. A chorus of barking broke out. A dozen Karakachan dogs stood at the base and barked at me with impressive maws. They were big-headed dogs with thick coats that reminded me of Tibetan Mastiffs.

One of them was chained to a rock with a crack in it. Everything here was attached to rock, hewn from rock, reclaimed from rock or possessed the qualities of rock. The river gully dropped sharply below the house, like a moat. The man came downstairs. Three puppies like furballs were barking like they meant it.

'They don't bite,' he said with an amused face that reassured me more than his words. This was Achilles.

I squeezed past them into the courtyard, like I was squeezing through moving furniture. A covered sheep pen stretched all the way around the house, some animals huddled in the back. Ram horns, chains and sheep hides hung everywhere in the yard, left behind after the death of an animal. It was a temple full of totems.

At the outside sink stood Kámen in a beanie, washing a bloodied knife and beside him was his mother, a petite woman with an acerbic face and elegant bead necklaces.

'Everything is interesting for you, isn't it,' she said acidly.

Kámen glanced at me sideways without a word. He was stocky and intense with brooding black eyes and stubble.

To enter a closed circle, you must do it on their terms, not yours, I reminded myself. The dogs sat in a circle around me, curious. The puppies climbed my legs. Kámen's mother invited me into the kitchen for a mug of raw goat's milk. It was thick and fragrant.

'Milking, till kingdom come,' she said. 'The goatherd is on holiday and Kámen is goatherd. But he can't do it every day so we feed them in the pen. Not cheap.'

She opened a big ledger and wrote something in it.

'But they are all good boys. When I shout: "bag boys!", they run and pick up a bag.'

Sacks of animal feed everywhere, loaded and unloaded from vans, trailers and human backs – sacks of dog food, goat fodder and birdfeed because there was also an aviary of pigeons, guineafowls, hens and other birds that laid eggs in the fig tree by the washing line.

'And of course, I move hay bales too, 100 kilos,' said the mother. I felt buttonholed already, a sign of having entered the circle.

On your own? I asked.

'No, not on my own, with the misery. I shout: Misery! And there she comes. Do you know how you tease out hay from a bale? It's easier to tease it out of this table. I was once an elegant woman. Now I am a bag lady.'

You are still elegant, I said.

'Come and stay as long as you like,' she said.

I'll just fetch my things from the rented flat, then. Where could I sleep?

'Anywhere. The whole village is ours,' she said bitterly.

There was nowhere else to stay in the village other than the centre for large predators, which the locals called 'the hotel', but it wasn't open to visitors. Ruined houses with collapsed balconies were everywhere.

It was just Kámen and his family, the farm workers, the grumpy man with the cats and a few other houses that were being used part-time. The family had three buildings in the village: the sheep house, the goat house with rocky outcrops that the goats climbed when they were not out on pasture and the centre for large predators on the hill, half of which had seminar rooms and hostel-style bedrooms, and the other half was used for storing haybales. It had once been a barn. Marina, a biologist and Kámen's wife, ran wilderness camps for children. Later, I saw them running around the centre's grounds. When they lit a fire, the place felt like it was coming back to life but when they left on the weekend, it once again became a village without children. And without adults.

Kámen went off on his sombre chores, still without uttering a word. Achilles played with the dogs, but only because these ones in the yard were domesticated and not working. You don't play with working Karakachan dogs, especially if they don't know you. Once, I played with a young Karakachan in a border village and she bit me on the hand as if to remind me: I am not a pet. These puppies were kept here for now, but some of them would become livestock guardians after the age of one. Then there were the three chained ones who didn't go with the flock and didn't roam the farm: Spintop in the rams' pen, Barut chained in his rock cave here and Griffy who was out of sight.

'Not long ago, it was normal to get bitten by the neighbour's dogs when you entered their territory and now you have to chain them,' Kámen muttered later.

But that day, I didn't know if there would be a 'later'. I didn't know how long I'd stay – a few hours or a few years. It was that kind of place. It had happened to others. Volunteers, enthusiasts, helpers, animal lovers and hired workers had come and gone.

Why did you come to this place? I asked Achilles. The road is terrible, there's no people left, and you are from another part of the country that's flatter and easier.

'An overdose of idealism?' Achilles scratched his beard. He was a good-humoured man, an aesthete who liked art, books, films and of course, his number one mission in life – dogs – and had a more academic approach to things than Kámen who was a practical man of few words. They were both cerebral and emotionally detached. Both had graduated from the Academy of Arts following in the footsteps of their artist father.

'It's classic transhumance terrain here, well-trodden. And we wanted something as close to traditional pastoralism as possible. From lower ground to higher ground.'

Actually, in transhumance it doesn't matter whether it's horizontal or vertical, as long as there is a change of pastures.

But this breed of sheep needed the vertical. As vertical as it gets.

Once it was up and running, the Orelek commune applied for pastoralism to become a legalised category of animal husbandry. This brought it into the present, at least on paper – and in law. Until then, pastoralism was simply practised. Perversely, legalising its status brought some terrible side-effects. One was the amount of paperwork it now involved. This made it prohibitive to people with low literacy skills and made room for entrepreneurs who couldn't care less about grazing animals but were good at paperwork – and pocketing subsidies. The bond between animal and human was bureaucratised and corporatised and this changed the face of pastoralism in just one generation. If you wanted to breed free-grazing animals, you needed someone to handle the bureaucracy.

It had all started with Kitan.

'We gave them pocket money as boys and they saved it up and bought a dog,' said the mother. 'Then another one. Then came Kitan.'

'Kitan was a turning point,' Achilles agreed.

The kitchen walls were covered in photographic calendars of Karakachan dogs from around the country and across Europe. Kubrat. Barut. Murat. Kuna. Yantra. Titan. Karakitan. Karamana. Nestor. Perun. They were all from Kitan's lineage. The dogs' woolly coats, the names, the trail – it all somehow reminded me of the plateaux and mountains of Central Asia, where I've never been.

'And we were happy, thank you very much, when they were just into dog breeding,' said the mother. 'But then they decided to save the whole world. And things became difficult.'

I leafed through a photo album. Kámen and Achilles at twenty, with dogs. Marina at twenty, then with toddlers, and dogs or wolves.

Still, though, there are many other empty highland villages. Why here?

'There was another man,' Kámen said, swinging in and out of the house. 'His father was a shepherd. Locals.'

The shepherd father and son had in fact been business partners to the two brothers and Marina. Then something had happened. They didn't appear in any photographs, but I found their image on an old rolled-up poster showcasing rare breeds. They held lambs, dogs at their legs. The father was a tall man in woollen trousers and rubber galoshes, with hands like spades and haunted eyes. The son was massive, with a set jaw and dark fire in his eyes. They were an old, dispossessed clan from Orelek. Where were they now?

'The father died,' said Achilles. 'The son is very much around.'

Kámen slammed the door.

Before the break-up, the brothers and 'the other man', as they called him, had restored the Karakachan sheep to a healthy number. Others bought from them and bred their own flocks, and there were even three associations dedicated to this sheep now. This was not good for the breed, because it meant that the criteria for what made the breed genuinely Karakachan diverged over time and the gene was distorted. This was called 'anthropogenic fragmentation' and was due to competitive breeding and disagreements among pastoralists.

'There is an argument in academic circles and among breeders,' said Achilles. 'By the books, there are some 16,000 of these sheep. But they are not pedigree.'

It appeared that the brothers and 'the other man' had the only authentic Karakachan sheep at present. There had been some excitement about flocks in Greece and Serbia, but the latest research showed that they were not the same breed.

'Unfortunately. Because if tomorrow a blight strikes our herd or the other man's herd, there is no reserve gene pool. It can happen very quickly.'

The Karakachan sheep had been down to a few hundred when the brothers, Marina, and 'the other man' started searching for them all over the southern Balkans, twenty-five years ago.

'What's so special about those sheep anyway?' I hadn't seen any yet and I also harboured the thought: what can be special about any sheep? They're just – sheep.

'The Karakachans said it: it's the oldest sheep in the world,' Achilles smiled. 'And scientists agree. It's adapted for mountain living like no other. More like wild goats than sheep. The Thracians raised them. And they used these dogs too. So there's a bit of history.'

'You have to see them in their natural environment.' Kámen swung through again. He drove between the goat house and the sheep house, loading and unloading sacks. The dogs barked every time. It was noisy for an empty village.

'When can I see the flock then?'

Kámen mumbled something and drove away.

The mother sighed dramatically. She was small behind the big ledger. The admin was constant. There were obstructive ministerial laws that made rare livestock breeders jump through hoops. It was one of many burdens. Another was the conflict with the national parks which allowed them to graze their animals for a price, then persecuted and fined them at every opportunity in a cat and mouse game. Yet another was mean vets who argued over small issues and abused the power they had over livestock breeders, because to receive subsidies for specific breeds, each animal had to be inspected by the vet. But the biggest þane was the lack of shepherds.

'I never told my children: go to the ends of the earth and spend the rest of your life carrying sacks. But that's what they chose,' said the mother.

Achilles chuckled. He didn't carry many sacks. The next day, he returned to their town in the north, which was reached by following the river upstream. Their town was near its source. They had literally come down the river with their animals. Their town was once known for its grazing herds that moved freely across the border with Serbia. Then the town became a hub of steel factories, coal mines and industrial-sized farms, then that collapsed too and the town's surroundings are now a ruined landscape. There, Achilles took care of the admin and another twenty dogs.

'I should reduce them to ten', he said, 'But I can't seem to. It's good to have some extras for the gene pool.'

To stay on Kámen's grounds, you really had to be part of the circle, otherwise it was entirely without comfort. The house was basic and to get phone signal you had to sit by the willow in the square. Downstairs was just the dark rustic kitchen with a wood stove, a narrow bed resting on a stone so big the ground floor had been built around it, a long table, two fridges. The outside sink was the only sink. Everything was washed there – dishes, bloodied knives, morning faces.

Upstairs were four rooms. Stacked with their faces against the wall were Kámen's old paintings in acrylic. Some were unfinished. He had not put the finished ones on the walls.

The farmhouse was built by workers, helpers and volunteers on the ruins of an old house. The family were not meant to live here full-time but the helpers and volunteers brought with them personalities, relationships and other complications. All ended up leaving. Yet a flock had its own momentum, the animals increased and workers were needed. Thirty years ago, it had been the Karakachan dog and sheep on the brink of extinction. Now it was the shepherd. Experienced shepherds and goatherds were down to just a few in the entire region. They rotated among livestock owners, changing employers every few years: a tiny pool with no extra genes.

The only bathroom was in the outbuilding. Next to it was the hired workers' room with its three single beds, a stove and windows with a sheer drop into the river gorge. It was empty because the hired shepherds were 'up' with the flock for the summer. That is, at Black Water. In fact, it was just one shepherd, and his helper had suddenly come down today and quit.

'Shepherding is simple but it isn't for simple people,' said Achilles, implying that the helper was 'simple'. It was an old saying.

A shepherd didn't just herd the animals. He lived with them day and night. He had to be good at milking, sheep care, dog care, and in winter, birthing lambs through sleepless nights.

'We've seen a stream of them,' the mother went on. 'They can't keep the flock together. They sit at the table and their noses run. They steal and eat too much, and they're all alcoholics. Gypsies, mostly.'

It was time to feed the few sheep in the pen. Among them was an

orphaned goat kid, wee Hector, who liked it here with the young
sheep, not with the goats. He bounced up to us with trusting eyes
and a curly punk's fringe.

'Wee Hector will grow into a buck. So what, we'll still love him!'

Her bitterness vanished as soon as she turned to the animals. Little
Hector was too beautiful and smart to be used for any human purpose and I hoped – I just hoped for him.

There was something exhausting here, and something compel-
ling. The never-ending difficulties, Kámen's impenetrable manner,
the brain-rattling road, the pre-historic land packed with history, the
vastness of the mountains, the passion that sparked this revival of
animal–human movement, the struggle that followed and hadn't let
up – everything was hard and meaningful.

It felt like something was required of me, and of everyone who
made it up that road which says: 'Abandon all ease, ye who enter here
and join the mission.' Visitors had a habit of driving up here, taking
photos of the animals and silent Kámen, like a monk in his animal
church, and leaving. The family were used to the attention and
enjoyed it but visitors only saw the surface. Some didn't even get out
of their car because of the dogs. The family cultivated their desert
island, surrounded by hostile seas.

Marina breezed in and out of the house to fetch jars of yogurt for
'her kids' and to eat quickly from a pot of soup, though she didn't
touch the roasted haunch of a goat kid swimming in its glistening fat
and melting in the mouth.

'You're not vegetarian, are you?' Kámen turned to me. He avoided
eye contact.

Marina had a permanent frown on her sculpted face. She had no
time for people unless they were on the same mission as her. After
her visits to the house, she jumped into her jeep and drove back to the
centre to lay out lunch for the kids.

When Marina and Kámen left, their son sat at the table and began
to draw a cat snake's head. Alex and his brother studied at the Academy of Fine Arts in the capital but Alex spent his holidays here. Any
work he could do in the city felt less meaningful than here where
everything you did made a difference.

'But I feel like there's always something more that needs doing,' he said. 'I can't relax.'

Alex grew up with men and women who compulsively drew, carved, built, shaped, imagined and controlled the world around them. Driven women and men, pioneers who could not rest or say That's enough, thank you. If he wasn't lifting sacks for his father, Alex was cleaning kids' rooms in the centre for his mother. His own needs took a back seat.

'I want to do my art. But I can't live without animals. And my parents need help.'

The family went on holiday just twice in twenty years. It didn't work, things started going wrong with the animals and the workers. Kámen had to rush back and the circle closed in on him again.

Alex fed the dogs. Two puppies, Malina and Kalina, fought over their bowl, baring their teeth. The third puppy, Sunny, was older and not related to them. His eyes expressed more than he could possibly know at seven months of age. Everybody was fed generously – dogs, goats, chickens, and when the mother was here, humans. But she was not always here. And Marina was only here in the summer when she lived at the centre with her dog Kira – a sandy dingo-like cross with wolfish ears – who followed her everywhere. Marina had found her as a puppy on a remote road, left to starve.

The young quitter sat sullenly at the willow with his rucksack, waiting for someone to give him a lift. Kámen asked me to take him down when I went.

''Cos I don't want to see his face again,' he said icily.

I assumed the guy was guilty of something nefarious. But this had happened before. Helpers didn't last at Black Water. The average was ten days. The head shepherd was now alone. Kámen visited him once a week.

'Can I come with you next time?'

Kámen looked sceptically at my sandalled feet.

'That's okay,' I said. 'I live in the Scottish Highlands.'

Kámen was surprised. He'd assumed I lived in a city.

'Are there flocks there?' He lit a cigarette and leaned on the gate of the goat house, ignoring the sullen quitter under the willow and enjoying making him wait.

'Yes,' I said. 'Sheep, cows . . .'

Once, my Scottish village was a self-sufficient Valliscaulian priory with large orchards. Then it became a village with livestock and crofts. Now it's a village of gift shops and hairdressers. The sheep and cows are in fenced-off farms up in the braes.

'Stationary farms, I imagine,' Kámen said.

Yep.

No shepherds, no large predators, no walking with your animals, no carrying luggage on your back, no guard dogs and no milking by hand. The cows and sheep of my Scottish braes grazed the same patches and ate fodder the rest of the time and nobody tasted their milk. They were there just for meat. They were always behind wire and the fields and braes could not be crossed, or you were trespassing. Everything was in squares, drawn across the land with a ruler.

'I miss the real village,' I said. 'The way it was. With all sorts of beasties like here'. Kámen looked pleased for the first time.

'I spent my childhood with my grandparents in their yards,' he said. 'That's where I learned to milk, shear sheep, build sheds, train dogs, chop wood, things like that. I felt a part of things.'

When I moved from the city to my Scottish village, my social self began to slip, and with it – many of the people I knew. Another self emerged, fresh and keen, looking for a different kind of pasture. My centre of gravity changed – from the man-made to the organic. The man-made was crowded. The organic was fringe. The social occasions in my life decreased and my adventures increased but I needed companions.

'You should have seen Orelek in the first years when we came,' Kámen said. 'There were old people. Donkeys, pigs, characters at the pub.'

Those people died and nobody new took root. The shop was closed by a mean mayor who wanted to sell it to the highest bidder but there were no bidders and it lay empty, with old calendars on the walls. The pub had been run by a man who died. His son Ugrin the Radio was a goatherd for Kámen for several years. When he quit and took his own goats down to Kresna, he sold the family house for a pittance.

'People who love livestock end up with their own,' Kámen said.

Kámen had frozen Ugrin out. He couldn't forgive him for leaving.

We stood in silence, surveying the hills, having the same thoughts. Ruined houses dotted the slopes like rotten stumps. Orelek was once made up of eight large districts and eighteen smaller ones spread across the hills. They were all named after clans, the places those clans had come from or local animals and plants. Drakolovo the Dragon, Kosovska, Barata where Kámen lived which meant 'warm spring', Wolfland, Prairie, Fat Oaks. At one time, each big district had its own school, craft workshops, logging station and of course, dairy houses. Until the middle of last century, these hills had been an animal city. One hundred years ago, there were 50,000 sheep, 20,000 goats, several thousand cows and buffalo, and innumerable horses and dogs – all belonging to Orelek. Most of the sheep were Karakachan. They moved around with their shepherds like a game of chess and the wolves and bears moved around them in an outer circle. At the time of collectivisation, the animal city had already shrunk to a quarter of itself.

'We are the last ones,' Kámen said. 'Pastoralism will die out in Europe. It will continue in Central Asia where it began. But European laws go against it and Europeans have forgotten where they come from.'

'This is not even Europe,' he went on, 'this is the Balkans but we're smitten by the same perverse laws, the same ignorant attitude and the same forgetting.'

'This is why people like me are the last hole of the flute.'

A shepherding expression that has entered everyday language.

The laws make it so that lamb from large stationary farms abroad is cheaper than the organic meat raised in labour-intensive pastoral terrain like this.

'We have imported lamb in the shops. Because their government encourages them, and ours blocks us. Pork is half the price of lamb, which doesn't help.'

The price of meat from free-grazing animals like these has stayed the same for ten years, while the cost of fodder has doubled. The mainstream market for goat and sheep yogurt and cheese favours large stationary farms, and the dairy station Kámen and Marina had built under the goat house at great expense suffered from a lack of water, so they'd stopped making cheese. The last of the weekend villagers still cultivated orchards and vegetable gardens, even if they lived in the towns. A rich incomer had diverted a brook to his own garden. The two, combined, caused water shortages.

'Don't be a pessimist,' I said, my heart sinking.

'I'm a realist,' he inhaled his cigarette and squinted against the tide of reality.

'Village life will make a comeback,' I said. 'People will be forced to return to small-scale living. Closer to the land.'

'No. Everything has a beginning and an end. And we're towards the end,' Kámen said. 'There used to be scores of sparrows. No longer. Swarms of bees on the plum blossoms. Not many plums this year either. Nightingales are shot. It takes ten nightingales to have a meal in a restaurant. And the storks. They shoot them in North Africa. We do something to protect them here, but once they go across the pond . . .'

'I know,' I said quickly. 'But I still want to come up and see the flock.'

'If you must,' he muttered and went into the goat house with buckets full of feed, the door slamming behind him.

'What happened up there?' I asked the glum young quitter on the way down in my car. On this road where a burst exhaust pipe was only a question of time, quitting felt inevitable.

'Nothing,' he said. 'The colleague broke his hand and drinks for the pain. No phone signal. And there's a bear with three cubs. I jumped on the mare and the bear chased me.'

He was done with Black Water and Kámen was done with him. At Warm Spout, I glimpsed the goats from earlier on and the goatherd, who was yelling into his phone. That had to be Ugrin, dubbed 'the Radio' because he was always on his phone. The goats were a mixed bunch – he wasn't into breeds, just goats.

Down in the gorge, the international lorries thundered past. At a roadside dump appeared goats. They had come from the river, long-haired, curly-horned and ancient-faced, the same breed as Kámen's. Kalofer goats, they are called, and they are one of the oldest animals in Eurasia. They looked it. I pulled over to watch them among the rubbish. Through the poplars glinted the river, its coils moving like a snake. Then a dog appeared, and I knew the man was not far behind. It was usually a man, waiting behind the animals. Gazing into space, lighting a cigarette or scrolling through his phone. A man with a crook climbed out of the grove, tall and dark-skinned like an Ethiopian herder, rubber slippers on his bare feet. Behind him was a woman with bleached hair and a small dog in her arms. She said something to him in sign language. When the last goats vanished under the road, the pair vanished with them.

KITAN

The wildfires in the mountains were put out, killing two fire-fighters. I said goodbye to my landlady and her grandson in the spa town, and back in Orelek the mother showed me to a room upstairs.

The dogs covered my legs in strings of saliva. This was my inauguration into the house pack. Hello, Sunny, Malina and Kalina, Muna the Monkey with her eyes full of premonition, Gutsi, Metsi, Glavcho, Loopy Junior and the rest of the Loopy family. The Loopies liked to dig holes in the sand under the laundry line. Daddy Gutsi lay in front of the kitchen door like a rug and didn't move when you opened it. When a chorus of barking broke out, he stood on the big rock by the washing line and howled theatrically, then flopped down in the shade like his job was done. Mama Metsi was mild-tempered and long-legged. Five-month-old Loopy Junior had short ears, wide-spaced eyes and a pig's snout and produced incredible amounts of drool. Black-headed Glavcho nipped your trousers for fun. Yellow-headed Malina and Kalina fought over food. They had earnest faces with slanted eyes. Kalina and Malina meant Ladybird and Raspberry. Their mother Kalina was a majestic bitch with wise eyes. Their father Redhead was away with the flock.

In the goat house was another pack of dogs. The working ones were Murat, Shaban and Mecho. The goat house dogs and the sheep house dogs rarely met. They kept to their own territory. At night, something would set them off – a passing horse, wolf or fox – and when one group started barking, the other group picked it up and the gorge echoed : *Awww. Woofwoofwoof. Baubaubau. Awww.*

It could last for hours. They barked past any point of usefulness. It was irritating, then funny, then irritating again. You had to sleep through it or not sleep at all in your bed of scratchy blankets. There were no sheets in this house. If you got up at night to use the toilet downstairs, you made your way through ten dogs who were either prostrate or barking.

'You get used to it,' the mother said.

I spent time with the dogs. I got it, how one of these dogs could change the course of your life. This is what Kitan had done. Kitan had brought the family here. With dogs and sheep, then horses and goats, plus the rescued wolves and bears, and a stream of humans who like Kitan were no longer here but had given the best years of their lives to build what was now here and rekindle the hut fire in the mountain kingdom of Orelek so that today you could believe it was merely asleep and not dead.

Kitan was born in 1993. He had a human head. His eyes, his thinking, his communication, everything about this dog was different. He was a true Karakachan. It dawned on Kámen and Achilles that Kitan was probably one of the last purebred Karakachans and that the whole lineage was on the brink. A lot of things were on the brink. It was the 1990s, a long decade known as the Transition. The regime had collapsed and with it the state-controlled economy, including animal husbandry and agriculture. Cooperatives were dismantled, the agronomists and shepherds lost their jobs and a whole nation of buffalo, sheep, cows, goats and horses had nowhere to go.

Then came the post-communist restitution: if your grandparents' property had been confiscated by the state, which was the case for almost everyone, you were entitled to receive a part of that lost estate which also included land and animals. But at this point, you had no idea how to milk a goat or care for a horse and you were living in a flat anyway. It was fifty years too late. So, you got rid of these animals by passing them on directly to the brokers who swarmed around animal auctions like vultures and gladly took them off your hands, then sold them to slaughterhouses and industrial farms abroad. Privatisation repeated the crimes of collectivisation.

Grazing animals had once been embedded in your family, with their own names and lineages. Your ancestors had slept with them and shared food with them. Now, just one or two generations later, their children and grandchildren were shipped off like slaves to some

faraway shore or down the road to the slaughterhouse. It was a repe-
tition of what your ancestors had already experienced first-hand.

And the Karakachan dog? Since the great Karakachan flocks were
disbanded in the 1950s, it had endured a brutal fate. By 1990, it had
been endangered for some decades. When the nomads were settled
and their dogs went wild, the state invented an 'anti-rabies' policy
which gave blanket permission to kill guardian dogs that were not
used. This caused the first sharp decline in the Karakachan pedigree.
It was further diluted in the 1980s by uncontrolled cross-breeding
with other large dogs from completely different lineages like the
Caucasian Shepherd Dog and Saint Bernard. This happened because
there was no established standard for the breed.

Against this backdrop, Kámen, Achilles and Marina criss-crossed
the mountainous countryside in search of more dogs like Kitan. They
found them with the last of the highland shepherds – endangered
indigenous breeds of dogs, sheep, goats and horses, and no one else
was interested in them because their commercial value was lost.

Over the next decade, the brothers' mission was successful: to
breed authentic Karakachan dogs and have the breed officially recognised and quantified, which had never been done before. Their dogs
from Kitan's lineage ignited interest, won competitions and began to
sell at home and abroad, inspiring a whole movement in the world of
dog lovers. This ensured the health of the gene pool. When Kámen
and Kitan were invited to a television studio in the capital, because by
then Kitan had become a celebrity, the dog walked the city streets on
a lead as if he'd grown up there. But the Karakachan dog is not a pet.
It needs a mission: to guard. The refinement of the breed over the
centuries had been merciless. I heard of cases from the 1980s when
Karakachan dogs who failed to react to a wolf attack were shot by
their owners : who cried as they did it. You cannot feed a Karakachan
dog that doesn't work was the brutal logic, but it was more than that,
there was a military ethic at work. You could not have deserters in
the ranks. In fact, these dogs were used by the army from the Russian–
Turkish War in 1878 onwards. Traditionally, shepherd dogs have one
of their ears clipped as puppies, the right ear for males, the left for
females, due to some antiquated belief that it made their hearing

better. This was still carried out in places and Marina said there was some truth to the bit about the hearing, but the practice was slipping into the past, thank God. One thing was certain – these dogs were made to be one with the tough mountains of the southern Balkans and their web of large predators, grazing animals and humans. They were adapted for these conditions and could survive, but not thrive, as house pets. Guardian dogs didn't just protect the flock from large predators. They also protected large predators from being shot by people with livestock.

If canine people like Kitan disappear, the mountain's web will be torn forever. Mountain dogs, mountain sheep, mountain goats and mountain horses go together, and human livelihoods and psyches have been woven into this web for thousands of years.

Twenty-five years ago, a retrospective exhibition in the capital showed photographs of the last Karakachan nomads with their flocks in the hills, before they were settled.

'These old men and women came, dressed in black,' said Achilles, 'they walked around the exhibition and cried.'

They were Karakachans who had been robbed of their animals and their paths fifty years earlier and put in apartment towers. Among them was a tall man who had spent ten years in prison for saying, in 1958, that the bandits who stole and slaughtered his animals on behalf of the communist state were – bandits. His white-haired wife was there too. Their daughters had grown up without him, just a plate on the table 'for Dad'.

Marina, Kámen and Achilles, soon joined by 'the other man', continued combing through the Bulgarian highlands and started buying the odd mountain sheep here, five there, until a small flock was harnessed. The young enthusiasts were interested in animals, not people, but inevitably they came across the last of the animal people. They were all marginalised, often from minorities or the traumatised survivors of collectivisation, communist exploitation, labour camps, post-communist anarchy and the contempt of a self-loathing society. Many of them were Pomaks in the Rhodope Mountains – the Bulgarian-speaking Muslims of the southern Balkans. Emin was a Pomak, and his father had got into horses in the 1940s when he was hired by a Karakachan family. Like the Karakachans, the Pomaks had suffered a brutal assault – the state had taken their Arabic-Turkish names and replaced them with state-approved ones in the 1970s. They held on to their animals because that's all they had left. The Pomaks were conservative and had remained close to the land, to old ways of speaking, old breeds of animals and old mountain knowledge. It was in these isolated communities that the young enthusiasts found indigenous dogs, sheep and horses.

There was the shepherd Zebeko, so devoted to his flock that he slept inside a dog's hut with his legs sticking out. His Karakachan dogs were bearded and speckled, and not for sale. They were a type of dog that disappeared with him. There was the crippled shepherd Sbirko (Motley), so called because he kept all sorts of animals. He lived in a hut above the pen and having lost the use of his legs, he watched his dogs take the flock out to pasture every day, then bring them back without fail, his army of orphaned animals. No help came. Sbirko was near starvation. After two years of visiting him and passing the tests he put the brothers and Marina through to see if they really cared, knowing he was at the end and that he'd found a good home for his animals, Sbirko gave his flock to the young enthusiasts. And died, taking the century with him. His black mountain sheep were the base of today's flock. There was a young shepherd called Tahir. They encountered him in the same state in which I discovered Emin: sleeping under a plastic sheet in rags, kept warm by dogs and hanging on to his sheep and goats. They brought him here and he became a super shepherd.

That was how the dying village of Orelek was reinvigorated by a bunch of smart, hard-working idealists. They threw themselves into rebuilding the metropolis of lost animals. The flock grew. Two human children were born – Alex and Theo – and many lambs, puppies and goat kids. Enthusiasts and volunteers joined in. Everybody slept where they could – caravans, ruined houses, and washed in the river.

'The other man' and his shepherd father stayed in Orelek for nine years. Tahir became like a son to the old shepherd but after a few years, he left to grow his own flock in his own mountain, where in every glade there had been a dairy house, and where in one wealthy estate in the nineteenth century – Agush Aga's estate – ceramic pipes had connected the milking dens to the dairy and through them flowed the milk of 12,000 sheep. One hundred dogs had guarded that flock. His mountain was the homeland of a man who wasn't a shepherd but who had walked the land with his flute, followed by animals: Orpheus. Tahir cried when he left Orelek with twenty-five sheep and two dogs in tow, along with the parting gift of a choice ram from the old shepherd.

 · After Tahir came other gifted shepherds. There was Vangel, a dog whisperer like Kámen, who became like a brother to 'the other man'. But when a volunteer fell in love with Vangel and the couple asked to stay on and work together, it was 'No'. There was no room for couples. More losses followed. The biggest one came when 'the other man' and his father left and with them, most of the sheep. An unhappy agreement was reached between Kámen and his now ex-partner, in which Kámen was left with a handful of sheep and two rams. He started all over again. And again, he grew his flock to the size it was now: 700. The other man and his father made their exit down into the gorge with their detachment of animals. They had a strong flock, but no base.

This happened fifteen years ago. The two men have been sworn enemies ever since. Kámen did not even speak his name – he was 'the other man'.

It was like lightning had split the mission into two parts that didn't talk to each other. Adversities followed, as if unleashed by a curse. Two devastating fires struck the goat house and they had to rebuild it from the ashes. The spirit of the place changed: workers kept leaving, volunteers decreased, Kámen and Marina drifted apart and there were no more wild parties under the moon. People used to come to Orelek and throw themselves into the mission, fall in love with the wrong person and leave too late, animals in tow.

But it wasn't over yet. The wheel of fate creaked audibly in the dead silence of Orelek. Something was unfolding out of sight, in the sheep pens, in the shepherds' huts, in the hearts of those who had given their all to nurture their world back from extinction and had been let down, but who had not given up. Dogs and humans, wolves and sheep, visible and invisible designs wove their tangled embrace and in just a few days, I felt that embrace tighten around me.

The dogs were the vital link. I became attached to the Loopy family, to greedy Malina and Kalina, noble Sunny and Muna the Monkey with her sensitive blinking eyes, even Barut 'the Tinder' chained to his rock, who barked half-heartedly as you approached, his face droopy, then suddenly stopped and went back inside his crack in the rock, indignant that he had to perform the same stupid routine every time. And in the goat house, Shaban and Murat who fought for your affection. Shaban was yellow-white with a foxy, intelligent face. He fought wolves and was normally kept chained to protect the rare visitors but when I sat under the willow in the square, he came and leaned his head against my chest and we sat like that, though I'd done nothing to earn his trust or he mine.

One morning, there was a bucket of raw meat in the shower.

'Goat throats for Vachka. I put it there away from the dogs,' Alex said, waking with a guilty look because his father didn't like late sleepers and there were sacks to move, goats to milk and a wolf to feed. 'Do you want to see her?'

Muna the Monkey jumped over the pen gate to greet us. She had a strained bark as if her voice was breaking. The Loopy family were jealous and crowded around Alex to claim their place. He batted them off with a bunch of dry broom, used for this purpose, and also to sweep the steps from pigeon droppings. Muna jumped back inside the pen for safety.

Seeing I was about to hurl rotten bananas into the gorge where food refuse was thrown for the chickens, Alex took them for the cockroaches he bred as food for the lizards, which he also bred.

'And the lizards, as food for . . .' his grandmother said.

'No! The lizards are too expensive,' said Alex.

We took the bucket above the village. The open sheep pen was empty. The flock is up with our shepherd, Alex said. *Our shepherd.* Not everyone can say this.

'Up there, in that hell. It looks nice now, but . . .'

We looked at the blue-white pyramid of Thunder Peak and the beautiful spine of Little Horse that led to it. It looked out of human reach.

The wolf enclosure was an open-air park. A wildlife organisation had built it for rescued wolves. Alex threw the meat over the fence and Vachka came over, her tail long and swinging. She looked subdued. Her companion had just died after fifteen years together.

We walked uphill to the empty bear enclosure. They'd given the bear away to an Italian zoo.

'He's better off there. It was getting too dry here and the fence was old and unsafe. But in Italy they castrated him.'

The bears had been two: a male and the Wee One, a pleasant female so ferocious when provoked that she killed a big male once.

'They didn't get on. He stole her food. Then she died and he got worse.'

Alex and his brother would pick apples and plums for the bears in the heat, but the bears' favourite snack was balls of peanut butter mixed with honey.

'I spent my childhood here,' Alex said. 'Sitting by a stone all summer, waiting for something to crawl out.'

It was reptile country – scorched, rocky, hissing with heat. Something darted between stones, but how can you tell a snake from a lizard when it moves so fast?

'Lizards have ears, little round holes,' Alex said.

There were four types of venomous snakes here: vipers, adders, rear fanged Aesculapian snakes and cat snakes, which have venom in their rear teeth and chew their victims with them. Alex was bitten by one but nothing happened, he said, just a swelling. And a scar – two holes for two teeth.

'Oh yeah, this is herpetologist heaven. I am one of many biologists to get glued to this place,' the small wizened-faced man with the cats told me.

I got to know him over time. His name was Velin. He was a veteran ecologist and the driving force behind the campaign to save the

Kresna Gorge from a motorway initially planned to go right through the gorge, a protected NATURA 2000 site. The campaign had lasted for twenty-five years, successfully.

'Tons of governments and nasty creatures have tried to destroy this gorge. Going against nature, against European law. We've held up. But for how long?'

He was battle-weary, knowing that the motorway would have to be built because of the heavy lorry traffic along this international Sofia–Athens route, and anywhere it was built would be an ecological disaster. There was something exceptional about Kresna Gorge, I knew it with my senses.

'Your senses are right,' Velin said. 'When I first came here as a young man, I became inebriated. Not on wine, on the place itself.'

People dubbed him The Grape because of his exquisite homemade wines.

'What south, what incredible south, I thought that first time!'

You have a river valley, he went on. You have two mountains. The first is a stable massif, the second is a dynamic terraced one. Glaciers slipped down from the north and brought boreal species that survived in the gorge and nowhere else. Boreal means northern. At the same time, species came up from the south with the wind because the gorge is only 150 metres above sea level and an open corridor to the Aegean. And due to the isolation of the gorge, everything that came stayed and began to diversify like crazy. You have endemic species that exist nowhere else.

'Eighteen kilometres along and a few kilometres across, and you have the richest biodiversity in Europe. Spain is Europe's most biodiverse country overall and Bulgaria is the most biodiverse per square kilometre. And this gorge takes the cherry.'

This is what was at stake with the planned motorway.

'You've come to the right place. Orelek is a gateway to a world that few get to see anymore,' Velin said. 'My story with this mountain is not a happy one. It's the story of a passion, and passion consumes you. You'll see.'

And by the way, he added, Alex is a shaman like his parents.

★

Alex grew up with dogs and wolves. In the family photo album is a
toddler hugging the first rescued wolf cub. The second one, Vacho,
lived with them for two months.

'Two months is the longest you can keep a wolf cub as a pet.
Because a wolf can't be a dog.'

What's the difference?

'The wolf needs a pack. She doesn't need you. The dog does.'

Vacho died choking on a bone. Then there was the Savage one
who bit Alex under the elbow. She was killed by the dogs right here,
by the wolf enclosure – before there was an enclosure.

'She kept attacking them when they returned with the flock and
they got fed up.'

There was the Red, poisoned by villains. And then the Good one;
a volunteer took her out for a walk on a lead, she overdosed on plums
and died. Now it was down to Vachka who was the granddaughter of
the first Vacho and the Savage one. They were looking for a new
companion for her.

'What's not okay is when people breed a dog with a wolf,' Alex
said. 'For hunting. But the result is something confused. A hybrid.'

They did not like hybrids here. By the side of the road was Griffy
on his chain. He had a huge, confused head, though he wasn't a
hybrid.

'I better walk him,' said Alex. Griffy had bitten everyone except
him. Griffy had followed Alex everywhere since he was a puppy.
'But I wonder if my turn will come too. He used to go with the
sheep, then something went wrong and he started biting sheep, dogs
and people.'

'There's nothing wrong with Griffy, he's a perfectly normal dog,'
Marina protested later. He was traumatised by shepherds who beat
him, so he goes mental whenever he sees a stick. But Griffy bit people
without sticks too. It had all gone sour for him, stick or no stick. He
reminded me of stressed humans who can't distinguish between
friends and enemies.

'See, there are five types of Karakachan dog, by colouring,' Alex
said. 'Griffy is mixed, black body with white paws, white tail-end
and white necklace.'

There were the white-yellow dogs like Muna the Monkey, the white and blacks like Glavcho, the greys and the three-coloured dogs, usually black-and-white with yellow on their face. They are the surviving types of Karakachan. And then there are the other ones not here — the moustachioed ones, the bearded ones, the speckled ones, the short-legged 'mean' ones dubbed wolf-throttlers, all those brave and loyal ones that couldn't be saved from extinction.

Alex unchained Griffy and put him on a lead. Griffy looked grateful beyond words and they climbed into the lizardy rocks, boy-man and dog-wolf, and they were lost in the cloud of dust left by the last logging lorry of the day, now thundering through the ghost village. It was piled with the long bodies of pines planted when the millennial beech forest was felled and sold cheaply to the Soviet Union, a forest so immense and full of life, known and unknown, that when the old shepherds entered it with their flocks, they took off their caps and said a prayer to the spirits of the mountain.

THE OLDEST SHEEP IN THE WORLD

Reports of the bear with the three cubs made Kámen go to Black Water sooner than planned.

It was a pre-dawn start after a barking night. The Loopies were now asleep, passed out on the stone patio and didn't move if you stepped on them, the scoundrels.

We drove in silence in Kámen's white van to the fork at Warm Spout and took the rough forestry road with the faded sign for hikers. The unsealed surface was dug out, unfixed for decades, but it provided the only car access to the transhumance trail. When dawn broke, a sheer drop below the road revealed the amphitheatre of upper Pirin, ready for the day's spectacle. The peaks ahead were drenched in golden light. The road joined the thunderous Orelek River. We passed a wooden bridge.

'The mandra,' Kámen broke the silence of the last hour. The ruined dairy house was in use until 1990. The 1980s were the last decade when the pastoral infrastructure was used properly, and men and boys from Orelek and Kresna drove the flocks up here, and to the huts where we were headed. Milk was brought from the sub-alpine pastures on horseback and turned into cheese in this, the last highland dairy to operate. Now all that was left was the name Mandra, which was used for the whole area. Dozens of highland locations were called Mandra, a nod to the mountain's milky past.

The road ended at an area called The Beeches. The river was fast and full of rapids. In antiquity, there had been a copper mine here. Above the river was an empty summer pen, and a hut with signs of use – stacked logs, a cardigan.

'Who uses this?'

'The other man,' said Kámen unwillingly.

'Where are his sheep?'

'At Sinanitsa.'

We took one of two paths, both submerged in greenery so that I wouldn't have spotted them at all. One led to Black Water and Orelek Lakes. The other led to Sinanitsa and Gergiyski Lakes. Sinanitsa and Black Water were neighbouring cirques below Thunder Peak. On the map, they looked like neighbours but on the ground, the ridge between them made them stangers.

Kámen bounced up the path in his shorts and beanie, a sisal sack swung over his back. Inside was a sensor lamp to guard against bears, and bread.

It was awesomely wild terrain, unrelentingly upwards. The forests made it dark and even more remote. We climbed the terraces like robbers scaling a cathedral. Meadows alternated with flagstone paths like something the Romans could have built, but they were natural. The river drowned out other sounds.

'This is where we take the flock up. And hope it doesn't rain. 'Cos the mare once slipped and fell'.

She fell straight into the gully. She survived, but the saddle broke in two. I could not understand how several hundred sheep could pass through these multiple obstacles and come out at the top, intact. But the shepherds of old had done it with thousands of sheep and hundreds of horses.

Beech, pine, meadow, pine, meadow. On a meadow called Kamen klet were ruined stone huts. A golden eagle flew out of one. Kamen means stone, and the name suited both this mountain and Kámen himself. Bears were often seen on Kamen klet.

Once, this had been an animal metropolis for several months of the year. These gorges echoed with barking dogs, men shouting over hilltops, boys milking and milk vats loaded onto horse saddles and taken down the bandit path to the dairy. Cooking fires were everywhere. The reason why people came this high with their herds was the fresh pasture.

Lupins, hellebore, mint and St John's wort shone in primal colours. After an hour we crossed the river down a badly eroded slope. Stones fell. We fell. We went on, and after one last meadow like a wall, in which Kámen's black mare Mimi was grazing with her brown foal and two other horses, we reached Black Water.

It was like turning a page.

A white amphitheatre opened, with massive pines for spectators. The whole of Black Water was skeleton-white and overlooked on both sides by a mature Bosnian pine forest – Black pines, they are called here. A black and white world.

The river was crystal cold. Thunder Peak and Little Horse loomed above, close yet far away. The valley was still in shadow. We walked past the first hut. A man with cows used it. He was known as The Privateer and his cowherd lived in the hut. The cows grazed high above a plateau with juicy grass, called Etip, after a great shepherd who had lived up there most of the year with his hired hands, dogs and one of those legendary flocks that ballads call 'uncounted'.

Kámen and The Privateer disliked each other but rubbed along out of necessity.

'When we first arrived, there was an old man with a few hundred cows. Of the small mountain variety that are indigenous to here. He pastured them himself every summer in this hut. Until he became too old to trek. He sold his cows and died.'

We reached our hut with its empty pen. The fencing and everything else was made from wood, except the stone base of the hut which looked solid like a real house. The ruin next to it was an open dump for tins and bottles.

'This is what's left of the old hut, the first one we built.'

An avalanche came down and the fallen pines had crushed the hut. There were rows of fallen pines still and the sight of them created a sense of chaos, like anything could happen at any moment. They built the new hut with what they managed to salvage from the old one.

'When we first arrived, this was the only available place.'

Not that it was busy, but everything was too damaged. In Black Water alone, there were the remains of several huts that had been swallowed up by the land so that you could stay here a while without noticing them.

'After me and The Privateer, there'll be no one,' Kámen said. 'Who wants to carry stuff on their backs but fools like us? You saw the path.'

The terrain was suited only to mountain breeds. The transhumance path and the hikers' path was one and the same, and this was another conflict between the national park on one hand and people like Kámen, The Privateer and 'the other man' on the other side of the ridge.

I peeked inside the hut. It was cosy: a big bed, a shelf, an iron stove. There were blood stains on the duvet.

'Where is the shepherd?' I asked.

'At the lakes. Or Etip's.'

Both were reached by a different incline formed by a tributary of Orelek River – there was a choice of two waterfalls to follow. There was no signal so Kámen couldn't call his shepherd. He'd have to telepathically connect with his sheep and follow his instincts towards them. He looked at some circling crows.

'I don't like those crows,' he said. A sign of dead sheep. 'Otherwise, it's nice to watch the crows ride air currents. Bandit crows.'

In a bandit mountain. Fit for bandit people. 'I'm a bandit,' the old cowboy, Kosta, with the horses and the cows said to me. 'I can't sit still. It's this mountain. It spurs me on.'

Sometimes, when there was pen fixing to do, Kámen slept here for a night or two with the shepherd.

'I can't begin to tell you how I dragged these logs here after the other hut was destroyed,' Kámen said.

He'd had sidekicks all along, and hadn't done these things on his own, but his narrative kept to the first-person singular. I guessed that he had always felt somehow alone.

We climbed through a grove of dwarf-pine, past a waterfall that sang a morning song. Dwarf-pine, juniper and an endemic type of yellow heather had taken over what were once wooded pastures. In the era of big flocks, the flora was more varied. Now there were just a few plants that were invasive in character. This is what happens when grazing animals disappear from an ecosystem and the balance is injured: some things disappear, other things over-appear. Quantity increases but variety decreases. Grazing animals create patches of self-renewing grass that alternates with woodland, something called a mosaic. It's the mosaic that is broken. It becomes more like a synthetic beige carpet. Or a dead forest.

'Every year, I lose animals here,' Kámen said. 'Last year, my shepherd got drunk on the last day of the season and twenty sheep were lost. We found six lined up here with their throats ripped.'

Wolves.

'I can't relax until I bring them down and count them.'

Wolves, bears, disease, drunken shepherds, and – reivers.

'Reivers! Are they still around?'

'You bet,' he said. 'In every highlands there is a clan of reivers. Everybody knows who they are.'

Here, it was the Tinder clan, he said. They prowled like wolves in the night, snatched the choicest sheep and cows, and drove them skilfully across the canyons all the way to the border where they kept them in hidden pens for a year or two, then blended them with their existing flock here. They had done it for generations, he said.

'Nothing you can do. It's in their blood.'

But counting horned heads and ogling choice lambs was in Kámen's blood too. His grandfather had been a serious livestock breeder and smuggled his flock back and forth across the Serbian border during the Second World War, before it became part of the Iron Curtain. His great-grandfather was a big dog breeder.

'Nobody could feed his dogs or hit his dogs, except him,' Kámen said. 'But there is no place for these kinds of dogs in our world anymore. Just as in Scotland there is no place for the wolf.'

'Well, actually,' I said, and told him about the talk of reintroducing the wolf to Scotland. He chuckled.

'But the wolf isn't gonna sit there. It means having guardian dogs, shepherds, large territories and hikers who don't freak out at large predators.'

A whole change of culture. Kámen had shed his dark mood.

The flock came into view. They were scattered like black dominoes on a white board and several Karakachan dogs came over to greet Kámen, regally, without breaking into a run.

'Keep close to me,' he said. 'The rest are fine but Balkán will bite you.'

Balkán growled. He was old and the leader of the pack. His eyes were inflamed – perhaps from staying up all night, keeping watch. He had that almost unbearably loyal look on his face, a Karakachan look, his chest prominent as if covered in medals of fur. It was the fate of the best shepherds, to put the flock first and suffer in silence.

The guardian dog is 'the only animal perfectly trained for the service of others,' said an unnamed naturalist a few hundred years ago. I saw this in Balkán's red eyes.

The sheep came into sharper focus. They were a mineral black-brown and with their small, dense, woolly bodies, they looked as old as the stones. Snouts to the ground, moving as one even when they were scattered – it was a scene I knew from some old life of mine. Their faces were distinctive, with velvet snouts under their curly hair, and as finely drawn as a pharaoh's head.

The cold breeze ruffled the dogs' coats. They looked heroic. It was an animal army, a complete world without humans. Everything went still. I wanted to kneel on the marble floor of the corrie because these really were the oldest animals in the world. You looked at them and you could see that they'd come through slaughter.

I tried to count them but gave up. Mountain sheep were the first grazing animals to be domesticated, but this lot looked pretty wild.

The Karakachans had preserved their animal breeds in a remarkably unadulterated state. This in itself was a sign of the long-standing nomadic existence of these people and animals: it showed that their contact with civilisation was merely transactional. Their deepest contact had been with the natural environment. This is why their sheep remained semi-wild. In the first half of the twentieth century, there were between half a million and a million of these sheep. In November 1957, army lorries blocked the roads and took the migrating nomads' animals, leaving three sheep per family. The Karakachans were literally pushed off the road and forced between four walls. This is called sedentarisation, to rhyme with homogenisation. When the flocks were taken, the dogs dispersed and went wild, howling like wolves. But they were in fact following the north–south trails – all the way from here to the Aegean Plains. And then, at the end of the season, they would come back along the trail. Without the flock. Without the humans.

This was foreseen by Karakachan seers.

'If the Karakachans die, everybody dies,' they said. Sheep, dogs, horses, donkeys and humans. It is not a coincidence that the animals they bred took their name.

By the end of 1958, the number of mountain sheep had decreased to 158,896. All Karakachan sheep were swept into the industrial project of increased production – of meat, milk and wool. They were immediately interbred with others, like Merino. In the 1980s, 33,000 tonnes of wool were produced for the textile industry every year. Forty years later, this industry was gone too. The odd artisan is left spinning wool.

Many died of broken health at the crossroads of fortune where their animals were taken away. Others resigned themselves to living between four walls while still wearing their thick woollen clothes and getting hired as the best shepherds around in the summer season. True, they were now employed by the very industrial-agro complex that had wrecked their way of life, but at least they were able to live in the open for half the year – the men, that is, not the women. In Greece, a handful of Sarakatsani continued to travel in summer along a south–north axis, but it stopped at the border. The annihilation of the last shepherd nation in Europe delivered a clear message: modernity had no place for free-moving people and animals.

This flock, these dogs, symbolised what was left of it.

The dogs walked with us, seven of them. With a crook under his arm and Balkán at his side, came the shepherd. He was dark and unshaven in faded tracksuit pants and a peaked cap. He smiled warmly and took my hand in his. His other hand was swollen and purple.

'What's with your hand?'

'Ach, it's on the mend,' he said breezily. A gap in his teeth dented his smile. But his eyes were hidden.

Kámen inspected two sheep bitten by an adder. They limped a bit.

'Kito, come. This is Kito. And Kasho. Gashta the pants. Baguer.

Redhead.' The shepherd introduced me to the dogs. 'Balkán is best
left alone, eh, my boy.'

Kámen sent the dogs off. He didn't like it that his shepherd was
introducing me to them. And when the shepherd said, jokingly,
'These sheep are only his on paper, otherwise they're mine,' Kámen
abruptly herded them up the corrie. The dogs followed.

We sat by the top lake and The Privateer's cowherd joined us. He
was a skinny young guy with blue eyes discoloured by sadness, or
booze. The tourist path passed along the ridge above and by law, the
grazing animals had to be 100 metres away from the path. People
came down from Thunder Peak, skirted the two glacial cirques and
continued onto the well-trodden paths of eastern Pirin. Hikers were
like pegs along the ridge, but this was an empty world. The two
shepherds kept each other company for lack of any other.

'Where's the bear?' said Kámen. 'I couldn't sleep thinking of that
bear.'

'She's around,' grinned his shepherd. He'd seen her on Kamen
klet, pushing her cubs one by one to the edge of the forest.

Last year, a bear came to the pen. The dogs barked their heads off
but didn't attack.

'I threw a stone at her, and she threw a stone back at me. Like a
person,' the shepherd recounted. 'Then she picked up a sheep and
walked off with it tucked under one arm. Like a person.'

We laughed. The shepherd was forty-ish and handsome, in a rakish
way, his skin full of sun and wind. When he took off his hat, I saw
the pain in his clear eyes.

The shepherd and the cowherd met here every summer and saw
nobody all season, except the odd hiker and Kámen and The Privateer who took turns to bring provisions. (Like the antibiotics last
week, when the shepherd's knuckles, crushed by a falling rock,
became infected and his temperature shot up. He washed down some
dog antibiotics with rakia, that's all he had. He sat by the fire, deliri-
ous, and seeing a worm peeking from the wound – like the sheep
who get worms in their wounds – he took the pincers he used for
removing leeches from the dogs' mouths and pulled something out.
'Blimey, it's a hell of a stretchy worm, and now I can't move my

fingers!' It was a piece of tendon. He told me this the following season. There was no question of going to see a doctor).

The three men smoked. A cloud darkened the greenish lake and a sigh went through the grass, and through us.

'Mamma Bear took two calves,' said Vasko the cowherd to lighten the mood. 'And the cows pushed a calf off the ridge. Not even the dogs wanted to investigate. A madhouse.'

'Mamma Bear never fails to show up,' Kámen's shepherd smiled.

'If you are afraid of the bear, stay away from the hills,' said Vasko.

'What happens if there's suddenly a storm and you can't take them back for the night?' I asked them.

'Nothing. I sleep with them here,' said the shepherd. 'I have a nice plastic sheet.'

Kámen expected nothing less of his shepherd. He pointed at the sheep which had gone higher and were getting too close to the tourist path. This meant that the dogs too were getting too close to the tourist path. It was the shepherd's and farmer's responsibility to avoid frightening hikers at all costs. The shepherd rose to his feet reluctantly. But then Kámen had been the one who'd needlessly herded the sheep up the slope just a moment ago. He had decided that his shepherd had enjoyed my company long enough.

'What happened with the helper who quit?' I asked the shepherd. There was something smart and intriguing about him, as if he was running from something by doing this job.

'Nothing happened,' he said. 'He missed the internet and dreaded the bear. It's not for everyone here.'

We hadn't been introduced. His name was Alexander.

'Or just Sásho,' he flashed a smile and climbed up the marble corrie, crook in swollen hand. He wore simple canvas sneakers like a hipster. I didn't think I'd see him again.

Shepherds are the invisible people, I thought, when we hiked back down to the hut and Kámen talked about himself. The flock, the dogs, the whole enterprise depended on them, they were at the centre of the circle. Yet shepherds were not seen or heard. They remained faceless figures who blended into the land. They had no names. They were looked down upon, even by their employers. They were not meant to be protagonists in the story.

Back at the hut, Kámen produced a tub of fatty lamb he'd brought from the roast at home.

'We should leave it for Sásho,' I said. He hadn't eaten fresh meat all summer. There were only tins and frankfurters in the hut, along with a pot of cooked butter beans.

'No, I brought it for you,' Kámen said. But he didn't touch it himself.

'As Carlos Castaneda's Don Juan says: "When in the forest, you mustn't overeat. A bit of dried meat, a bit of peyote." We have peyote in the house by the way.'

Yes, lots of cacti on the farm, I kept getting stabbed by them. Kámen set about mending the fence of the pen. The sun was already in decline. We'd be returning to Orelek in the dark. In the hut, I pushed Sásho's bloodied duvet aside and fell into a restless sleep full of barking dogs. Though when I woke up, the valley was quiet like a tomb.

CALLING THE WOLVES

Marina picked me up from the sheep house in another pre-dawn start. We drove fast, almost furiously, in the blackness above the village, along a poor forestry road. Dawn broke when we reached an area of terraced pastures called Prairie. A panorama of rolling hills opened. Prairie had been a busy neighbourhood of Orelek, you could tell by the size of the ruined school. The odd ruined house and some bungalows for hunters and shepherds was all that was left. Ugly and cement-grey, an unfinished new church stood in the middle of Prairie like a monument to corruption – a local politician had laundered the money that should have been used to fix the road or the water supply. Dogs ran after the jeep. There was an open pen with goats and sheep 'The other man' again.

'That's a lot of white sheep,' Marina frowned. 'Has he started a third flock?'

Marina had a permanent frown. It's hard to stop certain things once you've set them in motion, she said, meaning the last twenty-five years. A Spanish biology student was spending the summer helping her, but she had sprained her ankle on one of Marina's field trips. She was in awe of Marina and thinking of making wolves her thing too, but didn't know if she could keep up the pace. The wolves' pace and Marina's pace were the same thing.

With a rucksack of our recording equipment on and coffee flask in hand, we set off from Prairie, for the pine forest of Baba. This was the old transhumance route. Baba was the conical hill you climbed before you took off in the direction of The Beeches and the arduous trail to the huts I'd just covered with Kámen. The forest was cold and awakening with birdsong. We talked dogs.

'Dogs with pointy ears are closer to nature, more primitive,' she said, like her rescued dingo-like dog, Kita. She'd wanted to bring

Kita along but Kita had gone off into the hills to play with her friend, another hunting-type dog rescued by Marina and later adopted by someone in the village. She had found that dog on a forest road, with her ears cut off.

An animal's size and primitiveness – or being closer to the wild ancestors – are inversely related. Karakachan horses are smaller than other horses, and faster. They survive alpine terrain, hunger and predators better than others. Being smaller makes you faster. That helps in the wild.

'Labradors and huskies are big but they are more modern, bred as company for humans,' Marina said.

Guardian dogs like the Karakachan are not. And they don't have to be huge to be equal to the wolf, who also doesn't have to be big to throttle one hundred sheep in an hour. It's more about purpose than size. For example, the Romans bred enormous mastiffs just to sow terror but, like bodybuilders on steroids, those freaks were ill-adapted for sustained reproduction and died out.

The Karakachan dog retains its ancient genes. It is a Molossus descended from highland Asian canids close to the wolf, like the Tibetan Mastiff. They were brought over at various points by settlers, armies, trade caravans and pastoral nomads. This process began around 3,000 years ago. Alexander the Great's military campaigns in Asia, the Greco-Persian Wars before that and many other military and settlement campaigns opened corridors for the guardian dog. One of the earliest written descriptions of dogs that resemble today's livestock guardians is by Herodotus, who writes of the Persian king's vast army with its 'Indian dogs' from the Himalayas.

The nomadic Turkic Bulgars brought their dogs and horses from Central Asia in the sixth century and ten centuries later, the Yuruks came with their dogs from Asia Minor. It is thought that the prototype for the Karakachan dog and other livestock guardians in Europe came from the Pamir and Hindu Kush massifs. But there is also a link to the Molossus dogs of Epirus, described by Aristotle in his *Animal Histories*: 'In the Molossian race of dogs, those employed in hunting differ in no respect from other dogs; while those employed in following sheep are larger and more fierce in their attack on wild beasts'. A few centuries later, Pliny the Elder states that the guardian dogs of Epirus fight lions and elephants, but they too had probably come from Asia. In a passage about fabulous creatures in today's India and Pakistan, Strabo speaks of brave dogs that can overwhelm lions and bulls and 'do not let go of what they have bitten until water is poured down their nostrils.'

'True guardian dogs are rare now,' Marina said. 'There isn't much left for them to guard.'

The old shepherds said it: once, there was enough for everybody. For the wolf and for us. The flocks were larger, the dogs were tougher. 'Now they've become softies, like our lot,' Marina said. Yet she was pleased when she saw scary Shaban put his head on my chest. She was glad to see the dogs being at once tough and tender because that was the character of Karakachan dogs – aggressive to intruders, loyal to insiders. In that sense, they were like wolves.

'But a wolf can never be trained for the service of others,' Marina said.

Marina tracked the wolf population of western Pirin twice a year. There were several strategic places in Baba where she called the wolves. It was an hour's climb to the first one.

Wolves roam over large territories. They can cross 20 kilometres in a day without stopping. I hoped we wouldn't be copying them because I didn't have the stamina after yesterday and another night of being serenaded by the dogs.

We stopped to inspect some dried white shit full of bones and fur: fox or wolf. Marina collected it in a plastic bag to put under the microscope later. She could tell from the prey's fur what animal it was from. And a bit further on:

'Oh, someone's had the runs and it's fresh,' Marina crouched by a pool of excrement, happy to have found traces of what looked like bear. There were half-digested berries. She put some in a laboratory vial with a stick. Some minutes later, we heard a grunt just above the path and a heavy escape: a bear.

'Hello bear,' she said gently and clambered after it. I froze.

'We startled her. A small female,' Marina was excited. Her frown was gone.

I didn't tell Marina or she'd think me weak, but I have a fear of the
bear. In a recurring nightmare, I am chased by a bear or a bear blocks
my way. The bear rarely appears in the dream, I just know it's there,
and it fills me with dread. Marina didn't seem afraid of anything.
Except stopping.

'We've fought tooth and claw for twenty-five years. We can't stop
now.'

The sheep, the goats, the dogs – for Kámen, it was personal. For
Marina, all animals were about preserving the ecosystemic web for
the sake of the web. In nature's mind, there is no difference between
the survival of a wild animal and the survival of a domesticated one.
Tracking wolves to protect them from hunters and birthing a lamb
that might be eaten by those wolves – they went together in nature's
mind. Marina had nature's mind. She saw how fragile the web had
become and it made her frantic. She was running out of time.

'But it goes the other way too. Spontaneous recovery does happen.'

In Holland, wolves reappeared by themselves. In Spain, there are
2,000 individuals re-colonising the plains and hiding in what's left of
the forests.

'Mind you, the official count is an overestimate. It's the same here.'

There were around 800 individuals in Bulgaria, but the official
figure was double that. Hunting organisations in cahoots with local
authorities did this on purpose: they exaggerated the number of
wolves to justify indiscriminate hunting. This included farmers who
sometimes hired a wolf stalker to stop attacks on their livestock or
put out poison, which often poisoned the dogs. And the vultures.

'But even the vulture has made a comeback. In Pirin, we thought
they were exterminated, then a pair suddenly appeared last year.
Black-headed ones.'

This is prime vulture country but only when there is livestock.
And prime wolf country because of the forests, I thought.

'No, wolves don't need forests. Only to hide from humans. But
they're happy living in the open. Like in Scandinavia and in the
desert.'

The communist state was murderous towards wolves. In its
attempt to control the behaviour of all living things, and allegedly to

protect livestock, it poisoned masses of wolves, so that by the 1960s there were just 100 left, a borderline number. But the wolf recovered miraculously.

'Then, in the 1990s, there was one last attempt to legalise wolf poisoning, but it didn't pass in the end. Still, the wolf remains a neglected animal, the lowest of the low. Even to science.'

The wolf is the eternal enemy in folk tales, a misunderstood creature.

'I had to do something.'

That's when Marina started collecting data and thirty years later, she had so much of it, she was doing a PhD. But she was not an academic, she was a wildish woman, happiest in the woods on a tense mission with a flask of coffee and a notebook. In the final days of her second pregnancy, Marina still went out to track wolves, the mother told me, and the family were afraid she'd give birth and literally run off with the wolves.

You were not supposed to do this work alone, but biologists are a shrinking species, Marina said.

'Most of my students wanted to do medicine, but didn't get in. Biology was a second choice. Because it doesn't pay well.'

Most biologists were not into walking across mountains at dawn. They preferred to drive large cars and write reports in heated rooms.

'People with a real interest in nature are decreasing,' Marina said. 'Even among biologists.'

This surprised me. I thought it was the opposite. But here we were, the only humans on Baba. The bears outnumbered us by far. More signs of bear appeared. Large, overturned stones: they had been looking for ants. Crushed shrubs. Clawed trunks.

'Normally the bears don't use this path in summer. The fact that they are this year, means the path is virtually unused by the two-legged. That's good!' she grinned.

Even with Marina here, I was afraid of the bear. I understood that the wolf would not attack me, but I didn't understand that about the bear.

Marina was measuring a fresh bear print with a tape measure. Twenty-five centimetres long, fourteen centimetres wide. A large male had passed along the path just moments ago. Not the same one we'd surprised an hour ago.

'You asked why wolves? Because you can communicate with wolves.' It was obvious to her. 'They are highly communicative.'

That's why Vachka needed a new companion. During mating season, Marina separated her from her old mate with netting, 'because there's no point in having young ones doomed to a life in captivity.'

Marina grew up in the capital, but her happiest times were spent in her grandparents' villages. One lot of grandparents lived across the border in Macedonia – that's where her father was from. There were lots of horses, black buffaloes and dogs in the fields. She felt free. We moved on, fast. She was delighted with the density of bears, there were at least two in a small radius. Later in the season, she would come up again, with me and Kita in tow, to set up camera traps for the wolves.

'Wolves are conservative,' she said. 'They stick to the same territory.'

They had rendezvous areas where they raised their young, and core areas where the young were watched over by an adult, while the rest of the pack hunted. It was in these places that Marina set up camera traps. Like any hunter, she was happiest when on the trail of something untamed.

We finally stopped and she took out the recording equipment and set it up. Then she stood, cupped her mouth with her hands, took a deep breath and howled. Just like a wolf.

'*Awwwww. Awwww.*'

Once, wait. Twice, wait. Three times, wait. The mountain picked it up. It was a drawn out, melancholy cry. A fourth time. Silence. She packed up the equipment and we moved to higher ground in silence. Her howl affected me. It rippled through my body for the rest of the day. Again, she set up and called the wolves. Once, twice, thrice, four times. The mountain opened up below the meadow. We waited. I saw a small, white, fragrant flower, like an orchid. But it wasn't an orchid. In folklore, it's called nymph's flower.

'*Awwwwww*' . . .

The tall pines spin above us. It's like the mountain is calling to itself. The wolves are silent. It feels like they have gone forever.

'They have answered me in this spot before,' Marina frowned. 'We started late. We should've been here earlier.'

But there were other reasons why the wolves were silent. They might not answer out of fear that, if they spoke back, they would be tracked down and killed.

A memory came from the winter. I had been walking all day with Emin, looking for the horses, when we arrived at a hunter's lodge. It was full of men from his village, heated with booze. They had just shot a large grey female wolf. She was crucified on the bonnet of a jeep to be photographed, her dark blood dripping over the headlights, her head on the windscreen. I wanted to move on at once. But Emin was happy: 'Here, I'll give you 20 bucks for it!' He'd just lost a fowl to this wolf. The cubs, we didn't touch, the men reassured me, then one of them gave us a lift back to the village. Most of them worked as builders in England and France. This was their holiday back home. Home: where you can be a barbarian again.

Killing a parent is much more destructive than killing a cub. The couple is broken up, the surviving adult becomes unpredictable and is likely to change territory. If you want to damage a population of wolves and at the same time harass the grazing animals, kill one parent.

The last wolf in Scotland was killed in the mid-eighteenth century. Books are written about that wolf – a measure of how pallid life is without the full web, so pallid that the wolf becomes academic, but also a measure of the care taken with the wolf's ghost and a measure of understanding about what disappeared with the wolf: entire ecosystems. Better late than never.

Here, among the common people, men who kill wolves are still seen as sportsmen. One fanatical stalker spent fourteen hours waiting for the wolf without moving. He used infrared lights and nighttime cameras. He had shot over 100, not counting the cubs which he always shot along with the parents and lined them up for a photo shoot. 'Successfully removed' was the term. 'Game' for predators.

But the language of industrial farming across Europe is no different: 'culling' for killing.

Once, Marina caught some poachers killing one of the collared wolves. She made the mistake of sending a signal to the national park within sight of them. A week later, three of the family's guardian dogs were poisoned above Orelek – the hunters' revenge.

This is what Marina was up against.

'When Vulcan, our first rescued wolf arrived in Orelek, the town vet came up to see a sheep. He heard about Vulcan and said: Well, if there is a market for wolf hides!'

That's why she was putting all her efforts into the younger generation.

Marina placed tracking collars on the wolves to map their movements. If a collar was not active for more than four hours, it gave a 'mortality signal'. That usually meant that the wolf had been killed. There were hunters who, seeing the collar, tried to cover their tracks by dumping the body in water.

Another memory came to me. Kosta the old cowboy called the wolves too. Once, several of his calves had their throats ripped out. The word was 'spoiled'. He called the wolf, the wolf came from the woods. The cowboy waited with his rifle.

'Come, it's you I need, I said and blasted his brains.' Then he dragged the body into the river.

'The wolf is the most traumatised animal,' Marina said. 'Because it's been persecuted for centuries by the two-legged and it's running out of places to hide.'

That is why the wolves were silent.

The persecution of wolves across Europe has been a kind of natural selection, resulting in wolves that are forever mistrustful of humans. Twenty-thousand years ago, there were fewer humans and more wolves. Some of those wolves became scavengers and companions to humans and eventually, turned into dogs. In the Chauvet Cave in France, there is a picture of those early days of friendship 26,000 years ago: the footprints of a boy and next to them, those of a large canid like something between a dog and a wolf. Boy and dog-wolf had entered the cave to see the animal drawings that were already there, and already 5,000 years old.

Marina packed up the equipment and we began to make our

descent. And – another bear print. The smaller bear had passed along the path while we were at the top! Marina recorded the measurements and we traced the prints to where they had faded in the forest.

Kosta the cowboy did something different with bear prints when he came across them. He squared them with his crook and said: 'Where you step, there you stay.' A spell against the four-legged ones.

'You know, you're lucky with bears!' Marina grinned. And in that grin I saw the girl – who lit up when she ran to the buffalo and the horses in the fields of her grandparents' village. 'Bear is your animal, not wolf,' she said.

She had called the wolves, but the bears had answered. I told her about my dream then, and my dread.

'It's in your head,' she said. 'It's because you don't understand them.'

It was true. I didn't understand the bear. I'm not sure I wanted to. Us two-leggeds project our limited minds onto the four-legged: and their pastors. That's what Marina was – a pastor of wild animals. And because the impersonal nature of her mission was still incomprehensible to the masses, there was a conspiracy about people like Marina: that they 'released' wild animals into nature. Wolves, bears, snakes and dangerous creatures in general, just to be perverse, just to be witches. What else was a lone woman doing in the forest?

'How are you supposed to release them?' I asked.

'I dunno. Apparently in Turkey there are special breeding grounds for wolves and we are supposed to be taking wolves from there and smuggling them across the border, just to release them here and piss people off.'

We laughed.

'But it gets weirder,' she said. 'This conspiracy also circulates in Scandinavia. Colleagues there are accused of "releasing" animals too.'

I fell down the bear path and got up again, and I briefly felt like a woman who runs with the bears, not from them.

At the house, the Loopy family growled and didn't approach. They smelled the forest on me. Only Malina and Kalina came to play. Muna the Monkey came to say hello too. She blinked a lot with her albino lashes, as if life was a bit much for her. I would miss them.

By evening, everyone was milking in the goat pen: Marina, Alex, Kámen. The mother processed the milk in the dairy room. Marina went back to the centre to look for Kita and prepare the next camp with the limping Spanish student. Alex went to his terrarium and Kámen disappeared on some errand in his white van. He often drove at night, his eyes half-closed. Coming up the other way was a beat-up jeep with missing windows. The driver headed above the village towards Prairie without stopping.

The television was on in the dark kitchen. An American film that I hadn't seen for twenty years was showing and I sat at the table, picking at the roast in the tray and watched it to the end. The white men shot the wolf who communicated with humans, slaughtered the buffalo and desecrated their bodies for trophies, wiped their arses with the notebook in which the disappearing world of an old America was recorded, and next up for slaughter would be the humans on horseback who ran with the wolves and the buffalo. The fate of the Native Americans reminded me of the Karakachans. I don't know which was worse. The Karakachans had roamed longer in a boundless environment but when their animal nation was dismembered, they were put in houses and blocks of flats, not in reservations. Only the mountains of their birth were left, to roam in their dreams.

In the morning, the mother was moving a bale of straw above the goat pen. The goat kids watched her, munching under their fringes. There was no ladder. She had to push it down and jump. Why didn't Kámen have a ladder, at least?

'Oh, that would make it easier and it's meant to be painful,' she said. 'Have you had enough of us?'

No, I just need to get a good night's sleep. I hoped to be back next year.

'We'll read your book about the lakes. One will read, the others will listen, to save time.'

Giving your book to people who didn't ask for it is like giving advice. It is politely received and discarded.

'Don't worry, you're busy,' I said. But she had moved on already, back to herself.

She had grown up with a family cow called Elsa. They always had fresh milk. Then she married an artist who became successful and the glamour of it defined her. And now – this again. 'There are things you don't imagine would be repeated,' she said, 'but they come back in disguise.'

Shaban came over and put his head against my chest.

On the way out of the village, I tried the schoolhouse again. Velin was in a better mood. He let me in and we sat at a large table in a room where workshops took place before the pandemic. Mushrooms in jars, red wine in bottles – his hobbies.

'Are the wolves answering?' he asked. 'My favourite film of all time is *Dances with Wolves*. Because the protagonist is a kindred spirit – a man who runs away so they don't cut off his legs.'

'I watched it last night,' I said.

'How are things at Kámen's?' he asked.

'Well, you live next door to him,' I said.

But Kámen didn't talk to Velin. 'Kámen is as stubborn as a mule, otherwise this whole enterprise wouldn't have survived,' Velin said, 'it takes a genius of *inat* to do that.' Inat: a Pan-Balkan word meaning stubborn to the point of self-harm. 'So, hats off to him,' he said.

'But he expects you to read him telepathically, like the animals do. Without having to resort to words. And then he gets mad when you don't. It's the nature of the beast.'

Velin the eco-warrior knew Marina through the biology network and when they set themselves up here, he bought the ruined old school to be part of the mission and educate the next generation together. They did for a while but something in the human web was torn. Everyone was too self-centred for a supporting role.

He showed me his garden.

'It's not what it was, the last fire destroyed everything.'

I asked if I could eat a fig from his tree.

'It's not my tree,' he said. 'I'm borrowing it. Life itself is borrowed.'

Velin had a rare disease. All the bones in his body had been broken at some point. He was written off by doctors and learned to walk again, and even to build boats and sail the Pacific Ocean. He knew

about inat. He was a global soul, wise enough to cultivate local goodness. Velin lived here with his ninety-year-old mother, a bird-like
woman with dementia who took to wandering down the dug-out
road in a lace-embroidered dress with her stick topped with a carved
owl and stopping any passing driver: 'Excuse me, I'm lost. Would
you take me back to the capital?'

Once, the village eccentric, now dead, got into the house, unlocked
the window and the two of them escaped together into the woods,
holding hands like children.

That's why Velin kept the door locked.

'I didn't think it would come to this,' he said.

He lived here most of the time because you can't be an ecologist
and live in a city, he said. Growing up in the capital, he knew he
would study biology because that was a way to be close to interesting
things. When he spent holidays in his grandparents' village, he had
two friends: a cat and a raven. An early memory: the family are
hiking at Thunder Peak and he and his brother are small enough to be
carried in rucksacks, and from the rucksack on his mother's back he
sees the mountain below. Far, far away were little houses.

'And I said to myself, one day, I want to live in one of those houses.'

'And now you do,' I said.

'And now I do. And I carry my mother on my back. Anyway, have
you met Stamen of the Tinders? You should. He and Kámen pass
each other in the night like lost ships, but they started together.'

The other man!

Velin sat on the bench. Two cats jumped up on each side of him
and sat there with slitted eyes, making Velin look like a friendly
oracle.

On a field trip to the Kresna Gorge twenty years ago, Velin was in
a reserve of Greek juniper, taking a sample, when a huge man in cam-
ouflage startled him. Velin thought he was a poacher and the man was
about to fine Velin on behalf of the national park. A rainstorm broke
out and while they explained themselves, the river rose. Stamen took
Velin across on his back. That's how they met.

'Come and meet the oldest individual in Orelek,' Velin and the
cats got up.

The four of us walked to the church courtyard. Cemented into a platform like a monument was the mighty fossil of a juniper tree.

'This lady is a thousand years old and holds the history of the place,' said Velin. Juniper is feminine here. 'She burned in the last fire. I had her encased so people don't forget or she'd have ended up in their stoves.'

A wildfire had crept up from the gorge and reached Orelek by dusk. Seeing that the fire brigade was taking its time because of the poor road and that the few inhabitants were helpless against the flames, Velin did something he'd never done: he lay down by the fig tree and called to the spirits of Pirin to send rain and save the village from another apocalypse.

'Because it wouldn't rise from the ashes again. And neither would we.'

Within an hour and after a long dry spell, the rain came. Orelek and its creatures were given another chance.

THE OTHER MAN

Stamen had called to say he'd be late because of an emergency in the national park. The Greek juniper reserve had caught fire.

'But only along the edges so we contained it.'

There was a charred smell about him. I climbed into the jeep with missing windows and said 'hi' to his boys in the back with their eager faces. This was not our first meeting.

'This reserve is not natural,' he said. 'It was engineered by the communist state.'

Stamen was a park ranger.

'Communist-era forestry changed the face of the mountain for the worse,' he said.

Between the 1950s and the 1970s, forestry politics came into direct conflict with highland communities. It happened in the wake of traumatic collectivisation.

'The hills above this gorge used to be mixed. Oak, hornbeam, juniper. No pine. And cultivated fields. Rye, vines, later, tobacco. Fields were mown for hay. It was a biodiverse patchwork and locals grazed their animals throughout the year, moving them around to give the land a rest.'

This patchwork sustained itself naturally. People pruned the juniper which grew back, but without invading. Goats and sheep are drawn to varied pasture and they too pruned the juniper. The way people managed their land and their animals supported a habitat where all endemic species thrived.

'It was a spontaneously created juniper reserve, but with other species too.'

Then the communist state arrived to rearrange the mountain, felled the mixed forest, erected barbed-wire fences to keep out people and animals, and planted pine not suited to this lower climate belt.

'Then, they cordoned off large hillsides and declared them a juniper reserve. Illegal for grazing.' Once again, small grazing animals were pushed up to less accessible areas.

The short-term result was a war between powerful state agronomists and powerless locals. The state won, of course. And the long-term result was monoculture. It changed the soil and the microclimate, caused erosion and stripped bare the weave in which grazing animals were the key thread.

'The goats still love the juniper grove,' Stamen said. 'It's still illegal for them to graze there, but some things can't be stopped.'

'Why do they love it?' asked his younger son from the back.

'Because it's tasty to them. Just like these grapes are tasty to us.'

He pulled over to pick a bunch from the vineyards along the road to Orelek and we munched the amber Keratsuda grapes, sweet with south. I almost exclaimed, like Velin: What south, what incredible south!

'The Grape makes the best wine around here, have you met him?' Stamen said. 'Anyway, the reserve is now in a semi-chaotic state.'

And of course, a juniper grove burns like kindling. There is nothing to stop it. That is where the massive wildfire started some years ago, the one that almost destroyed Orelek.

'One of the biggest sins committed by the communists was the mass felling of the old mixed forest of Pirin. Criminal logging hasn't stopped ever since. And how are you?'

He gave me his usual quick glance. He wasn't one for smiles, but he had a way of noticing people and animals. He had an eye.

In Kresna, Stamen could be seen in one of two cars: an old Lada inside which he looked like a giant and the Nissan jeep in which he still looked like a giant, because he was. His sons, with their eager faces, were always in the back seat. Stamen's wife worked in the capital and their boys lived here and there. Now, I'd joined them on an errand to his pens in Prairie. Stamen seemed to have a pen in every fold of the mountain, but his house was in Kresna.

Kresna: I had taken a room here, in a riverside hotel called Strymon where I could sleep at night and have contact with the outside world during the day. It was only post-Orelek that I felt the full

Orelek effect, like a mild post-trauma – the gritted teeth, the sense of something separate and injured.

'Yeah, it's extreme there,' said Stamen. 'But you've got to be extreme in this game. Or you give up.'

The first time I met Stamen, he sat down heavily under the linden trees in the town square and skipped the small talk: 'You've heard by now that I'm the villain in the story. It's okay, I can take it. Kámen and Marina are visionaries. I'm more primitive. But I joined the cause with all I had – my parents, our animals, and I gave my best years to it.'

Knowing I was part of the Kámen circle, he was surprised that I was talking to him at all. And it's true that I felt a loyalty to Kámen's circle – so much so that I was a bit uncomfortable making contact with 'the other man'. He was obviously purged from the Orelek chronicles for a reason.

'Me, I'm of peasant stock. Greedy for land and animals, this is my problem.'

The dark fire was still in his eyes, like in that old photo. Only his body had grown heavier, with a limp that made him look like he had accepted some things.

'The point of my life is to be in the highlands with the animals, the dogs.' The coffee cup was tiny in his hand. 'You look at me here, but I'm up in Prairie with the animals. The dogs.'

The dogs were not exactly animals to him. They were more like humans.

In the 1990s, Stamen saw a newspaper article: two artist brothers in the north were breeding Karakachan dogs. Stamen was looking for good guardian dogs for his parents' sheep and goats. He took the train north and met the brothers – and Kitan.

'Kitan was something else,' Stamen said with feeling. 'In him you saw how the Karakachan dog is part of the mountain and the mountain is a part of it. For hundreds of years they were one. They can't thrive without each other.'

Mountain dogs and dog mountains.

'Kámen is this country's greatest dog breeder, full stop,' Stamen said. 'And when we met, I found kindred spirits. Until then, I'd felt isolated.'

They talked dogs, he ordered a puppy and told them about this highland village with still-trodden routes and empty houses, pastures everywhere, all waiting for something to happen. They were already rescuing sheep but didn't have a proper base or proper mountains for them. One day, the brothers and Marina took the train south to Orelek. The rest became history.

Stamen came from the Tinder clan of Orelek who had first arrived with their flocks and dogs from Albania on horseback. This was the case with many of Orelek's settlers and this stretch of the Struma basin. The settlers came in waves between the fifteenth and nineteenth centuries along two principle axes: west–east and south–north. This meant Albania and western Macedonia and Thessaly and northern Epirus. There were three main groups of settlers: Arnauts (Christian Bulgarians and Albanians), Vlachs (Aromanians and Karakachans) and Greeks (in fact Greek-identifying Vlachs).

They had been displaced by groups of nomadic Yuruks sent to the Balkans in a re-settlement project. The new colonists took over pastures and dislodged other people, like Stamen's ancestors who wandered off in search of new grazing land: a common story. They mixed with those who were already here. The hills of Orelek had had resident shepherds since antiquity. Roman rule had established a thriving settlement that later waned. But on the whole, this side of Pirin was available to newcomers. It was difficult terrain but fertile with abundant water and pristine pastures. Once here, groups like the Tinders lived in yurts for decades before they built permanent dwellings. Back in Albania, they had always lived in yurts.

In other words, the line between nomadic and settled was not completely firm at that point. All pastoralists moved with their animals and the direction and degree of movement was determined by the available pastures.

Every hillside and family name in Orelek tells the story of this migration. The Drachov clan is made up of the people who came from Durres (Drach) in Albania. There is also a Yurukov clan, because some of the Yuruks became settled. The Yuruks bridged continents but their yurt camps gradually disappeared from the land. From the early seventeenth century on, their movements decreased and their settlements vanished from the Struma region. Perhaps the 'Little Ice Age' forced them to withdraw to warmer places in the Aegean. In any case, in a typical turn-around of the pastoral chessboard, the pastures once colonised by the Yuruks were eventually re-colonised by the Vlachs, Karakachans and the rest of the population.

A word left behind by the Yuruks is still in use, but only just: *gins*. It means clan, seed, genus or a group of animals and people united by a purpose.

'Lots of Vlachi settled too. In my childhood, the best flock in Orelek belonged to a guy called Kolyo the Vlach. Small black Karakachan sheep.'

The Struma Basin was like a never-ending party at the genetic pool. Its people were descended from all over the Balkans, the Aegean, Asia Minor and Central Asia. The melting pot effect was obvious in the names and faces. Some like Sásho had Levantine looks, others like Stamen were large and fair like Celts. This is the region of Macedonia with its own dialect, late Ottoman history, politics of insurgence and counter-insurgence, schisms, rivalries and mountain escapades that were incredible but true. Shape-shifting and shit-stirring for fun.

'My grandfather said it: we're outlaws by nature. Separatists. Just for the sake of it, 'cos we can't sit still.'

It was the thrilling terrain. It spurred people on to passion and trouble.

Stamen's godfather Andrea was from the oldest Albanian clan, the Proko.

'There's a water fountain built by the original Proko. Haven't been there for forty years.'

Stamen's grandfather spoke fluent Turkish and taught his grandchildren to count in it. Turkish had been a language of trade for him and therefore not just survival, but worldliness and fun.

'Those two men instilled in me respect for the Turks.'

Animal-rich Orelek had traded with passing Turks, Pomaks, Jews,

Romani and other Gypsies, Yuruks, Karakachans, Aromanian Vlachs and all manner of travelling buyers and sellers, dealers and recyclers.

The Tinders were above all highlanders. Their nationality was the mountain.

'To have animals near you, this is our religion,' said Stamen and his jaw set. 'There are people in the family who go to the cities and make contributions to the world. But there must be one that stays behind with the animals in the hills. Dogs, goats, sheep, something. If you lose that, you lose yourself.'

Under Ottoman law, pastureland was sacrosanct. Until the last days of Empire, a decree held: 'A land that is primordial pasture may not be ploughed up. If this is done by force, it must be reinstated as pasture at once.'

In the country where small grazing animals are religion, pasture is church, the seasonal rhythm is the Bible and the barking dogs on the perimeter are choir, nomads and peasants alike had the right to expand grazing land by controlled tree felling and fires.

When the communist authorities arrived in Orelek, the Tinders' flocks were taken and their house in Prairie bulldozed, forcing them to the level of Struma as if they were falling on their knees. They had to start again and build a house in Kresna. Kresna started as a couple of roadside inns, then houses for the exiles of Orelek, then a train station, finishing as a planned town, though it was still a village at heart. A village with an international road cutting through it.

'My great-grandfather always had animals tucked away. There was money because of that. He built a big house in Kresna.'

That house was bulldozed later when the municipal buildings were erected. And again, the animals 'tucked away' saved the day.

'The old shepherds had pens in the remotest places. They were big, burly people with thick sticks. They were herbalists, medicine men and animal whisperers.'

He spoke in the third person, but that described the Tinders.

When Stamen joined the brothers and Marina on their mission, his parents kept a flock of sheep and goats in the gorge and when the mission set up permanent camp in Orelek, Stamen and his parents threw themselves into it with all they had – their flock, their intimate knowledge of the mountain, their experience from a lifetime with grazing animals, boundless enthusiasm and brute physical strength.

'We came up with our axes, our animals and the clothes on our backs.'

Early on, Stamen scouted the village for suitable houses for the mission. He asked an old woman: 'Where do we go so we don't get in anybody's way?'

'Up there, sonny,' she said. 'In the Bara neighbourhood 'cos there's no one left, but . . .' she trailed off. 'Go light a candle in the church.'

He did – Stamen is religious in an earthy way. In this mountain, it's the only way. A forbidding cloud hung over Orelek then, Stamen felt it the way I felt it twenty-five years later.

'The first houses in the Bara were built by the sons of Proko.'

They were watered by the Kosovska River and its multiple *bara*, 'warm spring'.

'The years in Orelek were the happiest of my life. We grew the flock.'

It takes time to grow a flock. They travelled up and down the country scouting for sheep, goats and dogs. They got a strong team together. There was Vangel, Ivan and a couple of other key players. There were women who came as volunteers and stayed.

'It was a team of like-minded people that got the whole thing off the ground. It wouldn't have happened without them all.'

Among them was a young, tall, determined woman who arrived with a rucksack and stayed for two years. She left due to relationship complications, possibly a triangle. Years later, Stamen visited her in her ancestral village in the Balkan ranges, where she had attempted to build something similar to Orelek out of her grandparents' ruined house with a partner and a handful of sheep. 'A sad sight,' Stamen said, 'they lacked help and there was no focus. You need focus.'

During his Orelek years, Stamen not only found his purpose and place, he also gained an education. It was thanks to the family book shelves that he started reading and went on to become a graduate in agronomy, with help from Achilles who claimed to have written Stamen's thesis on the long-haired mountain goat for him. Yet it was Stamen who got them fired up about that goat in the first place. Or so he claimed.

'I said: we've got to have these long-haired, curly horned goats. They're endangered. Kámen said: what are we gonna do with them? I said: I dunno but we've got to have them. He said: who's gonna look after them? I said: I will.'

They started gathering and breeding the spectacular Kalofer goats and he became a goatherd for two or three years. Busy in the day with the sheep, he'd take the goats out at night and sleep standing, propped on his stick.

'The moon was my sun.'

The volunteers at the predator centre were educated men and women from the city, with strong ideas about eco projects. The locals were bewildered.

'An old woman said: dearies, we are a village of two rivers and you talk of collecting rainwater with expensive equipment. Can't we harness the rivers?'

The locals were stuck in their ways and the incomers must have had a colonial whiff about them from the start, but the serious cracks appeared over ownership. The idea had been to run the place like a commune with a shared flock and resources. It's how pastoralism worked anyway. A community organised itself around the blended flocks. It was called *bachiya* by the highlanders and *company* by the Karakachans. It was a cooperative enterprise driven by logistical necessity. To run a flock in summer is very labour intensive and pooling resources was the way to do it.

It was a communal endeavour, but private property remained sacrosanct. Stealing somebody else's sheep was taboo – which doesn't mean that it didn't happen of course. Like the peasant bachiya, the Karakachan company was a group of loosely connected families who pooled their livestock for the summer and all the men and boys became engaged in animal care. The Karakachans were far more patriarchal than the highlanders, though, and power was much more centralised. A headman who was wealthier and more educated than the rest stood in the centre and made all the important decisions: communicating with the outside world, buying grazing land, supplying provisions for everyone and being a one-man elder council with a few close aides. It was a highly responsible position and open to abuse and corruption of all kinds because the other men were illiterate, innumerate and relied on him to keep the books. The women kept the camp going. An unwritten agreement between the head man and the hired shepherds was made for the whole season but if the hired hands found the boss unfair, they could walk away. In reality this was difficult. They would have to walk over multiple mountains in search of work with another company. Yet, if they wanted to, they could do that and ruin him.

The highland bachiya was the same, but with one difference. During the summer it was a men-only organisation; women and children only visited the highland pastures to bring provisions. The bachiya had a less hierarchical structure than the Karakachans. At the end of the season, the profit was distributed by the head shepherds and the flocks were split again for the winter.

The Orelek project had wanted to rekindle the pastoral commune.

'But it didn't work out,' Stamen said. 'Wolves don't eat shared prey.'

A shepherding expression.

'And private property separates people. This is what happened to us.'

Disputes over property, animals and relationships drove wedge after wedge into the project. Sparks flew, there were love triangles, creaking floorboards, the constant counting of animal heads and just one shared sink. Stamen got involved with a volunteer. The couple were suspected of plotting to break away with part of the flock. Stamen had been looking for a suitable partner with a similar interest in animal breeding, but who was socially superior because he was ambitious. And he was put in his place; he was getting above himself. Stamen, his father and all the others, paid and unpaid, had carried stones, logs and animals on their backs for years, but there was an unwritten pecking order and Stamen wanted more of everything for himself. Meanwhile, Kámen started speaking about Orelek's achievements using the first-person singular. This galled Stamen. The atmosphere became oppressive.

Then one summer things came to a head over some choice lambs that Stamen had marked as his own with the ancestral stigmata that is passed down in every shepherding family. In his paternal line, a cross was cut into the lamb's right ear. When you give your sheep to a new owner, you also pass down your unique stigmata. It's a tattoo in the fabric of time. To pass on your mark is like passing on your genes. In a shepherd's faux-pas, Kámen overrode Stamen's mark and made his own on the same lambs by cutting off the tip of the right ear; the one that was already marked.

Every shepherding family knows that if you tamper with another shepherd's mark on an animal, a curse will strike you and your animals. Why did Kámen do it? He must have been seized with lust at the sight of those lambs.

But this was Stamen's version of the story. Kámen's version would undoubtedly be the opposite: they were his sheep and his lambs to start with and Stamen cut into the wrong territory.

I believed both of them. And anyway, how could you tell yours from mine among hundreds of sheep? It was a movable feast.

'Anyway, the winter leading up to our break-up was terrible. A winter of death. The river froze. Bands of wolves walked with the flock like they were dogs.'

The few workers who were left were stretched to breaking point. Just like now. Being at breaking point was nothing new in Orelek.

'When I told my father we were leaving, he cried.'

On the last night they slept on the floor of the church and again, Stamen lit a candle. They left in the morning with their axes and in their rubber galoshes and cardigans knitted by Stamen's mother, taking an awful lot of sheep and goats.

'They were ours,' he said.

But it was water under the bridge now. Stamen wanted peace.

'No he doesn't,' Kámen said. 'He wants to wipe me off the face of this mountain.'

'We need to work together or there is no future,' Stamen said. 'We've got to get the pastoral laws changed to save this way of life.'

'Bullshit,' Kámen said. 'Stamen is part of the problem. He perse-
cutes me.'

'I'm building a hearth. For like-minded people to join me. I want
to rekindle the flame of the early years. I hope you come and stay,'
said Stamen.

'People don't change,' Kámen muttered.

'I've never stopped working for the cause since I came down from
Orelek,' said Stamen. 'And that's the main thing.'

Stamen's flock had become what is called a 'nucleus flock'. Ideally,
for the sake of the breed's survival, there should be three nucleus
flocks in three key places sufficiently distant from each other: here, in
North Macedonia across the border and in Greece or Albania. But for
now, the nucleus was in this mountain, one flock split in half by a
ridge.

In his big notebook from that time were fine drawings of animals.
'I'm not an artist,' he said, but here was a portrait of the ideal long-
haired, curly horned goat as an old shepherd had described it to him.
There were drawings and accounts of specific sheep and goats. Maybe
they were drawn by Kámen on the long moonlit nights they shared,
sleeping in barns and pens and looking for the Holy Grail with perfect horns?

During that winter of death, and with an obsessive precision,
Stamen noted how much each growing animal weighed, its measurements and his objections and frustrations. There were detailed
encounters with people and animals in remote villages. It was a passionate chronicle. Stamen was like two people in one: a mountain
lover but with a landed peasant's mindset that made him want to
accumulate past any point of usefulness. An excess of earth. That
inat again.

The day after he and his father came down from Orelek, Stamen
bought land for pens, huts and pastures above the gorge. He stepped
outside the Orelek circle and drew his own, back where his dispossessed ancestors had begun. His father died and his mother continued
to herd the flock in the hills of Orelek, knitting through rain and
sunshine with the dogs beside her, her lined face turned towards
some twilight weather full of ghostly flocks.

The volunteer who'd been Stamen's lover left too, and founded her own little kingdom of Karakachan sheep and dogs in the north. People who love livestock end up with their own, but somehow they also end up alone.

It was dusk when we reached Prairie. The boys jumped out. Dogs came over to greet us.

'Stay close to me,' said Stamen. 'Mind you, the toughest dogs are not here.'

They were up with the flock, one ridge over from Black Water.

'Nice dogs,' I complimented him.

'I'm trying to get Kitan back,' he said. 'All these dogs have a bit of Kitan.'

Stamen's shepherd Dimko was asleep in his shack, drunk. He was an emaciated retired builder who'd defaulted to the ancestral job.

'The drunk shepherd is the bane of our lives,' Stamen slammed the door and went into the pen to inspect a sick ram. He'd brought him down from the summer pastures on horseback, along a path similar to Kámen's. The boys were given a task: to fix the tap in the field.

'I want the boys to grow up fit for mountain living,' Stamen said after checking the ram. 'That's why I want them to play with the Gypsy kids who look after the animals. Because the Gypsies are the last savages. Still close to nature without the comforts most people have. And that makes them strong. Trouble is, there's no other kids like that. My boys are isolated.'

Like him, I thought. Next, he fixed the pen fencing. The boys joined in, bringing pieces of wood.

'Lately it's been storms or extreme heat. All I can do is fortify the pen and wait for the storm. Or the bear,' he said.

He loved it. He was in his element. 'And the wolves?'

'I'm pals with the wolves,' he said. 'Wolves belong in a healthy mountain. They're not an enemy. That's why we have dogs.'

The dogs are so in harmony with the flock that it's like a contract with the wolves. They know where the boundaries lie and respect them.

When Stamen was in Orelek, two dogs he trained killed a wolf in twenty-two minutes. He timed it. We looked at the sheep in the pen. They were the ones left behind after the exodus.

'Look at the expression in the eyes. It's completely different from other sheep!'

I'd never really looked at a sheep close-up. I had a poor basis for comparison with other sheep, but the look in their eyes was wild, not stupid as popular lore suggests. They didn't give a shit about anything but open spaces. They looked independent.

'They are primitive,' Stamen said.

Unlike other sheep, they were still in touch with their wild nature.

'And the wild is always beautiful,' he said. 'Feel the wool. This is what wool should be like. I can tell if this is a genuine mountain sheep just by the wool. There's not enough people left to talk wool with.'

Their wooliness was different from other sheep I'd seen. It was 'open-ended' wool: long-fibred, coarse and kinky, of a shade like no other. A lamb was born blue-ish-black, then with age it fades to grey-black with shades of brown.

'I get it,' I burrowed my hands in the sheep's coat. It felt like coming home.

How to identify an authentic Karakachan sheep? The tail should be very short. The animal should be no more than 60 centimetres in height at the neck. The colour should be even, either grey-black or whitish; no spots, no speckles. If you are still in doubt, feel the wool, a touch of softness tells you the animal is a cross. This is why they had been crossed with Merino by the communists – to make them softer. The mountain sheep's wool is pre-industrial wool. It requires pre-industrial handling. It is not made for factory machines. It is not homogeneous enough for manufactured clothes.

I told Stamen about the photograph of Kámen and the goats that brought me here.

His tired face twitched with emotion. 'You have an eye. You get what's special about these animals,' he said. 'That's rare.'

'And the white ones?' I asked, remembering Marina's frown.

'They are rough-woollen whites, another compact mountain breed.'

The nomads kept both types.

In the thirty-year journey this ancient sheep had made from the brink of the void to here, there were many turning points. One turning point was the discovery of Motley the paralysed shepherd, who had Karakachan sheep, but no pure-breed rams anymore. Another turning point was a trip to Macedonia across the border. It was Marina, Kámen, Stamen and wee Alex in the car. They drove to a remote abandoned army barracks, converted to a makeshift pen, to inspect a flock of sheep.

'When I entered the pen and saw those animals, my legs gave way,' Stamen said. 'Kámen and I just looked at each other. We knew we'd found something rare.'

The flock had been assembled by a professor of agronomy, a Macedonian Vlach. Professor Kozarski was his name, and this was a euphonic feat – because *kozá* is goat. Anxious to rescue the last of his people's animals and fully grasping their cultural value, Kozarski had put this flock together from three separate lots he'd located after extensive research, all of them in the region where three countries meet: Albania, Macedonia and Greece. This is a remote mountainous region of lakes and empty villages.

'Kozarski bought all three and made this spectacular flock of autochthonous Karakachan sheep.'

The young enthusiasts could just about afford to buy a couple of rams, though they wanted the whole lot. And, there were laws – border laws. A series of smuggling manoeuvres followed with Stamen and Kámen carrying rams on their backs across the border at night.

'It was like carrying a phoenix on my back,' Stamen said. 'I didn't feel the weight. I was flying. Then we mixed those rams with Motley's flock. When Motley's sheep were inseminated by Kozarski's rams, I was in heaven. Those sheep deserved the best. We had a new generation.'

After the Orelek schism, Stamen went back to Kozarski and smuggled two more rams over the border.

'No,' Kámen said. 'Those were *my* rams he'd taken from Orelek. To the secret pens the Tinders had along the border, rustlers to the marrow.'

One way or another, Stamen hung around that border with the

coveted rams long enough to be offered other smuggling jobs by Albanian traffickers who were impressed with his talent.

He could have ended up making a fortune trafficking animals, drugs and people but the rams were all he wanted.

'What happened to the rest of Kozarski's flock?'

'It was disbanded.'

Kozarski couldn't afford to keep them and the state took them off him. The sheep were expediently auctioned off: scattered, diluted, slaughtered, gone.

The boys fell asleep on the way down in the jeep, leaning on two sheep. Stamen had to slaughter them at home this evening. It was an order for someone.

'Sometimes I think I was born in the wrong century. I inhabit this body. I have a family but all I want is to be up there. With the dogs.'

We passed through a dark and empty Orelek. Stamen missed the old days. They'd grill a rooster, get a barrel of wine and dance in the snow. Marina led the dance, Stamen's father next to her, and the old women and men in the village danced too, those who then died, and the volunteers danced too, those who then left forever. Especially the women. No women volunteers came anymore. And all the hired workers were men.

'When the women go, everything falls apart,' said Stamen.

Stamen eventually married a high-flyer from the city. She didn't care for animals and didn't spend much time here, but she was his link with the world, like Marina was for Kámen. We passed Kámen who was pulling up in his white van by the goat house. They did not greet each other.

'We have nothing to say, but we agree that the plight of pastoralists is getting worse. They want us to disappear. We've talked to ministers but governments keep changing, it's chaos. I'm fifty. Then I'll be sixty. Then I won't be here.'

A few days later, we drove to a young woodland above Orelek in the Lada. Stamen wanted to find Proko's spring and invited me along. He carried an axe. The boys had sticks.

'It was somewhere here.'

He remembered a handsome wooden basin between two stones with a clear channel. Used by horses, people, all sorts. 'I'll meet you at Proko's spring,' people used to say. We wandered looking for signs. The boys looked for big stones that might be it.

'No, look for greenery, that means water,' said Stamen. There were self-seeded oaklings and hornbeam among the invasive juniper and stunted pine. It showed in action the consequences of the felling of the mixed woods.

'And these vines gone feral tell you that once people cultivated them here.'

Wild vines are stronger. These vines gone wild remind me of a passage in Plutarch's *Parallel Lives* describing how, in their first battle against the superior Roman army somewhere between Rome and Capua, Spartacus and his army of gladiator slaves surprised their enemy by jumping on them from a clifftop, hanging from ladders they'd woven from wild vines. They apparently won that first battle thanks to those wild vines, and to the many local shepherds and herdsmen who spontaneously joined them − 'sturdy men and swift of foot', Plutarch writes − and who must have despised the system as much as the gladiators.

Stamen limped ahead and hacked off branches to open up the closed path, threw them on the ground and pushed through scratchy juniper, going against the thicket of time and neglect. The boys and I found traces of rabbits, foxes and wolves − and the smell of carrion led us to a dead fox. 'Not killed by hunters, which is good,' Stamen said. He abhorred hunting.

We found it. The stone was split in two and blended with the forest floor. The fountain had become a bog.

'But look, Dad, there is water,' said one of the boys. The spring was alive. 'Don't disturb it,' Stamen said, 'or you'll frighten off the wild pigs and they need it.' We picked up a green bottle made from the kind of thick glass not used since the 1950s.

'We must come back and rebuild it,' Stamen said to the boys. 'Open it up again.'

'Yes!' one of the boys enthused. 'And then people can come and drink from it. Because now you can't drink from it.'

'Unless you are a wild pig,' said the other boy.

'And there is nobody here anyway,' said his brother. 'Unless we count the pigs.'

'Pigs are somebody too,' said the other boy. 'Aren't they, Dad?'

Dad was lost in the view that opened up from this strategic point in the hillside, to the hot mineral baths on the opposite hill. A story claimed that the mineral springs were once on the Orelek side but that an earthquake moved them downstream the Struma just a century ago. But the earthquake was political: the Balkan Wars. The village of the mineral spring was once Greek-speaking.

'My grandmother and her village women would stop here with their horses en route to the mineral baths.'

Not just to bathe in the baths, but to wash raw sheep wool. Then they would knit socks and make rugs on their looms.

'The women of Orelek were tougher even than the men. They worked till they dropped and endured without complaint. And nobody thanked them.'

Stamen's mother and grandmother had kept a garden up at Prairie. It contained flowers, medicinal plants and vegetables. 'Like an open-air pharmacy,' he said. Forced to live in town, they trekked 15 kilometres up through the hills, with mules, to look after their garden. Then they trekked back at night, in the dark, wolves and all. I could not imagine it. One stormy day, his mother trekked to Prairie, where her husband and another shepherd stayed with Kámen's sheep and where Stamen has his pen now. Both men were drunk in the hut. 'Bloody useless the both of you,' his mother shouted and took the animals out to pasture, the dogs in a circle around her under the cold rain and still knitting with the wool that she'd washed in the hot springs. Around her neck was yarn and in her hands were long needles. She walked and knitted, sat and knitted, the dogs keeping her warm. Her face turned to the hills, as if waiting for a sign.

'My parents were the last of the highlander kids. When my father died, she became permanently sad,' Stamen said.

She walked around in a daze and one day a harvester tractor mowed her down in the street, she survived but she doesn't tend the garden anymore, not even in her town house. She stands outside the gate and waits.

Is there food for the dogs? Have you fed the children? And the lambs? Are the little ones fed?

On the way back to the parked Lada, a thunderstorm broke out. We trekked in silence, drenched. I was leaving the gorge soon. Stamen carried the smaller boy on his back, over the eroded forest floor that was already running with mud. There was no carpet of leaves to absorb the flood.

I don't know if Stamen will rebuild Proko's Spring. There is too much else to do, too few helpers. That's why, when we walked away from the spring, he hacked at a self-seeded young oak so that its white core shone white in the darkening grove and said to his boys who nodded solemnly, as if looking back on this moment from the future:

'When I'm not here and you want to find the spring, look for this tree.'

PART TWO

COMMUNION

THE ORPHANED ONES

When I returned ten months later, it was food time, so the welcoming concert at the house was brief and everyone returned to their bowls.

Malina and Kalina with the rust-coloured faces! You are big now, but still puppies at heart, you wiggle your whole bodies. Yes, yes, yes. I can't see your mother and I can't see Muna the Monkey but the Loopy clan are all present: Metsi has lost a leg to a tumour and limps on three, Gutsi is telling me something with his big head, Loopy Junior wraps my legs in drool, Glavcho the Head punctures my trousers in welcome and two others are digging holes in the sand.

Over the winter, Kámen's father had died. He was everywhere in this house, Pygmalion-like: in the hand-made table and stools, carved animal heads and bunches of grapes like totems above the doorways, his delicate life-like sculptures of sheep and goats on the walls. He had spent his life at the altar of creation, seeking the union of nature and art.

At the kitchen table, Alex drew an eagle's head. He'd cut his hair and looked older.

'Golden eagle,' he said, barely lifting his gaze. 'Its wingspan can reach two metres.'

The golden eagle was the symbol of Pirin National Park and it was endangered.

Zebras and antelopes crossed the television screen.

'What day is it?' he asked. 'Must clean the centre for the next camp.'

Marina wasn't here yet, and the mother had just left Orelek. Kámen knew to expect me today, in fact, I'd just crossed him in his white van on the way up. He looked at me without seeing me, lost in worry. 'Ah, you're here,' he said and drove on.

'I didn't know you were coming,' Alex said. 'Nobody tells me anything.'

We talked snakes. There was a new one in his menagerie: a rescued one-eyed Aesculapian snake that he'd been feeding because it couldn't eat with its crushed jaw.

'Some wicked locals come to me, knowing I love reptiles and boast about how they killed a snake. How they waited for it to come out, rat in mouth and crushed it. I tell them: well done mate, but one day the rats will eat your house and there'll be no snakes to help you.'

Next door, in an open pen by a ruined house were the rams, guarded by a chained dog called Spintop, and kept separate from the ewes until the exodus to Black Water. So were the barren sheep, that is, the young ones under one year of age.

And the ewes? Out in the hills with Sásho.

'Just make sure you're not on the road when they come down 'cos the dogs will attack,' Alex said. 'What's the time? I must feed Vachka and the hybrid.'

We walked to the wolves, past Griffy on his chain. Alex carried a bucket of raw liver which he threw over the fence to Vachka. Then to the hybrid. He was grey, large and on edge. He'd turned out to be a cross between wolf and dog.

'We'll have to get rid of him and find her a real wolf.'

They kept them separate with a fencing net, but Vachka liked him and they licked each other across the net.

'He was kept on a chain. The problem with him is, he doesn't know what he is. That makes him unpredictable.'

It was part of his trauma. Wild one moment, docile the next.

And wee Hector? He was a buck now and didn't answer to wee Hector anymore. Not because he didn't hear, but because he didn't want to be singled out.

My room had three single beds. Oregano was drying on one. I opened the window, happy to be here again with no expectations except to join the exodus. The only information Kámen had shared on the phone was: the beginning of July.

'Are you okay for me to come?' I'd asked.

'If you like, but you know it's not a walk in the park.'

'It's okay, I'm prepared.'

'There are things you can't prepare for. It's been a bad winter and a worse spring. The cost of forage has doubled. They have cut the subsidies. No market for our animals. I've just met with some new people in the ministry with good intentions, but they don't get it. It's like speaking different languages. Sásho got drunk and lost animals. We looked for them all night and one of the dogs was shot by poachers.'

He did not ask what kind of winter and spring I'd had. Difficult, was the answer, for reasons of my own. Now I steeled myself for what lay ahead.

At the sink, a short wiry man of seventy was rinsing a tin can before pouring beer into it. His boots were unlaced. He had familiar, untrusting eyes. He nodded a curt greeting.

'I hope I won't bother you, I've got the back room,' I said.

'Not to worry,' he said.

His name was Anton and he was Kámen's maternal uncle. He spoke in a cutting northern dialect and the family all switched to it when talking to him. Everyone called him 'bai Anton' as a mark of his seniority. *Bai* is like 'uncle'.

At dusk, Thunder Peak went a pale red and the hills flushed with a light I'd not seen before, like another planet. A barking frenzy began in the gully: the sheep were coming home. Bells chimed but it took an hour before Sásho appeared.

He brought a rush of warmth from the sun-drenched hills. He unstrapped his rucksack, sat down by the sink opposite bai Anton and beamed:

'You're back!'

His hand was healed, though his fingers had lost some movement.

'Goats did me in today by the waterfall,' said bai Anton and poured beer into another tin can for Sásho.

'Sheep did me in. Mushroom,' Sásho replied.

'Aye, plums are bad,' said bai Anton who was hard of hearing.

Anton was the goatherd. He'd taken over when Ugrin left.

The dogs broke out in sudden indignation. A logging truck drove past on its way down, scattering animals. The geese and chickens joined in the cacophony of protest.

'Can I come with the flock tomorrow?' I asked Sásho.

'You don't have to ask! You're always welcome,' he grinned. 'Oh, there are two new puppies. You can see them tomorrow. They're also Kalina and Malina. 'Cos the mother was Kalina.'

'She died,' said Alex. 'She was so good. There's no other like her.'

They were bottlefeeding her puppies. Kalina's death had left two sets of siblings orphaned, both with the same names.

'Kalinka?' Sásho called out to the young bitch who lay inside the pen among the young sheep. She'd been lying there for two hours. 'Where is Malinka?' Malinka was eating scraps left by the chickens. Kalina lifted her head when he went to see her. Later, we found out why she lay away from everybody, because she was dying.

This is how my season of shepherding began – with a birth and a death.

The day started at 7:30 a.m., with bai Anton and Sásho sitting by the sink, leaning forwards with elbows on their knees and fags in hands, like soldiers in a corridor. They didn't eat breakfast. Their rucksacks hung from nails. Everything hung from nails because of the dogs. Inside the pen, the lambs were munching like crazy.

'Where are you taking them today?' asked Sásho.

'Same-same, along the river,' said bai Anton. 'You?'

'We might do Shemeto,' Sásho turned to me. I nodded, I had no idea. The hills all looked the same to me. There were several itineraries that the two men rotated, trying not to cross each other because of the dogs.

'I'll be seeing you,' bai Anton was off down the white dust road to the goat pen.

Anton was once a radio engineer in a mine. He took early retirement, but a man's got to work, he said, so he came and joined the mission. He never mentioned it, but I knew that everything in the three buildings here had his fingerprints on them, from the soil pipes to the stone flags. Sásho dubbed the whole family 'Steel Works Limited' because of their northern town, and their reserved temperaments. Anton had adult children and an estranged wife up north that he never mentioned.

Sásho and I passed the two sturdy puppies who were tied to leads behind the covered pen and they barked at us with their bear cub faces and adult eyes, guarding already. The new Kalina and Malina.

'Orphans,' Sásho said, 'It's all orphans here, like me.'

'Are you an orphan?'

'No, it's just when I'm up at Black Water I'm a bit forgotten.'

If you are a livestock guardian, it is the sheep that are your family, not your own blood.

In the open pen above Griffy's kennel, 500 sheep waited to be let out, with red-eyed Balkán in the middle. At the back of the pen was sturdy Kito. The other dogs roamed around the pen, ready for the day's adventure.

'Every day is an adventure.' They came to lick his hands. 'Keep close to me until they cover you in their smell.'

This happened quickly. My trousers were already covered in Loopy drool, just like Sásho's. One by one, they came to sniff me, rub past me and leave saliva on my clothes, wagging their tails and looking at Sásho for confirmation that there was a new dog in the pack. Only Balkán kept his distance. He was working.

The sheep rushed out of the pen as one and began to pull manically at the grass, then climbed through the shrubs and rocks. It was immediately obvious that you could not control their movement, you were outnumbered. The best you could hope for was to accompany them, but to do that well, you had to understand them. Sásho waited for the laggards to join the rest and we walked behind them with some of the dogs, past the wolf enclosure.

The hybrid cowered behind a tree. Vachka was out of sight.

'He has a wolf's head and a dog's body,' Sásho commented. 'His tail is curled. Wolves have straight tails. He is lost in his own life.'

When we climbed to an outcrop with a view that plunged down to Orelek, the dogs lined up like sentinels and barked in unison. The wolves answered with howls, but the dogs howled back and outdid them.

'From here on, it's us, not you,' translated Sásho. He reintroduced me to the dogs.

'Balkán you know, he's the leader. If I lose him, I lose the flock.

Muna the Monkey of the three voices. She barks, then runs behind me for cover, eh darling.

Karamana the Gypsy, who brays like a donkey.

Sunny was small when you were last here. Now he's a big boy. His father is Spintop and his mother is one of the Loopies.'

Who was Spintop?

'He's the one with the rams. He was bitten a lot as a puppy and became reactive. He just spins chasing his tail. And he hates brooms! If you show him a broom, he goes nuts.

Topi is Kito's son and the youngest. But look at his clever eyes, eh Topi.

Gashta the pants are very curious to know everything. Two sisters and a mother. The mother's got no fur on one side. Dogs change their coat twice a year and it hasn't grown.

Kasho! Kasho was an alpha since he was a puppy, but he likes cuddles.

Kito is named after Kitan. You know about Kitan. My hopes are pinned on Kito and Kasho to take over from Balkán. Trouble is, with Balkán here, the others can't be bothered.

Redhead has got promise too. Him, Kito and Kasho.

And Baguer the Digger is a good dog but hasn't come up. He's got worms.'

'Who's your favourite?' I liked them all already. Sunny walked beside me, making me belong at once. He had a head like the sun. The Gashti trio were interested too.

'They're all my favourites but I have a soft spot for Muna because she needs extra attention. And this is my other girlfriend, Breadie.'

Breadie was a communicative sheep with a broken horn from a fight. She came over and sniffed his hand.

'Most sheep are indifferent to humans. They relate with each other but there's the odd one who communicates. Usually older. Like Breadie.'

Sásho took bread out of his rucksack and gave her a slice to munch, then he dabbed her bleeding horn with green disinfectant from a bottle.

'It'll fall off eventually,' he said.

He carried medicine for the sheep and the dogs, and a loaf of bread and some sausage for himself which he sometimes shared with the sheep and the dogs. Plus, a water bottle because there were no springs.

'That's why we're going to Shemeto. There's a reservoir.'

The dogs hung by us, then scattered among the lizardy rocks. Out of this pack, Balkán, Kito and Kasho were alpha males who would actively protect the flock from wolves and bears. The rest were guarding the stock in a more low-key way, and the older dogs shepherded the flock by guiding it along the right itinerary.

The flock moved uphill at a steady pace and we matched it. The dogs matched it too. It was neither slow nor fast, a grazing pace. The dogs were happy to forage and hunt on the perimeter of the flock. And the humans had to entertain themselves as best they could. I started foraging for wild mint and yarrow. Sásho smoked.

'You can't rush anything,' Sásho said. 'Most of it is waiting.'

'What are the main things for good pasture?' I asked the basic questions just in case today was a one-off experience.

'Water. Shade for *pladnina*.'

Pladnina is shepherdese for noon rest. *Pladne* is noon.

'And enough varied grazing.'

That's why they have to be taken out every day, over a large territory.

'You mean on weekends as well? And in winter?'

He laughed gently. 'There's no weekends for the sheep. In winter, it's the same but without pladnina. They graze and you don't lie down. It's too cold anyway. Snow is the worst because they can't get to the grass.'

'Don't you get chilled being out all day in the rain and snow?'

'You do. But you can't get sick on this job. Kámen had pneumonia but didn't take a day off.'

And Sásho hadn't taken a break for seven months. Not a single day off!

'I'm used to it. And anyway, when I stop walking, my body feels like cement.'

A shepherd syndrome. The sheep set about eating branches of juniper and the round leaves of a spiky tree that I hadn't seen before. It tore your hair and clothes.

'Coin tree,' Sásho said. 'They're fruits, not leaves. Come this way or you'll be shredded.'

I'd never before seen Christ's tree or Jerusalem tree, so-called because Christ's crown of thorns was made from it. The golden-green coins were like padded tissue paper and rustled when the sheep munched them.

We walked across a hillside of sand and stone to an open grassy plateau which was like a viewing stage for Maleshevo Mountain ahead and Pirin behind. It was majestic, a chord struck before the full symphony of the day. Ta-ta-ta-taaa.

Ta-ta-ta-taaaaa.

The sheep moved in one big mass. The lambs were small, round, woolly and pulled at the grass with determination. Their teeth were sharp.

'Like razorblades,' Sásho said.

Breadie didn't have top teeth. I thought it was age, but all sheep only have bottom teeth. I was shocked when he told me this.

'There's no way to know these things until you experience them,' Sásho said mildly.

'Once, I was up at the lakes where we met last year. These vet students turned up, hikers. Very taken with the flock. I tested them: how many teeth does a sheep have? They thought and had a consensus. Six on top, and seven at the bottom. Okay, I said and opened a sheep's mouth, now count them.'

He grabbed a lamb and removed a spiky blade of rye-like stalk from its eye.

'Plant awns. Bad when it gets into dog paws and lambs' eyes.'

The lamb sprang from his arms and ran to its mother. They didn't like being handled and darted when I approached. The official description of their temperament is 'extremely lively'. They were dubbed *kamenarki*, stoners, because they are alpine animals.

They were difficult to milk because their udders were small, and sometimes there is nothing to take hold of, even for the lambs. You had to 'put the lamb to the tit' and teach it how to suckle. If it was rejected by the mother, it died within three hours. That's why winter was the toughest season. Summer was also the toughest season because of the migration and the ordeal of Black Water. Sásho and bai Anton were finishing off the sheep milking now, before the exodus. Sheep were not milked on high pasture.

Highland sheep were not as productive as lowland sheep and when he milked them in the spring, Sásho's forearms swelled up with inflammation from the effort.

'They have a yellow sulphur substance that protects the nipples from injury and ticks. When you milk, it gnaws away your nails and they can fall off.'

But he didn't mind, nails grew back.

'I heard an old shepherd say: what is the difference between sulphur and colostrum? It's like Mars and Jupiter.'

A cryptic gem of pastoral alchemy.

The hills kept opening like the pages of a book fluttering in the warm breeze, full of writing that I couldn't read yet, but I was beginning to adjust my eyes.

'Yea, this is where we hang out every day, me and the *kalimani*.'

He meant the ewes. Sásho spoke the playful Macedonian dialect of the region, full of archaic words, some of them Greek like kalimana. Here it meant 'godmother' and also any female being. Now when I looked at the ewes, they looked just like godmothers. They had authority. The flock was all female, except for the male lambs with their mothers. Another thing the people of this southern region did, when they liked you, was to call you 'dear'. *Milo*. Dearie. It was the neuter which made it diminutive, like you were a dog or a child. It was a trademark of the rough-and-ready, informal, affectionate south.

Everything about Sásho was of the south: his bristly black hair and darkish skin, his accent and the warmth he radiated. He came from the Roma slum downstream, a Turkish-speaking community that was mostly Christian, with some Muslims. But he was not Roma, although when he told jokes, he took on the accent and broken speech of the Roma: Please sir, the children is sick, and the wife too, he is very sick.

He grinned. 'You become the people you mix with.'

'So what are you if not Gypsy?' I asked.

'I'm like the hybrid that's not good enough for Vachka.'

He had in fact lived in Orelek for the past few years. Before that, he herded another flock in the Malashevo Mountain across. He had spent almost a decade as a hired shepherd above this gorge. Sásho was a qualified electrician but had done all sorts of jobs before turning to shepherding: in a wood processing plant, building work, in the many greenhouses of the Struma region and in Sicily, and in peanut groves.

Behind the easy smile was a harsh life. He was from a border town downstream, where three countries and three mountains meet. The town was famous for three things today: it was the hottest place, the crime capital of the country during the 1990s when smuggling barons built the criminal empires that are legitimate businesses today and it was also the hometown of a noted clairvoyant called Vanga. It was a place of intrigue and dark hills. Sásho and his older sister were born of a father from that town and a Pomak mother from the Rhodope. His father's family were pastoralists who came as refugees from Greek Macedonia in the wake of the First World War. They continued working with livestock until they were forced into industrial jobs on the railway and in mining. When Sásho was a toddler, his mother left.

'I like this job. There's always trouble down. Up here, if the mood takes me, I can swear all day at the sheep and yell at the hills. They forgive me. Until it's out of my system. Then I'm like new. No harm done.'

We walked for four hours, leaning on sticks and surveying the flock and the dogs who prowled the perimeter like wolves. We arrived at a reservoir built during the communist era for the large agro complexes, now ruined. The sheep lined up to drink and the dogs immersed themselves and floated, satisfied by this bath with a panoramic view, like the pool of the pampered people.

We sat at a small wooden table under an oak. It was built by Ugrin the goatherd to pass the time. The dogs lay under a willow tree, Sásho smoked. I smoked with him for company. The heat gathered like a presence.

'A few weeks ago there was a hailstorm. I sheltered here. But you can't shelter from hail. The meadow became a sea.'

He'd been more worried about the lambs. He called them 'wee mice'. After 35 kilos, a lamb becomes a young sheep and after giving birth, it graduates to a ewe.

At precisely noon, the sheep lay inside a shady grove. The dogs flopped down too, except for Balkán and Kito who patrolled the perimeter.

'Balkán's eyes, can you not do something about them?' I asked. Yet this was the lot of the guardian dog. With age, he went blind and anyway it wasn't Sásho who made decisions about the dogs, though he lived with them and fed them. A dog could be taken away, given away, sold, moved up north by the family or die, and nobody told him anything.

'The dogs all have a speciality. One goes for snakes. Another for wolf cubs.'

Sásho spread out a big plastic sheet that he carried rolled up and strapped to his rucksack like a mat. I spread my rain jacket out a couple of metres apart. A wave of laziness washed over us: pladnina. We nibbled our packed lunches.

Behind me, a sheep breathed heavily, as if she was choking. 'A lung condition, nothing you can do,' said Sásho.

The light is blue, the mountain is blue. It is a blue world.

'Blue like a sea,' Sásho said. His eyes were a light green, like a pond. 'But better than a sea. I saw the sea after I was kicked out of school. I took the train to a fairground and I got a job at the rollercoaster. There was this girl, like an Arab with blue eyes. We hung out for the whole three days and on the last day she kissed me. My first kiss.'

For years, he travelled from fair to fair, hoping to see her again. He had become a street kid by then. At school, the director's son goaded him for having no mother and poor clothes. Sásho had a little blue jacket. One day, the other boy poured water over his jacket. It was winter. Sásho picked up a stone and threw it at the boy's head. The boy survived, but Sásho's primary education was over. After a year, he left a school for children with special needs because he was too bright. His grandparents and absent father wanted to put him in one of those notorious state boarding houses, like prisons, for young delinquents. Sásho ran away from home. He was ten. At the fairs, he worked on the rollercoasters, see-saw boats and other dangerous toys, quickly learning the ropes, diving between the grinding wheels to fix the rides, leaping between gondolas and helping other children to have fun, watched by their parents. He was agile, clever and desperate. He travelled alone and ticketless, from bus to train, stopped by the police and dragged home to his border town.

'I loved being on the road but there's one thing I hated. You just get used to people, like family, and then you have to go. I better let you rest. I've talked too much.'

'Yes, my head is spinning like I'm on a Ferris wheel.'

'It's not often I get to talk to someone. When Moni the Mute was here, we talked a lot. In sign language, of course. We were together all the time, for six months. When he left I missed him. I started talking to myself. The worry is when you start answering yourself too!'

He laughed at himself but the sadness of the homeless fairground boy weighed me down. I lay down on my jacket. He lay down on his plastic sheet. Muna lay next to him. He turned over with his back to me and hugged her. Kasho stepped over me delicately, foot after foot, with his huge body, then again, then he lay beside me, his massive head and paw on my chest and yawned in my face with a mouth full of teeth.

In my slumber, I heard chatter, indistinct like in a café. But it was not humans: pigeons, sheep, woodpeckers – a coven. A sheep coughed like a smoker.

At four o'clock, I sat up, Sásho too. The sun had moved, Muna and Kasho had moved, the sheep had risen on their feet and were considering their next move. A few left the grove but returned.

'They remembered their lambs.'

They took an hour to get going. I was restless now. I wanted to walk.

'You can't force them. If you force them, they'll return to the grove but in groups, scattered, and make your job harder.'

They left the grove as one and moved quickly. We made our grazing progress back. Walk, wait, walk. Always behind the last animals or to the side. If you try and rush them, they get stubborn or scatter. You don't want them to scatter. The aim is to keep them together and gather them when they disperse. It was 8:00 p.m. by the time we reached the pen. A twelve-hour day. The late afternoon light painted the hills of Orelek a saturated blue. It was intensely beautiful and then the light shifted and it was different again, like a moving painting.

'Will you come again tomorrow?' Sásho asked.

'Yes,' I said.

On the way back, Muna split to visit a brook and when she returned, Karamana and the three Gashti attacked her 'because she washed and didn't smell like them anymore', Sásho said, and threw a stone to disperse them. The male dogs stood by. Muna came to him bloodied, and didn't leave his side.

Once the flock was inside the pen, Sásho fed the dogs. The two orphaned puppies whined at the big dogs but stood their ground.

The news of young Malina's death was delivered by bai Anton who sat outside, smoking. We all waited for it to sink in. Sásho cuddled the yellow-faced sister who wagged her whole body. Yes yes yes.

'Kalinka-Malinka, now you have no mother and no sister,' he said. 'And no one to fight with over your food'.

She became Kalina-Malina, two in one. When one of the new puppies died too, the survivor became Malina-Kalina. She ate and barked for two, small and determined with her bear cub face by the gate of the sheep pen.

I stayed up late to catch up with Kámen. He sat down heavily, filling the kitchen with smoke.

'It's a paralysis. Pandemic, war, pandemic. They alternate them,' he said.

They've cut down the subsidies for this breed because there are too many now. They're not endangered anymore. An irony. The hybrids aren't counted either. Fodder will cost 100,000 lev instead of 40,000. One lev is fifty cents.

'There's rice in the oven if you like,' he said. 'I have lived apart from my children and wife for twenty years. Visitors ask: where is your family? I don't know what to say. Twenty years, wasted.'

'They're not wasted,' I said. 'You're still here. The animals are here. And your family too.'

'There are 100 goat kids sitting in the pen. That's too many. No market. People prefer to blow 300 lev on a night in a hotel than on a goat kid. While waiting to sell them, they are on fodder which means that when they're taken out in the hills they go all skinny because they're not used to free grazing.'

Fodder, the sedentary life, reliance on someone to bring you food, this is how enclosed animals become effortlessly fat but unable to survive in their native environment anymore. They become like humans.

'When do you think you'll take the flock up?'

'No idea,' he said. 'I can't find the mare. She's given birth somewhere.'

He peered through the thick smoke. 'And how are things in Scotland?'

In the morning, the kids at the centre spotted a sheep wandering above the river. It probably split off from the rest of the flock, looking for mushrooms and followed the river. Sásho fretted, and I fretted with him.

Sásho opened the pen. The dogs came to greet us. Another day at Shemeto, because bai Anton was going to Fat Oaks where we were meant to go. The kids arrived at the wolf enclosure with Marina just as we were moving up with the last of the sheep. I stayed behind to see the kids. They were in a happy bubble here without contact with the locals, empty houses all around, like a hotel in the post-apocalypse, but they were fine with it. To them, this was how villages are: a museum where some exciting exhibits could still be met in the flesh.

'You see,' Marina was saying to them, 'The hybrid is confused because he was kept on a chain. He approaches but is afraid of us. Mixed signals.'

The kids threw meat to Vachka and the hybrid, their hands sticky with blood that they washed off with large tubs of water brought from the sheep house.

'They like each other!' a girl said.

'Yes, they do. We'll look for a real wolf for Vachka but if we don't find one, we'll put them together properly'.

'Why don't you put them together now?' said another girl.

'When I see them separated by the fence, I am sad,' said one boy.

Marina entered to see Vachka who had a swelling on her throat, a bite from an adder which was potentially dangerous and Marina frowned.

'Come, my love.' Marina turned to the wolf with a tenderness that I had never seen in her before and wouldn't see again. She crouched, and the wolf put her head on Marina's chest.

I caught up with the flock. Sunny was waiting for me with his clever trusting eyes and I felt a pang: one day, I will have to say goodbye to these dogs.

It turned out that the lost lamb this morning had had one of those plant awns in its eye. Blinded, it had gone round in circles, split from its mother and spent the night in the hills. Sásho was relieved to have it back, even with one damaged eye.

'Kámen has put all he's got into this flock. It's his life. It weighs on me, sometimes. When I lose animals, I feel sick with guilt.'

He overtly respected Kámen and Kámen covertly respected him.

'There aren't many left like Sásho,' he said to me. 'The rest just woo you at the beginning, then start playing their games. Money and booze. Sásho doesn't care about money and his drinking is cathartic. He goes on a bender for a week, then sobers up.'

'We help each other, somehow,' Sásho said. 'I can't leave Kámen. I see what he's up against, though sometimes I get sick of it. I'm hostage to the flock. Alone with my phone.'

It was just the three of them in winter. Each to one side, wrapped in silence and eating separately. Marina's summer kids glimpsed them from a distance. The shepherds were out in the hills with the flock. They were faceless primitives in the eyes of the city kids with their designer thermal jackets, double-insulated travel mugs and parents who constantly texted them. The meeting of worlds was skin-deep.

'Spoilt brats,' Kámen mumbled. 'They won't learn a thing from five days here. You need grandparents to teach you. A real village.'

'No,' I said, 'it's good 'cos some of these kids will become the new wolf people, horse people and even sheep people thanks to what you and Marina are doing here.' Kámen was pleased to hear it but hid his pleasure.

We reached the reservoir. The oregano and yarrow became brighter as you climbed. Suddenly, there was an outburst of excitement and the dogs took off to chase something.

'Rabbit or wolf cub,' said Sásho. 'There was a guy who came with me for a few days. A prospective shepherd. The dogs chased a hare. Is that a wild hare or a pet? he asked. I said: they're pets, but people release them to have a run around. And he believed me.'

Muna laughed with us. She really did have three voices, like a bagpipe.

'That guy didn't last. You've already lasted longer than some,' Sásho said. 'It's the climbing. And the isolation.'

This job requires three things: liking your own company, liking the animals and liking the outdoors, plus not being afraid of anything.

Suddenly, Kasho attacks Sunny who is walking next to me, almost pushing me over in a pile of angry fur. Sunny has followed me everywhere and it's the second such attack today – Kasho has it in for Sunny. They bite each other with teeth like sabres. It happens quickly. Sásho intervenes to separate them and is bitten on the calf.

'Jealousy. Kasho needs to be top dog,' he says, lifting his trouser leg to check, but there's no new bite, just an old scar from Barut. It's good to have thick trousers.

Not long after, the dogs ran off with frantic barks and then returned to us to report. They'd disembowelled a wolf cub. It lay on its back, small and tragic and when Sásho touched a stick to its mouth, its teeth gripped it in a final spasm.

'Luckless wee thing. There's a wolf lair in this grove.'

Sásho didn't like wolves. It's hard to like them when you're a shepherd. They take more animals than they need, like avaricious people, Sásho said, and they kill for fun. With the bear it's different – it takes one and makes it last.

At pladnina, we spread out our stuff in a different spot by the same grove. We ate olives, cheese, peppers and shared tea from my flask. Sásho smoked more than he ate. Anton and Kámen were the same, and so were all the other shepherds I met. When you eat, you can't walk, especially in the heat, and by nightfall you are so tired your appetite is gone. If you want to lose weight, become a shepherd. A sheep sniffed my bag of oregano. Redhead licked a sheep's face. Kito sniffed Muna.

'She won't let him because they're siblings,' Sásho said. 'But one of these days, she'll get pregnant. I can't keep her from it a fourth summer.'

The family didn't want more puppies, there were too many to feed and the excess animals were sold to Karakachan enthusiasts from around the country. This is the most expensive type of pastoralism and the most expensive type of farming. It is also some of the hardest transhumance terrain in Europe. These facts are connected. The arduous terrain required good roads but the roads were car-wreckers. It all added up in cost, effort and planning. You needed a full-time shepherd, additional workers in the busiest season, summer pens, winter pens (indoor and outdoor), huts that had to be fixed after the latest avalanche, guardian dogs and rented pasture each year. On the other hand, keeping a shepherd who took the flock out almost every day of the year was cheaper than keeping the sheep entirely on commercial cereals.

Sásho was paid 1,050 lev (525 euro) a month, and all his expenses were covered, including food, but excluding cigarettes, alcohol, clothes and shoes. It was the going rate. There was no extra pay for enduring the hardships of Black Water or the sleepless winter nights. No contract, just a gentleman's agreement. He was free to leave at any time, though the agreed notice period was a month and he could be fired at any given moment. This was the standard set-up between hired shepherds and their employers.

Sásho was content. He had seen much worse in his life.

'Any idea when we're going up?'

'Kámen is still looking for the mare. Usually we go before the village feast.'

In two weeks' time.

I liked this life. I wondered if I could take up shepherding, part-time in summer, like this. Why don't more people do it as a lifestyle choice? You don't have to be from rural stock, you can learn. You don't have to have hundreds of sheep, half a dozen would be enough to subsist and be outdoors with organic milk and cheese every day . . .

Sásho didn't think so.

'Most people just don't last. Plus, there's no one to learn from. The old shepherds are gone.'

Sásho got into livestock when he started helping a friend. He enjoyed working with grazing animals, small ones. Not horses. Sheep calmed him. The walking, the milking, the ruminant company, the dogs, the hills, the lack of social pressure and the absence of temptation to do the wrong thing. His first job was with a large flock of sheep, him and another guy. They were a breed indigenous to Maleshevo Mountain, tall and white. For five summers, he roamed the hills of no man's land along the border. In winter, he and the other shepherd lived in a shack by a big tributary of the Struma lined with shady old sycamore trees, without electricity: no fridge, no TV.

'But a beautiful spot. Here, it's luxury by comparison. And it's still beautiful. That's the thing about this job. You're always somewhere gorgeous.'

That employer was rubbish at paying and Sásho was owed money when he left. By contrast, everybody in Orelek was decent.

'If you stay longer and open your eyes, you'll see things in Orelek. That visitors don't see.'

'Visitors like me,' I said.

'You're not a visitor,' he said, 'I don't know what you are, yet.'

I didn't either. I covered myself and drifted, exhausted by everything, comforted by the smell of sheep droppings and wool. When I woke up, Kasho came and lay his head on my neck like a wool rug. The sheep hadn't moved. There was a breeze. Sásho was busy with his new phone after he'd lost his old one. This happened to shepherds a lot: you lie down, it slips out of your pocket or you run after an animal and it falls out, or you were drunk and don't know what happened. Sásho had a small radio and turned it to a local music station called Gaia.

'This song!' A folk song came on, drawn and sad. 'My sister sang it. We'd come back from school and sing. She sang Rhodope songs and I sang Macedonian songs.'

Then his sister was taken away to live with their mother and her new husband. There was no forwarding address. Sásho had no memory of his mother. Now his sister was gone too. His father and uncle both drank and Sásho felt like it was all his fault. 'Why, why did this happen?' he asked. But nobody told him anything. It was at that time that the trouble at school started. His quick mind, his facility with language, sport and music, it was all wrecked. With his sister gone, he fell into a void. Every time he tried to write something his hand shook and he couldn't finish the sentence. The same hand that was smashed last year.

'There was an album. I'd open it and my grandparents said: this is your mother. This is your sister. But why don't they come back? They were shadows. Everywhere and nowhere.'

One day, Sásho took the bus to the small town where he knew his mother lived. He had to see his sister. He found the street by asking. He was ten years old. His mother and her new husband stood at the door. His sister was there and they held each other so tight that nothing could prise them apart. Then they were separated and his mother said to him: 'You shame us by turning up like a vagrant. You have no right to be here. We are a family and you're not a part of it.' He could hear his sister crying in another room. He spent the night at the neighbours' and left in the morning: alone, down the street to the bus station, where in his distress he took the wrong bus and ended up at the seaside, at a deserted fairground; the one where he had his first kiss. He slept in an empty gondola until the police found him and escorted him on the train back to his border town where there was nothing left for him.

He never saw his sister or mother again. He remained on the move.

He liked places and faces. At funfairs, in strange towns and on trains, he scanned the faces of women and girls, looking for his original lost ones.

The sheep were at the far end of the field. I hadn't noticed them moving past us. We packed our stuff.

'I don't know why I told you all this. Maybe because you're interested. And not full of yourself like other people.'

He rolled up his plastic sheet. His right hand shook. We walked across the field to the reservoir, the dogs on our side like centurions, turning us into long-distance wanderers in stained clothes and with dusty hair in the golden light. Your clothes didn't stay clean for more than five minutes here, because to be clean is to be separate from the animals.

Sásho picked up something from the ground and rubbed it. It was a coin. A very old coin featuring a head with curly hair and feminine features in profile and on the other side, two centurion-like figures guarding something between them, like a grail. These coins were known as *constantinki* because they were from the reign of the Roman emperor Constantine.

'Your luck,' I said.

'I wondered where it had gone,' he grinned.

We walked in silence. After crossing the brook where the wolfling was gutted, the flock stopped and rocked as one. It was like a reed bed moving in the wind. Two of the dogs lay in their way and sometimes that stopped them. They will move, said Sásho, it's still early. Trouble comes when it's near dark and they stop like this and say *pfff* like a burst accordion, that's bad news. It means they won't move and you won't get them back. They settle there for the night, with the dogs.

'What about the dogs, can't they make them move?'

Nothing on the outside of the flock could make the flock do anything, but Balkán could prompt them from within.

'You can't force a sheep. If you hit them, it's worse. They start going round in circles.'

Sásho learned this the hard way when he was a beginner and hit a sheep with his stick across the back, breaking her spine. Her back legs collapsed and she died. It was terrible, but he didn't know that you must never hit an animal across the spine or anywhere.

'In the hills, if you carry a stick you are a shepherd. If you carry poles, you are a hiker. What if you carry nothing?' I ask Sásho.

'Then you are a plant gatherer, like you.'

Bai Anton told me there is summer savoury higher up. But the sheep lie down again, and we never make it to the savoury.

'I'm sorry,' Sásho grinned. 'We keep going to Rome without meeting the pope.'

There were leaders in the flock who went ahead and the rest followed. Then there were the middle ones and the rear ones. You can't count 500 sheep every time, but keep an eye out for the key individuals in the flock: the rear ones like the one with the split ear and the lamb, a few bad apples that strayed, the eight white ones which were scattered throughout the flock and when in doubt, he counted the ones with bells on which totalled nine. If all of those were present, the flock was intact.

They suddenly moved as one and rushed through a pine grove.

'Here comes the mushroom!' Sásho said. 'Mushroom is my enemy. If they get stuck here, it'll be a pain in the ass to get them going.'

But there was no mushroom, just a carpet of pine needles. The flock rocked, back and forth, deciding, like a fleet of black sails on a windy sea. The next distraction: mulberry trees. One long-legged sheep with a sexy strut split off and headed for it. A few more followed her. This is how the flock could split.

'This one's The Model, see how she walks.'

She gives birth to lambs and rejects them, but they get their fill from other sheep and grow bigger than The Model. They sneak behind other lambs and join in the suckling. Thieves, he called them.

'Like me,' he grinned.

Before the last rocky descent into the village, a terrific stampede broke out. The dogs were fighting, all of them except Muna. They all attacked Balkán for some reason. It was sudden all-out war. They reverted to wolfhood in an instant and Kasho my siesta buddy opened a maw with blade-like teeth. The noise, the collision of bodies, the clashing of teeth, it was staggering.

Sásho shouted and threw a stone at them. You couldn't get too close or you'd be caught in the melee. The dogs scattered. Balkán emerged, covered in liquid grey mud like a bronze sculpture, battered and bloodied, but still majestic with his medalled chest.

'What the hell was that!'

'The younger males,' said Sásho. 'They took him for another dog not with the pack. He washed and they didn't recognise him. It only takes a second for things to flip'.

This could happen with the sheep too. If a sheep fell crossing the steep brook banks, the rest could follow in a domino effect. One thing never happens alone.

'Come Balkán, give me your earie,' Sásho tried to apply disinfectant to Balkán's torn ear but he trotted off to catch up with the flock. You can't get sick on this job.

The next morning, stumbling down the steps with fatigue, I told the coughing ones that I'd be taking the day off and watched them melt quietly into the hills, each in a different direction. Cigarette in hand, Sásho was lost in thought.

Down in the Kresna Gorge, the stream of lorries never stopped. Roads, roads. The road to Orelek was an obstacle. It cut the mountain off from the rest of the world but the traffic along the good road was all one type, big global business, a monocrop that threatened to gobble up the quirky mosaic on the ground.

The hills pulled at me. I returned with provisions and only left Orelek once more before the exodus. Back at the house, the Loopies were finishing eating a hen's severed head. Kámen was unloading sacks at the goat house. Alex was sick with a bug but forced himself onto his feet because you couldn't get sick here. I picked up a book about guardian dogs in Europe and Asia from the kitchen shelf. It was written by an American pastoral farmer who toured the farms of colleagues in Spain, Portugal, France, Bulgaria and Turkey, and one of the places she visited was Orelek.

'It's recognised that in order to have a complete ecosystem, all components of the ecosystem must be present,' she wrote. 'Among those components are livestock, the large carnivores that want to eat that livestock, the guardian animals that actively challenge predators that dare to enter the flocks, and the human herders who live amid all these components.'

The mosaic again. We humans are just one component of that mosaic. We forget, as with Velin's mother's gradual slip into dementia.

I sat under the willow with my laptop. This was my office, by the monuments to the killers and the killed, and the silence was crushing. I answered emails but a day without the morning trek to the hills and the evening journey home is a day without history. I wasn't a component of anything today.

Come 6:00 p.m., I began to wait for the bells of goats and sheep and work out who was coming from where. The goat bells chimed at a higher pitch. After the first chimes, they took a while to appear among the stacks of rocks. When Sásho arrived, full of sun and dust, he joined bai Anton at the sink.

"The goats split in two, on each side of the river,' Anton complained.

'Let's go to Fat Oaks tomorrow', Sásho offered. 'We can hang out together.'

This was an in-joke. The flocks could not mix because of the dogs. I gave Sásho a plate of potato salad.

'I have some lentils from last night,' but he was pleased.

He didn't take cooked food from his employers except on feasts, and he wasn't offered any. In the first year, he began to feel like part of the family. Then one evening, not knowing that she was touching an open wound or maybe knowing it, the mother said to him:

'You know, Sashi, we're a family, but you'll never be a part of it.' Then she offered him roast lamb. He refused it and ate lentils.

He cooked in his room like a monk in a cliff-top cell. I ate in the kitchen with Kámen, Alex and bai Anton. The TV was on and few words were exchanged. The animals were in the middle. The humans were on the periphery. We served the animals, so they could serve us, so we could serve them.

'All the animals live well. They are well fed, well walked, well loved and have company, only the humans are deprived,' I said to Kámen and he thought it was funny. It hadn't occurred to him, he was so used to it.

It was a soothing monastic monotony, a balm for troubled souls, to know your purpose, follow an itinerary and bring the gang back, tired and satisfied after another day of fulfilling your mission. The days were beads in a rosary that passed through your fingers and you felt their texture and shape. The same, but different.

Morning prayer: milk the sheep and take the flock to pasture. Midday prayer: pladnina. Evening vespers: bring the flock home, feed the dogs. Have a humble supper, lie on your hard bed, then rise early and morning prayer.

Drink your coffee, lace up your shoes, strap on your rucksack, take your stick and in sickness and in health, in rain and sunshine, go. The dogs are waiting. The flock is waiting. The hills are waiting. You are needed.

I came down one morning and the coughing ones at the sink shouted in unison: 'Barut's unchained!'

Barut lay on the doorstep of the bathroom where I was headed. He'd been let off the chain in the night. Kámen and Alex were still sleeping. They alone could approach Barut.

'He looks relaxed,' I said.

'He looked relaxed last time too,' said Sásho and I remembered the scar on his shin.

I pee in a camping bowl in my room, throw it out of the window onto the chickens and get ready for another day in the hills. Thick trousers, sunblock, pocket knife, bags for herbs and other interesting things, notebook and pens. The heat reaches 40 degrees Celsius and makes the ink in the pens run. Water, raincoat. Leave phone behind. I don't know what day of the week it is and I don't care. I've entered a different timeline.

'We'll go to Wolfland,' says Sásho. 'I hope there's water. It's getting scarily dry.'

The burnt grass gives the sheep mouth ulcers.

'I'll take mine above the centre today,' says bai Anton. The camp is over, the kids are gone and it is safe to take his goats past the centre.

Otherwise, Mecho, Murat and Shaban might nip them and 'I don't wanna go to jail because of these bandits,' bai Anton said.

The local term for a dog bite is 'a nip'.

Yesterday, the two flocks met at a marsh whose level had been going down. Bai Anton was going to one side and us to the other when Murat, Mecho and Shaban launched themselves at our dogs at full speed.

'Stand back,' bai Anton shouted in warning. Murat and Shaban stopped and barked but Mecho attacked us. Muna barked with her three voices and hid behind me, and I hid behind Sásho. He grabbed my stick but we had seven dogs to defend us. It was all out war, an explosion of beasts.

Then, just as fast, the dogs shook themselves free, the three attackers returned to bai Anton for a pat of praise, then they're off with a bunch of oregano in the rucksack and it's a pastoral idyll again. Just like that.

The sheep and goats looked on placidly. Did they realise it was all for them?

No, they just watched the spectacle with glee. Goats are gleeful animals, said Sásho. When you try to get them home and they get stuck in a grove, they graze and look at you like this – he imitated, chewing, watching from the corner of his eyes.

Kámen is watching me from the corner of his eye too, like a stern patriarch with us his three children. Although he is my age and bai Anton's nephew, he is our senior. It's because he orchestrates the whole thing and does it without smiling. Not smiling makes you old.

'You still being a shepherd, then?' he says from the sink when I come down the steps. 'You haven't eaten with us lately.'

I feel guilty, but I always feel guilty around Kámen. He beams disapproval. 'It's that I'm in bed by nine o'clock and you eat at ten,' I say. He is doubtful, but he is always doubtful.

'Are we gonna get a shave one of these days?' bai Anton asks Sásho at the sink.

'Yeah, but when are we gonna go down?' Sásho comes back.

He hasn't been 'down' for seven months and bai Anton for four.

Not once, even to the town market or to a shop. Neither of them has a car. They rely on Kámen for everything and when they ask for a day off, he mutters: 'there's no one else, can't you see.' He brings them food, cigarettes, beer and if there is an emergency, like when Sásho had one of his attacks of high blood pressure and collapsed, Kámen takes them down, if he is around. One time, he wasn't and Sásho sat under the willow in the square and called an ambulance shortly before he collapsed.

'Or I might grow a beard,' Sásho goes on. 'Get a job as the village priest. But there's only three people left. Today you bury, tomorrow you're buried. Better shave and stick with this job, eh.'

'You've got a barber here,' bai Anton nods at me.

Sásho picks up sheep shearing scissors hanging from a nail and hands them to me.

Bai Anton picks up an iron comb for the dogs and hands it to me.

'We're sorted,' he says and collapses in giggles, his composure gone. It's the first time I've seen him laugh like this.

'Be seeing you,' says bai Anton and picks up his rucksack, still in stitches. And for the first time, he says to me: 'Enjoy your work.'

The next morning, they are both clean shaven with cuts from blunt razors, and I've cut my hair with blunt scissors. Everything becomes synchronised when you follow the flock.

'I've entered your rhythm,' I say to Sásho.

'And I've entered yours,' he says. 'Just because you're going with me and the flock, doesn't mean I'm not going with you. And seeing everything with new eyes.'

And we're off through the scratchy forest of coin trees, an army of oddballs. Every morning is a promise.

What will the light be like and the weather? What are we going to see and learn today? What sort of mood are the dogs in? Where will the sheep lie down, and us with them?

I have taken to asking, 'Is that all of them?' always worried that we're missing some.

'Please don't say that, you freak me out! I know my stock.'

You have to have a bit of trust. Sometimes they look many, sometimes they look few and either way, they're impossible to count when they move and impossible to count when they're still because they stick together.

You go up, always up. There is something higher, brighter, more saturated in colour, more perfect in shape, different from yesterday, although it's the same mountain every day. The dogs are by your side, they too are astonished by this moving picture and sometimes when you walk, you feel so light that your feet barely touch the ground, and you realise that these are some of the happiest days of your life.

WHERE THE SOUL CAN REST

Time with the flock is different from other time in the hills. When you hike, you are at your pace. When you shepherd, you are at their pace. You inhabit the round clock of the mountain with your animals and move clockwise with the sun.

When I check emails and world events on my phone, they feel far away, as if they are in the past or the future. Here, the only verifiable event is that of the hills which are solid but move all the time because of the light and because we move. It's a big enough event for me not to have room for any other events. Yesterday and tomorrow are falling away and giving way to above and below.

It's windy. We stand without speaking and smile at each other, we smile at the animals, leaning on our sticks by a ruined house that belonged to a herbalist. I wished he was still here to tell me about the herbs he picked and how he used them. My knee is sore. Orelekers suffered from rheumatic joints because of their unrelentingly outdoor lives and treated that with a strong tea of nettles, dandelion and birch root.

The dead herbalist's wooden balcony is still hanging on. The sheep graze among the stones and yarrow. The dogs scratch. Sunny is bleeding from his mouth because of a leech. We are heading to slightly higher pasture today. Where are my gloomy thoughts that blighted my winter? Nowhere. There is only this: cicadas, the peaks in the near distance and the air currents that we travel on like invisible highways.

The calendar of the hills is like no other. The horizontal line of industrial time is very different from the vertical vectors of pastoral time. Yesterday and tomorrow feel like the same day, but uphill and downhill are not the same place.

The movement is from hilltop to river, then hilltop again. The weather moves along vertical spokes in a terraced mountain. Everything comes from the sky. The rivers flow downhill. I learn to orient myself by sound and light and not to rely purely on form. When I can't see the flock, the chime of bells tells me where they are. The change in weather is heralded by a change of light.

In the night, there is a rainstorm. Should we check the weather today?

'Willitrain.com,' said Sásho. 'No.'

He and bai Anton agreed: weather or no weather, we must take them out. Just take a raincoat and your plastic sheet. It's an old shepherd thing. You stand in the rain, plastic sheet draped over you like a hut and you wait. Before plastic, the shepherds used felt capes. On especially cold winter days, Sásho lights a fire in the hills. I feel cold just thinking about it.

Every day looks the same but has a different flavour. It's the animals that give it the flavour, just as the flavour of their milk changes every few weeks because it has been infused with different grasses.

Today, I sit on a rock by the pen while Sásho lets them out. The sun is high. It's mid-July. The dogs come to greet me one by one, and I feel like a queen on a throne with her knights. A sheep comes over and looks at me, one cheek full of grass. In her eyes, I see that it's normal to be a sheep, but to be a human is odd. She wanders off, unimpressed.

Muna the Monkey didn't want to come today. She wanted to mooch around the pen but was sent up the hill by Anton with gentle kicks and: 'Sheep!' It's a word the guardian dog recognises. Muna barks like she has laryngitis, it's a whimper but she tries.

I begin to distinguish types of barks: how the dogs bark when they're about to fight, when they've found a wild animal, when they are warning us that something is coming and out of sheer excitement. On the way back there was frantic barking, like they'd found wolves, then we saw a black mass moving up a slope at the far end of the gully.

The rams! They've escaped from their pen and are making a break for it. It's near the end of the day, a bad time to be chasing twenty-seven rams and herding the sheep back at the same time. Sásho runs off to round up the rams before they move out of reach and become prey to the wolves that night. The rams are precious because of their seed. Sásho leaves me with the flock and Balkán. The other dogs run off with him – it is more exciting, though Muna and Topi return to me. I watch from a distance how Sásho and Kámen, who comes in the van, turn the rams around and herd them downhill but at the rams' pace.

For an hour, I wield the shepherd's crook. It's heavy. I feel a responsibility to keep the sheep moving in the right direction and not let them disperse.

Yaaraa, says a lamb. There's a consonant in there. It's a word. 'Mum, where are you?'

Beeree, answers the mother from another part of the flock. 'Over here, it's tasty.'

I notice cup-marks in the giant boulders, just like the druidic ones in Scotland. They were left behind by the early hill dwellers here, the Thracians. The boulders look at me with their empty sockets as the sun sets over Orelek: a reminder of those long-ago people who did exactly what I am doing now. The land has shifted since then, chasms opened and others closed, tributaries dried up and others filled but the sheep are the same. The dogs are the same. Am I the same too?

Did those people collectively known as Thracians really seek the same things as us? Freedom and adventure, purpose and belonging, and of course, food. The Thracian and Illyrian pastoralists are our ancestors.

In Herodotus's *Histories,* there is the following scene. Two high-ranking brothers from the Paeonian kingdom in lower Strymon went to the Persian king Darius with a ruse in mind that was meant to result in more power for them. They took their 'tall, beautiful' sister along to catch his eye as he passed a certain river, which she did like this: she went down to the river, leading a horse by a halter and spinning flax on a spindle. The horse drank, she filled a pitcher and walked back with it on her head, spindle spinning, horse in hand like an awesome mistress of plants, animals and the law of gravity. Darius was so impressed, he asked the brothers if all Paeonian women were like her. Yes, they lied and the terrible result was that Darius proceeded to deport the entire population of lower Strymon to Persia. This was in the fifth century BC, in Herodotus's own time. The woman with the spindle and horse halter in hand continued to walk this land without interruption until 1957, spinning the world's oldest wool like an oracle. And even after she was settled, like Stamen's mother she carried on knitting in the hills, leading her animal tribe. Before they were deported, the Paeonians downstream brushed against the Medi, a Thracian tribe who lived in this mountain until the Romans arrived and who probably left these cup-marks. They were semi-nomadic shepherds and in one such community, in one of the hills we walk now, Spartacus was born. (The only sure fact about his birthplace is this: it is a tributary of mid-Strymon between the Kresna Gorge and Sásho's border town). As a child he walked these hills with sheep and wolf-dogs just like these before he was taken by the system and became a Roman mercenary and later, the leader of the world's largest slave rebellion. His wife, whose name is unknown and who was from the same tribe, remained with him and died with him. Plutarch describes her as an adept in the mysteries. When Spartacus was first captured in battle and brought to Rome as a gladiator, a snake coiled around his face while he slept and in that she saw an omen for an exceptional fate, and being a Dionysian prophetess, she knew her snakes and omens; a memorable story that probably didn't take place.

The Romans built garrisons with towers and roads above the gorge. Their ruins are still here. When their army came up the river in the first century AD, the Pirin highlanders buried their gold and nine maidens pronounced the following before the hole was closed: 'As many hairs as there are on our heads, so many years shall pass before this gold is found again.' They knew the Romans were coming to stay. The new masters prospected for gold and although they found none, they found big veins of iron and lead ore, and roped in the entire population as miners. Inside their mines were found twenty or so children's swings from wood and rope, strung together. A woman babysat all the children belonging to the miners. Mining has been a method of enslavement ever since then.

Plutarch quotes how the king of the Scythians is called the 'basest of men' and 'robber chief of Nomads' by the Roman usurper-emperor Cassius, whose nemesis he was. The nomad barbarian – often a shepherd, and in the case of Spartacus a shepherd-turned-gladiator – is forever pitted against the emperor. Even if the emperor is in fact a usurper himself, and used the most barbarous methods. Cassius, who defeated Spartacus's rag-tag army of 120,000 men, women and children, crucified 6,000 of them. To walk with animals on the surface of the earth outside of imperial-industrial time is to resist the system that captures bodies and souls. I feel it in my bones, here, where the ruins of the Roman project lie under the ruins of the Ottoman project and on top of those sit the ruins of the communist project, overseen by the empty hills that signified the current absence of any project whatsoever.

The flock stands on the edge of the Coin forest but won't move on. They have a collective gaze, the stony gaze of the mountain sheep that says: we don't give a shit about your projects. Their rough wool flutters in the warm breeze and the breeze carries word of this exquisite texture for the world to know. When there is a breeze like this, their wool touches my skin even without touching me and I feel wind-proof and rain-proof with that wool. Threads of animal run through the flock and through me and I become one of them. When they don't graze, they look into space, at ease with emptiness.

The flock begins to rock, like a group reflection. I'm afraid that this reflection will lead to the dreaded conclusion that sounds like *pfff* and leads to being stuck here for the night. This is a risk they are prepared to take if the mood takes them.

Then, just on time, Sásho runs back and whistles. They rush downhill as one.

Every time we reached the shade of a grove for pladnina, I remembered the old Karakachan saying: 'where the soul can rest'. You enter the shade of a forest after the arduous climb, the heated plains, the river crossings, and you sit down and let your soul rest. The soul of your animals too. Do ruminants have a shared soul?

'They have a shared something,' Sásho said. 'The dogs have a soul. And an ego. I feel it, sometimes. It's a nice feeling'.

We sit on Sásho's plastic sheet in the shade and watch a 1980s comedy called *A Nameless Band* on his phone. I love the closing song. It's the end of the summer season, things are a bit desperate and the little provincial band sing by the seaside:

'We're staying, we are staying/ never mind that autumn's coming/ never mind the coast is empty now.'

I take off my socks. Sásho is embarrassed to take his off because his feet are blue, but you can't be embarrassed for long out in the open. You have to be what you are. His feet are blue from copper sulphate.

'That's toxic!'

'But it stops my feet falling apart. They put it on animals and on fruit so it can't be that bad!'

He applies it instead of foot powder. His job in the mountain over came to an end one night when he had to birth a lamb, milk the cows and then another lamb was bitten by dogs. Stressed, he called his colleague who'd gone to bed in their shack.

'How do we treat dog bites?'

'I'm not a bloody vet,' his colleague said. The employer wasn't around either. Sásho took care of the bitten lamb as best as he could and quit. After that, his employer couldn't find a replacement and was forced to sell his stock. Sásho's feet suppurated with wounds from all the hill walking in cheap trainers. He was hobbled, but when he came to Kámen's as a pen-cleaner and milker, Kámen spotted his talent and offered him a shepherd's job with Moni the Mute. Alright, but only for a while, he said, I won't stay forever.

'Just the sight of sheep makes my heart open. And dogs. I don't know why. It doesn't happen with goats. Or people.'

That was three years ago, and it was Moni who showed him how to protect his feet from damage. Copper sulphate stops the feet from ulcerating and sweating. It is ultimately damaging, but Sásho was used to damage.

After Moni the Mute left, Sásho became Head Shepherd. A helper was hired, one Bimo who was good with animals, but when he drank, he ate for ten. He'd go into Kámen's kitchen and raid the fridge, then start on the jars of honey and peanut butter, like a bear. Worst of all, he howled at night.

'Like a werewolf,' said Sásho. '*Aaaaaa. Aaaaa.* And woke up the house.'

You had to slap him awake, but he'd start again. Aaaaa. Why do you howl, Bimo? No idea. In the end, his howling drove them nuts, and they couldn't keep up with his eating. When Sásho told Bimo about his lost mother, it turned out that Bimo lived in the same area and knew her. 'Do you have a son called Alexander?' he asked her next time he went home. 'No, not me,' she said. Bimo called Sásho and told him.

'I'm dead to her. And sometimes, it's like I wanna be dead to the world.'

We packed our stuff.

'Wake up Balkán, you'll sleep your youth away. Get the godmothers moving. Let's talk about fun things, eh? Three guys in a pub . . .'

'No, I've had enough of your jokes!'

And we walked silently across the blue light of July, the two of us, plus the sorrow.

It's another day. We're off to Vachkovtsi, Wolfland. We walk in single file along a shady river and I hear music. It's the bells. The bells are singing. Then I hear distinct voices. It's the sheep, they have different voices and intonations. I hear words.

We pass a scorched area where the wildfire had passed en route to Orelek.

'There's good lucerne here but it's got to be mown. The first growth can't be digested and a sheep can die from it.'

'But who mows here anymore?'

'Exactly, so you don't take the sheep through here in spring to avoid it altogether.'

We pass rags, wellies, tyres, bottles, remains of the last people who'd used this place other than shepherds: the loggers. There'd been carts and caravans and evenings by the fire. They were Gypsies or disguised as Gypsies like Sásho.

'It's quiet without them,' said Sásho.

Here, the humans had always been a minority in relation to the animals but they had never experienced the isolation that Sásho had to endure. They had been a community because the pastoral world had been everywhere like a moving human–animal rug. Over the hill was your neighbour with her animals. At your heels came your other neighbour's dogs and below came the long caravans of the Karakachans – it must be May again!

Their caravans were led by a young woman who had recently married, who walked ahead of the loaded horses alone, spinning wool on her long witchy wooden spindle carved with arcane symbols: stars, crosses, spirals. You recognised faces from last year's exodus. You sold them potatoes, tobacco and woollen socks and they sold you their cheese. Children and dogs everywhere. The Karakachans crossed ways with other itinerants, like the Gypsies with their famed and feared fortune tellers and their bears on chains, offering to treat any affliction by way of a bear massage. Some Karakachan women had small crosses tattooed between their brows to ward off the evil eye and distinguish them from other nomads.

I met the last person in this mountain with such a tattoo: Kosta the old cowboy's mother, a woman of ninety who teared up easily when she talked about her life and who waited up for her son all night if he didn't come home from the animals, which was often. She'd been tattooed as a young girl and didn't remember it. Nomads had crossed this land for so long that her people were almost certainly settled nomads. In this tiny toothless woman I saw the link with the wandering Thracian and Illyrian shepherd women who tattooed their entire arms and legs with animals, snakes and sunbursts.

The sheep stop for their siesta in a meadow full of brambles with a ruined house that still has a roof and even a stove inside, and two single beds with stained mattresses. In winter, it's used by Sásho and a couple of other shepherds. On a small table are resiny pieces of pine kindling. Vasko the cowherd has lain them out to dry for his fire. He comes here with the cows in spring and summer before they take them up to Black Water. We survey the valley from the little broken veranda: the cows are there but no sign of Vasko. The Privateer, his boss, has thirty sheep missing. 'That's a lot!' Today, we're told to keep an eye out for them and if we see them, to blend them with our lot and bring them home.

'Either they've split or it's a wolf.'

We each lie on a single bed, like children in a communist-era orphanage, like the one they wanted to put Sásho in.

'If you leave, I mean when you leave, I'll miss you so much, I don't want to think about it,' Sásho says from his bed.

I'll miss you too, but I don't say it.

On the way down, the sheep eat plums and so do we. They are red-green, sour-sweet.

He shows me more cup-marks and crosses in the rocks and when the flock scatter in a big meadow, we sit on a boulder to wait. It's rare to sit down. You lie down at pladnina but you stand waiting for the flock, because as soon as you sit down, the dogs come and push you over with excitement or you lose track of straying animals. There is thunder but no clouds. The Orelek highlanders had a ritual for rain in times of drought. They'd choose an orphaned girl, cover her head in elder branches and take her from house to house, sprinkling water around her. They recited:

> God, give us rain!
> To give us wheat and rye
> to feed orphans and paupers,
> paupers and hired uns,
> hired uns and shepherds,
> goatherds and cowherds.

Shepherds, orphans, paupers and hired ones went together. The hired shepherds were those who didn't have sheep of their own or wanted to live away from their family for private reasons or had no family and no property at all. The best headmen of a shepherding cooperative were those who could promote their employees all the way through the ranks to headmen with their own flocks. To have a shepherd leave you, fully emancipated, animals in tow and bride on horse, was a sad occasion for a wealthy pastoralist but also an achievement. Only the most manipulative employers kept their hired hands in perpetual servitude. This still seemed to hold true.

We observe a huge rainbow without rain. To the Karakachans, the rainbow signified another realm beyond this one. The rainbow is a highway that bridges one mountain with another. On the rock, we lean on each other back-to-back like Janus twins.

'We're like good and evil,' says Sásho. 'You are the good.'

Sunny puts his head on Sásho's knee and smiles with a face like the sun. There is a big bite on his snout from the latest scuffle.

A sheep's lip is torn after an overly passionate kiss from a dog. 'What can we do?'

'Nothing, it will hang.'

Topi and the Gashta girls knock me down from the boulder with affection.

There is no evil in animals. Everybody in our rag-tag army is good. They don't know how not to be, even those who will bite you are good. When you are a shepherd, your soul can rest because of that.

'What is your ideal world?' I asked Sásho one evening when we returned by the winding forestry road. (I don't use roads, bai Anton boasts, roads are for lazy people.)

'Blue. My ideal world is blue,' he answered.

Air, water, mountains are blue, the colour of freedom. The colour of July.

Above the Coin trees, a sheep stopped, blood running from her nose. Sásho crouched by her and stroked her until she died. She was the one who couldn't breathe on my first day. Her lungs had collapsed. We left her there. It was too far to carry her. Later, bai Anton would come and rip her stomach open for the dogs. He got the worst jobs. I looked at the sheep's face one last time before we left her.

All I see day in, day out, is Sásho's face, the dogs' faces and the sheep who have distinct faces and the faces of the hills, the sun and the moon. Everything has a face. The moon's face is already showing in the dusky sky.

'Three days to the full moon,' I say, 'and we'll start howling.'

'The wolves already are,' Sásho says. 'This morning I woke up at five and looked at the moon, how beautiful it is. And I heard the hybrid, then Vachka joined in.'

I'd heard them too and thought they were dogs, but the line between dog and wolf is blurred now. They are one creature with two heads, like Janus twins.

Kámen is still looking for the mare but everything else is ready.

'Oh God, I hope Sásho won't start resting now,' Kámen moans in the kitchen.

He literally moans sometimes, with the burden of it all. Sásho is entitled to a break after seven months without a day off and before the ordeal of Black Water, where he will stay for two or three months. I will stay with him for as long as I can bear it but Kámen is afraid that once 'down', Sásho will go on a bender and become irretrievable.

'Those warrens in the 'hood, you've no idea. It's Bangladesh. Children and dogs in the mud. He doesn't answer his phone down there.'

The truth is, there is no one to replace Sásho, not even for a day. Kámen must become a shepherd himself, which he resents because it is a lowering of his status and he has a hundred other things to take care of.

These sheep are spoiled, I think. Do you have to have a full buffet every day and not let us do something other than look at you eat? Tyrants.

It's another day. We doze on the plastic sheet in a paralysis of midday heat. Faces pass through my sleep: Alex with his mother's unblinking face, turning into an owl then a snake, Kámen with loyal dogged eyes, the face of the dragon hill with its giant crevasse, the face of the hill with ruined houses like rotten teeth, the sphinx face of Thunder Peak, the face of the mild mountain across, the face of bai Anton with its foxy mistrust and the face of Sásho with gentle wolf-dog eyes.

Only my face isn't there because I have no face or body when I lie like this on the boundless bed of the hills, I have nothing at all. I am a vessel through which passes the breath of the world.

Last night, Sásho drank in his room. As he talks about his life and we become close, people and emotions crawl out of the box where he keeps them. They walk with us in the hills. There are his street friends in various towns: the girl who wore a wreath of garlic around her neck to guard against vampires; the girl who beat up all the boys and under whose bed he slept, hidden from her parents; the woman who took him in, aged thirteen, to live with her and be her lover; small-time dealers and narco bosses; glue-sniffers; strangers who beat him up; others who are beaten to a pulp before his eyes; the cops who are on his trail; the famous actress in a hotel lobby who took him under her wing and he became an extra in her film; the shepherds in the hills and the animals. Then his Gypsy family, his Orelek family, his lost sister and mother. All of these ghosts walk with us and the flock, and with all the other ghosts of Orelek.

By age ten, Sásho was sleeping at the central train station in the capital and selling newspapers on the trains, a boy with quick fingers moving through the draughty corridors with a stack, '*Daily Standard, Evening Standard, Good Housekeeper, Beautiful Today*'. He squatted in empty houses with other vagrants then in a halfway house for the homeless where a lot of marijuana was smoked or he would get on the train and get off in a rural suburb with empty holiday houses. He had several keys and if one of them would work, he'd let himself in and lock himself in from the inside, knowing that if he was found he could be battered to death. Street children were worthless. In the morning, he locked the door from the outside. He had no bag, only the clothes on his back stolen from washing lines and shop fronts with help from cats. He'd throw a sausage for the cat and it would bring down a whole line of clothes. He'd go inside a building and climb the floors to look for shoes left outside a door that fit him. This is how he walked through his youth. They called him 'Wolfling'.

'That's why the wolf's neck is thick, because he alone carries his prey,' he summed up. A shepherding expression.

But he realised theft was not for him. It was too cowardly, taking stuff behind people's backs, so he turned to robbery instead – where you face your victim.

'I wanted to be Robin Hood,' he said. 'Take from the rich and give it to the poor. I can't remember what arrived first, the drugs or the arms.'

Miraculously, after years on the street, he decided to return to school and got a diploma in electrical engineering. Then, due for compulsory service in the army, he was turned away for being underweight. 'How are you gonna hold a Kalashnikov when you're 50 kilos!' a general shouted at him to his relief. But he kept slipping back into vagrancy. When he accepted a job in cahoots with the mafia-like police – they give you the trail, you do the robbery and you split it – he ended up in jail. A year in jail that he could have cut in half had he told the court about the police ring, but he would be a dead man the moment he left jail; a dead man at twenty. Post-prison, he found himself on the road again with just the clothes on his back. This is how he washed up in the Gypsy 'hood by the river. A friend invited him, he stayed. The Gypsies are a closed community but he picked up Turkish, got a job at a wood-processing plant, moved in with a girlfriend's family and for the first time had stability. True, he was in a shack without plumbing or privacy but village life was a balm.

'To understand the Gypsies you have to become like them,' he said.

To live day by day. Not to accumulate things or make plans. To blow a thousand bucks on drinks and singers in one night instead of putting it in the bank. This is how he lived but a few years into it, he got restless. He wanted more, he wanted to learn something new, see faces and places and get away from the ghetto with its cycle of drinking and fights and its closed horizons, so he became a shepherd's apprentice.

This morning, his eyes are unfocused, his monologue is going round in circles and by pladnina, I am drained and we agree to be apart. I sit at one end of a meadow full of flowers and he stays with the flock by the reservoir. I listen to the wind play its chords through the flowers and impressions pass over me with their immaterial bodies. They are carried by the wind.

The wind is a messenger travelling from afar and I try to catch the message. Like a word that's not a word, it is a continuous movement of grass and light, of animals and the sun's orbit. The wind is alive like a being. The wind is the world's soul passing over me and its message is this, the world's soul. Anima.

It passes over us when we lie down with the animals. It touches us and moves on. I don't know where it goes but one day, I will go with it and not wake up anymore.

'You can't run away from your fate,' Sásho says today. 'You go around in circles, like the rams in the pen. I tried to build something but everything falls apart. I hit a dead end each time so it's better to be up here, where I'm neutral.'

Where the tired soul can rest.

There's an awful lot of waiting. What gets me through it is Sásho's company. But if I was on my own, I have no idea what would happen. I might become a sage or quit very quickly or I might take up smoking, and maybe drinking.

Surely, I should be doing something with my time, not standing here, waiting for a bunch of sheep to eat their fill for hours every day. God, I'm bored! But when I try to read a book, my eye wanders back to the hills. When I'm here, I don't want to be elsewhere.

But I am not patient. I rush towards the next moment. In the next moment, there is nothing better than in this moment. I know that, but it's ingrained. It's a neurological condition called being a Westerner. Patience is a forgotten art, like shepherding. Most people don't have any patience at all. The only thing that makes waiting bearable anywhere is to scroll through your phone. You the shepherd do this too, while you wait for the flock to graze their fill and move on and for the sun to complete its painting of the day.

But the difference is, you the shepherd must be philosophical because no amount of scrolling will fill the gaping time that belongs to the flock. You become a graduate of the Stoic school of time. Yours is a practical philosophy, like that of wandering bards and dervishes and homeless children and dogs. You can't get lost in your phone too long because you must be aware of every twitching dog's ear, every change in the wind, every bleat and every type of cloud.

It's all about body language. If you walk ahead of the flock, you block them and they will split on either side of you which can cause complications. If you are behind, you can encourage the last ones to

move along faster, like the sheep with the split ear and her lamb or
The Crocodile, the sheep that looks exactly like a crocodile in profile. If you stand to the side, they know you're there and feel free to
explore the pasture. If there's no human guardian, they stick together.
If you stand in the middle of them like Balkán, they will run past you
as if you're not there but wherever you stand, you must learn the art
of waiting.

'I don't mind waiting,' says Sásho. 'I'm reckless by nature. Too
impulsive. Drinking, fighting, shooting off my mouth, falling for
women not of my rug.'

Not of my rug. One of the many expressions that come from the
people of the rug, the chergari. Everybody knew that you should
marry someone of your own rug (social standing), that you should
live according to your rug (cut your coat according to your cloth) and
that you shouldn't pull the rug your way unduly (take more than
your due).

'But with the animals, I've learned to be calm.'

The good shepherd is calm. He knows what to do and when. Little
action is needed, except at the right moments. It takes cultivation. It's
like martial arts. The good shepherd doesn't get sick. The good shepherd
can take monotony, bad weather, wet clothes, lack of appreciation,
dog bites, ulcerated feet, being invisible, having no name, being
underpaid, lack of sleep, caring for something that will never belong
to him and walking through a beautiful world devoid of humans
with just the clothes on his back.

The good shepherd waits, even when it's hopeless.

'For example, I'll wait for you. Years will pass. We'll grow old and
I'll still wait for you. Up here.'

'You mean figuratively,' I say.

'Do I look like a figurative guy? I might get my own sheep. Ten is
enough, so I can wait better.'

This man is like no one else and has become dear to me. I dread
these weeks becoming a memory.

'I don't want this to be just a memory,' he says. 'That's why I'll
wait. Literally.'

We bring something out in each other. And something about these open hills makes you say exactly how you feel and makes you feel exactly how you must. It is safe to feel here and let your guard down, wear terrible clothes or no clothes at all, laugh, cry, sing and be touched by everything.

Today has been peaceful, like gliding on a smooth sea with just enough wind in the sails. Everyone is at ease. No dog fights, the sheep are mellow.

'Well done girls, that's how I like you.'

We're a fleet of moving legs and ruffled heads. We know each other now, all 540 of us. That's 500 sheep, 8 dogs, 2 humans and 30 young sheep that are no longer lambs and that have been let out of the covered pen to mix with the older ones. It's their third day and after the initial mad rush to pasture, they have settled into the rhythm of the flock, though they are still the first to come out in the morning, like runners who can't wait for the whistle.

Tomorrow, Sásho has a day off and we are going to Kresna in my car. It's an adventure to be in the lower world without the animals, like parents skiving off without their children.

We stand in the forest of coin trees, scratched, sunstruck and moonstruck, Orelek at our feet. The hills spread out all the way to the future which is unstable and blue like the light. Another beautiful day has passed.

'Can you imagine these hills without any more flocks or dogs?' I say.

'Well yeah, it wouldn't take much. If Kámen and Stamen give up, that'll be it.'

I imagine the hills of Orelek empty like the Scottish highlands and I imagine the rest of the earth like that. I see anguished humans going around searching for something but not knowing what it is. They are scaling the hills. They think they are tourists but they are pilgrims. They have forgotten how it looks or what it's called, the thing they've lost. They will suddenly remember when they see it.

They are searching for the mountain sheep with a head like a pharaoh, the horse that reads your mind, the Karakachan dog with human eyes, the golden eagle drawn by a boy's hand and the wolf that answers your call. They are searching for communion. When they cut the forests and slaughtered the horses for meat, they did not understand that everything was connected by a living breath and now their souls can't rest because they are orphans of this earth. Wondering if they even have the right to be here.

LOOKING FOR MIMI

Mimi the mare was spotted at Warm Spout. The Privateer told Kámen on the phone and he jumped in the car. I joined him.

'I went looking for her yesterday. I got close to her in the woods but she bolted 'cos of the foal and I lost her.'

Above the Orelek canyon, it's a spiky, steep jungle. It's impossible to look for anything here, big or small. There is no trail of dung on the road and the hoof prints lead nowhere. We drive past some high pens and huts with hired shepherds. They belong, once again, to Stamen. How many pens does he have! But there's nobody home.

'Otherwise I'd pay them 50 bucks to find the mare and save me a day.'

Between them, Kámen, Marina and Stamen own twenty Karakachan horses above the gorge, although you can't own a wild horse. You bought it but you don't own it.

The horses roam as a commune, even if their owners don't talk to each other. Out of that commune, just two mares are tame enough to obey humans and carry luggage; one for Kámen, the other for Stamen. Kámen's mare Mimi only works at this time of the year, then she rejoins the rest and goes semi-wild. What makes her difficult to track down now is that she has split off to give birth, but her roaming territory is still vast, a wooded canyon 10 kilometres long with just one forked road. Kámen must find her or there is no exodus. He drives slowly and we scan the woods for moving shapes.

'If I have to, I'll go back and get some water and food to last the day, then I'll comb this jungle again. How was the day off?'

Yesterday was Sásho's day off. Just one day.

We drove into the gorge. Two weeks in the hills for me. For him, seven months. Everything looked artificial. There was nothing but

cement, metal, plastic and glass. Plastic everywhere! We ate lunch in
a roadside restaurant, feeling like aliens among the truckies, the locals
and the holiday lunchers. People looked lethargic, lost.

'So many sheep, and they're all scattered. I must gather them!
Prrrr, prrrr.' Sásho mocked himself. 'And so sad. Even when they
bleat and graze, they're sad.'

Faces, colours, restless movement.

We were on a high, the only happy people I saw all day. We had
been let out of a boarding house with pocket money and a day to fill,
then we'd go back at curfew hour. Two black storks circled above us
in a dance.

Sásho said 'They're beautiful. They remind me of us.'

We kept looking up. Everything at street level was too busy for
our senses. People who go on long retreats feel like this when they
break their fast. In your super-sensitised state, everything is height-
ened. The mechanical noise causes you pain. Everything is sealed
shut with gravel, brick and metal and people's faces are shut too, and
they're metallic. The horizon is hemmed in. You don't know how to
live in such a world.

The lower world looks like an unsuccessful experiment in which
the green-blue earth was turned into a cement plant. The experiment
is over, factories lie roofless and storks make their nests in them and
the experiment's former employees have nowhere to go except perhaps to the hills.

'I feel unprepared.' Sásho's eyes were like plates.

Seven months with the flock, seeing nobody but Kámen, bai
Anton, the animals and lately, me. He was doing well! But we were
laughing a lot. At lunch, we began to laugh when the waitress brought
plates of kebabs and salads and a beer for him. It was all so orderly,
but stilted. The waitress hates her job. People sit in uncomfortable
chairs, wear uncomfortable clothes and have uncomfortable relationships with each other. Everyone is bored. Everything is square. Tables
and buildings have sharp corners made to harm you. The glossy menu
overwhelms us with a choice of dishes, yet they are the same foods
differently mixed. For a moment, the prices mean nothing to us. We
have forgotten the value of money.

This is not the longest time that Sásho has spent on a shepherding 'retreat' without a break.

'That was in my previous job. Those hills over there. The colleague and I stayed with the flock in a highland area called Sleepy Field for one year and four months.'

Sixteen months! It was warm enough in winter to keep the flock there. Provisions were brought up to them once a week. They lived inside a derelict military base close to the border, underneath which were sealed medieval dungeons and antique mines.

'Remember when we were kids and you tried to tune into a foreign radio station and got static? That's where they silenced Yugoslav radio signals, in that base.'

When he came down to the village below for the first time, it was like landing on another planet. All these people in the café with their funny faces and voices. He laughed like a lunatic for two days, his inhibitions gone, then got used to human society again.

I'd have a permanent change to my personality after sixteen months like that.

'I *have* a permanent change,' Sásho grinned. 'I just don't know if it's for better or for worse.'

We visited that village, where he had lived in a riverside shack with the other shepherd, after Sleepy Field. It was the mirror image of Orelek, but with people living in it. Millennial sycamores lined the tributary that led to the village. The people there were descendants of refugees from Greece, like Sásho's grandfather, and had drifted here along the river. The village had been populated by Pomak pastoralists but they were purged around the time this lot arrived. Nobody talked about it but Sásho showed me the remains of a mosque in a garden. Hybrids see more than pure breeds.

We drove the length of the gorge to the nearest city, past the roadside goats with the invisible herder.

'Moni the Mute,' Sásho said, though we didn't see him. They shared everything for half a year but now they never saw each other. Each lived embedded in his own flock.

So many trucks! So many things in the shops that nobody buys. So much food and alcohol. So much danger and distraction. Wind

turbines turn by the ruined Roman fort above the gorge where
Spartacus was born. What a long road he travelled. What a long road
Sásho and I have travelled to be here in this lost world twenty centur-
ies later.

'Who do you think you were in a past life?' I ask.

'Robin Hood,' he says at once. 'And you were Spartacus. 'Cos you
fight injustice with your books. But you do it in the open and I do it
in the woods.'

We pass a disused coal factory which was about to reopen because
of the war in Ukraine and fuel shortages. The lower world is in paralysis. It thinks it's moving forwards, it looks like it's moving
backwards, but it is not moving at all. Our civilisation is a collapsing
leviathan.

'This is why I prefer it up,' Sásho said. 'Because down here I lose
myself.'

Like everybody else.

'I fall into traps. I become a pretender and a user,' he said. 'It's
better to come down as a visitor.'

And it's nice to visit. We visited a shop for outdoor clothes. He
bought: canvas sneakers, two pairs; bars of soap; cigarettes, twenty
packs; a new rucksack; T-shirts; socks; chewing gum and a pair of
plastic clogs for me, for the hut.

'Anything else?'

There are hundreds of things we'll need at the hut, me especially.
But everything is carried on your back and my rucksack is already
packed. When the visit was over, we stopped at a roadside restaurant
for lamb soup and sheep's yogurt, neither of which was up to the
standards of Orelek and drove up the poor road with relief and
regret.

'Did you visit Bangladesh?' says Kámen in the car. Kámen had been
surprised to have his shepherd return sober and back at work this
morning.

Kámen is forced to employ men from the Roma 'hoods because
they are the only people willing to work with animals for the money
offered.

'Sásho is very smart,' Kámen adds. 'But he went to live with the Gypsies.'

'But he lives here now, with you.'

Kámen grunts. His presence puts a damper on things and I've been avoiding him. At the house, Sásho plays the happy-go-lucky hireling from the 'hood. In the 'hood, he has a persona that speaks Turkish, showers people with his hard-earned cash like a demented king and leaves without sobering up. With me, he is chivalrous, articulate and his impersonations of people and animals are so funny I have to sit down. This chameleon quality makes Kámen nervous.

Sásho lives in his house like a nanny, yet their inner worlds don't touch. Kámen assumes that Sásho has no inner world. Adept at reading environments and people, Sásho sees right through Kámen and has the power to disappear in a fugue or lose animals and ruin Kámen. In turn, Kámen keeps Sásho in the dark about everything, criticises him even when he gives to the point of sacrifice and strips him of autonomy. Sásho appears not to mind but he reserves the right to pull a trick on Kámen. It's their dance.

This new bond between Sásho and me galls Kámen. Perhaps he worries that my presence will tip the balance. Maybe he is jealous. Maybe there can be no bond between people from different social milieux and he is the realist checking the idealist, but his reality depresses me, so it can't be that real.

Kámen pulls the car over and we get out to look for trails in the thorny woods.

The Orelek commune got into horses because you need them to carry dog food to the summer pastures, and if you have Karakachan dogs and sheep, you must have the horses too.

The Karakachan horse is an old mountain breed from the Balkans, one of the few indigenous types that have not disappeared, although it's gravely endangered. It is descended from a wild mountain horse that travelled from Asia to south-east Europe at some unknown point in time.

'Twenty years ago, we went to this guy, a Vlach called Yanko.'

Yanko was a legend, one of the last great horsemen. They bought eighteen horses from him and walked with them for several days over two mountains, but the horses went back to their old stomping ground. It was impossible to stop them wandering off. Then Yanko himself joined the effort and he found them and brought them here himself. They stopped returning to him then.

'Yanko connected with his horses remotely. He knew where they were. He was old but ran like a young man.'

It was normal for Karakachan horses to travel great distances. They liked it best living separately from other animals. The pastoral nomads used horses during their migration from winter to summer pasture and once they arrived at the summer pastures, the horses were taken to remote peaks for the season. Donkeys, not horses, were used during summer to take food to those shepherds who were far from the base camp and these donkeys grazed with the sheep all summer. The Karakachans were 'fanatically consistent' about the purity of their breeds, in the words of an early equine scholar, and never bred horse with donkey.

The Karakachans had three main types of animal men: shepherds, milkers who were also pen workers and dairy masters, and horsemen. The horsemen were single men who didn't mind living in primitive conditions without the comforts of a hut and seeing nobody but the horses for months. The horses were not hand-fed and relied on pasture only, with the odd treat of salt mixed with cornmeal. The horsemen's diet and everyday life was even more monotonous. By the end of the summer months of free grazing, usually from May to November, the horses would go wild again and the horsemen would catch them with simple ropes called lasso.

Yanko lived in Rila Mountain to the north, near the great pastures of Belmeken where Karakachan and other herds have grazed for centuries.

Just fifteen years ago, you could witness a spectacle like no other and Kámen, Marina and Stamen were taken there by Yanko. In a big pit like an arena were twenty wild stallions. Men gathered on the edge of the pit. They had to go in one by one and catch a stallion the nomad way, with a lasso. The first man who went in was kicked and had his arm broken but this didn't stop the second man from jumping in. He was nearly crushed to death. And on it went, a gladiatorial game in the theatre of the mountain. They were mostly Roma and Pomaks, the last of the horse people.

'Those horses and those men are gone,' Kámen said.

But they were not, not quite. There was at least one such man and a clutch of such horses. Two, counting the old cowboy. I saw how Emin caught a wild young mare. He ran with her in a circle on a high plateau, the other horses in the middle, then, as she slowed down, he walked and talked to her, holding a rope. After forty minutes of this she stopped and regarded him out of the corner of her eye. There was no force. Emin's rage disappeared with the horses and he gave to the point of bankruptcy, the way I had given to him or that's how it felt by the end. He was emaciated like a convict and after walking with him, I became the same. You end up like your animals, that's all.

I saw him trip with sisal rope two young stallions who were mounting the mares and kicking everything in sight. Once the front legs were tripped, the horse couldn't walk far. Emin avoided doing this because he wanted the horses to be free, even if that meant they were hard to find and more mileage for him. Thousands and thousands of lonely miles along high roads and low roads over his lifetime. If his footfall was combined, he would have walked around the earth more than once. 'What do you say to them?' I asked him once. 'Just my usual garble,' he said. 'They don't mind I'm a lunatic. 'Cos they're lunatics too.'

It is desolate to be the last one, to live on the cusp of the void with the full knowledge of it. Surely living post-extinction would be easier. No more farewells on high roads and low roads.

For several million years, a three-toed grazing pony called Hipparion roamed the Strymonian plains. When it became extinct, there was no one to miss it. I wonder if this will be the fate of the last horse on earth: none of us will be left to miss it.

'There she is!' Kámen said.

On the low road by Warm Spout she was grazing in full view of us, beautiful and shiny with her fuzzy black foal beside her. Kámen was almost pleased.

'I have a telepathic link with her.'

We abandoned the car and Kámen put a bucket of feed and bread

down for Mimi before approaching her. When he managed to put
the halter on her, we walked them all the way to Orelek along the
heated road. She wasn't keen on being led on a rope after nine months
of roaming free and kept stopping to say 'No.'

'Now Mimi, don't be a stubborn mule,' said Kámen.

I walked at a safe distance behind her with a stick, urging her on
but not hitting her. The foal walked on his shaky new legs and kept
tabs on me from the corner of his eye. This was his first meeting with
a human. He was only a week or two old. They stopped every twenty
minutes for him to suckle.

Every summer, Mimi gave birth, and every summer her child was
killed by predators at Black Water. Like the brown foal I saw last
year.

'Let's hope this one's luckier,' said Kámen.

Kosta the old cowboy had told me that highland cows grieve for
their lost children for a long time but wild horses don't. They have a
completely different psychology.

'Horses are the most complicated animals,' Kámen said.

According to spiritual researchers like the theosophist Rudolf
Steiner, the horse is the animal with the highest level of conscious-
ness. I can believe it.

'I don't know why but one of Yanko's horses kicked everyone in
the family. Even after years of knowing us.'

All the horse people know each other and I'd heard of Yanko from
Emin and the old cowboy. He was dubbed 'Crooked Yanko' because
he told small lies all the time. 'Where're you off to, Yanko?' 'Heading
north.' But he was heading south, and so on. Maybe he did that "cos
he'd been swindled too many times and didn't trust anybody', Emin
said, 'and the horse world is full of crooks, thieves and lunatics like
me,' he said.

'I think horse people are complicated too,' I said to Kámen.

'That reminds me, this specimen came in the spring,' Kámen
turned to me. 'I don't know how he got here but he arrived on foot.
Tall, gaunt and deranged. A friend of yours. Or an enemy. I couldn't
tell. Interesting, at first. One of those invisible people.'

Emin was capable of crossing a mountain just to drop in.

'He rocked up and started helping me round the pen. Talking non-stop.'

Impressed by Emin's horsemanship, Kámen thought of giving his horses to him. He couldn't keep track of them and had too much else on his hands but after Emin sat at the kitchen table all night, Kámen just wanted rid of him.

'Yes, I've had those sleepless nights,' and I told Kámen about my expeditions with Emin in the snow. Kámen was curious.

Where did you look for them?

We didn't find them at the glacial lakes.

Where were they?

In the western Rhodope, two days later.

Kámen knew what this meant. For the first time, he looked at me as if he really saw me.

He and Marina had the same problem with indigenous horses as everyone else: they were not used in the rural economy anymore. They had lost their cultural value too. Some owners kept special breeds just for the subsidies but had no love for the animals. Every winter, as they pocketed the latest wad of cash, herds of cows and horses were left in remote places to starve and be eaten by wolves.

'And I can't let the Gypsies have my horses,' said Kámen. 'They will put them to the axe. The last of the indigenous horses are in the hands of the Gypsies.'

This was not entirely true. Several hundred wild Karakachan horses with a protected status roam the Rhodope and there are good breeders too, like Emin and the old cowboy, but it is true that the Gypsies are the last people who live *with* their horses.

Traditionally, four groups held horse knowledge, all of them nomads: the Aromanian Vlachs, the Karakachans, the Gypsies and the Yuruks. The Yuruks were called Konyari in the vernacular – meaning horse people, but also referring to their homeland of Konya in Anatolia. The Yuruks treated their horses like family and even kept them inside their tents. One ethnographer writes of families wearing rags while their horses are covered in splendid capes. Unlike the Karakachans, they did not leave behind a particular breed of horse because they were more lax in their approach.

The Karakachans owned large numbers of horses and kept them in
a military-style regime, like the dogs   no treats and splendid capes –
because for them, the horse was in service of the flock: just like the
human. I have never seen this with my own eyes but wild Karakachan
horses have a method to defend themselves against wolves and bears:
when a predator approaches, the herd press together with their heads
and chests facing out, ready to bite and kick the hell out of the
attacker.

The fate of the nomads and the fate of the indigenous horse go
hand in hand. By 1920, the last Yuruks were expelled but many had
already settled and mingled with the general population. The Aromanian Vlachs settled earlier, by choice, and even had their own
towns. The most famous of these was Moskopolje in Albania, which
had several splendid churches and even its own coin minting centre
and is now a semi-ruined landscape whose beauty hasn't left it. The
frescoes are still there, and there is even a lone priest in one of the
churches, who speaks Albanian and Greek.

The Roma were the last wanderers to hold on to horses but today
they were no longer rug people but slum people, with slum horses.
A hundred years ago, some Roma were settled craftsmen in the
towns, but most Strymonian Romani were wanderers with horse
katuns (travellers' camps). There were no ghettos. The last Gypsy
katuns were disbanded at the same time as the Karakachan katuns –
in the 1950s. For centuries, the katun camp settlement had a major
role in the social, cultural, political, economical and ecological landscape of the Balkans, as it did in Central Asia and the Caucasus or
anywhere where pastoral nomads were major players. The word
'katun', like *cherga* for tent and rug, probably came from Central
Asia, brought by the Turkic-speaking horse nations who came with
their shamans and khans. They were the Bulgars who founded Bulgaria and later, the Kumans who came with their flocks and large
guardian dogs, continuously forging the evolution of the Karakachan
dog and horse.

Like the Karakachans, the Gypsies were wrenched from the road,
stripped of their horses and shoved into concrete ghettos. They were
less amenable to homogenisation than any other group and never

recovered from being settled. Settlement ruined them. To this day, it is difficult for state education and cultural assimilation to reach them, and their levels of literacy remain low. Industrialisation and urbanisation under the communists stripped the Roma of their traditional trades and pushed the men into slave-like labour units deployed in large building projects such as the construction of roads, railways and ship yards. The country's infrastructure was built by anonymous Roma men, whose life expectancy remains the lowest in Europe.

The professions the Gypsies lost were horse grooming and trading, blacksmithing, copper smithing, ironmongery, small-scale trade, wood carving, musical instrument making and many other small crafts, like wooden-combmakers called *grebenari*, spindlemakers called *vreterani* and of course, bellmakers for animals. Of their typical crafts, all that is left now is music, basket weaving and selling vegetables. The rest is logging and heavy manual labour for the men and low-grade service jobs for the women, and lately, shepherding. This is how a permanent underclass was created out of dispossessed wanderers.

We arrived in Orelek. Kámen tied Mimi up in a small clearing by his goat house. Later, he would move her and the foal somewhere safer because wolves came down in the night.

To live in the mountain has always meant horses grazing nearby. At the end of the nineteenth century, there were around 394,000 horses of four or five indigenous breeds in the country's territory (one breed was the Karakachan). In 1940, there were a quarter of a million left. Before the seizure of the Karakachans, their horses alone numbered around 100,000. When the Karakachan herds were confiscated in 1957, the horses became useless and were slaughtered en masse and given to pigs and chickens as food. The genocide of the Karakachan horse was Europe's final act against nomadism.

This is what you resisted by keeping mountain horses. Emin, Kámen and Marina, Stamen, the old cowboy, some took subsidies, some didn't. Yet they all kept these horses because they knew that without the mountain horse, the mountain was incomplete. Without the horse, all other animals are orphaned and most of all, the human animal.

How do you know you're a true horse lover and not a recreational one? You must be ready to do a bit of what Emin does for his horses: walk the earth for them. The horse lovers of this world are few.

I sat under the willow in the empty square where you can get signal. Sásho called. Muna the Monkey was not with him today.

'She's not here and you're not here, and I can see my future,' he said. 'Will you come fly with me?'

'You're drunk, dear,' I said.

'I'm desperately sober. Will you come and fly with me for the rest of our lives?' he said. 'And make a better future.'

'When you sober up, we can discuss it,' I said.

'I'm drunk on a realisation, dear,' he said. 'That when I'm old and impotent, I'll still choose you. Because you're an endangered species called a true friend. It terrifies me.'

'How are we going to say goodbye?' I said.

'That's what terrifies me. The godmothers are lying in that pine forest like a cathedral. I've got an old tyre for a pillow. You're next to me and yet you're not. I must learn to combine the two or I'll go mad, like Spintop.'

I span too, groundless under the willow in the empty village, as if an air spiral had lifted me up and there was no safety net to catch us when we fell.

The next day, the church bell rang. Orelek was having its annual feast. Cauldrons with kurban – 'sacrificial' lamb broth – bubbled in the church courtyard, a blatant scene of nature worship as the mountain itself demanded. Even industrialism couldn't completely destroy the dominion of nature and the Church had long submitted its doctrine to the cult of the mountain. Here, the blessing and smudging of summer pens at the start of season was not carried out by a priest but by the head shepherd who assumed the magical powers of Pan the demiurge. Long tables were laid out in the empty square. It was the feast day of Saint Marina, the old goddess of fire, medicine and snakes – and her cult overlapped with that of Saint Elijah, which made sense in this electrical mountain. Orelekers had also worshipped Saint Katerina, the protectress of bears. This was the one day of the year when the sleepy kingdom of Orelek awoke with a jolt.

People drove gingerly up the broken road. They had come out of their towns with offerings: stuffed pastries, cakes and salads, someone had gifted the lamb for the kurban.

These were the descendants of Orelek paying their respects to their lost homeland. Their parents and grandparents were humiliated, robbed, battered, killed and exiled along with their animals and these orphans came to check up on the old house, check up on the roofless ruin and fill a bucket with figs from the family garden. These were tattered people without teeth, women in black who'd lost husbands and sons and men who worked abroad, remnants of highland clans, the faces of a pastoral civilisation that was only smashed in the last seventy years by the military-industrial complex whose ruins were now everywhere. Two men were so drunk, they crawled through the church courtyard, one of them barking like a dog, their mothers hovering beside them with guilty faces.

When you are traumatised, you feel guilty about everything, including the crimes committed against you.

There was a man who stood out in this crowd with his lined mahogany face, frizzy hair and clever eyes. Within minutes of meeting him, I felt like he could sell me anything in a language of my choice because, being a horse dealer and a Roma, he spoke four. His name was Orhan. His ancestors were one of a handful of Roma clans from Orelek and were expert horse cobblers, smiths and ironmongers. They were Muslims. The entire highlands had depended on their skills, from horse cobbling to crafting cauldrons and ploughs, and they'd been greatly respected. Orhan lived in Sásho's border town and was one of the region's horsemen and general animal people, sometimes he helped Stamen who was not here today.

He told me that well into his grandparents' life, which meant until the Balkan Wars of 1912–1913, Turkish and Bulgarian merchants trekked here with their horses to sell olives, fish oil and raw cane-sugar cubes. They sold their goods in large leather sacks with strings.

'Adapted for horse saddle,' said Orhan, ''Cos everything went on horseback. The Karakachans made sacks from goat skin called *tulumi* and filled them stuffed with fresh cheese, butter and ghee.'

You bought these by the bagful when the nomads passed through.

'We have the mountain horse to thank for everything but the most handsome horses are the Danube and the Arab breeds. Of the heavy-weight ones, the Ardennes and the Russian Don that the Cossacks used.'

'Balkan indigenous horses have straight ears. Indian horses have their ears pointing out,' he went on.

'And do you know the best milk? It's donkey's milk. An immune booster, like colostrum. Thick like that of the Karakachan sheep. Sold to big pharma to make drugs. It's the next big thing, I tell ya! Want me to get you some?'

I told him about the mare and he asked to see her. We walked over to Mimi and the foal in the clearing. 'Pure Karakachan,' he said. He pushed her lip up. Fourteen or fifteen years old.

Now, I understood the expression 'don't look a gift horse in the mouth'. It's because you can tell the age and health of a horse from its teeth. Free-grazing horses wore down their teeth faster than horses fed on forage because they had to work harder in the wild and their diet was more sporadic. Years are counted in the upper and lower teeth. When the bottom teeth begin to wear out, the horse enters its second decade.

'You can tell character from the teeth too. Milder horses wear off their side teeth faster. Hard-headed horses, slower. And you want the milder one. Like her.'

He patted Mimi. The foal kept away from us.

'Ach, it's hard for the indigenous breeds now,' he said with pain.

It was the same with all grazing animals. The indigenous breeds were existentially threatened. Commercial, more productive breeds have flooded the market, pushing out indigenous breeds. They are all hybridised because no native breed is naturally 'productive' in any industrial sense. It is too close to the wild. Sheep that are a mixture of six breeds have been created expressly to give 2 litres of milk, instead of the more modest yield of the mountain sheep, 300 milli-litres per milking. Horses that are bigger and more spectacular, so you can show them off at a rally. But these bigger, cosmetically enhanced animals with larger udders are not adapted to survive long-term, just like those atrophied mastiffs bred by the Romans. They have no kinship with place and no resistance to endemic diseases like the autochthonous breeds do. They are used as food machines, trophies and toys that feed into the industrial model of growth and profit, whose aesthetic expression is the culture of deep fake and all of which is collapsing: genetically, ecologically, economically and ethically.

'Commercial breeds, commercial people. Nature rejects them all,' Orhan summed up.

And in the meantime, the final breeds of horse, sheep, dog and human that are adapted to organic living are pushed to the brink. Orelek was this brink. Several breeds of indigenous sheep, horse and buffalo have been wiped from existence in just the last few decades.

Vital: that's how I felt around these animals. They were vital and they made me feel vital. I discovered that this is also a term in zoology and biology. The 'vitality' of these breeds is described by one scientist as an 'excellent adaptability to local ecological conditions, high degree of resistance to disease, reproductive success (including the complete survival of offspring), absolute suitability to breeding conditions, and accommodation to different types of feed.' This vigour, absent from commercially bred grazing animals, is the result of the indigenous ones' 'eternal harmony within nature'.

One look at Mimi and her foal confirmed this.

'This mare and her foal don't look much but they're tougher than other breeds. The Karakachan horse doesn't sicken, doesn't die of starvation and never buckles down.'

Alpine conditions and long-distance treks shaped this breed. During the Balkan Wars and the First World War, bigger, more impressive horses collapsed in the muddy Armageddon. Not the Karakachan horse, and how did the twentieth-century human thank the Karakachan horse for its millennial loyalty? By feeding it to chickens and pigs.

'But, any horse you want, I'll find it for you,' Orhan perked up. 'You wanna know about horses? I'll take you places across borders, no passport needed. Show you things you'll never forget.'

I was tempted. Orhan had the battered but unbeaten verve of the eternal traveller. In *The Iliad*, Homer describes Hector of Troy as 'a tamer of horses'. A tamer of horses is an old thing to be and though commercial movies use actors with square jaws and blue eyes for this archetype, I think that horse tamers have always looked like Orhan.

'Are you married?' he lit a cigarette after scanning my fingers for rings and probably counting my teeth too. I laughed.

'If you weren't, and if I didn't have a great wife, I'd throw you on this horse, take you some place no one can find us and ask you to marry me, no passport needed. 'Cos you darlin' are a rare breed worth a million.'

By mid-afternoon, everyone was gone and a blanket of silence fell on the village again. White napkins fluttered in the empty square.

The family didn't go to the feast, they kept their distance and had their reasons. The remaining few villagers complained that it smelled of animals. They were so damaged by dispossession that they couldn't see it was thanks to Kámen and Marina that their village was still a village and not just stones and wolves. Some of them were jealous of the incomers' success, not appreciating the sacrifices they had made to be here. Yet the stand-off was not between incomer and local. It was between different world views. Among the feasting villagers were local functionaries who closed the last village shop and prevented the road from being fixed by siphoning off funds into churches in the middle of nowhere. There were hunters who laid poison to kill guardian dogs out of meanness, and people who believed that Marina 'releases' bears into the wild because she has a van with a bear painted on it.

But it was also that Kámen held himself apart from all of the other villagers out of sheer pride and had never given a lamb for the village feast.

Today, he had been cooking all day. I made a salad and we sat at the long table for our own village feast: haunch of goat kid, crispy and tasting of meadows and rice pudding with goat milk and melon. The flesh of these animals is like nothing else. It has more of the earth's flavours in it than any other meat. At the table were Kámen,

Achilles, bai Anton, Alex, his brother Theo who had just arrived, Sásho and me; a last supper before the exodus.

'Eat up 'cos there are animals. Animals there are,' Kámen quipped. We all smiled but not happily. The surplus was due to the paralysed market.

'I've got everything ready,' Kámen said to his boys and his brother, ready for a preliminary trip to take the luggage up to the hut. They hadn't been to the hut since the season closed last October.

His boys looked at him without seeing him. They were in their own world. Theo had been making sand sculptures at a seaside festival and hadn't mentally arrived yet. He was a radiant teenager with an acute awareness of others. We'd already chatted outside where he fed the Loopies and Alex chided him, in their father's gruff voice, for taking too long.

'I've got the saddle too,' Kámen went on.

His boys nodded. On the TV was *Snatch* in which Brad Pitt is a Gypsy with horses. It made us laugh in the wrong places. None of us could quite believe it.

Achilles was his affable self, doing everything slowly and irritating his brother, but it was good to have somebody who laughed in the house. Then, Kámen lay on his narrow bed by the fridge and fell asleep as if after a battle: or before.

Late one night at the end of the week, Kámen knocked on my door:

'We go tomorrow.'

EXODUS TO BLACK WATER

The night before the departure, there is commotion. Lamps, footsteps, engines whirring into life, dogs barking. I lie in bed and worry
that we lost part of the flock when we came back along the tricky
river path from Wolfland yesterday, and that they are now coming
down into Orelek, setting the dogs off. It's one thing to lose sheep
when drunk – then you're an idiot – but losing them sober is
unforgivable.

I sleep and dream of sheep on a meadow, their throats ripped open.

'Don't,' whispers Kámen in the morning. 'I haven't blinked all
night.'

There was no sheep crisis, just something he remembered in the
middle of the night and went to the goat house to get. He can't sleep
before the exodus or he has the same dream that I've just had.

'I'm not gonna blink tonight either, 'cos I don't know what prowls
at Prairie,' says Sásho standing at the sink, smoking a last fag with bai
Anton who is too stoic to say he'll miss us.

Sásho goes to fetch the flock and Vachka and the hybrid howl in
farewell. They know it's exodus time. They will miss us too. Without the sheep and the dogs walking past every day, it'll just be the
two of them, kissing through the mesh.

The rams mingle with the sheep for the first time since last year
and are already mounting them. They are horny – now I get the
word! Their crowned heads are impressive. Some have been fighting
and green branches are stuck in their curly horns. 'They've dressed
up for their wedding night,' Sásho laughs. There's a commotion on
the road when the flock comes past the house: the guardian dogs
attack the house dogs who are in their way. Twenty dogs go to war
in seconds. There are clouds of dust and blood. Chained in the cave,
Barut doesn't take sides. He is too old for this sort of thing. I shrink

to the back of the yard, Kámen whacks them with a broom and it's over. The Loopies assume their place in the yard, licking their blood and the others continue with the flock. There is collateral damage, a guineafowl.

'Kasho, you shit, you killed it!' Bai Anton picks up a ragged bird and the Loopies fall on it, delighted.

'It's turning into a Gypsy wedding already,' Kámen allows himself a smirk.

And then we're off. Rucksacks on our backs, across the river gully and over a wooden bridge. There are over 600 sheep in the flock. Between now and the end of the season, there are many liabilities: the aggressive rams who can wreak havoc, the young sheep who've never done this before and don't know where they're going, the lambs who might be too small to keep up without injury, the dogs who might be wounded by predators, the horses who might slip and fall into the gorge, the weather that could do absolutely anything and finally, us humans who are in charge of the whole thing but not in control of it.

Today's mission is for Sásho and I to get the flock to Prairie and stay there overnight. To me, this is an adventure like no other, mixed with grave responsibility but I am not thinking 'danger'. When I look back, I understand why Kámen hadn't slept. It is like this every year and it has been like this since the beginning of transhumance: you've done it before, you know the terrain, but you have no guarantee of reaching Black Water intact, surviving the summer and making it back in one piece. None. And when everything is connected, things go wrong in a chain reaction.

This departure is a rite of passage but there is no one to mark it. When the mother is here, she pours a bucket of water on the road for good luck. Once, families sent the flocks off with bunches of flowers and gunshots, like to war. Then, a branch was placed on the door like a wreath and over the coming months the remaining ones checked on its state; if it kept well, their dear ones were safe. If it wilted quickly, it bade ill. A ritual itinerary was followed out of the village to avoid bad omens. Those who stayed walked some of the way with the departing ones, to a threshold outside the village where the thread connecting the flocks with home broke. Farewells were said and the departing ones walked on without looking back. When the shepherds brought the flocks home a few months later, the village knew what kind of season they'd had even before the mass of animals moved into their field of vision. If gun shots were fired, it meant a good season. No shots meant a bad season and bells removed from the animals was the silence of death.

Kámen sees us off from Barut's rock, swearing. This is his threshold.

'Not that way you sod!' he shouts at Sásho who annoys him with his good mood and Pied Piper confidence, 'not to Bangladesh! Move them to the left!'

But Sásho knows exactly where he is driving the flock. It has been hard, being in Kámen's radius, like carrying a heavy sack at all times. With each step away, I lighten up.

'They don't look as many as I thought,' I say to Achilles.

'Yeah, they look a few and suddenly there's an awful lot,' he chuckles.

Sunny is next to me but when we climb the first hill, Sunny turns back. He has decided to stay down in the pen with his girlfriend Karamana. I'll miss him. Muna the Monkey is meant to stay down too. She is useless as a guardian dog, with her laryngitis and fear of everything and dog food is heavy, but she manages to sneak past Achilles and rejoin her beloved Sásho who tries to send her away with 'No, I don't want you,' but she knows he doesn't mean it.

Achilles climbs with us to the edge of a pine grove and when it's clear that the flock is on its way, he turns back. Catching up with the flock, I get disoriented among the pines. It's amazing how quickly the flock can zoom out of sight and earshot. One moment they're not moving, the next moment you are running through woods, your flock lost.

'It's not the flock that's lost, dear, it's us.' Over the phone, Sásho instructs me how to reach them by following the edge of the grove. I am relieved to see the black crowd of animals and the human with the crook, grinning as if all is well in the world.

And it is. The trek to Prairie is pleasant, past wild orchards, ruined houses, brooks and across open pastureland. I can see why this was

Orelek's most coveted district. There is lots of water, pasture, light and shade. When Stamen's grandmother agreed to get hitched to his grandfather, already a widower, she did it with typical peasant pragmatism: because his house was 'top of the brook'. You didn't want to be at the bottom of the brook after everyone had used it.

The flock is dwarfed by the open spaces. The gently cascading landscape is arcadian. It's what we imagine when we say 'pastoral'. After Prairie, everything will change. This is a threshold, the last area where you can see what is happening in all four directions before the mountain engulfs you, and if you can read the landscape, there is always something happening, if not now, in the past or future. In the distance is a shack where Vasko the young cowherd stays in the warmer months with The Privateer's cows. Vasko is already up in Black Water.

In the other direction, we see black and white sheep and a man who is too far away to discern. When you can't make out the person, you make out the sheep and dogs, from the size and breed, and the direction of movement.

"That's a guy you don't know.' A hired shepherd for another farmer. His dogs and our top male dogs are already involved in a barking face-off. Sásho recalls our gang. The man directs his flock away from our trajectory, he knows we're going to summer pasture. The mixing of flocks is to be avoided at all times and the dogs are the first stop. The dogs' perimeter is large and they shoot across the land like arrows.

Herding and grazing is all about territory. People managed tens of thousands of sheep and goats here. The nomads and their armies of animals crossed the way of the Orelek highlanders with their own animal communes, like a game of chess on a giant open board with white pieces and black pieces, and once you made a move you couldn't take it back. There was only one way: on and up. How did they avoid complete chaos?

'They knew their animals very well. And they were good at tactics,' says Sásho. 'It's about knowing your territory and not straying out of it. Like in the street. You must know which gang you belong to, and where their turf is. If you cross the line, you're done for.'

Like him, that's how he ended up in jail.

Then Vasko calls: 'Hey plague, where are you?' They call each other plague. Soon, I will discover how apt that is. Shepherdese follows.

'You gotta give me back that pen gate you stole from me,' says Sásho. 'I haven't got time to make a new gate.'

'Yeah no worries,' says Vasko. 'I don't need a gate. Our sheep are mongrels anyway, not like yours.'

Their thirty sheep that went missing ten days ago were not found. They went missing because someone was drunk.

Sásho stole that pen gate in the first place.

'But I had to carry it!' he tells me.

There's a shepherdess with a child in the hut with Vasko. This is a surprise. Sásho doesn't know her. I'm glad. Another woman! Sásho doesn't mention me at all to Vasko.

''Cos I don't want him to have thoughts about you,' Sásho says. 'I know what's in my territory and I'll protect it. That's you and the flock.'

'You didn't bring the kittens!' He wanted to bring two kittens from a litter that lived on his roof, to chase the mice in the hut.

'I took pity on them,' he said, 'I saw them together and couldn't split them.'

I stop under a pear tree to check my emails one last time, and lose the flock again. This time for an hour and in the open! It's like the earth opened up and swallowed Sásho and the flock. Not even the sound of bells. Only Topi lags behind, but not for me. He is chasing something. He is the youngest in the gang, just over a year old. As with the lambs, a year is the youngest age for a dog to join the summer exodus.

Topi and I are alone among rolling meadows. Sásho calls to explain where they are: 'after the deep gully, look for the unfinished church and a house.' There is a basic one-room house that belongs to a cowherd, and there is Sásho. I've lost my water flask already. I'm flustered, the heat is sapping. The sheep look few again.

'Don't worry,' he grins. 'Leave the counting to me.'

He has a reassuring effect on me. Nothing fazes him. He smiles and everything falls into place. We flop on a couch: a house with a couch in the middle of nowhere, like the last dwelling in an abandoned world. A beer chills under a running tap connected to a spring.

'One shepherd for six hundred sheep is out of balance,' I say. Until recently, there were enough shepherds to ensure a more even spread – say one per two hundred.

'I don't want a small flock,' says Sásho. 'Six hundred go wherever they like and I go with them, but a hundred and fifty are hopeless. You can't walk with them.'

This means: 600 go a long distance because they mow a meadow in a day and need fresh pasture and 150 stay on the same meadow day after day, and that's boring. Sásho likes roaming. Today, he has a crook that he twirls in his hand like a street performer.

I left mine behind because it was lent to me by Anton.

'I'll buy you one en route,' Sásho grins. 'The shops are open.'

For a moment, I imagine chalet boutiques in the woods. We have no money, of course. On the couch, we enjoy Prairie's open-air concert: the running tap, the wind playing a major-scale sonatina on the corrugated tin roof, the buzzing of flies that Sásho tries to keep from my face when I doze off and the bells of our flock.

'Why are there so few bells in such a large flock?'

'Any more would startle them,' Sásho said.

Bells were chosen carefully for each flock. Not too many, or the sound would unsettle the animals. Not too few, or predators wouldn't hear them and you wanted them to hear them and keep away. The bells were chosen for their musicality and ideally, the set composed a spontaneous melody as the sheep moved. Like the dogs, the sheep were a walking orchestra. It was good to put a bit of silver in the blend, if you could afford it, to make them sound sweeter.

Later in the afternoon there are different bells; thicker, bigger. Cow bells. The cowherd on whose couch we sit is approaching. Yep, there comes a stream of vicious invectives. Shepherds swear at their animals like they are possessed. It's tradition. It's time to get out of his dogs' way. Our flock has already moved in the right direction, towards the night pen, one meadow down and we follow them. The cowherd appears, a tall man in a checked shirt, who waves at us, surprised to see a woman. He knows we are migrating. He is a retired miner, another one. It's no wonder retired miners want to spend their remaining years in the open.

'There's bear!' he shouts.

The bear is confirmed later by Stamen's shepherd Dimko. En route to the night pen, we go past Stamen's pen but don't see Dimko. The two pens are 500 metres apart, just enough for the dogs not to clash. The first thing Sásho does when we reach our pen is make a fire. I bring stones to encircle it and stop it spreading across the dry grass. Dry grass is the reason we are migrating.

Kámen and Alex arrive in the van at dusk and Theo and Achilles arrive on foot with Mimi and her foal and tie her up by the pen. Darkness comes, the flock is inside the pen, but the fence has collapsed and Kámen and Sásho set about fixing heavy beams with rusty nails in them and with no hammer. It's a big job that takes an hour, during which sheep escape and we get them back in. If a ram escapes, it's much harder, but fortunately the rams are busy on top of the sheep. The fence of these open pens is low, up to your waist at most. It would be easy for a bear or wolf to help themselves to a sheep in the night. That's why we have eight dogs with us. The only thing the fence does is to keep the flock together. The real protection comes from the dogs. And the fire.

We've been on our feet for ten hours and I just need the day to come to an end, but it's not about my needs, or anybody else's. It's about getting the job done. I stand by the horses with the boys and Achilles. They have brought us food and sleeping bags and mats.

Stamen comes over in his jeep, boys in tow, to see what we're up to. We haven't seen each other since last year.

'We're going soon too, you could've come up with us,' he offers. 'Mind you, our hut has a whole family in it. You need men, women and children for this or it doesn't work.'

That comment rubbed it in for Kámen who only has Sásho. The two swap information about sheep, dogs and the resident bear of Prairie, and Stamen and his boys drive off. I'm surprised to see them talking to each other but they have no choice: there is no one else in Prairie and they have to coordinate their movements to avoid chaos.

'I used to enjoy coming here but it's become an extreme sport,' says Theo, picking up on my exhaustion. 'My father says there's no workers but if there were workers, he'd double the flock. There's something in our family that needs to push things to the limit. I don't know why.'

The fence is fixed. Then, Kámen pulls a leech out of Kito's mouth with his bare hands, which could have lost him a hand, and they leave in the van.

It is cold enough for hats and jumpers. We eat raw green peppers stuffed with fresh goat quark and a tub of goat meat from the roast. Sásho leaves the meat for me because there will be no fresh meat for the next few weeks and I don't eat the processed frankfurters favoured by shepherds as an easy snack. We roll out our mats and sleeping bags on the spiky heath by the pen, a few metres from the fire.

When they were on the road, the women, children and some of the men slept in instant shelters made from wooden poles and *chergi* (rugs). Their katuns were set up at previously agreed strategic points along the journey. This is how the flock met with the caravan, because the shepherds drove the flock ahead of the human caravan that moved more slowly with the horses carrying all the luggage. Every couple of days they met in these stopping places with running water, a spring and sufficiently inclined ground so that sudden rain wouldn't flood the camp and drown animals and small children. The horses were unloaded and allowed to graze.

These overnight tents had to be made and unmade every day or two and the caravans carried all the materials strapped onto the horses, including Y-shaped stakes. This is how it was done: two stakes were driven deep into the ground and another one placed on top. One rug was stretched over this Π shape and fastened into the ground with hooks. Two more rugs hung on each empty side to make a four-walled shelter. The luggage was placed at the back end and a fire was lit outside the entrance. This is how they lived on the road until they reached their summer huts to discover what was left from last season. I saw a highland camp of Roma mushroom pickers once and they used this same method for their shelters. Unable to afford shop-bought tents, they did it the old way, with rugs and plastic sheets draped over wooden poles.

As late as the first half of the twentieth century, when the settled ones heard the *katunari* were coming, it could be Gypsies, Aromanians, Karakachans, 'Gypsy Vlachi', Tsintsari (Cincari), or Kutsovlachi (both meaning Aromanian Vlachs) or even Gyuptsi (from Egyptian for Gypsy). This was exciting and alarming news in equal measure, because it meant tasty and exotic things for sale, different faces and clothes and a gust of the open road. Yet, the open road was grubby and unpredictable and it meant that fields were trampled by the caravans, which announced themselves with a terrific din of bells and dog barks, the flocks so large that they could take hours to file past and from time to time, things went missing from houses too, and fortune-tellers cursed you if you pissed them off, and a curse from a woman of the rug is nothing to laugh at.

The impermeable rugs were woven from felted goat and sheep's wool. When a son split from his parents, the one item his mother gave him above all was a super-rug like this, spun by her. That rug symbolised the house he had to provide for his family. These rugs were also thrown on top of the loaded horses to protect the luggage and children.

Dimko is shouting something in the darkness. Maybe one of our sheep has wandered off to their pen? Sásho goes to investigate with the torch and sure enough, Dimko rocks up to our fire, a flask of booze in his hand and dogs in tow. We sit down and the two canine gangs fall on top of each other, on top of the fire and on top of us for fun with a terrific gnashing of teeth. Only Muna hides behind Sásho. The two shepherds shout obscenities until they stop. The air fills with the smell of charred fur.

Then, unfazed, Dimko and Sásho discuss moves across the chessboard.

'When you go tomorrow, we'll take this lot up to Mary's Pear for a while,' says Dimko. 'Stamen's other lot goes up in a couple of weeks. Which route are you taking? That's crazy, man! You'll lose the young 'uns, they won't know what's happening. Us, we always take the forestry road.'

'Nah, forestry road takes ages. And the young 'uns are well blended now.'

Then, Dimko wants to tell us about his time in the capital, when he was careful stepping over the tram lines in case of electric shocks – we can't tell if he is joking – and how he quit the city because it's like an open catacomb. He makes us laugh but I am exhausted and he is playing high-energy music on his tablet. Sásho sips tea with me, but I know he'd rather sip something stronger.

'Why do shepherds drink so much?' I ask. They consider the question.

'There's not much else to do,' says Dimko. 'And you're always alone.'

'You pour yourself a dram while you cook,' says Sásho. 'You listen to the radio or watch TV and by the time you've eaten and gone to bed, you've sobered up or you're plastered. I don't know a single shepherd that isn't a heavy drinker.'

'But I don't use when on the job,' says Dimko. 'Not me.'

'Goodnight,' I rise and he stumbles away into the dark with his dogs.

In the morning, when we walk to the water spout by his pen, accompanied by our dogs who no longer have bones to pick with his, he comes out of the shack on shaky legs and offers us coffee. His father, dubbed The Buck, was one of the great shepherds of Orelek, but the son cannot carry the staff; something is broken.

Shepherds have always drunk hard and the bibulous shepherd is as old as Pan the goat-legged god of wilderness and pastors who was lecherous half the time and legless the other. But I imagine that previous generations of shepherds didn't use quite as much – and on the job – simply because less of everything was consumed then. Wine, bread, dairy products, everything was home-grown. Resources were finite because they were local, even the olives and caviar you bought from passing traders could only be acquired in the warmer months when the roads were passable. When you ran out of supplies, that was it for the season.

The night is full of stars and animal noises. Next to us is a thicket of bushes and I am worried about the bear, but the dogs prowl the perimeter and continuously bark near our heads, so there's no chance of a bear or of sleeping. Mirni is an outline in the moonlight. The foal is lying down.

People like the Tinders lived in this place for generations. This is where Stamen's mother and grandmother kept a garden until they couldn't. I understood how, once here, you didn't go down to Orelek more than twice a year and to the gorge only when you had business with the external world or married away.

Herodotus wrote about a wandering tribe of shepherds who were 'constantly on the move' in their home mountain of Pindus and continued to move after they were displaced by others. They were the Dorians, who may or may not be ancestors of the Karakachans. Being constantly on the move was the lot of all pastoralists and the line between wanderers and settled people was not so sharp in pre-modern times. A bit like the line between wolf and dog in pre-historic times. If you were a highlander living in Prairie, you would constantly be on the move, never mind that you had a house, because the flocks had to move. It's just that your movement was within the contours of this mountain. Our exodus to Black Water traced these contours.

This mountain was fully occupied by the settled highlanders but for centuries, the Karakachans' route passed through Kresna Gorge on the way to summer pastures in Rila and the Balkan Ranges.

After the First World War, new borders between Greece and Turkey to the south and Bulgaria to the north hampered their movements. Until then, they'd had two wintering regions: Eastern Thrace with its principal towns of Edirne and Kirklareli (which fell into Turkey) and southern Macedonia with its principal towns of Salonika, Kavala and Serres (which fell into Greece). New border bureaucracy and land competition between nomads and settled ones increased, especially after the mass exodus of Bulgarian refugees, like Sásho's grandfather, then a baby, from Greece. More pastures were ploughed up as agricultural needs increased. By the 1930s, border crossings were a nightmare for the nomad. The Greek side counted heads of cattle with mean precision, the Bulgarian side carried out paranoid searches looking for contraband tobacco and the Turkish side slapped heavy taxes per head of sheep, then banned crossings altogether. Some families started loading their flocks onto cargo trains to avoid this. Then came the Second World War, the Cold War and then the Iron Curtain fell so fast that many Karakachan families were separated for the next fifty years – some remained in Greece, others in Bulgaria and yet others in Turkey.

The last nomad itinerary before 1957 went like this: overwinter in the dark hills of Sásho's border town, come May you travel along the Struma, up the Orelek River to Prairie, Fat Oaks and then on to the north until you reached summer pastures. The pastures were negotiated in advance by the headman.

When the Karakachan herds stopped in Prairie, the headman and his aides, draped in black hooded felt capes, visited wealthier houses like those belonging to the Tinders. The region was famed for its tobacco and wine and the nomads wanted to stock up on the best products that money could buy. The Karakachans didn't often rear pigs but the Orelek highlanders did and now was the time to stock up on bacon and lard. Meanwhile, the highlanders bought the famous nomad *strombotiri* cheese and ogled the black rams.

'Hey, colleague, sell us one of your rams,' the Tinders asked the Karakachans. These were the black mountain rams that Stamen and Kámen would carry on their backs over the border two generations later.

'Nah, no chance,' said the Karakachans and went on their way in the morning. They were notoriously stingy about selling their breeds. It was part of their insularity. If they sold you a horse, you could bet it wasn't one of their pure breeds; the same with the sheep. They guarded their animals jealously. Animal and human endogamy went hand in hand: the Karakachans never married outside of their group until they were settled.

But during the night, a man and a boy, covered in sheep skins and smeared in ram semen so as not to alert the dogs, crept in and stole away with a choice ram on their back. They were Stamen's father and grandfather. Next season, when the Karakachans once again passed through Prairie and crossed the Tinders' flock, the lambs looked familiar. The stolen ram was, of course, tucked out of view.

'Hey, colleague. That looks like our sheep.'

'Nah,' said the Tinders, 'not yours. No chance.'

And they went their separate ways across the chessboard of the mountain. This was recounted to me by Stamen.

'It's always been like that,' Sásho said, 'with sheep, dogs, and people.'

His cigarette was the only light in Prairie other than the eyes of the dogs.

A seed is snatched in the night, blown by the wind, and it takes hold in unexpected places. And here we are. Blown to Prairie by some mysterious current: Sásho, me and 600 ruminants, eight canines and two horses. Here we are in this ghost mountain, breathing as one. The air is as cool as liquid. The sheep are completely still, as if petrified in moonlight. Above us are the cities of stars. Sásho gets up to stoke the fire, it soothes the flock and keeps predators away. A flock without a fire is like a church without incense, they say.

What will happen in Prairie if these last flocks disappear? The dogs will go wild and mate with the wolves and new hybrids will appear, like in 1957. Things will still happen, just without us.

I sleep for a couple of hours. I am zipped up in my sleeping bag and during the night I see that Sásho has covered me with his too. He is lying next to me, uncovered, smoking.

'Your arrival has awakened me,' he says. 'I was asleep. I didn't know why I took out the godmothers in the rain, why I roamed like a lost soul. Now I know. So I can share this with you. And remember how beautiful everything is.'

I wouldn't be here without you, either. I'd remain safely on the edge of things. The book of my life would be different, but a force propels us: anima. When something chimes between us, the whole field is enhanced, like turning up the volume. Prairie, Orelek, the whole side of the mountain vibrates with it. Because we're here.

At dawn, Sásho boils a tin of coffee in the embers. We are too tired to eat breakfast. He smokes and we pack our stuff, ready for when the others arrive in the van. The flock has coped well on its first night together as a team. Never again will *these* animals be together: these rams, ewes, lambs and the young sheep that don't know where they are going.

Kámen won't walk the trail with us. He will bring the saddle and our luggage to The Beeches where the road ends. It's eight hours from here to Black Water if all goes well.

There was immediately a momentum. Six hundred sheep took on the sandy slope like a kamikaze detachment. Then, we entered the forest and the sheep slowed down. This was Marina's wolf trail, but it felt like a different place because the rhythm of movement was different. The sheep set it – a steady, munching forest rhythm, nose to the ground, leafy, mushroomy, sun-spotted, needle-carpeted and cool. Sásho moved among the flock, popping up here and there like an elf. Achilles and I kept to the path, recording the event with camera and notebook. Alex and Theo stayed ahead with the mare and the brave foal. His legs looked too fragile for this terrain, but they were Karakachan horses – they were made for this.

The dogs hunted along invisible trails. I missed Sunny but today all the dogs were smiling with heads like the sun.

The flock scattered through the trees, then it assembled along the path and multiplied before our eyes. They looked like thousands!

Achilles and I talked about dog viruses and vaccines and the qualities of the Karakachan dogs. 'Brave, independent, self-starters, aloof', went the official description.

'They're valued above all as a pack that works together. Everyone has a role.'

There must be synergy in the pack. Those that were embedded in the flock, like Balkán, those who stayed with the flock at all times like Gashta senior, Topi and Muna and the frontliners, like Kito, Kasho and Redhead.

Transhumant movement is exactly what it says: across the land, moving like a symphony on the stage of the earth. Everybody has an instrument and plays from the same score. Communication is key. Today, we had what it takes to play this piece. Everyone did their best, despite lack of sleep and the rough terrain and we communicated by moving together in the right direction, in tune with each other and the ground beneath our feet. Everybody was in a good mood. Crossing the land puts you in a good mood, your body hums.

The Karakachans travelled with new-born foals and human babies. It is said that women gave birth standing, with their hair and undergarments loosened, and could be back on the road in a couple of days. The caravan must go on, the momentum was unstoppable. I found this hard to believe, then I read a book by Turkish writer Irfan Orga who stayed with the Yuruks of the Taurus Mountains in the 1930s. He was in the camp when a woman returned from grazing the goats. She had just given birth and the newborn was strapped to her back. She immediately set about milking the goats. The next day, the baby on her back, she was out with the goats again. These people were tough in a way that modern humans can't comprehend. They were tough like their animals.

The only luxury for the woman giving birth during transit was a couple of heated stones at the feet and the belly to ease the pain, and an exception was made for her on horseback. The Karakachans are the only Balkan peoples who forbade horse riding for women, for reasons that must be to do with 'shame' around women's sexuality or some other superstition. Only brides rode horses on the night of their departure from their home tent, or sick women on the road. The Karakachans were the most rigidly patriarchal of the wanderers. The Aromanian Vlachs, the Yuruks and the Romani were much more relaxed and women were more empowered, but all pastoral nomads lived lives based around gendered tasks for practical reasons. The able-bodied men went with the sheep. The women went with the horses and built the camps.

Exoduses occurred in two separate streams. The human caravans followed the migratory routes: the horses carried the luggage which was tied up inside impenetrable woollen bags. The perishable foods like flour, salt and sugar were in wooden boxes. The most important items of luggage were the milk kits: copper cauldrons and pots, trivets, cheese kegs, straining cloths and dishes because this is how the nomads made a living. They also carried bundles of sheep wool, which women and girls continuously spun on long spindles as they walked. The women in their loose black headdresses mounted on a felt braid like a crown were inseparable from their carved spindles. The men in capes were inseparable from their carved shepherd's crooks. They moved with their animals, like witches and wizards of the woods.

When a woman got married, her father-in-law gave her a small cohort of animals, perhaps a horse and a few sheep. They would remain her personal property for the rest of her life. She could lose her husband in an avalanche or her children to sickness but she would have her animals. What a long road she had before her and what a long road she had covered since her birth many mountains ago.

A single family had anywhere between four and seventy horses. In the late Ottoman era, when Vlachs, Yuruks and other transhumants were at their strongest and kept the Ottoman army supplied with cheese and wool, it could be up to 200 horses per family. You could see a caravan of 8,000 horses carrying the luggage belonging to a single company of 1,000 people. The sheep went with their drover-shepherds and milkers, off-road through the forests, often moving at night to avoid clashing with other flocks, run-ins with hostile villagers or being seen trampling fields. Everything was dictated by the animals' needs and the nature of the terrain, which changed dramatically day by day. The flock and the caravan would then meet at stopping places and set up camp for the night.

This trail from Prairie to Black Water had not been trodden by the Karakachans in the last few hundred years, although it might have been at an earlier stage, before other settlers arrived. It was part of the Orelek grazing grounds. The highlanders of Orelek walked it twice a year with their flocks and you didn't want to mess with the Orelek highlanders over pasture.

We climbed through forests, each like a city.

Pine is rational and streamlined in its Gothic architecture. The floor is made of soft needles and mushrooms but not yet, it's too early. The sheep lingered, hoping. Sásho whistled to get them going.

Beech is full of secret floors, an old beech forest is a metropolis. There are all sorts of inhabitants and everything gets recycled and reused.

Oak is musical, the leaves trill and light passes through it like waves. Oak is a sun city.

The lambs called to their mothers across the forest in voices that were sweet and comical, like chipmunks.

Eeeeee

Beeeee-reee

'Like babies,' I said.

'They are babies,' Sásho said. 'They're only a few months old. That one was a tiny mouse but it's chunked out. It'll be bigger than his mother when we come down. That one, number 4318, is too skinny. Kámen should take her down in the van or she won't make it. The orphan is too small. I'll keep an eye on him.'

The orphan pulled with his teeth and kept up at the back.

'Do they know we're going on a long journey?'

'The lambs don't. The older ones do. The dogs too, except Topi.'

The forest hummed. Sásho and I were light-footed with the euphoria of exodus. He went ahead, then waited for me. I went ahead and waited for him. Alex asked Sásho for a cigarette.

'What, the air too clean for you?' I teased. Later, I asked Sásho for a cigarette too. 'What, the air too clean for you?' Alex came back at me. The mood lifted the higher we climbed. We were cutting short through the mountain while the road snaked around. Dimko had no idea what he was talking about when he suggested taking the road.

It was like all of life in one day – highs and lows, deciduous and coniferous, cool and warm, rest and effort, river-crossing barefoot and chuckling like a forest elf, then hours of silence. The pace didn't change. It was like having a metronome. You could speed up if you wanted to but then you had to wait for the rest to catch up. Or you could sit on a stone and nibble something, but in no time the forest closed behind the caravan like the gates of a city. The sound of bells vanished and you didn't just lose linear time, but linear distance too. Time and space become one. You move in a straight itinerary but within it, there are circles. You try not to get lost in one of those circles.

In their heyday, when there were no borders and the nomads travelled great distances between the plains of the Aegean and the highlands of Bulgaria, they could be on the move between winter and summer pastures for thirty days. They had their stopping places, like Prairie. In their twilight years, after World War One, they travelled shorter distances but along the same routes.

Transhumance has UNESCO status as intangible cultural heritage of humanity. Yet, most of humanity has forgotten about it. We have forgotten that this too is something we can do, if we fancy it: walk with animals, live with animals, care for animals and be cared for by them. Even make a living from it. Today, it is just as difficult to make a living from pastoral farming as it is from making non-commercial art, music or literature. You must be fuelled by a devotion that can't be dampened by rain or burned up by fire.

Subsidies may also run out, governments could collapse, laws may become unenforceable and the towns of the plains may be flooded as the waters rise, yet the animal mountain will be here, its portals open.

All of this reached my mind through my feet when I walked with the flock.

We arrived at The Beeches in high spirits. Kámen was waiting for us in the van but his face spelled out bad news.

'Sásho,' he whispered with self-loathing, 'I forgot the most important thing. The saddle.'

This meant that he must return to Orelek and then come back along the awful forestry road, causing a two-hour delay. This is what happens to people who don't sleep.

'You three take the flock up,' he told Sásho, 'and the boys wait here with the mare.'

But the others were not informed and they tied the mare up where the steep path began. This blocked the sheep. Instead of rushing up the path, the sheep rushed into the beech forest to look for tasty things and then began to go round in circles. This wasn't the intended move across this tricky part of the chessboard, but Kámen was gone and we needed a rest, the lambs did too.

Sásho stood for the next two hours, keeping a watch on them. Alex clambered into the woods to look for interesting-shaped branches for his snakes and Achilles and Theo zoned out by the horses. I dozed in a spot of sun and listened to the thundering river. The river was compressed in the gorge as if the banks ground closer and something choked in the gullet of the mountain, and if I weren't so relaxed and safe, I wouldn't want to linger. Only three people regularly drove this far: Kámen, Stamen and The Privateer. Even the rangers from the park didn't make it more than once or twice a year.

Kámen returned with the saddle: why were we all still here? He expected the flock to be at Black Water by now. We explained, guilty until proven innocent. He pushed down his frustration and he and Alex saddled Mimi, strapped on 150 kilograms of dog food, we took our big rucksacks from the van and the ordeal began. The Karakachans loaded their horses with up to 200 kilograms on the flat and up to 150 kilograms in this kind of terrain. For a small horse, this seemed a lot, but they coped well.

Kámen carried a heavy white sack on his back, like a furious Father Christmas. He tried to speed up the flock because it was getting late but the trail was narrow and all the animals went off-trail, all 600 of them, as if to spite us. Demented with rage, he roared and picked up some of the sheep and threw them on the path, which involved stopping and putting his sack down first. Sásho herded them quietly and they moved at a glacial pace.

Tired and fed-up, I rushed onwards to get away from Kámen's fury but along the path I heard a growl: a bear-like growl, like the one I heard when I was with Marina. The river roared. The others with the mare were far ahead. I retraced my steps and waited for the sheep to catch up with me. No, I am not a woman who runs with the bears.

Floor after floor, the never-ending terraces of Pirin delighted the hiker, but not the shepherd. On the steep meadow called Kamen klet, I threw down my two rucksacks in anger. The meadow was ablaze with yellow mullein like candles in a church. I flopped down among the candles. The hardest bit was yet to come: crossing the river down the eroded slope. Why does it have to be so hard, why does pleasure turn to pain every time Kámen turns up? He flopped down a few metres away from me with his Sisyphean sack. It was right that his name meant 'stone', just like this stony mountain.

'Did we tire you out?'

'I'm fine.'

'Don't worry,' he said, 'after a few climbs to Etip, you'll get fit.'
'I am fit!'

'The family annoy me,' he suddenly let off steam. 'They can't think and act independently. I must think for everyone and . . .'

'Your expectations are too high,' I cut him off. 'No one can live up to them.'

Dark woods rose on all sides. We were climbing into a narrowing funnel. Thunder Peak loomed ahead, a spectral white. Its western flank was already in shadow and that's where we were going. I cut some mint for tea.

'When I used to stay at the hut, I'd contemplate every flower,' Kámen reminisced.

'Shepherding is a philosophical occupation,' I agreed.

'Only if you have the brain for it,' he said. 'If not, you fill it with alcohol.'

Tired and smiling, along came Sásho with Balkán and Muna at his side, the sheep graze-walking like crazy around him.

'How are you?'

'I can't complain,' he said and seeing that I was deflated, he took one of my rucksacks on top of his two. Inside his rucksack was a duvet and a 2 litre bottle of red wine – for me, because I said I liked wine. We munched crackers that I passed around.

This was the last time the three of us would be friendly together.

That all the sheep survived the river crossing was a miracle. The eroded vertical bank had no grip at all, everything slipped down: stones, humans and animals. You slipped and reached for solid ground but it was sand that ran through your hands. I had a flash of premonition: this is how it's going to be from now on.

Then the last steep meadow, where The Privateer's cows grazed among summer savory, St John's wort, purple-flowering mint and thyme. And here was Mimi and the heroic foal, unsaddled and grazing next to The Privateer's mare and foal and the stallion father. I crawled across the white stony desert of Black Water. The pieces of marble were difficult to walk on, and worse when you stepped between them and twisted an ankle.

The Privateer's hut had two adults and one small person standing outside it. Vasko waved and shouted welcomes and I waved back. And there, at last, was our hut.

'Culture shock,' Achilles chuckled at my face. 'Like arriving in a foreign country.'

He showed me the food. It was in sacks hanging from nails. There was an outdoor tap that didn't work and the river was a few metres away. The two boys sat by the lit stove inside.

'It's cosy,' said Alex.

At some point in the past months, the hut had been burgled of all bedding and kitchen utensils left behind from last season. Kámen lay out the camping mats. We had my thin sleeping bag and Sásho's duvet.

It had been another ten-hour day. The family had a three-hour return journey to Orelek, in the dark.

Sásho arrived last with the flock and herded them into the open pen. They rushed in keenly, tired and full. The dogs looked excited to be here, like Marina's kids at the summer camps in Orelek.

'Home sweet home!' Sásho grinned, and stumbling with fatigue he went to fetch more wood behind the hut.

Kámen had dropped in on the other hut and was concerned about the drunken 'lowlifes' that I'd be stuck with.

'There's a woman,' I tried. 'She might be half-decent company.'

'No,' they said as one. 'Not if she's here.'

And they were gone. We sat at the table outside with our packs and watched them melt into the darkness. I won't last long here, I thought.

But the exodus had been a success.

PART THREE

BLACK WATER

TWO HUTS

I woke up and the hut was shaking, as if from wind or rain. Something roared.

'It's the river, dear,' said Sásho who was making tea on the lit stove. 'It won't be here for long.' The river would retreat later in the season. Its marble bed sucked in the water.

He'd visited the other hut last night while I slept. They'd had a dram or two.

"There's a long-suffering woman and a gifted child who'll be ruined by shepherding,' he reported. 'We'll have visitors today, just to warn you.'

It had been a long time since there were women in these huts, or children.

I stepped out and was dazzled by splendour. Our valley was flushed with early sunshine. The river had risen in the night and was closer to the hut. Thunder Peak glowed like a golden pagoda. The dogs prowled the perimeter like mythical creatures. Sásho lifted me up and we span.

But I also had the sniffles. All night, cold air blew through the cracks on my side and I wore a hat. 'We'll insulate the hut!' Sásho declared but got distracted by the dogs who ate the oatcakes I left on the table. Hut rule one: don't leave food on the table. We had two tables, the outside one and a nice square one with benches in the little covered porch by the door. The porch is fenced off with a little gate. It's a sheltered space and a buffer zone for the hut. This is where the dog food was kept, the human food hanging from nails, the stack of logs, the horse saddle beautifully cobbled from red-dyed leather and wood, the washing line and it's where the dogs liked to hover and must be chased.

The door of the hut itself can be latched from the inside and padlocked from the outside. Above the stove, there is no wall – a cooling system of sorts, to stop the hut burning down. You can see into the hut and the wind blows in.

I insulated my side of the wall by stuffing empty sacks into the gaps between the tree trunks that made up the hut. I used my folded clothes too. Sásho's side was more protected but there were sacks of food there and my side had space for toiletries and clothes. This side was comforting too, because only a wall separated me from the sheep in the pen. I've never slept so close to so many animals. During the night, I heard music. The wind squealed with small shrill voices, lots of them, next to my head but in the daytime, they sounded like mice.

'I should have brought those kittens,' Sásho said. 'Don't leave any food out. I'll investigate later.'

Sugar and coffee left behind from last year were nibbled and the packaging was shredded. Only two items were intact: a tin of thyme gathered by Sásho and a jar of quark. We opened it and it was still fresh. This was because of the cold, but also because of the quality of the milk. We ate some of it and gave the rest to Muna the Monkey who was always near. I organised my things. My pile was ten times bigger than Sásho's yet I was unlikely to stay to the end.

Sásho had brought three T-shirts, a jumper, a hooded sweatshirt, two pairs of tracksuit bottoms and a thermal vest. He'd forgotten his towel and waterproof jacket. We had one bar of soap, washing-up liquid, plenty of dried and tinned foods, lots of white bread, biscuits, cheap sugary snacks, Vienna sausages, good coffee, no milk or yogurt, some sheep's cheese and yet lots of things were missing. We needed warmer bedding, towels, pots and pans. The only pot left after the burglary had no handle and was almost worn through. There were no mugs except an enamel one I brought and just two tin plates.

'It's enough for starters!' Sásho beamed. 'And what's needed, Kámen will bring up.'

How do we let him know what's needed? Up there, Sásho showed me a high rock at the bottom end of the valley opposite the other hut, a ten-minute walk: the rock with phone signal. Later, I managed to send a message to Kámen, with a list. The other problem with the phones is that we only have a small solar battery to charge them. It takes all day to charge a phone battery halfway and the cable is nibbled by mice.

Sásho climbed into the pines behind the hut to reconnect the long hose, trodden on by wild animals, between the spring and our tap. When spring water coughed through our tap, all was sunshine. We had the best drinking water and could wash dishes and clothes, and it wasn't as icy as the river which was also besmirched by the odd cow patty.

It was bad practice for sheep and cows to share pastures. The national park should not have allowed this too-close cohabitation. Where sheep graze, there is fresh grass the next year. Where cows graze, there is thistle, Sásho summarised. Sásho was waiting to see where the shepherdess would take her small flock this morning, to avoid a mixing of animals, but it was only a matter of time before it happened.

She took them uphill across from their hut, past Signal Rock.

'Look at them, skin and bones,' Sásho commented. They were too far to make out but it was obvious they were inferior to ours. 'Like owner, like sheep, like shepherd.'

This was the last year that the national park allowed cows on its territory and The Privateer had bought these sheep to keep his pasture at Black Water. Cows were given five times more pasture than sheep and subsidies were given by the square mile, which is how this mountain had turned into a giant cow farm, or so complained the sheep and goat owners. Cows were not brought up here until recent decades. Locals like Stamen recalled up to eight flocks of sheep and goats, but no cows. This was pure profit-driven expediency and an example of how the European subsidy, blithely applied, can corrode ecology. A similar thing had happened in Scotland with subsidised sheep who have nibbled the land to a desert.

There was also a suspicion that The Privateer's sheep were ill. The thirty heads that went missing might have died from a virus. The park should not have allowed sick animals to threaten our healthy ones.

Sásho let the flock out. One sheep had a bleeding ear and he pulled her to one side to apply the green liquid. We were not going anywhere today, or tomorrow. The sheep would graze in the valley while we found our bearings. They were full after their two-day banquet anyway.

I took stock of our provisions and made the hut homely by unpacking everything and lining it up on the single wall shelf. The family had brought sixty eggs in a plastic tub and not a single one had broken! There was a bag of fresh fruit and vegetables. Above the bed, suspended from nails were two labelled bags: 'Medication for dogs' and 'Medication for humans'. I like travel apothecaries and had brought my own. We were well stocked in case of accidents and illness.

Speaking of which, here came Vasko the cowherd, child in tow. Our dogs barked at them from across the river where they mooched around with the flock at our higher end of the valley. The cows grazed at their low end of the valley.

It was windy so the guests sat at the indoor porch table. I watched them from inside the hut. The child was self-contained and chubby with bright observant eyes. Vasko was not completely sober.

'Give the boy something sweet,' he grinned toothlessly like an old man. 'To make him strong so he can get it up.'

'Don't be a plague,' said Sásho, mildly.

Vasko peered through the gap with his hyena face. 'Is someone in there?' I realised that Sásho hadn't told him that I was here at all, in a desperate attempt to delay the inevitable: a territorial face-off and a clarification of my status. I came out. He didn't remember me from last year.

'Welcome to the refugee camp,' his eyes swam at me.

We offered tea and biscuits, but Vasko wanted something stronger and reluctantly, Sásho poured him a dram. 'Just enough for tooth ache,' they joked. Vasko had brought disposable cardboard cups, knowing that the hut was burgled and bare.

'Everything here is communal,' he said and I didn't like the sound of that. I also didn't like it that Sásho wore a stud in one ear just like the stud in Vasko's ear. They'd done a little bonding ritual to mark the start of the season. I was losing Sásho already.

The boy was aware of Vasko's problems and looked embarrassed.

'Teach him some English,' Sásho pleaded. The boy had been teaching himself everything from YouTube.

'What's your name?'

'Constantin.'

'How old are you?'

'Ten. What's your name?'

Sásho beamed but now Vasko was afraid of losing the boy to our intellectually superior hut. Constantin's mother had pulled him out of school to help her at work and the boy was keen to get back in. Vasko had no say in the matter; theirs was a casual relationship. The three of them arrived in the hut two weeks ago with 120 cows (calves included) and 130 sheep. The child's mother, Vanya, was a cowgirl who knew Vasko through the herding network. This was her first time here and her first time dealing with sheep.

'You need a few more things,' Vasko said. 'Like a pot to cook in. I'd give you ours but Vanya needs it. She's a good cook, eh Consti?'

'Not Consti, Constantin.'

'Alright Consti.' Vasko ruffled his hair and the boy rolled his eyes. 'You're the best.'

A coil of rope hung from a nail.

'At least you've got rope,' Vasko said. 'To hang yourself when Kapka leaves.'

'You can borrow it after that,' Sásho came back.

Hanging is the traditional method of suicide for mountain shepherds.

Constantin offered to help me chop vegetables while the two men set off to gather dry wood for our hut. Vasko had brought a plastic tub of the precious *borika*, pine shavings with resin on them, the finest fire starter and the best welcoming gift for a hut dweller but when they returned, Vasko sat down again and put the radio on loud.

'Now,' I said firmly. 'You need to turn that down.'

'How long are you staying?' he leered.

'Not long, if you keep sitting here drinking and not letting me rest.'

'Rest?' he cackled. 'There's no rest for the wicked, eh plague?'

Sásho looked worried and tried to manage the situation diplomatically. Constantin watched with an expression that was not ten years old. He and his mother were on the run from the father, a violent alcoholic. Constantin chewed the chocolate bar. He didn't want the sweet treats but sugar was how the adults drugged him.

Then, our English lesson interrupted by loud music, he went home. By lunchtime, I was fed up and feeling unwelcome on my turf before I'd even had a chance to make it mine. I went up into the woods to sit by the spring with its pleasant babble. The water sneezed into the hose, chuckling to itself. I would get to know this spot well. Muna the Monkey and Topi came with me. There's always something interesting to hunt for in the forest. Among the tree trunks felled by the avalanche was one that had unmistakably been clawed by a bear.

From my observation spot in the wood, I saw a man propped up by a child, stumbling along the nettle path that connected the two huts. It was safe to return.

Stuck in the outside table was my kitchen knife. 'What happened?'

'We had it out,' Sásho was sombre. Wanting to protect me from gossip down the shepherding grapevine, Sásho told Vasko that we didn't know each other. Vasko said: 'Fine then, I'll come sleep with her.'

Sásho told him that if he ever bothered me, he'd drown him in the river. Vasko stuck the knife in the table and vowed not to cross our doorstep again.

'Good,' I said, feeling dread.

We can't be at war with our neighbours from day one and I wasn't used to kitchen knives being waved around.

'This is the Wild West,' Sásho said, not reassuring me with the following story of two summers ago when he was alone and The Privateer was in the other hut. Before Vasko there was another hired cowherd. The Privateer had it in for him and hit him regularly. Sásho couldn't stand it and one night when visiting them, he grabbed The Privateer and dragged him to the river where he put his head into the water for 'long enough'. They were all drunk. He then ran back here, but afraid that The Privateer would come and batter him in the night, he climbed into the dwarf-pine grove where he spent the night with some of the dogs.

'Don't mention this to Kámen,' Sásho said. 'What happens here stays here.'

The Privateer stopped beating his worker, and he and Sásho remained on friendly terms. The following summer Vasko was hired.

'It's just the two of us here, all summer. He's all I've got. And when you leave, and when Vanya leaves with the boy, 'cos that's guaranteed, it'll be the two of us again.'

The season was three-months long, but this would be a short one because we were late bringing them up and once into late September, the weather would get too rough for the huts.

'Vasko is obnoxious when he drinks, but he works hard and he's generous. I've never seen him hit a man or an animal.'

But it was Vasko's creepiness that worried me, not his aggression.

In the afternoon, Sásho rebuilt the collapsed stones of the outside fireplace and went to the other hut on a peace mission. He told another lie: 'we've been together for six months.'

'It's not a lie,' he said, 'it's how I want it to be and in five months' time it'll be true.'

Sásho hoped that would cement our territory and I hoped that there would be no more visitors overstaying their welcome. I made stuffed peppers on the stove, relishing the peace, then the chimney started smoking and the plastic roofing around it began to burn. I ran to fetch water from the tap but didn't have any large vessels. The valley was hot and the sun baked the thick plastic sheets of the roof. Sásho turned up just in time, child in tow. Birds had been making a nest in the chimney so that the twigs and feathers were a fire hazard. He swept them away and put the fire out at once. I realised how dependent on him I was here.

'Not to worry, dear,' he reassured me. 'It's adaptation day. It'll be better tomorrow.'

'My mother said you can visit us,' said Constantin. 'That's why I came. But I'm going now.' He didn't want to go. 'What are you writing in the notebook?'

I told him.

'Holy shit!' he said in English. He smiled and looked up to his right side, as if there was something hovering above him. 'That's a coincidence because I like to read but I don't have any books here. It's boring. Can I read it when you finish?'

'Of course,' I said. 'Do you want to eat with us?'

'No, thank you.'

'Any time you get fed up with them, you can come and stay with us,' Sásho said. 'Okay?'

The boy nodded politely. 'Bye,' and he made his way down the nettle path.

The huts were out of view of each other and all we could see was the smoke from their chimney. At night, they shot rocket fireworks to ward off predators and they shouted at the animals like they were at a rodeo. 'That's poor practice,' Sásho said, 'animals don't need being shouted at and the dogs get stressed.' He had learned from Moni the Mute that you could manage your dogs and your sheep and goats without making a sound.

'*Ow, ow ow ow,*' yelled Vasko at the cows, come dusk, to herd them into the electric fence that was their night shelter. Then, '*Ow ow ow ow,*' Vanya shouted at the sheep. Constantin was trapped with savages.

In the evening, Sásho whistled once and our entire flock turned around as one and moved back across the valley, filing into the pen as if under a spell. The dogs were quiet all day, but during the night they barked at the cows in the field and at the horses who moved from one end of the valley to another. There was always something moving across their field of awareness. There was nothing we could do except learn to sleep through it, or not.

'That's a bear,' Sásho said in the middle of the night. Large stones tumbled down the steep forest behind us and landed with a thud behind the pen. Only a bear could turn such large stones. The dogs normally bark at a bear and howl at wolves, but now they growled in fear. A chill went through me. Sásho went outside. It seemed that two rams had jumped over the fence to explore, but the large stones were bear. Let's hope Kámen brings up a sensor lamp, I thought. The same large stones tumbled above the other hut, Vanya heard them in the night. The same thing happened on the second night and the third and Sásho started checking for blood in our pen every morning.

Blood would mean a sheep had been taken. A week later, the bear came to the others' pen and stood a few metres from it. Vasko and Vanya both came fearlessly out to the pen. It was a female bear. Their dogs barked from a safe distance. 'I look at her, and she looks back at me. Cheeky!' Vasko summed up. Then the bear turned around. 'You must have been so pickled,' I said, 'she just wanted to get away from you!'

'Aye,' he agreed. 'Animals hate the smell of booze. Horses throw you.'

Every morning, Sásho lit the stove, made me a coffee and sat on the corner of the bed, smoking. He was always in a good mood. For a day, we had no visitors to the hut and all was well. I so wished Vasko wasn't here.

'Me too. But he is,' Sásho said. 'He'll be the last to leave.'

The mice turned out to be new-born puppies, ten of them. One of the other dogs had given birth here in quiet, just before we arrived, and now found herself surrounded and at the mercy of our dogs. She had put them inside a felled barrel behind the hut. Kámen wouldn't feed anybody else's puppies and The Privateer didn't want them either

'I have a bad feeling about their chances of survival,' Sásho said.

This morning, we let the flock out late. Sásho watched them file out, looking for signs of illness or wounds. He grabbed a ewe by the horns and felled her to the ground. I used all my weight to hold her down while Sásho fetched the green antiseptic fluid and poured it into a gaping wound in her neck, white worms crawling out.

Mountain sheep rarely sicken. The Karakachans famously said that predators killed more of their animals than illness and that the worst illness for the flock was a cruel shepherd.

We herded the flock up the slope to the dark line where the dwarf-pine began. There was a way through that led up to one of the waterfalls and on to the lakes but the path was not maintained by the national park, only by Vasko. He had pruned the dwarf-pine to make a passage for sheep and humans and at the same time, strung sisal rope across it to bar the cows from going up. The only people who made a small mark on this place and who knew it down to the last shrub were the shepherds.

We would leave the flock up here and keep an eye on them from the hut. I didn't have the energy for a big climb and we needed to process the firewood, cook and recover from adaptation day. We sat on a rock and surveyed our new home. The Bosnian pines here were one of the last indigenous forests around and the mature ones were several hundred years old. They had echoed with the voices of 8,000 sheep and hundreds of horses at once, well within my lifetime. They had seen men with long moustaches on horseback and wolf-whispering women, like Stamen's mother. They had witnessed fights between wolves, dogs, bears and humans.

Our two huts with pens backed onto the forest. I saw the ruins of several other huts, like archaeological digs revealed in the earth. Across from the huts was more forest and above that, the rock stacks collectively called the Eagles. Several streams disgorged into the main river of Black Water which lower down turned into the Orelek River. Today, the river was low and ice blue. I could see how the whole valley was its basin, clean, like the dawn of the earth.

In springtime when the snow melted, its volume was ten times what it was now, a spectacle only ever seen by wild animals. In heavy winters, snowdrifts could reach 14 metres in height.

The cows had wrecked the floor of the valley but there was still some grass, the purple of wild mint, big tufts of nettle, the green-black of dwarf-pine and the dusty olive-green of Siberian juniper; all of these are invasive plants that thrive easily in the impoverished soil left by cows or completely abandoned by grazing animals. The five horses were here, moving around and always in a different spot. We looked for Mimi and the foal every morning. The others' sheep were white dots in the distance, like stones.

'That sheep is ours,' Sásho pointed at a black dot standing apart from their flock. 'Nothing we can do. We must wait for their flock to return home, then retrieve our sheep from their pen and drag her home.'

A skinny figure crawled up to the pines, after the cows. Then he crossed the valley, stick in hand, naked from the waist up and climbed up to us. Red faced from the sun, all sinew and muscle, feral, sober and sad. This is how I imagine the long-term survivors of an apocalypse – like Vasko.

'My solar battery's fully charged if you guys need to charge up your phones,' he offered. We did.

'That godmother worries me,' Sásho pointed at 4328 who was lagging.

'See if she's got a temperature,' Vasko said. 'Give her an antibiotic shot, plus those other drops and she'll be good as new.'

But Vasko had no experience with sheep and Sásho wasn't so casual with antibiotics.

'I don't know where to take them tomorrow,' Sásho said. 'It's hard through this dwarf-pine. Plus, can't take them to the lakes 'cos of the park checks.'

'Yea,' said Vasko. 'Up is too high, down is too low, my marrow is too narrow, sideways is too wide. That's why we're here, plague. Got any doping?'

'No doping,' said Sásho.

'This is life in the refugee camp,' Vasko turned to me. 'It's lonely. We've got to help each other.'

Before Vasko came, Sásho spent a summer alone. The Privateer came up from time to time to see his cows, otherwise he'd call Sásho and ask him to keep tabs on them. As a thank you, he brought lots of alcohol. 'But on my own, I'd have a dram at night with my lentils,' Sásho said. The heavy drinking began with the next helper. While here, word reached him that his wife had gone off with another man.

'And he started drinking from the morning, crying and banging his head. One day, he climbed to Signal Rock and called Kámen and said: Boss, I need to go down, the wife is dying.'

He was too ashamed to say. That was the last they saw of him.

'That summer when I was alone,' said Sásho. 'Do you remember when Kámen hadn't come up for ages and my nails got so long, I said: Bro, I'm like an eagle, I can pick you up and carry you over the hills'.

They laughed. Vasko had lent him his nail clippers.

'You see now,' Sásho said to me. 'How after three months here, you go down and you're an alien. You want to go down, but when

you do, there's nothing there for you. You speak another language.
You've dropped out.'

'Better to drop out,' said Vasko. 'Pandemic, war, pandemic. Here,
it's safe.'

'Here, the pandemic is you,' Sásho said.

We laughed and took in the majesty of the valley. 'The landing
strip' is what Sásho called it. Because you arrive but then must take
off or suffer the madness of limbo.

The shepherds came in waves and their departures marked the end
of a small era, and of a relationship like no other. For example,
Kámen's old hut had been home to Stamen's father during the many
years he had shepherded the Orelek flock. The Privateer's old hut
had been home to the old cowherd who had died straight after selling
his animals. Then, after the schism, Stamen's father took up that hut
with their own flock and Ugrin the Radio moved into our hut. They
were to each other as Sásho and Vasko were now, except Stamen's
father was like a father to Ugrin. This is a man's world. Women
appeared briefly, in erotic dreams, in supernatural guise as samovili
nymphs or more mundanely, on a donkey's back with provisions. In
ballads, the shepherd in distress is saved by a clever maiden or a loyal
dog who turn up at the eleventh hour to wrench him free from bears
and bandits.

But bandits and shepherds have always been like wolves and dogs,
sometimes they fight, sometimes they fraternise. They come from
the same seed. For the Karakachans, summer pasture, milking and
dairy-making was strictly a man's job, and the running of the home
base was down to the women. Even settled societies like the Orelek
highlanders led a semi-nomadic life, at least the men did. They were
away from home half the time in places like this, with other men and
boys. It was the pastoral dance: in summer, the human males and
females separated but ewes and rams mated and in winter it was the
other way around. If you were a gay man, the shepherding life with
its homoerotic undercurrent was a way out of marriage. If you were
a gay woman, you just hid it.

Stamen was not exaggerating when he said that to be a shepherd
you must be a semi-military type. Pastoralism and pacifism are not

synonymous. At their weddings, the Yuruks and the Karakachans waved recycled one-time war flags and fired their guns in all directions. There ran a continuous line between pastoralist, soldier and rebel outlaw.

It started with the Romanised and Hellenised Thracian pastoralists hired by the Roman army (like Spartacus) and later by the Byzantine, Bulgarian and other dominant armies. This continued in the Ottoman Empire. Medieval Vlachs and other pastoralists had their own auxiliary unit in the imperial army and formed a privileged social-military class: the *voinuks* (meaning soldiers in southern Slavic languages). After the sixteenth century, this gave way to the Christian *spahi* category, under similar terms. And the terms were this: able-bodied nomad and semi-nomad shepherds fought the empire's wars in exchange for owning their grazing and agricultural land rent free or tax free. If they abandoned this duty, they had to pay again.

The Yuruks' situation was similar, even if they were Muslims with the privileges that came with that under the Ottomans. They were armed from their arrival in the Balkans during the fifteenth and sixteenth centuries because they came as militant colonists and the men were committed to a special reserve unit in the Ottoman army. But the nomads' commitment to central power was patchy. They were animal soldiers more engaged in local pastoral wars than imperial ones and concocted all sorts of ruses and evasions to escape military duties over time (while still not paying tax, of course). Eventually, the Yuruk unit of the Ottoman army was disbanded in the mid-1800s due to a lack of interest and shifting politics and gradually, the Yuruks faded out of the landscape and the culture.

The nomad shepherds were master tricksters. They could pack up camp and disappear with their families and flocks, leaving no trace. They could put leather moccasins on their horses and sheep, backwards of course, to confuse the enemy, and this is a true story, or flee to higher ground, abandoning their flock and inadvertently donating it to someone else. A wealthy Yuruk once vanished from his pastures at Rila Monastery, leaving behind 2,000 sheep complete with dogs and shepherds. In fact, pastoralists were employed as armed guards for monasteries, large estates and mountain passes

like the Kresna Gorge with their flocks and families. It was a more
pleasant alternative to being a soldier and getting yourself killed.
It was also a way of controlling the otherwise uncontrollable, large
and elusive population of wandering pastoralists by giving them
gainful employment and stopping them from plundering and plotting coups.

The plight of today's pastoralists is even starker when you know
that for centuries, they had special status. Their work was essential to
running the empire. They kept the population *and* the Ottoman
army in meat and milk products and in wool and felt, horses and
dogs. And when the empire was gone, they remained essential to
running the economy of the newly independent nation states. This is
why shepherds of all stripes, nomadic and semi-nomadic, Muslim
and Christian, had permission to go where others couldn't and carry
arms at all times. Yuruk women in particular were adept at using
guns. They often passed through tough mountain terrain without
their men and elected one among them as a chieftain: and she never
missed the bull's eye because they knew that the line between outlaw
and gatekeeper was blurred. It still is. The likes of Stamen's mother
always carried a knife with her and had scissors in her mobile knitting
kit. Part of the Karakachan women's bridal wardrobe was a knife
attached to a string that hung from her heavy black headdress along
with the beads and coins. She wore her bridal dress for a year after the
wedding. This was up to 20 kilograms of wool and silver-gold coins
and jewellery, in the summer too, but she began to use the knife
immediately. There were plenty of hidden folds in her layered dress
for a discreet gun. Over their wraparound woollen belt, the men
wore a kind of builder's leather belt with pockets for the staples of
shepherding life: a knife, a gun, tobacco, flint and stone, salt and a
needle and thread for those emergencies when the dog-wolves bit
through your trouser leg.

Blood feuds around stolen animals and stolen 'honour' were
common. Pastoral living was a razor's edge, now and always. There
was nothing genteel about it. The shepherd, bandit and outlaw were
practically synonymous in the nineteenth century when the Balkan
national movements produced a tangled network of revolutionary

bands who used the mountains as their strongholds and fiefdoms. As a shepherd, you could join them or support them but you couldn't fight them or escape them. You were destined to be crossed by them and watch them help themselves to your animals and sometimes, your sons and daughters. Many Sarakatsani in Greece took up arms against the Ottoman Turks. Though 'took up arms' is not quite right because they were never without arms and yesterday those arms were in service of today's enemy. It was the same wolf in a different dog's clothing.

Shepherds continued to carry guns even during Communism. Guns were still used today by some old shepherds but younger ones like Sásho and Vasko didn't know how to use a gun, it was illegal anyway, and with all the alcohol sloshing around that was a good thing. I heard that Vasko was wanted by the police. He was here instead of in jail.

The horses moved across the valley.

'Our mare had her foal spoiled last year,' Vasko said. 'Spoiled' meant killed. 'It was pretty, spotted. I hope this one lives.'

We could see where the avalanche had come crashing down, below the Eagles, and wiped out a whole suburb of pines. The ripple effect of the avalanche had felled the row of pines behind the huts.

They discussed pasture. 'The grass at the lakes is huge, they'll have a banquet!' But we can't go to the lakes yet because there are inspections from the national park. Even though we have the right legally to be there, they can still fine Kámen for grazing his sheep too close to the lakes.

'Once, this parker comes up to me,' said Sásho. 'And goes: are these sheep grazing? I said no, we're just passing through. He said, but are they eating the grass? I said, right now they don't have their masks, but I ordered 600 masks for them, and one for me. Tomorrow I'll put them on. What with this Covid. He didn't bother me after that.'

'So where *can* we take the flock?' I asked.

'Etip, behind that ridge,' Sásho pointed at the Eagles rockfaces. 'Where all four winds meet to fuck. You don't want to be there for that rendezvous.'

Sásho asked Vasko about his daughter. Vasko was divorced, with a ten-year-old girl he saw for a day or two, though he sent her all his earnings. He had no living expenses up here, other than booze and cigarettes. He used to work abroad as a builder – insulation – but 'I got insulated from my wife instead.' Then he drove a vegetable van between here and Greece. His father died young in an accident, followed by his mother.

'Ach, I wonder when this life is gonna finally end,' he summed up.

'Don't say that,' said Sásho. 'That's down to fate.'

'When your time comes, it comes,' said Vasko. In his watery eyes I saw the expectation, and even hope, of a short life.

Our flock safely ensconced by the dwarf-pine, we descended to the hut, picking up dry wood. You could tell what kind of winter it had been from the amount of trees that had drifted down. Snow and avalanches meant more wood. I cooked a vegetable stew on the newly rebuilt fireplace and the two guys sawed the wood into chunks and stacked them up in the porch. There was an electric chainsaw under the bed that Sásho was afraid of using after witnessing something as a child. Vasko had no fears at all, except of sobriety when depression crept in. We sat at the outside table and listened to our favourite radio station Gaia, with the folk music, and drank cold Nescafé and tea.

'Get your cows off my nettles,' Sásho said when a few cows came to graze the green barrier around the pen. 'I need it as extra buffer.'

The cows were eating the nettle because that's all that was left for them down here. Down here meant our valley, which sat at 1,800 metres.

'I'll have to take them up soon,' Vasko agreed. 'Up' meant the high plateaux under Thunder Peak. These cows were of an indigenous variety adapted for extreme terrain like this. The Privateer had had other breeds before, but they fell off the cliffs. He had learned the hard way that only alpine cows can live in alpine places.

'The sheep is a mower, it maintains a pasture,' said Sásho. 'The cow is a destroyer. It pulls out everything, root and all.'

Vasko shouted: 'Ow, ow, ow, ow! Milka, come darling, stop pulling everything, root and all! Leave Uncle Sásho's nettles.'

Then he sang drunkenly, though he wasn't drunk:
'Milka lay dying, on the high mountain.'
'Look at these pretty eyes she's got for you,' Sásho teased him.

We were avoiding mentioning the new-born puppies, to give them more safe time here, but Vasko knew and later he came with a sack to take them away.

'How did you do it, darling? You're an amazing mother,' he spoke tenderly to the bitch while he put them in the sack. But when he got distracted by the cows, the mother started taking them out of the sack one by one and bringing them back to the shady barrel, squeezing through the porch fence. They were mice-sized, blind and squealing, with their umbilical cords hanging.

When Vasko took them away, she brought two of them back, one by one to the barrel, the next day, squeezing through the fence with desperation. It was safer here and our dogs left her alone, but she could not save them. The other hut didn't own up to it, but we knew that Vasko had left them out for the wolves and foxes. For weeks, the mother trotted around looking for them and dripping with milk. It was the humans on the perimeter, not the other dogs, that killed her children.

Tonight, no firecrackers disturbed the silence of the valley. Left to itself, everything speaks its own language. Sásho took the stud out of his ear. He brushed his teeth with a finger dipped in salt. He'd forgotten his toothbrush, a habit from his street days.

'You can't carry around a toothbrush when you're constantly on the run.'

The nomads did the same, their toothbrushes were their own fingers. I imagined their teeth were terrible but reports say otherwise, that they had excellent teeth.

'You're like pre-historic man!'

He grins with his rather good smoker's teeth, two are missing but there is not a single filling.

Mood is a language. The moods of the animals reflect our moods. For example, on serene moonless nights, when after a calm day you step out into the staggering blackness, you are met by several hundred headlights looking at you. Who knew that sheeps' eyes glow yellow in the dark? The dogs' eyes glow green. These are the only lights on a moonless night in Black Water.

'Am I here because of you or are you here because of me?' you ask as you brush your teeth next to a curly-horned ram who steam-breathes through his nostrils like a dragon.

And they answer with their collective mind: We will not abandon you.

LANGUAGES

While I eat porridge and Sásho smokes by the stove, we listen to the morning radio. It is only day three but it feels like we have been here a week.

In the lower world, it's over 40 degrees, there are wildfires and citizens are advised to wear white clothes and avoid going out. The war in Ukraine scorches the earth and the soul. He turns off the radio.

'Dearest, the world has gone insane,' he says.

'We just have to make sure *we* don't,' I say.

'We'll be fine, we have each other,' he says. 'And Muna, eh Monkey.'

Muna is keeping a low profile under the bed and also digging up the earth that I sweep away from the floor stones several times a day.

Mornings are cold. Our valley remains in shadow long after the sun rises behind Thunder Peak, striking a golden tuning fork for the rest of the day. A dirty white glacier in the shape of an angel sits in a dip above our valley, like a coat of arms. Every morning, the world is brand new and brilliant. The rock faces are turned towards us like spectators. Did someone say something?

Beeereee – in the pen.

Van-van-van says Balkán. Out-out-out.

'Balkán, it's always out-out with you,' Sásho quips, 'you never say in-in.'

Balkán looks at him, indignant: I'm a guardian, not a party host!

Every morning, Sásho opens the pen gate and talks to the animals.

'Come on Breadie, I've got a treat for you.'

'You're a piece of shit, you are,' to the aggressive ram who attacks the competition, causing havoc in the pen.

'Kasho, why the long face today?'

'Get lost Muno, you're spoilt.'

'Come on Mouse,' to the orphaned lamb.

'Oh, is that her majesty the Model!'

'Hard to get you out, hard to bring you back, you're a pain in the ass, all of you.'

'Topi, I see you, keep away from the food sacks.'

'Hey, 1365, stop eating the dog food!'

One-three-six-five has taken to jumping out of the pen, trotting in front of the hut and then to the small clearing with the dog troughs. They were nicely carved out from trunks by Kámen.

Every morning, we check who's here and who's not. The foal is with Mimi, at the far end of the valley: good. Our sheep that joined the other flock has returned on her own, but now enters the porch, breathing heavily: bad. 'She doesn't know what planet she's on,' Sásho says.

Every other day, we do a count. The only time to do this with so many animals is when they return to the pen in the evening. I stand by the gate and count the key individuals that tell us if the rest are here too: sheep with bells, nine. White ones, five. The first ones: present. The last ones like the one with the split ear and the lamb: present. The middle ones like Breadie: present. 4328 is missing, just as we feared.

Gra-gra. Crows circle, a bad sign. Let's hope it's one of their sheep that's dead, not ours. The crows attract wolves and wolves are the second worst news after illness in the flock.

Our flock will graze down here again. We stand and scan the far slope where Vanya is taking out her flock, child in tow. One of theirs has joined ours too and yesterday, Vasko dragged her by the ear to their pen but later, the sheep came back. He repeated the exercise, but the sheep liked it with us and he gave up. We don't want Kámen to see this or he'll worry about illness spreading. We are worried too, but some things can't be helped. Karakachan sheep are highly resistant to viruses and we wouldn't worry had The Privateer's inferior sheep not been here.

And today, we are expecting Kámen. Word has reached us through The Privateer who called Vasko because Kámen wouldn't call to tell us and anyway, our phones are turned off to save battery. We rely on

Vasko's large car battery for our phones, which means leaving them at their hut and using up their power. Vasko doesn't mind. Everything here is communal, after all.

We stay close to home, remove leeches from Muna's mouth with the pincers that hang from a nail – and that Sásho used last summer to tear off his own tendon – eat lunch, heat water to bathe quickly in the nettle, for privacy because there are hikers like pegs along the spine of Little Horse today and some of them use binoculars, Sásho says. We are doubly nowhere here, too far down from Thunder Peak and too far up from the rest of the world.

To pass the time, we attempt a language lesson. Sásho understands a bit of English, I understand a bit of Turkish, let's improve it.

'I want to see the lakes,' I say.

'Senin gibi guzel bir gun,' he says.

We already share a language beyond words. We pick up each other's thoughts and emotions. We communicate about the flock from different ends of the basin using sign language that Sásho learned from Moni the Mute and I from him, but it's really just a shepherd's dance you learn after a few weeks with the flock.

Kámen appears in the early afternoon. Naked from the waist up, climbing the riverbed with a heavy sack slung on his back like a convict. He dumps it on the ground. He has no breath for greetings. There is a shocking slash down his forehead from his hairline to his nose, martyr-like. What happened?

'I got drunk and fell,' Kámen jokes drily. A plank with a nail hit him in the face yesterday.

'Pure luck,' Sásho comments. Meaning that his eyes are intact.

Kámen wants to know why the sheep are down here and not up at the plateau with the lush grass. Sásho, who has switched into his hireling persona, explains in a guilty-till-proven-innocent voice that he's wary of getting them mixed up with the other flock.

'What do we care about those low-lifes and their crappy sheep?' Kámen says. 'There's only a hundred and something of them, and we are six hundred'.

Sásho promises to take them up tomorrow.

'I smelled carrion on the way up,' Kámen comments.

We read between the lines: a sheep or more was lost during the exodus and it's Sásho's fault, even though Kámen was there, throwing animals around.

'There's bear in that spot,' Kámen says.

The spot is exactly where I heard the growl and turned back. We don't tell him about our bear, he'll just worry and there's nothing he can do.

Kámen takes stock of the bags of dog food and tells Sásho to give them less than half a bag, not a whole bag. A bag is ten kilos each. We have eight dogs and they should be given 400 grams a day, not a kilo. Sásho is doing with the dog food what he does with his money and, I will find out later, with his luck: spending it too fast.

In the sack are goodies, as requested: a duvet, a large pot, a second knife, tin mugs and plates, a tub of honey, fresh green peppers, a new cable for the solar battery and a 2-litre bottle of rakia, when we could do with laundry detergent and goat milk.

'Why did you bring so much rakia?' I ask Kámen who smokes and frowns at the circling crows: for whom the crow circles.

'Not our sheep,' Sásho reassures him. 'That's why I don't want to get them mixed.'

'Payment,' Kámen answers me tartly about the rakia.

'It's okay,' Sásho reassures me and decants some into a small plastic bottle for Vasko. 'Hide the rest. As if it's not here.'

I hide the bottle in my rucksack in a far corner of the hut. It seems cruel to pour it out after Kámen has carried it on his back and I don't want to start making new rules. Everything is precious because someone has carried it. We save every plastic bag, twisted fork and garlic clove, and tea bags are reused. I get it, why the shepherds used to sow potatoes in places like this. I offer Kámen bean stew, water and tea but he wants just one thing: to take the mare down to The Beeches and do two courses with dog food because he's got 240 kilograms of it in the van. Two courses!

He is insane, I think. It's already four o'clock. And off he goes, the heavy saddle propped on one shoulder. The horses are one floor down from Black Water. Sásho grabs his rucksack and a pack of bread.

'Just make sure they don't start moving downhill,' he instructs me about the flock. 'I'll be right back.'

And he runs to catch up with Kámen. I am suddenly alone. There are no goodbyes and hellos here, because there are no beginnings or ends. Just terraces to be climbed, seasons to be survived, animals and chores. The only luxury is the nights, when you don't have to carry anything or count heads and even if the bear comes, there is nothing to be done.

I take my stick and go across the valley to check up on the flock in a flush of responsibility. The dogs come up and greet me one by one and I'm proud to have stepped into the shepherd's shoes. The sheep look awfully few, though. I climb onto a high rock for a different perspective and Muna climbs with me, and we agree that they still look awfully few. Later, when they move downhill, they look many but now I'm worried that they'll keep going and I won't be able to stop them. But they stay and move back up again to the dwarf-pine line. Hours pass. I cook, sweep the hut and the porch again, write in my notebook and monitor the flock's movements. They scatter, then gather again. A few cross the river upstream, then cross it again but one remains on the wrong side, too scared to go across again because of the water and then heads uphill. I run after it for an hour, but you can't catch a mountain sheep any more than you can a mountain goat. It won't let me get close, all I know is that it's one of the young sheep, not quite lamb, not quite adult. It's confused. *Beeee.*

'*Beeeee,*' I call out.

'*Beeeee,*' it answers and stops then turns around to re-join me and the flock, but changes its mind just as I congratulate myself on speaking Sheepish. This goes on for a while – 'beeee, beeeee' – uphill and downhill until I give up, drained and frustrated.

'You stupid sheep, you deserve to die!'

I'm afraid that other sheep might follow this errant one up the wrong way and then there'd be no stopping them. I'm reminded of an old Karakachan shepherd called Yani who was asked what he made of it all when they collectivised his flock and appointed as headman the slowest member of the company who'd been a manure shoveller, simply because he'd taken Communist Party membership. 'Well,'

Yani sucked on his pipe, 'when the flock goes haywire, the loopiest sheep comes out at the front.'

We're lucky tonight, the flock doesn't go haywire. But it gets stuck. It's the home-coming hour and a few of the dogs enter the empty pen expectantly but the flock is motionless at the upper end of the valley. I have no idea how to get them home. I try whistling close to them. I try to direct a few leaders but they ignore me. I feel invisible. Once the sun leaves the valley, twilight comes fast. Only the peaks are illuminated, like another world.

I decide to feed the dogs at least, and when I pour granules into the troughs there is pandemonium. The dogs fight, Muna is injured and takes refuge in the hut, Balkán looks at me surprised, because this is the wrong order of things – I realise it too late – the dogs are fed once their work is over and the flock is safely home. Balkán eats with the others and lies in the empty pen, then, being a professional, returns to the flock. The other dogs roam aimlessly across the white desert, looking at me with confused faces, and I have no control at all, over the dogs or the sheep, and soon, not much control over myself either. Night falls. It has been many hours and it's clear that something has gone wrong. Is Sásho on his own or with Kámen or with Vasko? Nobody told me anything. I light the outside fire, to help him get home and give myself some company. Then, I march across to the flock again, with a torch. I whistle, they ignore me and rock. If they say *pfff* now, it'll be over. They'll be exposed to predators all night.

The mountain is a white wall. The forest is black. It isn't just control that you must surrender when daylight goes, it's understanding too. I can't fathom where I am, other than this, I am a dot moving slowly across a sea of stones in the night. The other hut smokes and they are firing off rockets.

I sit by the fire and try to eat. I wait for the dogs to bark, a happy sound when you're waiting for someone. They bark many times in the next few hours, at things that move in the forest, and each time I'm disappointed, my heart plummets with fear for Sásho. I am gripped by anger. This is Kámen's doing; everything done with force, pushing everyone to breaking point, no mercy.

'Tyrant!' I shout without a voice. 'You wanna kill us with your pastoral utopia!'

I get a sense of distress from the lower terraces of the mountain. Something has happened with the horses, I know it.

Beeeee, the lost lamb calls in the distance. I know how it feels. The blackness is complete. I turn on my phone to see the time, but it's even worse knowing that Sásho has been gone for seven hours. I could walk down to the other hut but it seems a long way in the dark, and there is the bear.

Before midnight, a distant light appears, a torch then two. But they are at the far end of the valley. Sásho would surely be following the path closer to the huts. They must be lost tourists. Some hikers miscalculate distances and end up lost in this valley. I am suddenly afraid of strangers, even with the dogs at my side. When they have crept closer, I shout at them. They shout something back that sounds like English. The dogs rush at them with mad barks and I can't tell if these are 'welcome home' barks or 'warning, stranger' barks. And it's not English at all.

It's them! Two mares, two foals, the stallion who has followed them and two men with faces like death. Vasko has a bleeding wound in his temple and his shoes are in tatters. Sásho is haggard but not injured. I burst into tears of relief. They cut the ropes of Mimi's saddle and six bags fall to the ground, twenty kilos of dog food each to add to the pile in the porch. Sásho unsaddles our mare and sends her off. They take the saddle off the other mare who is bleeding from the haunch and dump it here. She is not loaded. Vasko takes her and the foal and stumbles off.

Before he can tell me what happened, Sásho brings the flock home from the far end of the valley which he does with a single whistle. They file across the river. Slowly.

It is only when the gate of the pen is closed that he sits down on the bed, swallows some mouthfuls of food and tea, and speaks.

To save them doing two courses with one horse, Sásho suggested doing one course with two horses. Kámen agreed, it's common to combine resources between huts. This meant taking Vasko along, and the payment was booze. They trekked down to The Beeches, loaded up the mares and waved Kámen goodbye after Vasko was given a half-litre bottle of rakia – which he started to drink immediately and continued en route. These homebrews are anywhere between 40 and 60 per cent alcohol. It was slow going because he kept falling and Sásho had to drag him up each time, in the dark. They miraculously managed the river crossing where everything slips and the accident happened closer to home, where the path is steep and there is a ravine on one side. At some point, Sásho realised that Vasko was not behind him anymore. The mare had vanished too, only her foal stood on the path, trembling like a frightened rabbit. Sásho knew what had happened. The river roared below, the blackness was complete. With his headtorch, he scaled down the river bank and searched for the fallen man and horse. They lay in a bloodied heap, the mare stunned, the man unconscious.

'He is dead and I'll go to jail for this,' Sásho thought. 'Again.'

Vasko didn't come around for ages. It was agony. Sásho cut the ropes of the saddle and left the six bags there. Somehow, he managed to drag Vasko up onto the path, the injured mare was reunited with her foal and painfully, step by step, they walked the rest of the way, with Sásho propping up his mate whose shoes were torn so that his feet were bleeding too.

'Mimi and her foal were troopers. And the other mare didn't deserve that,' Sásho concluded. We held each other all night.

In the morning, Balkán was irritable. He barked at the horses and bit two lambs who looked at him in shock. 'You piece of rubbish!' Sásho shouted at him. The flock rushed out of the pen and instead of going to the river, they overran the front of the hut, trampled the fireplace, crapped on the stones I'd swept, pushed over the washing-up liquid and drank from the soapy tub where I did the dishes. We were overrun. We were a minority.

'We're in their way!' Sásho said.

'We have to seek our human rights!' I said. We were laughing. It was a new day.

The dogs looked distracted, like before a storm, but the sky was clear. There was a general restlessness. I was getting claustrophobic and wanted to climb out of our funnel. Sásho was as fresh-faced as ever, but unfocused.

'Let's go up to the high pastures today, get away from here,' I suggested. 'We can swim in the waterfalls!'

'Whatever you say, dear.'

It was a brilliant sunny day and all the rockfaces looked down on us with benevolence. I was keen to move on to greener pastures, for the ordeal to be behind us.

'Almost behind us,' Sásho said. 'We'll have to go and fetch those bags from the river before Kámen comes up next. Don't mention this to him, please! What happens here stays here.'

'I don't like this secrecy,' I said. 'He should know what happened.'

'But then The Privateer will find out too, and Vasko will get in trouble.'

'Vasko almost died! And your hair has gone greyer. You shouldn't have had to go through that. It's hard enough as it is.'

Sásho sighed. 'It's the nature of it. And his drinking has got worse since last year. I'll get them across the river.'

By the time he came back, Vasko was already sitting at our table, his cut head bandaged and mixing cold water with Nescafé. Vanya and Constantin were climbing up their slope with the sheep. He'd come to drop off some rope and pick up his horse saddle. He had a netted bag for gathering herbs.

'I'm off for herbs in Kamen klet,' he said and I laughed, but he was serious. 'Vanya wants some St John's wort. She's got earache. Her ex beat her and her ear's damaged, poor thing. God!' he suddenly yelled with desperation, 'When is this life gonna end!'

'How's the mare?' Sásho asked.

'Ach fine, she's got a scrape.' Vasko got up to leave on his herb expedition.

'Don't go, bro,' Sásho suddenly got up and asked me to go inside the hut with him. 'Where is the bottle?' he asked me. I took it out of the rucksack.

He put it on the table in front of Vasko. I couldn't believe my eyes. I pulled him back inside the hut. 'What the hell?'

'I want rid of that bottle, for your sake,' he assured me. 'He'll have a drink and leave, with the bottle.'

'I thought we were off to the waterfalls!'

'Please, I want to prove to you that I can sit with him and not get drunk,' Sásho told me. 'I'll cook something. What would you like me to cook?'

'I thought you were off for herbs,' I said to Vasko outside.

'The herbs'll still be there tomorrow,' he said. 'I'm peeling potatoes now.'

They were making chips. He put the radio on and began to sing. I put on my rucksack, blinded with anger, left them at the table and headed across the white desert of rocks into the pine forest opposite the huts. I clambered, collecting juniper berries and chewing them to calm myself. But I couldn't calm myself.

Kámen pours alcohol down the shepherds' throats to keep the status quo. Sásho pours alcohol down Vasko's throat to feel sober. That way, neither of them had to look at themselves and the problem remained outside of them. And Vasko dumps his misery onto everybody. The mare probably fell last night because of his boozy smell. Horses can't stand it.

I sat on a fallen pine and to calm myself, I drew Black Water in my notebook; the loop of the river, like a noose, the two huts, two desolate shepherds with a bottle between them and a woman and a child by a cauldron. A nettle path connects them. At the high end of the valley lay our blanket of black sheep. At the other end, their handful of white sheep. The horses are out of view. The pines are severe. There is nothing more sober than a pine.

I felt separate, like a part of me was missing, had gone down the gorge uncollected, lessons were unlearned, trust was betrayed, a creeping insanity was taking hold of the valley. We are all orphans in the refugee camp, trapped by our passions.

All the dogs in the valley barked at something and the echo made it reverberate as if it was many dogs from different peaks. Cerberus the three-headed dog that guards the underworld must sound like this. Black Water is a purgatory. I saw Sásho cross the bone-white valley towards me. He came up and sat next to me among the flowering wild thyme. He was not drunk and not sober. There was a whiff of rakia.

'Last night I dreamt that you fell down and I went to catch you,' he said. 'I suddenly panicked in case something happened to you,' he said.

'It has,' I said.

'I don't want a bottle between us. That's why I gave it to him. I'm between worlds. I want to be with you but he is here too. I'm trying to combine.'

'And I feel stuck. When you drink, it's like you're not here,' I said. 'I want to explore but I can't do it alone. I should leave before something really bad happens.'

'Please don't leave. Once this bottle is gone, it'll be over.'

Until Tuesday. On Tuesday and Thursday, The Privateer and Kámen brought more booze up. 'Why do you do it?' I asked The Privateer. 'Because if I don't, he'll quit the job. And I need him.' Kámen did it because he was used to controlling his shepherds with booze and he was a man of habit. Vasko drank from Tuesday to Friday, then he ran out and went sober until the next Tuesday.

'Please don't go any higher. You know where I am. There's beans and chips.'

Sásho returned to the hut and I walked to the waterfalls where I took a plunge, gathered thyme and began to feel like myself again. It was day by day here. You could not even plan a decent end to the day. The best you could do was keep your wits about you. When I returned, a bowl of hot chips was waiting for me. Vasko crumbled some feta cheese on them but his movements were in slow motion.

'Eat up,' he smiled apologetically. He was too drunk to eat or walk home, so Sásho helped him down the nettle path, then helped Constantin get the cows back while Vanya herded the sheep home. Then he went to collect our flock, feed the dogs and gather more wood.

Our chores were set now: he took care of the animals, firewood and basic maintenance of the hut and pen, and I cooked, pointlessly swept the dirt floor and did dishes and laundry, mostly mine. The dogs chewed my rubber gloves. There was always a pot of warm water on the stove. I couldn't do anything without warm water and we were already running out of washing-up liquid. I am filled with respect that Karakachan women did laundry in one of two ways, for both of which you needed arms of steel. The heavy woollen rugs and clothes were soaked in copper cauldrons of hot water with lard soap and stirred, then beaten in the cold river with long wooden bats. The lighter textiles, like linen cheese cloths and undergarments were soaked for a week in wooden vats with dry manure in them. They stirred them every day and after a week they washed them sparkling white. The sheep shit scoured them like a mild bleach.

When you live in an alpine hut and don't have a cauldron or the guts and arms of a Karakachan woman, things that you've never noticed before become precious: like washing-up liquid, resin kindling, lighters and matches, lots of them, sisal rope, for your laundry line, for tying sacks to the saddle, for sheep when they get injured and you have to carry them (which hasn't happened so far), for re-attaching broken fencing and, when all else fails, for hanging yourself.

Small splinters too. I saw a pile of them in the hut and nearly threw them out before Sásho said: 'no, I need them'. When a sheep breaks a leg, which can happen when a ram mounts her too forcefully, you need one of these splinters to bandage the leg until it recovers. These sheep have worryingly thin legs.

Hats, preferably beanies. Not just for the wind but to protect your hair from the dust and earth that the animals kicked up every day. Our hair became like felt. Sun hats are no good because the wind blows them off.

Some things don't change in an alpine hut. For the shepherd nomads, the most precious items in a hut were a knife, a copper pot for heating milk and water, soap, flint, an axe for chopping branches and wood, those big goatskin bags called *tulumi* in the shape of a bag-pipe and with retractable openings for keeping cheese in, and of course, rugs. Lots of rugs. And a weaving loom for making the rugs and almost everything else they wore. The Karakachans slept on the ground of their huts, which in the posher huts was covered with bark and on top of that, rugs. Along the walls of their huts were bed-like planks where the milk and cheese slept. The humans slept on the ground, on thick layers of rugs and sheepskins. The children were often riddled with fleas from the goats.

That morning, Sásho woke up with horrendous spider bites on his arms that quickly swelled up. His blood was sweeter than mine.

'Their revenge. For taking away the cobwebs,' he grinned. 'They spent nine months making them and we destroy them in minutes.'

Constantin came down the nettle path.

'Can I come for a bit?'

'I'm so glad to see you!' I said and we drank tea with honey.

'I don't want to be begging for treats,' he said, taking the chocolate waffle I offered. 'I didn't come for that. May I ask how the book is going?'

I told him I was still taking notes and didn't have a title yet. I showed him my drawing of Black Water.

'Thank you for including me. Why not call it just *One Summer in Black Water*?'

'I think you'll become a writer, don't you?' I said.

He jumped up. 'I don't know but right now I still have energy and would like to do something for you.'

He went to the side clearing with the dog troughs and called me in five minutes: 'Ta-da! This is your writing table and chair. When those two are sitting there talking rubbish, you can come and write in peace. And it's sunny.'

He had placed a nice trunk as a table and another one as a chair.

'Thank you,' I said. 'That's the best writing station I could have.'

Then, he drew a picture in my notebook. Three recognisable figures with stumpy arms and above them, a fourth with wings. A big, jagged crystal like a sword pointed down from her to the three. The only person missing was his mother. He wrote their names.

'That's you. Watching over us with the giant crystal of the mountain, so that we don't hurt each other.'

'Why do I have wings?'

'Because you are our angel,' he said and looked up to his right again. He drew another picture. It featured two trees with big nests in them, birds flying above and a field of flowers, leaning to one side from the wind.

'This is a proper picture with nature and without people,' he said. 'It's more real.'

'Are people less real?' I asked. He shrugged.

'When they drink, they are less real. They shrink and you can't find them.'

He showed me a quartz pendant around his neck. It protected him, he said, from 'her' and other dangers.

'How do you find it living here?' I asked him.

'It's okay,' he shrugged. 'But my tablet has no power. I look at the mountain a lot.'

We looked at the rock stacks across.

'Do you see a mouth and eyes there, like someone is looking at you?' he asked.

Yes, I did.

'And on that rock, something is written, but I don't know what it means. Because it's in another language.'

'Yes,' I said, 'I think so too.'

'Do you sometimes feel like there were people here, but then they left and now the whole mountain is like an abandoned house?'

'Yes, I do.'

'What? Holy shit!' he said to himself, thinking of something. 'Do you find it strange that there are so many abandoned buildings in the world, yet people don't have anywhere to live?'

'Absolutely.'

'And also, abandoned numbers. For example, 1,000 is an abandoned number. I've called it and nobody answers. Sometimes, I feel like the number 1,000. I used to have a notebook like you'.

Then his mother pulled him out of school.

'If you want a break from your hut, you can always sleep here,' I said. He liked the idea but shook his head.

'Do you want to see my cartwheels?'

He cartwheeled across the clearing.

The next day, his mother invited us for bean soup. Like me, she favoured visits by invitation. We sat at the outdoor table by the water tap. Their hut was pointy, round and fully covered in branches, like a real nomad's hut. The edges of the wide bed were lined with cush-ions and the ceiling hung with furry blankets that Vasko had carried on his back to make it nice for Vanya and the boy. Geranium grew inside the walls and filled the place with its presence. I had hut envy. (Yes, Sásho said, but our hut lets in air and light.) They too had been burgled. When they arrived, they found the door open.

'At least close the door when you leave!' Vasko commented. He had risen from his drunken stupor. Who were these burglars in the middle of nowhere? 'Shepherds. Tourists. Who knows.'

The burglars took dry food but left half a bottle of French cognac. This was the language of the mountain: you have to leave something in exchange. The stone bases of old buildings were still contoured on the ground. This more open part of the valley was sunnier and hotter and the land went downhill more sharply.

Vanya was a fit, handsome half-Roma woman — a mongrel, she said — who had suffered so much hardship that she was in permanent survival mode. She kept an immaculate hut, washed, cooked and held her child hostage to her own injuries. She treated Vasko with pity and contempt.

'Vanyaa,' he smiled sheepishly, 'where's the rest?'

'Give 'im the poison,' she instructed Constantin and he glumly handed over the last 200 grams of rakia in a plastic bottle. One hun-dred grams, two hundred grams, fifty grams, have a wee dram, it's for toothache no more, I don't touch the stuff on the job. There was a language around drinking. Lying and drinking went together.

Drying bunches of herbs hung on nails.

'Look, we found blueberries today,' said Constantin. They were in a small cup.

'It's too early for blueberries,' said Sásho.

'Lots of thyme, but,' said Tanya.

'Juniper berries too,' I said. 'Good for the nerves.'

'There's no nerves here,' Vasko leaned against Tanya affectionately but his balance was off and he fell off the bench. She didn't help him. Constantin rolled his eyes.

'Yea, I took out my nerves with the pincers,' said Sásho and wrig-gled his hand. They laughed at the fond memory.

'Vanya's a bit nervy sometimes,' Vasko said, 'And I tell her, Van-yaaa, leave me alone, my pockets are empty like my head.'

'Behave yourself or I'll send you up for blueberries,' Vanya said sternly.

'Blueberry wine, eh plague?'

'You're a plague, you are,' Sásho said.

It was almost enjoyable, sitting here eating bean soup in the balmy dusk, with a tomato and onion salad. Tomatoes!

'From a can,' Vanya smiled and I saw that most of her upper teeth were missing.

Along the marble spine of Little Horse were two dark pegs.

'Look! Two Talibans.'

That's what shepherds called distant hikers. When hikers came down to us they became visitors. The section of the trail visible from our valley was notoriously perilous, with ropes.

'A bit late for hiking, it'll be dark in an hour,' I said.

'They're out for thrills.'

'I'll give them thrills when I pick up their shoes in the waterfall tomorrow,' said Sásho.

'Remember that time when we found shoes and poles? And they found the body later?'

'Aye. Someone looking for thrills.'

'Heeeeeey, Talibans! Come down! Or we'll come up!'

Laughter.

'One rainy night, I was on my own in the hut,' Sásho said. 'This woman turns up with a young boy, with torches. Where did you come from? Down some rocks, she said. But it's all rocks here! They were sodden.'

They'd dried themselves by the stove and eaten the stew Sásho offered, but the woman refused to stay the night and continued uphill to the lakes in the pitch blackness with the torches and he could not stop them. I couldn't imagine what that woman was thinking.

'You must have been drunk and she didn't feel safe,' I said.

'Not true,' Sásho said. 'She was weird. I felt for the boy.'

'Consti, fetch some olives for the guests,' Vasko burbled. 'You're the best.'

'No, he and I are gonna look for the old chimney in the river, eh?' Sásho said to the boy. 'The one that was swept by the avalanche.'

Constantin lit up and they went down the dry riverbed. And it was completely dry, at this lower end of the valley, the river had hidden itself! But at our end, it was still going.

'How come he's not going to school?' I asked Vanya. She didn't meet my eyes. She generally avoided eye contact, like Vasko, like Kámen's family. That's why they were in this profession. Invisible animals, invisible people.

'He helps me,' she said. She was not experienced with sheep and it showed in her rough herding style.

'He's gifted, you know,' I said to her. She was pleased but her jaw was set.

She grimly scanned the slope across the valley, although the sheep were safely in the pen. She expected nothing but bad things from life. 'You know me,' Sásho liked to say, 'I always expect the unexpected and the unexpected is usually bad.' He had learned that in childhood. Trauma did that to you. You expected the worst because it had already happened.

If Constantin continued to help his mother like this, he would be forced to educate himself through the internet. The shepherding life barred you from a worldly education, in the past, and Constantin's mother was stuck in the past. This was the dark side of a bucolic childhood not adapted to its current era. In the past, apprentice shepherds skipped the alphabet and the children of nomads remained illiterate except for those of enlightened and moneyed parents who could afford to pay a teacher to come up from the nearest village. It was an oral, archaic culture, a cult of the mountain. If you were a girl, these mountains were your fate. You were perpetually on duty: being pregnant, spinning wool, weaving and making and unmaking huts. The Karakachans only became literate and numerate en masse when they started to settle in the early twentieth century and entered the state system of housing, schools, citizenship and health care. And many appreciated the opportunities that came with it. This is when intermarriage with the rest of the population became commonplace and children no longer received the ancestral shepherd's crook: they

went to school instead. The nomads became civilised and homogenised, like their milk.

Constantin and Sásho were back from their small adventure. They
had found the old chimney and a dead sheep, one of theirs. We listened to Radio Gaia, the news. Visitors to the capital's zoo were
encouraged to give the resident bear ice cream, to increase interactiv-
ity with the animals. We laughed.

'And our bear is encouraged to take lambs,' Constantin said.

Constantin and Vanya saw a bear's rump today but were more concerned for the sheep.

The boy sprang to his feet. 'I still have energy and I'd like to do
something.'

He picked up a hatchet and hacked at the wooden trough that
Vasko was carving for the dog food. He whacked it with full force for
half an hour, letting out all the pent-up emotion. It was scary to
watch and nobody stopped him.

'Great job, Consti!' Vasko shouted. 'You're the best.'

Then his mother shouted, 'That's enough, you plague, come here.'

Constantin threw the axe on the ground. 'I am not a plague.' And
he went to hug one of the dogs, tears in his eyes. I wanted to console
him. Sásho held my hand to console me. He was trying not to touch
the drink before him and when Vasko wasn't looking, he poured it on
the ground. But when I wasn't looking, he sipped from it. Our
phones were lined up on the table, waiting for their turn to charge at
the battery. The radio played folk songs and we hummed along.

The bitch whose ten children were gone went around in circles,
her teats hanging. In the field, the cows measured something with
tails like pendulums. The dogs prowled the perimeter with distant
expressions. The stone mountain was bathed in a golden light for
which there is no word. It glowed like an open treasure chest, like the
interior of the earth, like something that cannot be forgotten.

'Vanyaaa,' Vasko briefly awakened from his stupor, 'is there any
ice-cream?' Blood seeped through his bandage.

Another day at Black Water was coming to an end.

VERTICAL PASTURE

Out of the top three components for good pasture, we were running out of one: grass. It was time to take the flock higher. Shade was not crucial here because it was cool enough and we had water since the river had not hidden itself yet.

Everyone was lazy and domestic this morning, but the imminent change in regime was felt. The booze was finished, a few peaceful days lay ahead of us. The sheep took a while to come out and had to be cajoled with bread.

'Breadie is out but a single swallow doesn't make a summer.'

The sick one, 4328, was still not here.

The dogs led the way, smelling an adventure. It started immediately with the wolf cubs they chased a few hundred metres upstream.

'The parents will be close,' Sásho said. 'And uncles and aunties too. Good for the wolves, bad for us.'

There were supposed to be just a few dozen adult wolves in the entire national park, but when you had grazing animals, they seemed to be everywhere. These ones were drawn to the valley by The Privateer's dying sheep. We knew 4328 would be our first casualty, and not our last. In the past, sheep had been attacked near the dwarf-pines at the top of the valley, like the six sheep throttled and lined up by the wolves last year.

It took thirty minutes for the flock to cross the valley and start their sharp ascent. Here was the other waterfall. Soon, we were so high up the cascades that the huts became dots. There was a path, but the terrain was almost vertical. There was quartz and granite of every size and shape, everywhere, and as the sheep ran up, scree fell. You had to scale it sideways. A bigger stone could knock you off balance and send you flying. It was ascetic terrain, classic siliceous scree stripped of all comfort. We entered the natural sculpture park of The

Eagles. Mushroom, Red Rock, Eagle's Nest. Our daily chorus of
faces, but now I was seeing them closer up they looked even higher.
This escarpment led to a series of steep panoramic plateaux with
juicy pasture. The whole area was called Etip and the cascading river
was one of several that led up to the mountain's long spine with its
glacial cirques running down it like ribs. We had to remain on the
west side of the spine at all times. Black Water, Etip's, the lakes, that
was our territory. We were meant to rotate the flock between two or
three grazing itineraries, all of which were vertical and involved scaling escarpments. If we didn't want to climb, we could stay in Black
Water where the pasture was exhausted or we could take them a
couple of floors down from Black Water, but that involved the perilous river crossing where everything slips.

We climbed, and stones fell. The sheep were at home here. It was
good to be climbing again. I took a quick dip in a rockpool under a
cascade with Topi who looked like he had grown up since Orelek.
Everybody was in a sunny mood to match the weather. We might
even see the lakes today!

'See that? That area once had big summer pens.' It was a bare patch
in the distance below.

Etip, the legendary shepherd, once had extensive pens and dairies
and it was said that he and his shepherds and thousands of sheep lived
here for most of the year, making cheese and sending it down the
mountain on horseback.

And now, a new problem: false hellebore. The sheep fell on it with
gusto. False hellebore is a green leafy plant that's nutritious and psychotropic. 'The sheep froth at the mouth from it, like they've eaten
laundry detergent,' Sásho said. The first time he experienced this, he
freaked out and called Kámen who told him that it wasn't lethal, just
poisonous. We were late in the season though and the strongest green
leaves were over.

And here came the first case of bad tripping. One of the young
sheep was stuck mid-cascades, eyes glassy, mouth frothing. We tried
everything but he wouldn't budge.

'Doesn't know what planet he's on', Sásho said. The flock suddenly shot quite high up the crags, mouths frothing and enjoying an

influx of kookie energy and we ran to catch up with them and stop them going the wrong way. Now, we had a dilemma about which way to go back. To the right and on to the lakes, then down through the other waterfall and the dwarf-pine grove, which meant leaving the stoned sheep behind for today and risk losing it to predators. Or to the left, and retrace our steps on the way down this evening, picking up the errant sheep. This was a very difficult descent.

But the route via the lakes was longer. 'What's an easier way down?'

'There isn't one,' Sásho grinned. Our late start at 9:30 and the flock's uncertain movement meant that we were better off retracing our steps in the late afternoon.

A whistle came from the ridge above. A tourist, I thought, but there was no human access. It was wild goats. The bucks whistle like humans to warn the herd.

We couldn't see any, but when Topi and Redhead zoomed off on a chase, two surprisingly large goats with big horns appeared at the top. The young dogs shot like arrows up the vertical cone but the goats went one better: they could actually fly.

'Topi has no chance,' said Sásho. 'But if they throttle a goat, I'll take it down on my back and we can eat it. Fancy fresh goat meat?'

No. I could picture the blood and guts in front of the hut and drunken Vasko disembowelling the animal, and himself accidentally. Surprisingly, the Karakachans were not hunters or even fishers, despite dwelling in places rich with game and despite their monotonous diet. They only began hunting when they became settled later in the twentieth century. Hunting just wasn't their thing. They preferred to buy cured meat from settled peasants and seemed content with cheese and legumes. Occasionally, they reared pigs during the summer, which they slaughtered and cured towards the end of the season, taking the preserved meat down with them to the winter huts. The same went for agriculture: they were forced into it by sedentarisation. They joked that no nomad can make a good ploughman. It was a painful joke, for one of their points of pride was that while the shepherd walks upright, the peasant is bent over the land. To swap the shepherd's staff for the hoe of the peasant was never a choice. It was an ideology.

Goats and sheep mix well and once, they had moved to higher pasture together, ensuring milk and yogurt for the shepherding families. Karakachan shepherds who pastored the 'barren' flocks far from camp kept a few milking goats for sustenance. Yet because of some obsolete law, the national park now disallowed livestock goats from its territory. The goat became a maligned animal in the early twentieth century when industrial forestry became influential and started cordoning off areas and either clear-felling millennial forests, or designating them as reserves, like with the juniper.

'I wish I could lure a goat or two to join the flock, then we'd have a little goat kid and fresh milk every day!' said Sásho.

I liked the idea. It wasn't impossible. If we spent a few days and nights up here with the flock, the goats and the sheep would sniff each other out, the dogs too. Our sheep had been wild once too, like these goats. If we abandoned them, they would go wild again and then life might be easier for everybody.

More than once, Sásho had slept by the waterfall escarpment. It went with the job. Twice, the flock got stuck in the evening and he couldn't abandon them. He wrapped himself in the plastic sheet and somehow made it through the small hours. Seeing the pen was empty, Vasko came up to look for him. He saw that Sásho had ripped his shoes and went back to get him his own second pair, then they took the flock down.

Your neighbour meant the difference between life and death.

'The worst thing on those nights was that I ran out of smokes. Bro, I said, I'll kill a man for a cigarette.'

The thought of spending the night in this crevasse appalled me. Even with the dogs. The gradient and the isolation were extreme. A huge dirty chunk of icy snow from an avalanche sat in the river. A hawk flew metres above our heads, then a golden eagle, then an aeroplane so low I could see people in it. Maybe they could see us too.

'It's not that it's low, it's that we are high.'

We caught up with the flock at a crossroads. It wasn't a visible crossroads, but the sheep always made up their mind here, whether to turn east to Thunder Peak or west to Etip's. They rushed to cross the steep escarpment banks, which meant east.

We spent the afternoon on the steep green slopes beneath the marble sphinx. Above us, creeping along its spine, were lots of peg-like Talibans. It was a madhouse today.

At some point they all stopped to take in the view from up there.

'Hey, come down or we'll come up,' Sásho shouted.

Someone threw a stone that bounced back and nearly hit Kito. The dogs barked, too right!

'Why are they doing that?'

'To see the sheep scatter, wretched Talibans.'

Some did it because they thought the animals were wild goats and wanted to see them leap. But today, the two shepherds were on display, there was no mistaking the sheep for wild goats and it was plain meanness.

'I've heard there's a cave here,' Sásho said. 'I want to explore it but haven't found it yet.'

'An abysmal cave,' I said. 'Stamen told me about it. The outlaws kept weapons stashed in it. And the shepherds their cheese.'

'Yes, that one! Wanna look for it sometime?'

It was unmarked on the map and unknown to anyone but the old shepherds, which is how Stamen knew about it. One day, he and some park rangers came to look for it and found it, its entrance a near-vertical descent into the mountain's interior. The speleologists who came with them deemed it too risky. 'Shall we put a plaque with your name on it?' his colleagues said. Stamen was not interested. He just wanted it to be known that this cave existed, for bandits, shepherds, outlaws. I hope Sásho never finds it.

Hours passed. At our feet was the blue world. The lakes were tucked out of view in their cirque. We would not see them today. Maybe tomorrow. The old pastoralists had had much more of an infrastructure than we do today. The present-day tourist trails were created over the centuries by animal caravans. Hikers followed in the hoof steps of the animal tribe without knowing it.

And now it's just us, The Privateer and Stamen.

'And we still have to play hide and seek with each other and the park rangers,' Sásho said. 'It's crazy isn't it.'

The sheep weren't hungry and lay down, the dogs too. I cut some thyme. We munched crackers with cheese. I was always hungry here but oddly, the more you walked, the less you could eat. Your body became lighter, more self-sufficient, and could do more on less fuel, just like the mountain goats. Topi kept close to me today and looked at me searchingly with his adult eyes. How quickly bonds were made in the mountain.

We won't always be like this, Topi, but now we are. We are completely together.

'I want us to always be like this,' Sásho said. 'Together.'

Different but equal. Sásho, me, Topi. The higher you went, the harder physical survival became, the more equal you felt to everything. Personas disappeared and essence remained. There is just one essence in all of life. Anima.

Last night, Sásho played me his favourite rock song: *You won't be seeing me low down. I cannot live without my dreams. Come, come and fly with me . . .*

'I want us to go higher. This is not enough. Tomorrow we'll go to the lakes. The godmothers love it there. They balloon like bagpipes at the lakes.'

Going higher was an addiction. At my feet, I could see where my journey began last year: the Kresna Gorge, then to Orelek. Then to The Beeches and on foot to Black Water. Black Water was a small white dip far below.

At four, the flock rose and began to pull at the grass with gusto.

'Now you decide to eat!'

To get them moving down to the river crossing with the melting snow, Sásho whistled with a leaf, a piercing sound. A false hellebore leaf. 'Just don't chew it or you'll start frothing at the mouth,' I said.

'Too late,' he grinned, nibbling it.

The sheep slowed down, time sped up. The sun was setting over the other mountain. Just when the flock gathered nicely and moved downhill, a rush of libido went through the twenty-seven rams and they started mounting the entire flock. As if they hadn't done it constantly for the past week!

The flock began to rotate, anti-clockwise in a spiral and locked itself shut.

'Now you decide to fuck them, you motherfuckers!' Sásho shouted. The rams that weren't busy mounting sheep after sheep were fighting. Horns clashed, heads smashed. A madhouse. Lambs bleated, trapped. The dogs could do nothing about it and wandered off to look for adventure. Only Balkán stood his ground inside the rotating mass of bodies. It went on for ages. Six hundred animals locked in an orgy. Sásho broke his stick on a rock. They could not be wrenched from their lust. We faced a real risk of getting stuck in the escarpment as night fell. The flock did not like to move after dark and Sásho would have to stay with them overnight. I'd be damned if I had to scale down this wall in the dark.

The only hope was to break the circle at its lower end, by getting a few sheep to move down and the rest to follow. We managed, and a trickle of animals began the long trail home, which took another three hours. On the way down, some sheep lingered in the patch of false hellebore again.

'Don't you start helleboring now!' We laughed. I was exhausted.

A few hundred metres above Black Water, the flock got bottlenecked at the most dangerous place in the descent. The path narrowed and two large flat rocks flanked it, each with a sheer drop. The sheep that weren't filing down went up onto the rocks as if taking their cue from the stoned one. Even Sásho looked worried. I couldn't watch, the suspense was too great. If one sheep fell, more would follow because they moved as one. They may not all die but smashed bones were certain and that was the same as death. Those splinters in the hut would not fix them.

A story from several decades ago was still told, about a flock of mountain sheep like these that fell off the ridge above the lakes – the whole flock. The shepherd, who was hired, hanged himself.

'If I lose these godmothers, I'll hang myself too,' Sásho said. 'Kámen and me, together.'

They would, too. Kámen out of despair, Sásho out of loyalty – and for fun.

To get the flock on the level of the trail, Sásho ran downhill and whistled from the low end. They came down from the rock and fell into line. I stayed behind to gather up the laggers. My nerves were rattled. Our valley was plunged into a cold shadow and I fell on my hand and bruised it on the sharp stones as I scaled the last slope. Slipping and falling was unavoidable here and without phone signal or a helper in the hut to wait for you, injury was a stark prospect. This was the lot of the isolation shepherd. Sásho never complained or demanded more. He had never been entitled to comfort in his life and the concept of ready-made safety was alien to him. The only time he snapped was last summer before my visit, when his smashed hand caused him agony.

'Bring me another headtorch, why don't you!' he lashed out at Kámen, 'I'll strap it to my dick so I can work day and night when my hand falls off. I've got another hand, don't I!'

He had not asked to go down and see a doctor, and Kámen had not offered it. Later, Kámen commented to me: 'He wouldn't have smashed it had he been sober.'

By the time I reached the hut and lit the stove, it was dark. Topi and Balkán came with me, their job almost done and the flock almost home, though Balkán was really skiving. Everything felt difficult now – getting the fire going, getting the food reheated, bringing tubs of water from the tap, even making tea took ages. The last lighter fell apart in my hands and the matches were damp. The flock advanced slowly across the white valley and blended with the dark. Sásho arrived and fed the dogs, then, with our headtorches on, we did a quick count of the flock as it entered the pen, by which time I was angry. This amount of hardship was not normal. 'How can you sustain this for three months, alone! No way.'

'It's just how it is, dear,' Sásho said mildly.

It was ten o'clock before we ate, on top of the bed. This job requires two people with the flock and one person at the hut, like it used to be. One to cook and boil milk to make yogurt and cheese. The others to take the flock out.

'Yes but there's no one left for this job, you can see for yourself,' Sásho said. 'I can't do this forever, but I dread what Kámen will face after me.'

The dogs barked like mad all night, not letting us sleep. The wolves were near. I went outside several times. There were so many stars, I couldn't bear it. Maybe the dogs couldn't bear it either. I shouted at them to stop but they didn't. I looked at the stars, stop it! But they kept being billions and burning brightly.

'Do we have any rights around here?' I said in the morning. I looked for a missing shoe again and collected my towel and freshly laundered T-shirt from the dirt.

'We are in their way,' Sásho grinned through the cigarette smoke, fresh and affectionate as ever. 'It's the nature of it.'

The nature of it is, someone had ripped open a bag of dog food and helped themselves during the night. My washing-up sponge was chewed up and the bar of soap had teeth marks – bottom row only. Someone had crapped in my clean baking tray, a weasel or a rat. The rams had butted the fence of the pen and it needed mending but we were out of sisal rope, the last piece of cheese was nowhere to be found, we didn't have a battery for our phones and my hair needed a wash but after the last stampede there was no shampoo left.

'I'm not going anywhere today,' I declared for all to hear. 'I'm a person too!'

For some reason, the sheep coughed like old smokers today. Sásho pointed at something in the pen. A ram had pushed his head into an empty plastic tub looking for food and now it was stuck on his head like a top hat that covered his eyes. He span and the others regarded him without sympathy. We collapsed with mirth.

'It serves you right!' I said to the ram.

Sásho opened the gate: 'I'll take them out. They'll graze stones today, to teach them.'

They liked stones. That's why they were called stoners. Sásho climbed the steep banks with them. These sheep would survive the apocalypse and not even notice.

And here came Vasko down the nettle path, with a plastic cup of something: shampoo, because the other hut heard that we lost ours. Their task today was to collect the bags of dog food lost during the accident the other night.

'Couldn't blink last night,' Vasko said. 'Dogs, wolves, bears. And no doping. You don't have any left by any chance?'

He was timid when Sásho wasn't around. I nearly said 'sheepish' but my view of sheep had changed by now. There was nothing sheep-ish about these mountain animals.

We drank tea and cold Nescafé, an 'extra' for which shepherds paid separately, God knows why.

Sásho took the flock to the dwarf-pine line, collected Mimi and tied the foal to save him another trek, but Mimi kept stopping and turning. There was no choice, the foal came along. The two guys saddled Mimi and were off, joined by the stallion further down. I sat down to read, but there is always something to do in the hut: sweep, heat water, cook, add something to the list of things we need, fix the broken latch of the door — and it was only then that I noticed the faded chalk writing on the door:

WE ARE AT ETIPS

A message to Kámen from a shepherd in some other summer. He'd had no paper and pen, and no phone signal.

We were ideally expected by Kámen to take the flock up on verti-cal pasture every day, but it was an inhuman expectation. You got fit very fast but you needed mental rest in-between these ascents and descents. The thrill of herding these animals was too great to sustain day after day.

A bunch of dog chokers hung by the door. The wooden baton attached to the chain collar was called a 'tripper', because it hit the dog in the face when it ran, to stop it charging too fast at passers-by and killing wild animals like deer and rabbits, but they are like a medieval torture instrument and it was agreed that they prevented the dogs from fighting off predators and the law was changed in favour of the guardian dog. I wouldn't want any of our dogs to wear it. At the same time, the dogs could be a real danger to tourists if the shepherd was not around and mean hunters used this as an excuse to shoot guardian dogs.

Muna the Monkey had been circled by the others' male dogs for days, but she was only interested in Balkán who had started circling her today. Balkán is supposed to be castrated by Kámen but there is some doubt about the success of the operation. The other dogs crossed and recrossed the valley aimlessly, Sunday-like. Today, ani-mals and humans were peaceful. On Tuesday, the booze would arrive so we had one more day. I draped the duvets on a large dwarf-pine shrub, to rid them of the fine wood dust that came down from the beams of the ceiling; the wood larvae are hard at work.

I lay inside trying to read a book but fell asleep. The sun filtered through the plastic roof weighed down with pine branches. The seasons roll over, the snow melts and Black Water roars and fills with water, the bed floats. Then it's summer again. Dogs cross my mind. Black herds come down from the top. Then, thunder rolls into my dream and I get up to collect the duvets and move the latest pile of logs inside the porch. I light the stove and put potatoes on to boil, and black tea, with luxurious honey.

And there across the white desert comes a figure clad in black, black mare in tow. The foal is still fragile but has kept up with many gruelling treks. Mission successful. Sásho cuts the rope and the bags fall to the ground. They found three bags in the water and three on the bank. I help him carry them and throw them onto the growing pile of dog food. Then he goes to bring the flock back. God knows why it takes them an hour to cover the few hundred metres from the top of the valley to the pen, and he must wait for them. He is patient, that much I know. Then it's time to feed the dogs. He removes a leech from Muna's mouth with the pincers and is nearly bitten on the hand, then the dogs erupt in a fight and collapse one side of the fireplace so it's out of use again.

We sit on the bed and laugh for no reason, except relief that another day has passed without incident.

The thunderstorm comes after dark. Rain drums on the roof and a cold breath rushes in. We light the stove again and step outside to see the staggering contours of our world against the marble sky. The flock is becalmed and huddled against the rain. For the first time, I see a sheep and a ram kissing. Balkán is inside the pen. The younger dogs sneak into the porch, but the older ones remain at their post by the pen gate and get soaked. Electric bolts strike and our valley is flooded with light like a stage with a giant projector. A lightning bolt splits Thunder Peak in two.

'I don't want this to become just a memory,' Sásho says.

★

I've started writing down the same date in my diary, every day. It's been over a week but I am not sure how much over. We don't have a calendar except on our phones which have no battery left since Vasko plugged his battery into the electric fence for the cows. Now I understand why the old shepherds always asked for bread, matches and a calendar. Why the Karakachan shepherds carried big round Turkish watches on gold chains in their pockets. And why bread was taken to them once a week. A week is roughly the time in the wild after which something shifts.

My hands have become a bit like Sásho's; thickened by carrying stuff, soot-stained because cold water doesn't wash off soot or grease, covered in cuts and splinters and with scuffed nails. Everything has become sooty from the stove inside and the fireplace outside, which Sásho fixed this morning.

'Today, we'll make another attempt to visit Rome and see the pope,' as he put it, meaning either Etip's plateau or the lakes where the views are best. But down the vertical slope comes Vasko, after taking his cows up early. He has two items of news: our sick sheep has died in the woods between the two pens, and don't go to the lakes because park rangers are doing inspection rounds. One of the rangers is Stamen. He likes to stand on the ridges and survey the corries with binoculars, hoping to see some of Kámen's sheep in the wrong place and slap a fine on him. I wonder if he has taken his flock to his hut that is over the ridge. Does he fine himself when his sheep go wandering?

Days later, when I have a phone again, I find a message from Kámen; the only time he ever wrote to me: 'DON'T TAKE THEM TO THE LAKES TODAY OR TOMORROW! KEEP THEM AT ETIP'S!'

There is a much better flow of communication between lower and upper earth at the other hut than there is at ours, plus a good flow of communication between the two huts, which saved Kámen a hefty fine today.

Today, the stench of carrion is in the pen and on the way up to Etip, we comb the flock for the sheep with the rotten wound, but her wound has healed, something else is causing the stench. The sheep circle the juniper bushes to nibble them and look like pilgrims at an altar. I pick some juniper berries for calming tea tomorrow, booze delivery day, when I know I'll need it.

Today feels different. The sheep climb the rocky wall slowly and I have a feeling that once again, we won't reach Etip.

'Something tells me that we won't see the pope,' Sásho says.

We sit on a panoramic rock with a sheer drop and survey the rock characters.

The Mushroom. When is it going to fall off its thin stalk? Eagle's nest with its flat top. Red rock, which is not red.

We creep up the high pasture, the sheep graze. It's the dogs that stink of carrion and we realise that they've dismembered the dead sheep and snacked on it. Hikers crawl along the spine above, but we don't call out in case someone throws a stone.

We roam the land with our eyes. Black Water is squeezed and claustrophobic. The blue folds to the west remind us that there is another mountain beyond ours.

'See that peak? That's Sleepy Field. Where I stayed for a year and four months.'

I count the mountains to Sleepy Field: nine. This is the source of the expression 'over nine mountains to the tenth', this landscape. The tenth mountain is the one you never reach, since nine is the number of completion. At nine, you are done. Then you start all over again, from one. There is a song about a company of shepherds who travelled between the Aegean coast and these highlands: nine shepherds herded their flocks for nine years, passing golden mountains and golden fountains before they reached home.

The tenth mountain is not home. It is the land of dragons where the impossible is real. Like in that other song where the protagonist loves a dragon-shepherd who takes her to his 'highland pen with midnight sheep and black dogs' and plays the flute all night for her. She ends up giving birth to 'two wretched dragonlets'.

We turn east and scan the land for the lakes. There they are! It takes me a while to distinguish them. They are well camouflaged, a blue one and a brown one, like eyes in a face that is not like other faces.

'I had a dream last night,' Sásho says. 'It came back to me now. We are at the blue lake. That's the deepest one. You are bathing. Go deeper, dear, I say, there are people coming. You go deeper, but I realise there are no people, it's sheep and now you're in the deep. I panic and wade in after you.'

The sheep draw geometric shapes as they zigzag uphill, black against the white scree. Rhombus-like, a moving harlequin pattern, like something you see in a child's kaleidoscope when you shake it. Now it's diamonds, now it's a star.

It's an unstable kind of day, and now the fog creeps over the spine of Little Horse and moves our way like a slow, white, woolly flock.

The fog is grazing, a shepherding expression. Will the flock be lost if the fog eats us?

'They won't get lost. They orient themselves by smell and sound,' Sásho says. 'But we might get lost.'

The sun is gone and the pleasure of the outdoors is gone. The fog grazes, the sheep graze and the day sags in the damp fog.

We sip tea from a flask, eat everything we have, smoke and when I start to freeze because I haven't brought a jumper, we agree that I'll go down to avoid catching cold. I do it reluctantly. I'm afraid to leave him behind in the fog and I'm afraid of losing the path on the way down. But at least the direction of travel is clear, you go down and just try not to fall off a cliff.

'Please be very careful. Go slow and don't fall,' Sásho says, hood up, standing. Every time we part is wrenching because you just don't know.

'Go Topi, go with her!' But Topi is in the mood to stay. Not one dog comes with me.

I lose them from view. I orient myself by The Mushroom, Red Rock, Eagle's Nest. I fall and get up. I lose the trail and end up wading through a sea of dwarf-pine, then arrive on the edge of a cliff. I turn back to look for a different way. Two wild goats stand on the ridge looking down at me, big like cows. They're not goats but chamois, that's why they're so big. They don't whistle, so I can't be a threat to them. The cold and damp envelop me but I know I'll make it just fine. I am not sure how Sásho will make it and I know I won't relax until I see them coming down in the evening. God, what a long day. What a long life. It could end any moment.

I got it, how it was for Sásho those months when he was alone and talked to the mountain. Days like this, weeks. I could not do it. I like solitude and I often go for weeks at home in Scotland without talking to anyone face to face but here it's different. Here, it's you answering yourself, with the ghostly backing chorus of all those before you who were sheltered, judged, killed and saved by the mountain. You rattle around in a haunted palace with hundreds of marble rooms and the silence is crushing.

'Nobody is interested in my life, why should they be,' Sásho said. 'It's just some little person's life. I don't mind. That's why Kámen doesn't know anything about me that matters. I prefer it. Don't write about me. Find someone more interesting.'

'There isn't anyone more interesting,' I said.

'You're pretty crazy too,' he said. 'Rare and bold like a white rose in a sea of red roses.'

What was this kinship we had? We both had an excess of fire and air in our makeup, no earth. We were restless romantics in search of something. I'd grown up in order and security and channelled my gifts. He'd grown up in chaos and danger and scattered his to the winds. But in some way, we were cut from the same cloth or indeed, rug. Maybe it was the south. The south was unsettled, untamed still. The migrating birds dropped seeds between Africa and the Danube and things happened.

'We've walked our paths alone,' Sásho said. 'The difference is that you're important to the whole world. And I'm important to my godmothers.'

But the whole world is here, now. I am not convinced that there is a world beyond here. And with just the two of us, Sásho literally means the world to me.

The hills that rise above the huts are more daunting seen from up here. One is called The Unknown because a body was found there and never identified. The two huts are little squares, with bigger squares next to them: the pens. I can see how far it is to The Beeches, and then even further to the Mandra dairy. Milk was carried on horses and mules this way. Shepherds from the 1950s recalled making trips like this, four hours with the horse in the morning, deliver the milk at the dairy station, then trek back for another four hours. In the morning they repeated the exercise. 'A dreadful, pointless, money-losing affair,' they said. A bit like keeping sheep in Black Water on a cold foggy day.

I am rushing though I have nothing to rush for. I want to get home where it's comfortable and safe from bears, fog, rain and fear. But if I was a nomad, this here would be my home, this moment, this crumbling ground without safety. All our lives, we try to arrive somewhere. Where are my ambitions now? I can't find them. They were never real. How can something unreal take up so much of my time on earth when the only thing that's real is this mountain? I can't fathom it.

Pirin was named after the old divinity of thunder and fertility, Perun, who is covered in dragon scales. I can see why humans worshipped mountains when they wandered over nine mountains with their flocks. Thunder Peak is the original cathedral. When Notre Dame burns, Thunder Peak is here every morning. The fog wraps the upper floors of the cathedral like an installation by the artist duo Christo and Jean-Claude but our valley is spared.

And here comes Constantin down the nettle path, with a shepherd's stick.

'Can I ask you something? But don't tell anyone.'

I promise.

'Can my mother and I come down with you when you leave with your boss?'

They think I'm employed by Kámen, otherwise why would I be here.

'But I don't know when Kámen is coming up. Probably Thursday. Your mother said you weren't going down for another ten days.'

'Yes, but we want to go sooner. We'll go down anyway.'

'You can't do that. There are bears!' The thought of Vanya and Constantin running away on their own, with luggage, all the way to The Beeches and without phone signal, is desperate.

'We're not afraid. It's just there are dogs with the other flock.' He meant Stamen's.

'What's happened,' I ask, but he clams up. 'Is it Vasko's drinking?'

'No,' he says. 'Can I do another drawing in your notebook?'

He draws a figure with his hair parted, holding a train – Sásho.

'Why is he holding a train?' Constantin shrugs.

'I don't know, but I see him on a train.'

Next, he draws a small figure with short hair who hands Sásho a bunch of flowers.

'That's me,' he says.

'Why are you giving him flowers?'

'Because I like flowers. And I want to give him something. And I have a question. How is the book going?'

'Well, I'm thinking about who the main characters will be.'

He lights up. 'Without being too presumptuous, I'd suggest three main characters: Sásho, Vasko and me. Like the three musketeers. And let's not forget the grand countess, Kapka!'

'I like your idea,' I say.

'The other night, did you worry about Sásho when they were late with the horses?'

'Yes,' I said.

'My mother worried too. But you shouldn't worry.'

'Really?'

'Yes. Because it's all for one and one for all. I better go back. Ah, Uncle Sásho is returning. Remember, don't tell him anything.'

And he disappears down the nettle path, past our pen, urging away the pesky cows eating our nettles.

The flock rushes down the hill without warning. *Beeee. Van-van-van.* The valley comes to life. Sásho is at the back, dry wood on his shoulders. He kisses me, feeds the dogs and rushes on to the other pen to collect the numbered ear of our dead sheep.

A mug of spiced wine would be nice tonight. But after drinking some of it or all of it, Sásho 'poured it out' to prove that he is not a drunkard. I fill the bottle with water at the tap.

In the rising sun, the rock columns cast gigantic shadows down the valley. They pointed at us like beaming messages. We couldn't get away from them. We sat at the little table. Tuesday. Vasko had already taken the cows up the slope and taken himself down the terraces to

The Beeches, to rendezvous with The Privateer and pick up a 30 kilo
sack on his back, booze included.

'I've grown to dread Tuesdays to Fridays,' I said.

'I know. Try not to get upset. I don't get upset 'cos I expect the
worst.'

True, perhaps my expectations were too great. Speaking of great
expectations, Kámen was coming. Probably on Thursday, and I'd go
down with him for a break. Black Water could only be taken in small
doses.

It was a day for making things. The rocks made shadows, Sásho
made a bean stew, I made notes, the dogs made love not war and the
sheep made drawings on the white vertical slopes. They drew a balloon that became a noose that became a spider's web. They'd had a
taste of vertical grazing now and it would be hard to keep them in the
lower parts of the valley.

I told Sásho about Constantin's secret question and he said: 'They
want to do a runner without Vasko knowing. They can't take his
drinking. Don't get involved.'

'How can you say that, it's their safety at stake!' But Sásho's idea of
safety was different to mine. He thought it was perfectly safe for
anyone to walk from here to The Beeches. Even to Orelek.

'We'll go and find out what's going on. But I told you at the beginning, they won't last the season.'

After lunch, we went down the nettle path for a visit. The three of
them sat inside on the edge of the bed, huddled together like grounded
children. They were happy to see us and share some of the new provisions. The stove boomed with a friendly fire. Vasko was already
finishing a small bottle of rakia. We ate black olives from a plate and
he gave us handfuls of small, round green peppers that were delicious
fried or raw. Vanya had varnished her nails. Vasko had a new pair of
canvas sneakers. He wore through a pair in a couple of weeks. He and
Sásho paid for their own shoes, which was rather ungenerous of their
employers, I thought. We listened to the radio. No news.

Their hut was the closest you could find to a Karakachan hut. The
nomad huts used to come in two types: round and conical like this or
square with a thatched roof. Summer and winter huts were similar in

structure but built from different materials and a hut could be very roomy. It was the women's job to build and decorate the huts.

This hut was built following the old technology, but using thick plastic sheets instead of impermeable rugs. A branch-woven skeleton, similar to a woven basket, was covered with a waterproof sheet and branches of whatever trees were available were arranged layer by layer on top of the scaffolding, like one grass skirt on top of another. Here, it was pine. In lower lying places, the nomads used fern. In summer, it was oak branches and the fragrance permeated their dreams. Their huts had no chimneys; the smoke exited through the breathable skin of the hut. A fireplace built with stones was placed near the entrance, like the stove here, and a small iconostas with a candle in a jar was placed in a corner of the hut: it was always the Virgin Mary. This was their only light. The middle of the hut was empty. Everything that counted as furniture was close to the wall: the raised cheese beds called *krevati*, luggage shelves and weaving loom. The bedding was made and unmade on the ground by the walls every day. The Karakachan huts could be very large and everybody slept together inside the one room, up to three generations. If a couple wanted to have sex, they had to wait for the others to fall asleep or go to the luggage hut next door. Or in the woods. As a rule, everybody slept fully dressed and only took off their socks, gaiters and handmade moccasins (later shoes). Between sleeping and waking, between the bare earth and the open sky was just a rug.

When the last nomads were settled in the 1950s and given houses with iron beds in them, they didn't use mattresses or duvets. They slept in their rugs. One rug underneath, one on top of them or if you only had one they just wrapped themselves in it and dreamt of the meadow.

'So when're you going down for a break?' Sásho asked Vanya.

'Coupla weeks,' she avoided his eyes. 'But we don't want to leave him alone,' meaning Vasko. 'Or he'll fall down and kill himself.'

'Who, me? Nah. And Milka and her friends are gonna be flying in the clouds soon.' He was taking them up to Etip's for the rest of the summer.

'Two of your rams are here,' said Vasko. We knew. Kámen shouldn't see that.

'But you tell me how to get them back,' said Sásho. 'By the balls, maybe?'

'I'll help you bro,' said Vasko, but he wouldn't. He was going on a bender for the next three days. He had 2 litres to drink. In the afternoon, he turned up at our hut, legless, to help Sásho chainsaw more wood. I couldn't watch. Afterwards, they sat at the little table and I read my book inside the hut, trying not to listen to them. You don't send a guest away in the mountain, Sásho had told me.

An hour later, Vasko couldn't move.

'Vanya should come and pick up her stock,' Sásho said.

'Vanyaaaa!' screamed Vasko, like he was being slaughtered.

'Don't scream,' I said.

'Vanyaaaa,' he whispered and fell off his seat.

Sásho almost carried him down the nettle path, then helped Constantin with the cows, then climbed to round up our sheep who were not making shapes anymore.

God, I can't fathom where all the pain in this world comes from.

We heard through the grapevine that Kámen is expected today, a day early. The grapevine was: Kámen told The Privateer who told Vasko on the phone and Vasko told Sásho.

Sásho is taking them up to the lakes and wouldn't see Kámen. We are trying to delay the moment of parting but the flock is butting the fence and wants out.

'See if there's a suitable ruin for us in the gorge,' he says. 'If I save up for a few years, I can buy it and do it up for us.'

He opens the gate. The dogs are already ahead, sensing the itinerary without being told. Sásho leaves a present for Kámen: the sheep ear with the numbered tag.

'You can leave me a note before you go, if you like,' he says. 'Come on, darlings, let's go,' and they're off.

That's how it is. You take your stick and you take them out. You don't look back, you don't turn around to wave. These are 'extras' you can't afford. Looking back has been a bad idea ever since Orpheus went to fetch Eurydice in the underworld.

There is something humbling and awesome in this daily exodus without a day off. It leaves me without words. Dogs, sheep and man, all for one and one for all. I watch their slow progress up the white riverbed, a lump in my throat, until they disappear into the dwarf-pine.

Muna and Topi stay with me. Thank you darlings. In the crushing silence, I take stock of the hut, looking for something, not sure what it is. Sásho's small pile of clothes, folded. Mine, bigger. The food that's here, the food we need. The things to bring up.

The sensible thing would be to pack up my stuff and leave for good but I've gone past that point. I sit at the table to wait for Kámen. Many times during the day, I scan the upper valley – for tourists and horses – and the lower valley – for Vasko, Constantin and Kámen. Sometimes, I scan the white hump of the peak for little pegs, but they are remote and irrelevant to our valley life. Whoever is coming near will be announced by the dogs before I see them but the eye seeks to meet something that moves in the emptiness.

I have learned to tell the time of day down to the hour without a watch from the movement of the sun. Between three and four, Kámen and Alex appear, rucksacks on backs.

When, on the way down to The Beeches with them, Mimi and the foal and Vasko and Constantin, I lag behind at the other hut talking to Vanya and lose the path and cross the river gully at the wrong place, it is the child who hears me shouting over the roaring water. He and Vasko wait for me. We continue our English lesson. His canvas sneakers are wearing out. 'Holy shit! It's no wonder, look at these stones,' he says. But he is not fazed by the stones, the forest, the bears or the drinking.

At The Beeches, the summer pen is full of Stamen's sheep that I last saw in Prairie. The shepherds are in the hut and wave to us. They're a Roma family with two small boys, two horses and a foal and their dogs bark at us from inside the pen. They are taking the flock up. They are even later with it than us.

'Any bear?' Vasko shouts to them.

'Yeah!' they shout back. 'Took two sheep. Big male.'

Kámen and Alex load Mimi with dog food from the van. More dog food! I beg Kámen not to give Vasko more alcohol but he has already taken it up with the luggage. There is something sick about this but they have a system. Kámen fears the whole system will fall apart if one component is removed. His forehead slash is still raw.

'He'll be alone now. He'll pine for you,' Vasko says while we rest by the river for ten minutes with cans of juice Kámen distributes from his van. 'Will you come back?'

'Yes,' I say. Vasko smiles toothlessly. Constantin beams. Kámen wears his mocking face.

And then man and boy are off with the loaded Mimi and the brave foal. It'll be a long ascent, a favour paid with booze. I feel closer to my lowlife Black Water tribe than to Kámen and Alex who are from my social milieu and fellow artists to boot, but haven't even made eye contact. Not even a simple: how are you? Alex collects branches for his snakes and on the way down in the van, they talk to each other about animals. I sit in the back as if I am not there.

The lower world really is burning. It was abstract on the news and now it's real. The heat is crushing. The air doesn't feel clean. There are too many houses, even in empty Orelek where I spend one night before moving downhill.

I find myself staring at a dot because there is too much to take in and I need to slow it down. In my high room, I can't sleep from the heat. The house is empty. I get it now, the full house–empty house effect of the pastoral chess game. There is always a missing part of the tribe. Either the farm is full and the hut is empty or vice-versa. The exodus is never complete, someone stays behind; some sheep, some dogs, a few humans. The vertical movement is constant, only the distance varies, and separation between people is inevitable because the pastoralist goes with the animals.

'You can leave tomorrow,' Kámen says at the kitchen table. 'Marina can leave. Alex can leave. Sásho can leave. My mother can leave. Even bai Anton can leave, only I can't leave.'

The emotional pain of separation and the physical pain of being together: a seasonal dance that only ends when the last one of you dies.

'Sometimes, I think of setting fire to this whole place and driving away without looking back,' Kámen said. I believed him.

Even then, he would still have the dogs and home is where the dogs are. If you have no house to return to, if you return and your house has burned down, then you lie down on your plastic sheet or your goat hair rug and you sleep with the dogs. Once again, you become chergar, a soul of the rug. They would not abandon you. In one song, a collective of shepherds return with their flocks from winter pasture in the warm plains to their village in the mountains. The head shepherd is missing. The others lie to his wife about his fate but the head ram tells her the truth:

> The dogs they stayed
> they stayed to bury him.

Sunny is in the dark pen with Karamana. He comes to say hello and I hug him over the gate but the jealous Loopies bark him off.

'Where have you come from?' Bai Anton shakes my hand by the sink. Nobody has told him anything.

'Black Water,' I say. He nods, impressed.

I have graduated.

IN THE LOWER WORLD

In the shimmering heat, the sandy pyramids look like a place where there was once a town that the desert then reclaimed. Yet the town is still here from time to time. In the gorge, present, past and future all blur together and you can't be sure which of these you partake in, and you don't mind.

The hot wind rattles the lorries which let out hot fumes. The train rattles the gorge. The two black herons are at their post on the river. Red plums wither on the branches before they've ripened, only small tart apples survive the heat. People in immaculate clothes pick through their food.

You take a room in Hotel Strymon by the river, with a blunt view of the Melo pyramid and Thunder Peak beyond. Behind you is the milder mountain where Sásho spent sixteen months without coming down. The room smells of chemical detergent and makes you sick. You notice that your clothes smell of sheep and smoke. There are three big roadside restaurants to choose from. You order a feast of five salads in the Turkish one, hungry for fresh vegetables, but you can't eat much unless you walk. Walking along the flat road doesn't feel like walking. Your body has changed, your perception has changed. You scan the perimeter for signs but all you find is people moving in and out of doorways, chairs and cars. It is a blank, horizontal world. Everything feels disconnected, like neurons firing at random without quite making up a brain. People look like they've lost something, but what is it? A blanket of ignorance covers the world.

After three days without walking uphill, you are gripped by shepherd's syndrome: your body feels like cement. Your hips and legs are stiff. The animal in you wants to break out and run. You are alarmed at the thought that this is your normal life. And if you want to change that and take up walking as a way of life, you have two choices:

shepherd or vagrant. Once, there were more options: travelling bard, itinerant this or that, soldier, healer, geographer. Many sedentary professions used to move.

'Wow, I don't know anyone who's been as high up as that,' says the young hotel receptionist. 'I've never even been to Orelek.'

But her grandfather was a shepherd who spent months in happy isolation with his flock. Just bring me bread and a calendar, he said.

'It's incredible you went up there,' says a seller at the market stall when I tell her it's a shepherd I'm buying T-shirts for. I also buy a wicker mat for the dirt floor of the hut. 'I wouldn't go to those places if you paid me.'

'It's good there are still people who do such a thankless job,' says another stall seller.

These market peddlers used to travel constantly. A Gypsy woman sells rugs and bedding out of a van and spends her time driving from one town market to another, sleeping in the van. I realise there is a whole circuit of small traders like her who follow in the footsteps of the nomads. They are poor but they get to see places and faces close-up. The last of the rug people.

I open my laptop and my fingers struggle to type. They are too thick and have almost forgotten their way around the keyboard. Must I squeeze my experiences into such a small space when they are so much larger? As large and layered as the mountain. I look the same as ever, but I feel like a giant. Something has expanded. I don't know how to explain this. Between the lower world and the upper world there is a problem of language.

And all the time, the earth is trying to make contact. I sleep in the afternoon heat of the gorge with the balcony door open to the Melo. The peaks beam a message, the risen ground hums. Not the humans. They have nothing further to add. It sounds like a river, like I'm in Black Water again but it is the hot wind running through the leafy crowns of the linden trees. The same wind I heard during my afternoon naps in the meadows of Orelek. The wind travels from impossibly afar, like another time. Anima comes in the balcony door to stroke me and go on its way. It is still travelling now. One day, I will go with it.

I sat at the computer all week, only leaving the hotel to get take-
away food and walk down the hot, shaking road. At night, bored
teenagers in skinny jeans went up and down the street, listened to
music, looked for adventure and finding none, ate takeaways and
went home. I imagined them at Black Water with the animals. They
wouldn't be bored there.

Countless times a day, I scanned Thunder Peak. There was nothing remotely as interesting in town. The peak changed with the light
and the weather, and never looked the same twice. I wondered where
Sásho had taken them today. I saw him sitting on the edge of the bed,
smoking in the dark with Muna under the bed. When he didn't call
at all, I knew his phone battery was flat, then a thunderstorm struck
and Thunder Peak disappeared. Hail hammered the gorge, trees bent
down, Melo looked like it was about to fall and bury the town. The
higher floors of the mountain seemed to move. If Sásho had taken
them up to the lakes, they would be stuck without shelter. The stony
path to the lakes became a slippery cascade during rainstorms. The
wind was like a hurricane and up there it would be strong enough to
pick you up off the ground.

I had to admit that the desolation of not knowing was more bearable down here where I could play soothing music and have small
comforts. Even if comfort was an illusion. Sometimes illusion helps.
I called Kámen for a dose of reality but when I reached him, I felt
worse. He hadn't heard from Sásho either. He too thought they
might be stuck at the lakes without shelter. The difference was, he
only worried about the animals.

I asked him when he was next going up. Sometime next week, he
said. In the gorge, Kámen was the stuff of legend and rumour. People
asked if he still made cheese. Some weren't sure if he was still there in
his wuthering heights.

The storm lasted for two days and two nights. On the local news,
a shepherd went missing. The dogs took the flock home and he was
found under a tree four days later: heart attack. What they didn't say
in the news is that his last thought was about the animals: will they
make it back? I was angry at the sheep. It's for you, you spoilt godmothers, that he and the dogs risk their lives and you won't even say

thank you! But it was displaced anger at Kámen, and the anger displaced something else.

The hotel was empty and I let myself in and out of a back door when the owners went home. After the storm, I walked down the road with the hot wind blowing in my face and looked for the two black storks above the gutted factory. The lorries were big like deadly ships. Cypresses, rosemary, fig trees, vines and willows. The river was turbid. Trees had fallen, roofs had come off. I looked for a suitable ruin. There were many. Is there a place for us in the lower world?

'For you, yes,' Sásho said. 'But I've become unfit for human society.'

I read the brand names on the lorries: Ljubljana, Global Sistem, Veliko Tarnovo, Magdak, Romania, Ultra trans, Polish beef, Greece, Papadopoulos Limited. A babel of products. Lorry drivers stepped down heavily from their cabins and crossed the road in flip-flops to buy bread, salami, beer, olives and spare headlights. They are a nation in themselves who live between Sofia and Athens, Hamburg and Istanbul, an existence parallel to the mainstream. Transhumance on wheels. The lorries are their horses, they complain of this dog's life but can't give it up and only their colleagues understand. The goods they carry are made in one country, transported through several others and make their way into my shopping list: small clock, charging battery, kitchen sponge, coffee, chocolate.

In the shop, I saw Marina who was buying crates of provisions for the next camp. She was frowning with stress and limping from some injury, and since I couldn't help her, it was best to leave her to it. The next day in the shop I ran into Stamen and Orhan. Stamen had stabbed himself with a steel rod and was getting a tetanus shot. Orhan was helping him.

'One lot has got to go from Prairie to Fat Oaks. The main flock has just gone up to the huts. Six hundred heads. Six dogs.' Stamen summed up his chess moves. 'And already there's trouble. Sheep reported missing. I've been up at the ridge for two days, patrolling.'

He asked how things were in Black Water.

'Fine,' I said, 'apart from the drinking.'

'You've done well in that boot camp. You need military training for it. Rivers, wolves, drunkards. It's not for everyone.'

When Stamen lived in Orelek, several shepherds met sudden deaths. One fell into a ravine chasing an animal, two others had heart attacks.

'When you next go up to Horse Plaza, remember it wasn't always empty like that,' Orhan said. 'Imagine hundreds of Karakachan horses. The only ones that can make it up there.'

Then he shook my hand. Once you'd done time in Black Water, people in the club treated you differently. It was a very small club but I was proud of my membership.

Stamen squeezed into the Lada and I saw the gory wound on his forearm. Even in their injuries, Stamen and Kámen were like Janus twins.

It's been a week in the fully human world where there is no place for animals. It has shown me something: we are a monoculture. Like those fields of single crops that go on for miles. The single crop is Anthropos. We have built a flat, boring world for ourselves on top of the original one in which we were just one component of a web that constantly moves, like plasma. This is what the shepherding life has shown me.

I see that most of what we do is try to fill something that can't be filled. I can't fill it either, in the lower world, and I realise that the only way is up. It's an instinct. It's the way of the free animal, to go up and down and up again. There was a wolf Marina collared when he was a cub and she followed his peregrinations over a decade. She called him Etip, after his birthplace. Etip left his family before he was two, to seek out greener pastures. He came down from Etip to the Orelek hills, crossed the gorge and for a while roamed the other mountain, then returned to his native one with a partner. When you're down, you want to go up. When you're up, you want to come down. You like this mountain, but you yearn to reach the other one. You need both, the variety nourishes you, it makes you alive. There's a language that goes with it.

When are you going up?

He's coming down for a day.

We're not taking them up for another week.

When are you bringing them down?

And always, you are adding items to your list then crossing them off. Sásho finally calls, from Vasko's phone, and it's been so long I don't recognise his faint voice. The relief is like putting down a heavy sack.

'Is that a waterfall roaring?'

'No, the river has risen like crazy.'

'How are you?'

'Fine, but it's a bit tragic with the sheep.'

A sheep was crushed by a rock so badly during the storm that he couldn't even cut off the ear with the number. Worse yet, two hikers called the national park to report four black sheep along the ridge that divides the two cirques.

'But they're not ours, I counted the flock,' Sásho says, sounding strained.

The communication blackout has made him anxious and blue, like me. He relies on The Privateer and Vasko for all information. He can't sleep, wondering where I am, worried that I'll be worried and that Kámen is worried about the missing sheep.

'Have you been drinking?'

'No! Just a bit of wine. I told you, I don't have a drinking problem. The other news is, the foal is no more.'

Then we get cut off. My mind is made up. I will move back to Orelek tomorrow and go up with Kámen, whenever that happens.

Outside the shop, I ran into Velin.

'Ah, you're still here, excellent!' he said. He was wrapped up in worries about his mother who was in the capital with a carer but he invited me for a wine tasting at his house and offered me a bed, seeing that my direction of movement was up.

'I have beds,' he said. 'It's visitors I don't have.' I slept in a room with twenty beds.

The road to Orelek was strewn with fallen rocks that nobody had cleared. I stopped to move the smaller ones. Trees were splintered.

Velin's reds were some of the finest I'd tasted.

'Kurt Vonnegut said: "When I look for a book I want to read but can't find it, I write it." I'm like that with wine.'

We sat at a big table in his laboratory-like kitchen and swirled the ruby wine in our glasses. One was the robust local Mavrud grape, one of our blackest wines, he said, and the other was a Georgian variety called Saperavi. It tasted of tart berries, leather and – what is it?

'Hawaiian cigar,' he said. Exactly.

'Every drop here is from the grape, I'm proud of that. It's been sitting for thirteen months so we have to let it breathe a bit.'

His dream was to make Pinot noir, but it wasn't an autochthonous grape. It's the finest wine, he said, like being touched by a silk hanky – it's there and not there. Velin had grown up with parents who loved the mountain and took their boys on blueberry and raspberry gathering expeditions, then made wine at home.

'There were fermentation processes around me,' he said. 'I inhaled wine before I could walk. Even my porridge was made with wine, 'cos my mother didn't believe in cow's milk.'

The wine tradition in this region is old, the Thracians famously drank their wine undiluted, unlike the Greeks. But the Georgians are older, he told me. Like us, they made their wine in clay pots but they never had the vine extinction that we had. In the eighth century, a puritanical ruler called Khan Krum banned the cultivation of vines to eradicate drunkenness, literally, for he decreed the uprooting of all vineyards.

'But a little something always survives.' Legend claims that the one kind that survived was Mavrud because a woman grew it secretly and fed her son with the grapes, then with the wine and called the boy Mavrud.

'But the native web was destroyed and it was never the same again,' said Velin. 'The only guaranteed autochthonous sorts we still have are Mavrud, Pamid and Keratsuda which is a white grape, dry but sweet and traditionally picked until first snow.' It was best kept in barrels with 'the mother'. I snacked on Keratsuda grapes every time I passed the roadside vineyards in the gorge.

'In Georgia by contrast, there are 550 native sorts. In biology, whenever there is so much variety, you know there's something ancient going on.'

During Communism, Georgian agronomists visited the Struma region and two Georgian vines were planted: Rkatsiteli and the Saperavi we sipped.

'I'm just a biologist. But this is my art.' We savoured the wines and snacked on the fresh goat's cheese I had bought in town from a cheese maker called Andrea.

'Now, here's something,' said Velin. 'There were seven so-called blue zones on this planet. They're down to five now. Where humans and animals can live a completely healthy organic life. It's about air, biodiversity and, get this, the consumption of goat, sheep and buffalo milk products. Not cow. This region used to be one such zone until the communists wrecked it.'

Corsica and Sardinia still qualified as a blue zone, in part because of their surviving transhumance and their montane biospheres.

'Cows were never kept for milk here.'

Cow's milk is the hardest to digest for humans and other animals and has none of the health benefits of the other milks, which is why so many humans have an intolerance to cow's milk. The rise of cow milk in the Western world's diet is a result of large-scale stationary farming, nothing more.

Among the nomadic shepherds, drinking cow milk was unheard of. Pastoral communities kept goats for domestic needs, but cows were a sign of settled shepherd farmers and were only kept for meat. The Yuruks were the most open to having animals other than sheep, and the Karakachans the least.

Everything was connected. The transhumance trails overlapped with the wine and gourmet trails. The animal people and the wine people met along those trails and exchanged goods: cheese and yogurt for wine, sausage and sheepskins for wine.

People fell in love on these trails, ran away with another tribe, swapped clothes, stole rams, horses and wine barrels wrapped in goat-hair blankets and always, some seed was blown by the wind and ended up in unexpected places. Between lower earth and upper earth, creatures met and exchanged currencies.

Wine trails, animal trails, rug trails. In this thrilling geography, life was tough but never boring. The Balkan Wars and First World War emptied the wine trail, and the Second World War emptied the pastoral trail.

'I'm towards the end,' Velin said matter of factly, like a biologist. 'I don't know if I'll make Pinot noir and it doesn't matter. What matters is that someone carry the torch.'

In the morning, he saw me off with a pack of dried ceps and a lump of kashkaval cheese.

'Take these,' Velin said. 'An offering to the spirits of the old trails.'

The cheese was made by an old man in the milder mountain across, a hereditary sheep's cheese maker. This was once a profession and there were lineages of *mandrajii*, dairy artisans. He was the last in his line, his son took care of the family sheep. He operated out of old dairy rooms where the elaborate alchemy of kashkaval took place: the 'sweating' or bathing of the fresh curd in hot water, the maturation which took several months, the checking, the wrapping and unwrapping and spell-muttering, like with a baby. His nutty kashkaval with a subtle undertone of olive-oil was in equal parts crumbly and stretchy and rivalled the finest pecorino of Italy, the only difference being that it sold for 5 euros a kilo, had no geographical appellation and the cheese maker didn't have a mobile phone so you had to drive up to his village past the beautiful tributary of the river lined with millennial sycamores, past the remains of the mosque, enter his rose garden where he sat at a table with a sad face and a strong drink, and ask: 'Got any left?'

'None left,' he'd say, his jaw set. Then, he would shuffle into his lab to double-check, seeing that you'd come all the way from the other mountain.

Kámen sits at the table, head in hands, too exhausted to even smoke. He has just driven around the mountain the long way and hiked up over Thunder Peak, down to Horse Plaza and to 'our' lakes, in search of the four reported black sheep. In the rain. Then he'd retraced his steps, a twelve-hour day. The park have issued him with a trespassing act for the four sheep. They do this to flush out livestock owners from the highlands and even when it's a groundless accusation, by the time you prove that it's groundless, you've lost time, money and strength. Today's wild sheep chase was typical. I met a breeder elsewhere who'd been hit with fifteen fines in one season.

At the moment, the existence of the four black sheep on the ridge can neither be proven nor disproven.

'It could be a false signal. Some hikers see wild goats and think they're sheep and vice versa,' I try to reassure Kámen but he can't be reassured.

He hasn't spoken with Sásho by phone. Why not? He shrugs. He'd rather trek for twelve hours in the rain. And anyway, he doesn't believe Sásho when he says the flock is all there and suspects one of three scenarios, I know it even before he says it. One, Sásho lost the sheep without realising. Two, Stamen's shepherd stole four sheep from our flock, with Sásho's connivance. Three, someone from the park is doing Kámen a nasty turn by putting in a false report, and the number one suspect is Stamen.

'Well, Sásho is not an idiot not to realise that he's lost four sheep, and in the second scenario – no, he wouldn't do that to you,' I say.

And Stamen has better things to do than steal your sheep, I think but don't say it.

'Or could they be Stamen's sheep?' I say.

'He is capable of anything.'

Kámen sees betrayal and subterfuge in all directions. What do I know, maybe he's right? There *is* betrayal and subterfuge. It comes with the territory.

Tomorrow, we go up. I know it from the list on the table: bread, cigarettes, voucher, frankfurters. It is unfair that Kámen must drive and trek 2,000 metres two days in a row for no good reason except corruption in the system. Some senior management in the national park were clueless. All they did was count tourist heads.

'The other worry is, the flocks got mixed, just as I feared,' Kámen says. Yep.

'That's why Sásho was not taking them up the same route as the others,' I say pointedly but he ignores my point.

'It puts my animals at risk. All I can do is trust the collective immunity of the flock. If they catch The Privateer's disease, it might show up in winter. Lambs are born but there's no milk and they die. It can decimate the flock. Twenty years of my life.'

I go to bed with a hollow feeling. The next day, I sit in the van with Kámen and Theo and leave the lower world behind. Theo gives me the front seat like a gentleman. In the van, Kámen and I try to have a conversation but he rejects everything I say, I disagree with everything he says and silence is better. Tolerant Theo sits in the back, not taking sides, waiting to be a beast of burden. What great sons Kámen has, I think, I hope he appreciates them, at least.

The last section of the road to The Beeches is almost impassable. The storm has dug out furrows and trees have collapsed but luckily, someone has passed before us and cleared up a bit, either The Privateer or Stamen.

The path is still strenuous with 10 kilos on your back. Theo waits for me and we even allow ourselves a short break on Kamen klet. Once when he was younger, he got lost here carrying luggage with his father, who went ahead and didn't wait for him. It was dark and scary.

'But I survived. What I've learned here I couldn't learn elsewhere. It'll serve me for the rest of my life,' he says. 'But I need to do my art.'

He shows me his latest pencil drawings of Michelangelo's David on his phone, and they are hugely accomplished. We climb the panoramic terraces with our packs and discuss how notions of beauty have changed over the centuries.

By the time we arrive at the hut, Kámen has saddled Mimi. It's a shock to see her without her brave foal who climbed these terraces like a trooper.

And now they're off on another course with Mimi! For dog food. There is dog food in the porch but more is needed.

This is a nightmare, I think, and sit down to catch my breath and wait for Sásho. Three hours later, father and son are back at the hut and unload the dog food. Mimi is freed from the saddle and slowly moves away, followed by the faithful stallion, parents without a child.

Another Herculean task accomplished, Kámen inspects the fencing and picks up a broken plank with displeasure.

'Nothing gets fixed. He doesn't care,' Kámen says. 'They're not his animals.'

I grit my teeth. One day, Sásho will walk away with nothing but the clothes on his back and his final wages if he's lucky, and you will have your flock and your dogs and your whole cursed kingdom of Orelek.

'I'll fix it,' I say, hoping that Kámen goes away quickly. And they do, because this is not the end of their day. As soon as they get to Orelek, Kámen must drive his son to the capital because Theo has an exam.

'Come on,' he says to Theo. 'Enough lazing about in front of the telly.'

Even radiant Theo is too drained to smile goodbye and anyway, we're not into niceties here. They're off across the valley, walking fast, separate and bereft.

Sásho has been doing laundry. A duvet is being aired and there is a pot of butter beans, without carrots. Beans, lentils, beans. And I forgot to bring carrots. I have difficulty lighting the stove, everything is damp. The sheep have been passing in front of the hut and their droppings are inside the porch and the hut itself. I sweep, and place down the wicker mat. When I unpack, I see what I should've brought: more veg, more towels, more tin mugs. It's almost like starting again. Kámen has brought up the usual, for Sásho: white bread, waffles, cigarettes, the awful frankfurters and of course, a large plastic bottle of rakia. I immediately pour out half of it and hide the rest.

If there weren't hundreds of kilos of dog food to bring up, we could have had more comforts for the humans, like blankets to line the drafty sides, a few jars of yogurt or wellies to wade through the mud. On Sásho's side, a bramble has pushed through the plastic lining. Its leaves shout with sap. Everything is frantically alive.

A skinny figure, stick in hand, descends the vertical slope, his cows out of view. I walk across the riverbed to meet him halfway in the valley. He is sober and I am almost glad to see him.

'How are things?'

'Same old,' he smiles shyly. 'A madhouse. Your foal is gone and two of our calves.'

But Vanya and Constantin are still here. I see the boy on the slope, coming down with a stick. I have brought him a notebook with a pen and give it to Vasko to pass on.

And finally, at dusk, a dark blob spills down from the dwarf-pine. *Beeeeee. Van-van-van.* The energy changes at once, as if liquid lava has run into the empty cup of the valley. They've been to the lakes. Behind them, a two-legged. He won't see me but will see the smoke. An anthropologist said: one of the basic human needs is to have someone wonder where you are when you are late coming home.

The dogs run to greet me in a homecoming euphoria. Sásho carries driftwood on his shoulders. A tired smile flashes in his baked face.

'Every day I imagined smoke from our chimney. But today it's real.'

LIKE DEVILS

Mimi had never done this before, but now she came up to the table where we sat with tea watching the morning spectacle of the sun and looked at us sadly, as if asking: Why? Why did they take him away? The stallion was behind her.

'I wonder how she feels,' I said.

'Bad,' Sásho stroked her nose and gave her slices of bread which she ate, sadly.

'Was it a wolf or bear?'

'I thought it was wolves 'cos they've set up camp by the dwarf-pine. But look.'

Across Mimi's chest was a raw scrape, exactly like a bear paw. It could be that she stood up to the bear who took her child or an injury from yesterday's trek with the luggage. The other mare came over too, and her wound was still there from the precipice accident. She had just been unsaddled and freed by The Privateer and Vasko who used her to bring up provisions from The Beeches. It was my first day back in Black Water and it was a Tuesday.

'Oh God,' I said. 'Black Tuesday.'

'Yep. The Privateer is staying the night so we'll have the boy with us.'

Another guy had come up with The Privateer, an ex-cop turned herbalist. He and Sásho hung out one summer when he came up for herbs, and liked each other a lot.

'Kámen brought up rakia but I poured it out,' I said.

'Good. It's better that way.' Sásho opened the gate to let the flock out. White mucus like snot came out of their noses. False hellebore again?

'No, something else. Just a cold, I hope. I thought Kámen would see them and tell me what to do. But nobody tells me anything. And if I wait for him down here when he comes, he'll complain.'

All this could be solved with a simple phone call but simple things were not favoured in Kámen's kingdom. I'd brought up two charging batteries for our phones but they too had to be plugged into the mains after a few days.

While the flock grazed close to home and the dogs chased long-legged wolf-cubs that I first thought were hares, we caught up on lower earth and upper earth matters. Last night, when they came down with me watching them, Sásho found a dead ram. Dead from a head butt with another ram. His brains were dripping out and 'his torches missing', as he put it. Too heavy to move, the rams weighed 70 kilos, so we'd leave him for the dogs and the wolves to distract them from the sheep and the surviving foal.

And the four missing sheep?

'Bit of a riddle,' he said. He was coming down with the flock one evening when Vasko told him that The Privateer had called to say that half a flock had been seen on Horse Plaza. Half a flock! No way, he thought, that's not mine!

That same day, Sásho was up at Etip's when four men came up the track who looked to Sásho like park rangers because hikers didn't know this trail. The dogs frightened them. Sásho wondered if they had taken revenge with a report of phantom sheep.

'Or they might have seen chamois and thought them sheep,' I said.

'No,' Sásho said, 'it was malicious.'

He'd counted the flock that evening and yes, a few seemed to be missing.

'Bloody hell! I counted them again the next day. And I've got them all, this time. Nine bells, eight white ones. But it'll be my fault, no matter what. I'm prepared for the worst.'

Any chance Stamen could have done something, just to make Kámen's life hell?

'There's always a chance of that but my animals are all here, for the record.'

Later, it was whispered on the grapevine that four of Stamen's sheep were missing but that couldn't be proven either and it was not clear who originated that rumour. The Privateer and Vasko, perhaps.

'So that's it, same old,' he summed up, 'at least you had a bit of variety.'

I told him about Velin and his silky wines that Sásho has never tried, about running into Stamen, my work deadlines I'd caught up with, the market in town, my anguish during the storm. He couldn't sleep either. The first few nights, he thought I was still here.

'I heard you say: You're snoring! But I'm just clutching your sleeping bag. I lie awake and smoke till I can't breathe. I worry that you won't come back, that I'll never see you again. Everything is shaking in the storm. I brace myself for the worst. Then, just as I drift off at dawn, that plague starts shouting at the cows.'

In the evening, he'd bring the flock down and look at the valley for signs of life. The other hut is smoking like crazy but our hut is cold and empty.

'Did you drink a lot?'

'No, not me! Just a glass of wine or two.'

I didn't ask where the wine came from.

Muna and Balkán are an item, except at night when she still sleeps under the bed.

'Muna, go sleep with your boyfriend. You've cheated on me!'

At night, the stove at our feet was hot but cold air blew at my head again. I could hear the flock breathe with their collective breath, occasionally a ram butted the fence. Sásho snored with his arms around me, Muna snored under the bed, the bramble plant sprouted new leaves, the dogs growled. I had forgotten how it felt when everything is alive all the time, inside and outside. You sleep differently. Your sleep bristles with things. They move through your sleep as if you never stopped moving across the land.

And now I couldn't sweep the sheep crap that was everywhere. The sheep drank from my tub of hot soapy water and pushed it over. Muna bled all over the place because she was in season and the tap was too far and I had to walk through mud to get to it, then the mud went into the hut and Topi and Redhead had taken to lying in front of the door, so I tripped over them. I threw the broom on the ground.

'Don't get angry, dear, it's the nature of it. You've forgotten,' Sásho laughed mildly and hugged me. 'Tomorrow, we'll go to the lakes and see if you fancy setting up camp there for a while. Just us and the animals. Will you come fly with me?'

Yeah! He lifted me up and the valley span around us. Muna laughed with her three voices. It was a perfect world again.

The tent was on the agenda every summer. Sásho had done it on his own. That way, the flock had the juiciest pasture without the dangers of taking them up and down between Black Water and the lakes. The tent and sleeping bags packed onto saddled Mimi, rucksacks on backs with provisions and a small camping stove, we would migrate to the lakes and live there for a week, undisturbed by Black Water problems. I began to daydream.

The euphoria of our reunion helped me readjust to life in a muddy pen with six hundred sheep, eight dogs, a bear behind us, an unknown number of wolves on the perimeter and crows circling the carcasses of sheep who may or may not have a contagious illness.

But by the afternoon, things had turned and all our plans were scattered to the wind. It was not day by day here but hour by hour, I remembered now. It started with Sásho going down the nettle path to the other hut. I followed, curious about the visitors.

'Thanks for the notebook,' Constantin said. He was subdued and his mother looked more glum than usual. Sásho, Vasko and the cop-turned-herbalist were fixing the pen.

The Privateer was a tall, hunched man of fifty, with a tragic face that had seen things best not discussed. The Privateer and Kámen badmouthed each other, but when it came to Black Water, it was friendly phone calls: 'You going up this week, colleague? I've got some stuff for the hut.'

A lot of The Privateer's sheep were dying and he scanned the slope. Later, when our flock were in the pen, he came over to check there weren't any of his mixed in. There were, two. His had red paint marks on their backs, ours had blue and pink.

The flocks had got mixed in the fog. Several of ours went to their pen, to join our two rams who were still there. Sásho retrieved the ewes but couldn't get the rams back. It was impossible to drag two rams across 500 metres against their will, though eventually he and Vasko did it. In the meantime, our rams inseminated The Privateer's ewes. He had sustained big losses, and there's enough for both, Sásho said, why shouldn't he have some nice lambs in winter? We shouldn't be selfish! This annoyed Kámen no end. 'Those are my finest rams!' he complained, 'and The Privateer is probably tipping Sásho,' which I knew not to be true. Kámen couldn't fathom pointless generosity. He also hadn't spent a summer at Black Water lately and had forgotten the implacable laws of the place.

Another of these laws was that what happens here, stays here. This is why The Privateer looked at me askance, not sure of my intention, and reaching the conclusion that he'd rather I weren't here. I pulled him aside and said: 'Life is peaceful until you and Kámen bring the drink. Then all goes to hell and there's a child here. Please stop it.'

He shrugged: 'If we don't bring it, they'll go trekking to the alpine lodges to buy it there,' he said. The nearest lodge was a three-hour trek, the same length as a return trip to The Beeches.

The Privateer was not a livestock lover like Stamen and Kámen and he had other businesses in addition to this. He was typical of the pastoral entrepreneurs benefiting from the subsidy system but he'd been into cows for many years and unstintingly put in the gruelling legwork and all it took to keep this operation going: the upkeep of the hut, the care for his cowherds, the difficulties with the national park and with Kámen and Stamen who both regarded him with contempt, and the general cliff's edge of Black Water. He may not love animals but I could think of any other enterprise that was easier than this, and he chose this.

I sat at the table with Vanya and the child while sheep were being counted and pens fixed, nervous about the imminent drinking. Two hours later, I came back to find Vasko slicing salami in slow motion, the ex-cop herbalist smiling soberly, The Privateer busy somewhere and Sásho with a glass of rakia in front of him. When he saw me, he tipped it on the ground, but it had started. 'Come, join us dear', he got up from the tree trunk so I could sit down. Everyone was ill at ease, each for their own reasons. Sásho was torn between wanting me to stay and wanting me to go so he could drink properly, but also torn between wanting to show me off to these men yet not wanting them to look at me too much because it was hour by hour here and territorially speaking, there were three of them against him.

'Consti, tell Kapka that I only drank wine when she was away,' Sásho turned to Constantin.

'Not Consti, Constantin. You drank wine and rakia,' the boy said. 'Quite a lot.'

Sásho ruffled his hair.

'The flock needs to be brought home,' I said in a stern voice.

'They know the way, I'm not a nanny,' Sásho said.

Vasko laughed like a hyena. The cop-turned-herbalist regarded me with friendly interest. Instead of storming off, I should've stayed. If you can't beat them, join them.

Back in our hut, I lit the fire and cooked a courgette and tomato casserole. At dusk, the flock and the dogs simply brought themselves home. They surrounded me and the fire, drank from the soapy water and entered the pen, sensing that the humans could not be relied upon tonight. I closed the gate on them and fed the dogs who were mellow. They knew the score. The fire kept going out. I sat at the table and all eight dogs, even Balkán, lay in a circle around me. The smoke stung my eyes.

I was descending into it and couldn't stop it. The kind of anger it upsets me to see in the world, that sparks off war and can't stop its own momentum, the anger of the spurned, the wilful and the mean. It starts off like fire, becomes cold like steel, then explodes and burns everything, leaving ashes behind. Some old wound was reopened here. There are no alcoholics in our family but alcohol is separation and separation is like death.

I climbed to the dwarf-pine where the wolves were camping and sat on a rock to survey the land. I'll observe myself as if from the outside. The other hut puffed away and our fire was a thinning ribbon, like a farewell, like the last day of the season.

A forest of symbols, this is where I was. Baudelairean territory. Black Water, *mon semblable, mon frère.*

On a stony ridge below Etip's, four animals stood, looking my

way. The missing sheep? No, they were chamois, majestic like mountain queens and kings.

'We're in the upper world,' I said to Constantin later in our hut.

'Yeah. But it's not that great in the upper world.'

'Do you love being with Kapka?' Sásho would ask.

'Yeah!'

'Me too. Is it okay being with me?'

'Yeah, but when you drink you're like a beaten dog,' said the child.

Darkness falls and the towering rockfaces assume identities I've
never seen before because I've never been in this spot at this time.
They are the intelligent faces of a planet we have inhabited without
really knowing it.

Once, I went through a period when living symbols appeared in
my dreams and a voice said: 'I am animus.' A lion's face that was the
sun. An eagle's face that was a lion, pulsing with an unearthly light. 'I
am animus.' I was trying to read Carl Jung's collected works, that's
what it was. But I had never had a dream that said: 'I am anima.' The
anima is hidden from my view. In Jungian psychology, animus is the
male part of a woman's psyche and anima is the female part of a man's
psyche. They are part of the contents of the collective psyche but
they have an autonomous life, which means that anima and animus
would exist even if humanity didn't. Either way, they take the shape
of moving images and infuse all our relationships. Even after reading
Jung, I am not entirely clear about this, but as a child I sensed that
somewhere, I had a brother and had lost him. I looked for him in the
faces of boys and men.

What civilised dialogues you can have with the wilderness, but
wilderness is sophisticated like that. It has all the components of civilisation. The four chamois were still there, like sculptures. First they'd
looked black, now they were grey. Sásho told me about a shepherd
who had lived alone in our old hut before the avalanche and ate a
mushroom he didn't know. During the night, he clearly saw ten wild
goats line up in front of the hut, like bearded devils with yellow eyes,
tongues out. *Eeeeee. Beeeee*, they mocked him. He ran inside, then out
again but they were still there. One, two, three, ten of them, like
devils!

In the open theatre of the mountain, your daimons come out to play. I blink and I am a grain of sand in the soil of Pirin. I blink and the two huts are not here, the fire has gone out. I blink and there are no more passions, just rocks, and four goats, like gods.

'There are hundred-year-old trees but there is no hundred-year-old power,' said the Karakachans. But emotions last thousands of years, without change. I walked down to the hut, past the eyeless ram and past the jaw and spine of a sheep. It looked like a fossil but it was alive just a few days ago and going *Beeee* in the cascades. It must be the loopy one that split from the flock.

I rekindled the fire. The dogs all came and lay their heads in my lap, even Balkán. 'The working Karakachan dog is aloof to humans, even its own master,' the breeder literature says. Balkán was the most aloof of the lot, but maybe I wasn't entirely human to him anymore.

Sásho and Constantin came down the nettle path. Sásho was unsteady and his eyes swam. I wanted to do with him what Kámen had done with the straying sheep during the exodus: pick him up and throw him on the right path again.

All our dogs barked at the new arrivals. Picking up on the disturbed mood and though she'd never done this before, Muna bit the child on the arm.

'He should've stuck closer to me,' Sásho declared, and sat at the table.

Constantin was crying from the shock. I hugged him and rushed to get the rakia from its hiding place and poured some on the puncture wound. It was just bruised and there was a little blood. Dazed with stress, I dished out some ratatouille for the three of us.

'Is there any more rakia? I need a drink!' Sásho declared. 'You want me to go back there, you want rid of me. But I want to drink at home.'

Constantin sat, unable to eat. He had endured another evening with drunken adults. He was brought here for safety by a drunk man and got bitten by a dog. And Sásho didn't care.

'Where's the drink?' he burbled on. 'I wanna be free!' He chased courgettes around his plate. 'You're always me, me, me. Think about me for once.'

A curtain fell before my eyes. I picked up the bottle and uncapped it. 'You wanna be free? Here.'

I threw the spirit in his face. There was the stillness of shock and I knew that something serious had happened. The rakia went into his eyes.

I held him immediately and he held me back in blindness, then he laughed, screamed and overturned the grill in the fire so that my casserole flew into the air. He walked blindly around the patch where Constantin had placed my writing table that the two men had overturned in a drunken log-cutting afternoon and when Constantin said 'That was for her, I'll fix it again,' they said 'Don't bother. It's in our way, we'll kick it again.'

Nothing could be built here. It was a casino. Constantin and I looked at each other, and he was the more composed. I fought back a panic attack. Sásho's eyes and eyelids became inflamed, like in a chemical burn. And now he wouldn't wash his eyes because that would make it worse, he insisted, like with pepper spray. As a child thief, he tried pepper spray on his own eyes to check the impact. It blinded him for half an hour but water made it worse.

'My eyes hurt but my heart hurts more,' he turned to me, blind and suddenly less drunk. 'I didn't think you'd do this. Now I know you're mean, mean, mean. And you're still perfect.'

None of us ate and Muna hoovered up the priceless kashkaval from The Grape. I extinguished the outside lights and we went inside. The sight in Sásho's one eye gradually returned but the other was not good. I was sure the damage was worse than he realised, anaesthetised as he was, but I tried to keep a cool head for the child's sake. I was racked with remorse: for doing this to Sásho, for doing this in front of the child, for adding to the chaos instead of dispelling it but Constantin was calm, he'd seen much worse. I took the torch to walk down to the other hut. I needed advice on spirit burns to the eyes.

'Don't go,' Sásho squeezed my wrist, 'they're drunk. They might attack you.'

'Yeah, don't go,' Constantin said. 'We could've Googled it. But now we have to sleep on it.'

He was the only adult here. I organised our three bedding pods with a duvet each. Child, me, Sásho. We sat on the bed, Constantin holding his notebook, me holding my sanity, Sásho holding a fag and sprinkling ash everywhere, and we ate peanuts.

The jokes that followed – Sásho with his terrible inflamed eyes making us collapse in hysterics with his Turkish and Gypsy accents, the late-night sharing of dreams and notebooks, it was all done on sheer nervous muscle. I laughed to stifle my horror that I might have damaged Sásho's eyes but we wouldn't know it until later, that I was now bound to Black Water and had a duty to stay until Sásho's eyes recovered. If they did.

And that the single thing that frightened me most in Black Water was – me.

'You are no different from me,' Sásho kept telling Constantin. 'You're gifted, you have zero support and I bet you have a sister somewhere that you're not allowed to see.'

The boy flinched.

'I don't want to talk about it,' he said.

'Stop it!' I said. 'He's not like you. He is his own person.'

'Tell me about your sister, do you miss her?' Sásho went on, and I could have thrown another drink in his face.

Then he taught the boy how to take a banknote from someone's trouser pocket. He put a fiver in the boy's pocket and talked him through it. Constantin listened politely, then took out the fiver:

'Let me give you this back, because it's not mine.'

Sásho looked at me and burst out laughing.

'Is that the best you can teach him?' I frowned.

'He's got to know some tricks. He can't survive from writing books!'

The two of them slept soundly. I put a cold compress on Sásho's eyes. The child slept, curled up and facing me. I lay on my back between them and prayed to any spirit that hadn't given up on us yet to help his eyes recover during the night, like the sheep who might be infected and must fall back on their collective immunity. The night was an abyss, I kept falling without reaching the bottom. I saw Sásho blinded, in hospital, with me at his side, bound like invalids for the rest of our lives. I saw myself explaining to everyone what I had done. I saw Sásho with his stick, a blind shepherd in the hills, a wreck because of me. My God, how much is wasted on this earth. This man, this boy. They were complete originals. The pool of the pampered people is full of the dull and the talentless, and here are brilliant fallen angels.

At one point, my anguish intolerable, I left my body as I fell down the abyss of Black Water. It was an impersonal thing, this abyss. It was my own psyche but my own psyche wasn't mine. It was everybody's. Rockfaces reconfigured and rejigged in the kaleidoscope of some cosmic magus. Everything shapeshifts, just give it enough time.

I lay between wizard-poet and rebel-fool in my forest of symbols. Storms, opiates, making love among gods and animals, nothing less than ecstasy could do for Sásho. I had joined *mon semblable, mon frère* and this was the price.

('What did you learn?' I'll ask Sásho in the winter.

'That I can't stop suffering,' he will say.)

At dawn, I climbed to Signal Rock and called an old friend who is an optometrist. She was in bed but I explained the situation.

'He should see a doctor. If not, start treatment with three types of drops. The main risk is chemical burn and infection. Of course, he washed his eyes for ten minutes with cold water?'

She told me to update her later. Kámen moaned down the line. 'Get Sásho to call me,' he said.

How lonely it was on top of that rock with the cold sun rising over the sphinx. The Privateer and Vasko were up early, surveying the cows. They looked at me across the white wasteland in an unfriendly way or maybe it was that everything looked hostile. I swung by their hut where Vanya offered me a coffee and sympathised, but 'you shouldn't have done that,' she said, 'my ex the alcoholic lost sight in one eye after an accident like this.'

'Put slices of raw potatoes on his eyes,' she advised, but neither hut had any potatoes left. I went down the desolate nettle path.

The sheep were snotty and pathetic in their pen, like children in a grotty orphanage deserted by the social workers, and the dogs were licking the remains of the ratatouille from the exploded fireplace. The pot lay on the ground.

Much of the day was spent on Signal Rock. Sásho came too. One eye looked terrible.

'What happened, mate?' Kámen asked.

'Nothing,' Sásho said sheepishly, 'the mistake was mine.'

'Can you see?'

'Like an eagle,' Sásho lied.

'Good,' Kámen said quickly, 'she made a drama out of nothing.' Then he hung up.

We were alone. What happens in Black Water stays in Black Water.

Between my anguished visions of catastrophe, my friend the optometrist who said the cornea could be damaged, Kámen who treated his own injuries the same way — by not treating them and Sásho who downplayed it, there was no middle way but somehow we found it. For the next twenty-four hours, Vasko kept to himself. We consoled each other, I put allergy drops in Sásho's eyes that didn't work, he took the flock out and brought them back in the rising wind, we laughed a lot in a pained way and I cooked with Muna and Topi who always stayed behind with me in the hut. I even fixed my writing table and chair that Constantin had made, though I didn't use it and it looked like a monument.

I began to enjoy things again but stayed in survival mode. It was the way Sásho had lived his entire life: in survival mode. That's why I was in trauma and he wasn't, because trauma had been his default state since the day he walked alone from the house where his mother and sister lived and took the wrong bus down nowhere road.

'That's why I drink, dear, to dull the pain but it makes it worse. It turns me into a lowlife. I'm a prisoner, going round and round. Please don't cry or I'll start too. Why are you crying?'

'Because I'm sober and sad, and I'll be leaving soon,' I said. And that puritan Khan Krum had been right to uproot all the vines in the land.

When my two companions woke up that morning, we breakfasted sitting on the bed: health bars and mugs of hot chocolate, except it was cold because Sásho was too hungover to light the stove.

'It's only one eye that's dodgy,' he reassured me. 'And you're still here. That's the main thing. Eh, Consti?'

'I don't know. But do you find it odd that this hut is so warm despite all the open spaces?'

'Consti,' Sásho said. 'Where do you learn to speak like this?'

The boy shrugged. We continued our conversation about dreams from the previous night.

'What are your dreams, my boy?' said Sásho.

'Well, I often have this dream where something is chasing me and I sprout wings and fly away, like a bird. But I'm not a bird.'

'I have the same dream!' I said.

'My dream is to break out of my drinking chains,' said Sásho. 'And then we can adopt you and put you back at school.'

Constantin rolled his eyes.

'I don't know,' he said. 'But today is a day for apologies.'

'Your mother needs to apologise for shouting at you,' Sásho said.

'Everything she does to me will come back to haunt her,' the child said.

'This applies to all of us,' I said.

Constantin did an illustration in his notebook, a figure with parted hair and wings being attacked by a homunculus.

'This is Uncle Sásho and a man like a horror who wants to grab him.'

Sásho laughed. Now Vanya called for the boy outside and I saw them off down the nettle path. His bite from Muna had darkened.

His mother stopped, 'where's your notebook?'

He'd left it behind but they were in a rush and I'd bring it to him later on, but they left that morning with The Privateer and never came back.

I opened his notebook and read:

'My sorrow, a short story:

I am a shepherd, and the stupid sheep keep scattering. Sometimes I want to kill them but it's not their fault. I, Constantin, will never give up on my dreams.'

There were vivid drawings of sheep and stars, flowers and trees and us, the protagonists of Black Water, fighting with our demons which appeared outside of us. In an act of generosity he gave us all wings, so we could fly away when the going got tough. Like now.

I drew in his notebook too and when I left Black Water, Sásho took over and noted each passing day in it, counting down to the exodus. The book of Black Water. We were all writing it, each in our own way.

THE WIND

The wind rose and didn't come down for three days. We tried to keep the flock close to home. The vertical slopes looked too risky in the strong wind. Sásho let the snotty-nosed sheep out of the pen, their coats fluttering.

The wind picked up soil from the ground and water from the river and threw it into the air. The smoke from the chimney and the water from the tap blew sideways. I opened the porch gate and the wind smashed it against the fence and broke it.

A lone skinny figure climbed among the pines after the white sheep whose number had shrunk by half. It was just the three of us now. Vasko was left with the sheep in the wake of Vanya's departure, having taken the cows to the high plateaux. We saw them sometimes at the top, motionless like Stonehenge.

Sásho moved the tap closer to the hut. We ran out of vegetables and I picked nettles to make risotto, clutching the bag from the wind. Strong wind unsettles me and I kept to the hut and the porch, only going out to fill water from the tap. I picked and burned the hundreds of fags left under the stove by the shepherds.

The sheep liked the wind, it gave them something to overcome. They really were Kámen's sheep! They ended up climbing towards Etip's and in the afternoon, Sásho climbed after them to get them back, leaning against the wind in his black clothes, and I didn't relax until I saw him coming down three long hours later. Walking home in his black hoody with driftwood on his shoulders and the black sheep behind him, he was nearly knocked sideways by the strong gusts. Mimi, the stallion and the mare with the foal sheltered in the pines, out of view.

After the accident with the eyes, everything had a hyperreal quality, like we were given a second chance. And the wind made it more so. Sásho wasn't blinded, we had forgiven each other, though not ourselves, and we had no idea when Kámen would come up but Sásho guessed it would be in another week or so. We held on to each other against the wind, grateful that the tribe were alive and unmaimed by end of day.

At night, we listened to Radio Gaia turned up loud against the wind. A regional talk programme was our favourite because of its practical concerns. One caller was selling black buffalo, another a tractor, another a corn field. One evening, a shepherd called with a song request. We could hear the wind howl and his dogs bark on the crackling line. 'Where are you?' asked the host. 'The Jackal,' said the shepherd, in Rila Mountain.

'That's north of here,' said Sásho.

The Jackal was an area of summer pastures once used by the Karakachans. Eleven thousand sheep had grazed there until the 1950s.

'You're in the eye of the storm,' said the host. 'How many sheep?'

'Four hundred.'

'Amazing. I love calls from people like you. 'Cos you're doing something real.'

'Aye. I wanna dedicate this song to the colleagues out there,' said our colleague. 'Aye. And the dogs. 'Cos we can't do it without them.'

'Muna, are you listening?' Muna was asleep under the bed. The song played. Sásho beamed. There were tears in his eyes. Mine too, I believe.

The next morning, Vasko came to tell us that there was another dead sheep, already dismembered. He sat on the floor of the hut by the stove. I was putting drops in Sásho's eyes.

'You wanna kill him with these drops,' Vasko croaked. He was convulsed by stomach ache and missed Vanya and the boy.

'Nah, don't need them,' he said. 'I'll find other ones, eh plague?'

'No plague, you won't.'

'Want some mint tea for your stomach?' I offered.

'You wanna kill me with your brews.' Vasko said. 'Got any doping?'

By now, I could predict it, like the carrot dialogue in *Waiting for Godot*.

The wind died down a bit that morning and we went to pick resin kindling behind Vasko's hut. You did this by hacking at one of several pines that had already been hacked. You aimed for the resiny core. The bark was tough like elephant skin and the old pines resisted giving up their essence. It was a war and we were the evil ones. If you hacked at it many seasons in a row, the tree was killed. Vasko had hacked a ladder into a massive old pine.

'Can't you find a younger one? These are valuable!' I said.

'There ain't any young ones,' he said. It was a mature forest. 'It's a shame but we need heat.'

It was hard going and dangerous, and after a few attempts with the axe I gave up and collected the fragrant splinters Vasko hacked off into a tub. Sásho avoided the hacking too. He preferred banter to heavy lifting.

'When Stamen and his father left, Kámen hired a shepherd called Nik,' he said, beginning one of his stories. 'Nik taught the shepherd-ing job to Moni the Mute. Anyway, Nik and another shepherd lived in the old hut before the avalanche. There was a bench on the porch. One night, they're lying dead drunk in the hut and Nik hears this banging noise outside. It's the bear, I tell ya, and gets up. And bloody hell, there's the bear lying on the bench, and snoring! He picks up the axe. Goddamn bear, now you'll leave my lambs alone! He lifts the axe, then the bear sits up and growls: Don't do it!'

The shepherd from the other hut had rocked up in the night and bunked down on his neighbours' bench. He wore a sleeveless fur jacket with a hood that he had sewn by hand himself. From a Karakachan sheep hide.

'It was a moonless night,' Sásho concluded.

Even I laughed, with my trauma from all their drinking. Here, experience becomes myth. You don't need time, it's instant. That's the shepherding life for you.

Vasko filled two tubs with resin kindling and gave us one, gener-ous as ever.

A fine rain fell. It felt like Sunday but it couldn't be, the alcohol hadn't run out yet. The whole mountain was empty. No pegs on Thunder Peak, just black crows and grey clouds that turned to fog.

Everything smelled of pine. The weather and the mood were almost stable, an unusual feeling in Black Water. It is hard, moving against the wind day after day. The last of the nomads did it for years.

Even after border crossings became a hazard, many nomads continued to move against the winds of change. But even within the national borders, in the final decades it became increasingly difficult for Karakachan companies to get permission for winter pasture. The authorities deliberately made their lives difficult. In 1944, a well-known family, the Kleftoyanakis, were trapped in snow for two months while waiting for permission to move their camp somewhere warmer and their entire flock died, 1,500 sheep. The owner, Yanaki, died at once. A few years later, a similar thing happened to another family, but some of were rescued by locals who dug them out of the snow and took them home. The owner, one Kosta Chilingirov, went off to buy winter feed from the nearest town, but when he saw that most of them could not be saved, he immediately sickened and died. Worse, in the final act of the destruction of the nomad, families were given no notice by the communist authorities. 'Otherwise, we would've sold our animals to have some cash at least,' said one man, recalling the final assault. But they were given no warning. Their animals were taken and they received nothing in return. This is how it ended for the last of the die-hards.

'Where do you get your gift with animals?' I asked Sásho.

'You don't need a gift. Just a feeling.'

When I did some research I saw that his mother's ancestors were likely settled nomads. His father's lot were displaced pastoralists. Their trails had crossed to produce Sásho then toss him back to the winds of fortune to fend for himself along the old paths. Some lines are indelible from the inner map.

On the stone floor of the ruined hut next door, we picked up a sheep label from the latest casualty.

'4328. She was not long for this world.' Sásho collected it for Kámen.

In the mid-afternoon, all three of us went up to Signal Rock to make phone calls but the wind cut off all signal and the wind had risen again. Enthused by the adverse conditions, our flock had gained too much altitude and were heading in the wrong direction.

'I'll get them,' Sásho said. 'You keep warm.'

He pulled up his hood and went after them, up into the steep pine woods where Vanya and Constantin had seen a bear, to Etip. With his black hoody and quick escape, he looked just like a Karakachan, a black fugitive.

He had to stop the sheep heading to the lakes and get them back down the same way, or some way. Vasko went back to his hut to resume drinking.

Two, three hours later, I'd cooked and enjoyed a siesta with Topi and Muna. I dreamt that a dead forest was closing in from all sides, covering pastures and sunlight, gobbling up space, squeezing us out so that we must make an exodus from this place by forming a thin black ribbon like the oldest sheep in the world, past the lakes to the head of the sphinx which is the end of the road or maybe just a launching pad.

Now I'm scanning the cliffs for signs of them. The wind has increased. The wind is a shapeshifter. One moment it's a caress on a sun-struck meadow, then it's a slap of acid in the face, followed by an erosion of confidence, until you become used to the seesaw of the fairground. The other day, I was desperate to leave. This morning, I was happy to stay. Now, the plastic covering of the hut flaps like a bunch of flags without a message. The wind tramples the hours in a funfair of wind. It keeps rising. I put on my windproof jacket and cross into the centre of the valley, leaning against the gusts, to watch the sun blaze one last time over the other mountain.

When I see Vasko struggling uphill to round up the sheep, I go towards him.

'He's not back!' I shout.

'He'll be back,' he shouts in reply. There is nothing more to say.

I cross the white bone desert to our hut and try to keep anguish at bay with chores, but I've run out of chores. I open an empty bottle to fill it at the tap and the wind plays a tune inside it. The porch gate screeches like it's about to break out of the fence and turn into a galloping wooden horse. I put a pot of water on the stove and it sings.

Inside the chimney, the wind screams at a high pitch, amused at how it is testing my sanity. Everything is alive in the wrong way. Our hut flag from the mountain rescue team is flapping like it's about to take off. A fat lot of good the rescue team are on a night like this.

I fear the wind because I don't know what it's capable of. I fear that, once unleashed, anima has no limits. Like me. Sásho went out in tracksuit pants and a hoody, with no jacket or hat, no water or food, four hours ago. Cold rain falls diagonally as if it is crossing the valley out from the map of the living. I stand outside and look at the glacier in the shape of an angel. And next to it, for the first time, I see an awesome creature. Two twin rock faces are divided by a funnel and there is a pre-historic dragon with its eyes rising from a reptilian snout. I want to show it to someone – look, that's incredible! – Sásho would appreciate it but he is not here. Something has happened. I scan the vertical faces until darkness falls.

The emptiness of the mountain is suddenly unbearable. I light all the torches we have and hang them outside, to help him orient himself. It's a moonless night. I drink tea and invite Muna inside. She is waiting too, pricking her ears at the slightest change of sound. And there are lots of sounds, but the wind makes them all. Topi is asleep by the bags of dog food. I feed them bread. The empty pen gapes like a wound. The bear-sensor is set off by gusts. A new roar of a thousand air drums rises. The wind begins its nocturnal military games.

I remember a folk song called 'The Mountain Has Overturned'. The vocal uses only a few notes, making your flesh crawl and your heart ache. I always wondered why it was so eerie. Now that I'm inside the song, I know why.

> The mountain has overturned.
> It has buried a pair of shepherds,
> two shepherds two friends.

The first shepherd pleads with the mountain: let me out, my lover waits for me. The second shepherd pleads: let me out, my mother waits for me. The mountain comes back: Hey you, pair of shepherds, a lover mourns you till tomorrow, a mother mourns you to the grave. End of song. We can guess the rest: she, the mountain who is always feminine, only lets out the one with the mother. Maybe she wants to keep the other one for herself.

I'm pretty sure I'd mourn Sásho to the grave. I've started already. I go out into the dark and begin to cross the valley with a torch. He is up there, several hundred metres from the valley floor. I try yelling 'Sáshooo' at the top of my voice but I can't walk against the wind and the dark and I can't even hear myself, the wind drowns all. The dogs at the other hut howl. I cry on the way back. My nerves are in pieces like the marble floor of our valley where I try not to twist an ankle. I wade across the icy river. I know why this is called Black Water. It's a geography of desolation. Had we been on Prairie or Fat Oaks, it would be different.

I lie on the bed with a small torch and the booming stove, Muna at my feet, and I calm the thump of my blood with relaxing music on my phone but battery is precious and I might need to climb Signal Rock in the morning to call Kámen for help. I turn it off. I turn on the radio to find our station, Gaia, but I can't get any station, just crackling as lower earth slips away.

Time passes without going anywhere. I run out of familiar things to think about. Everything begins to feel unfamiliar. The little clock tick-tocks to nine, five or six hours since he said: I'll get them. Everything slips away until all I have is faith, a little flame for all to end well.

The wind makes two dreaded sounds. When it passes through the pines, the pines lean and howl, like waves crashing in. Everything is water and air, no ground. The other sound is when it gallops down Black Water like an army of marauders or buffalo.

I go outside. Should I walk down the nettle path with a torch and see if Vasko and I can go looking for Sásho? Gosh, that's a torch coming down the nettle path! No, it's the eyes of a dog or a wolf. I'm not afraid of wolves but Vasko is drunk and I'm afraid of what I might do to him if provoked. The axe is right here. I pick it up, then put it back.

Sásho is the ultimate survivor and he's done this before. How little that helps.

It's fifty-fifty here with the animals, Sásho said. How right he was.

This work is penance. The shepherds do penance on behalf of the rest of us, for all the wrongs we have done to animals. How pointless that feels.

Nobody appreciates it. We are invisible. How desolate that is.

At 9:30, stars appear from behind clouds. How cold they are.

Muna barks with her feeble triple voice but Topi is quiet. I scan the super-familiar dwarf-pine line and see a black blob. Could that be the flock, coming down the wrong way? Half an hour later, it hasn't moved. It's just dwarf-pine. I hate it. The sky is a grey sarcophagus and a cloud hangs over the white sphinx like an omen. A double roar of wind and river blocks out any other sound, so there is no hope of hearing the bells or his voice if he is calling me. I know that the flock is stuck somewhere dangerous and won't come home until the morning. The question is, will Sásho spend the night with them. And whether he is stranded with a broken leg or a hypertension attack.

The black pines rise like pillars of the world. The torches of our hut illuminate the perimeter. I realise with shock that another thing Sásho doesn't have is a torch. Maybe he can use his mobile phone.

After ten, I hallucinate a human figure in the torch-lit valley but it must be the shadow of a cloud. In Karakachan folklore, Haros is the keeper of the underworld. Haros appears only to the dying. If you see him, your end or someone's end who is close to you is near. Haros is dressed in black, rides a black horse, has a black dog and not far off is his flock of black mountain sheep. He carries a scythe or sabre and he does not play the flute.

It is anima that plays all the instruments in tonight's orchestra. Yes, this wrecking force is the world's soul. The flame in my stove can turn to wildfire. Passion can lash out and blind you. There is nothing you can do.

I take a pointless inventory of the porch. There's the saddle. When there was a difficult birth or difficult death in a nomad camp, someone would take a saddle and uncobble it; to release the force that was stuck. I'm tempted. I look at the saddle. It is intricately cobbled and stitched and to dismantle it would take time and skill. The Karakachans bought hundreds of saddles from special saddle craftsmen, called *samardjii* from *samar*. Saddle making has been an extinct craft since the last saddle-maker, a Pomak in the Rhodope, stopped making them.

The nomads found that births, deaths and even cooking could not be completed until the flock came home for the night. It makes sense. With a missing Sásho, flock and dogs, everything is falling apart.

I lie and stare at the shaking roof, carried by the waves of the ocean, marauding armies galloping past, the river rising. If I stayed here for three months by myself, I would definitely turn to drinking. Or to God. Or to *something*. It's not the bear behind the hut or the wolves at the perimeter. It's not the storm or the cold. It's the void. I am inside a void and there is a void inside me. In this void, a little flame flickers, a breath, a soul. Psyche, the Karakachans called it. *Pshi-hee*. Not the standard Greek *psi-hi*. Nothing about them was standard. That's the whole point of being a wanderer. You cannot be standardised. When you stop wandering, you fall prey to the standard.

Pshi-hee. It is small but inextinguishable.

To dwell in the void for long periods of time, you have to be one of two things – a sage or a desperado. My years of meditation did not make me a sage. I am still terrified by the void but the little breath observes the moment and that is something.

Muna and Topi must have been asleep because they bark just as Sásho rushes into the hut. He looks like Haros. He has a thick piece of wood in one hand, like a weapon, and an unhinged look on his dirty face. I'm still hallucinating.

'Where is he?' He's looking for someone else, not me. He has lost his mind.

'Who?'

'Vasko.'

'What?'

'Did he come here?'

'No!'

He drops the wood on the floor and takes off his hoody with shaking hands. He hasn't quite seen me.

'His lights are off,' he says.

'And the flock?' I can barely speak, the nervous strain has stiffened my jaw.

'Up.'

The dogs too. They are stuck for the night. He is frozen, famished and paranoid.

On the way down, seeing the darkness of the lower valley, he thought Vasko had come to assault me or that I'd left Black Water with him, leaving only the lights on and an empty hut. To punish Sásho for his drinking, for everything being his fault.

'How could you think that!' I say.

But you could think anything here. He wolfs down some food and hot tea, refocusing his feral gaze and returning to language and sanity. The sheep could not be turned around on time and got stuck in an escarpment as night fell. It was neither up nor down, complete darkness, rocks everywhere. He'd stayed with them for a while, wet and freezing without shelter or even a lighter, then left them with the dogs and headed downhill but there was no orientation point in the black night. He shouted my name and looked for the two lights of the two huts, to show him which way to go and avoid falling off a cliff. Eventually, he saw one light. One, not two. When a shepherd is late with the flock, the other one always leaves a fire on, it's a law you don't break.

'And I thought: something's gone bad down there.'

'I thought you trusted Vasko with your life,' I said.

'But not with your life. And not when he's drunk. And deep down, I don't trust anybody in this world.'

There is no line between one thing and another here. Our innards are turned inside out and the outside comes in unfiltered. When even the hut fire is gone, little pshi-hi is the only beacon against madness.

In the morning, Sásho trekked against the wind again, to get the flock down and keep them close to home. I couldn't watch him walk away anymore. Fortunately, they were already coming down with the dogs, we saw the dark blob at the top of the cliffs.

'These sheep are nuts! They enjoy vertical rocks, rain, wind, height, everything that's hard – they love it!' I said.

Sásho laughed. 'That's why they're stoners.'

'You're a stoner too,' I said. 'Stoned even when you're sober.'

He lifted me up and we spun and laughed with the wind. We always ended up laughing for no reason, a wave of life force rushed through us when we were together, as if time opened and we fell in a swoop through this perfect blue world, like the two golden eagles we saw the other day when the wind first rose. They shot down like bullets and suddenly locked feet and surfed the crazy air currents in a skating dance.

'They remind me of us,' Sásho said. 'When I look at you, everything is alive. You make me fly.'

'You make me fly too. Then crash.'

Life with him is in bright colours. An old happiness flourishes in me, and an old wound. The rollercoaster, the merry-go-round, the plunging gondolas, the feeling of instant family that you could scream at and be forgiven, the desperation and the relief, then the moment that tears you apart, the vacated patch of grass and the life-long search for the lost face.

It was recovery day again. Sásho taught me some essential phrases in Kalderash Romanian, for example: 'Tomorrow morning you can fuck my daughter.' He didn't tell me where he'd had these language lessons, but hanging out with Roma for so long, you picked up the lingo of the road which was many-forked and many-tongued. Once, the road ended with yurts, now it comes to a dead-end in the ghetto where daughters are for sale. The wheels had come off the painted cart and span without direction.

Mimi and the stallion were on the other side of the river, in plain open wind, manes blowing as if they were running while still. They stood and looked at each other eye to eye, like before a wrestling match or a decision or maybe they were remembering their brave child. They held this position for half an hour, then they put their heads down and grazed again.

'I dreamt that the flock split at the top of the cliffs and just when the cliffs crumbled, they reunited and pulled back,' Sásho said.

I'd dreamt that my teeth were loosening like rocks in a storm.

The porch gate was smashed again and after Sásho fixed it, we stood against it inside the porch and watched our wind-whipped valley, leaning out like on a train. Toot-toot. The wind burned our faces red and whipped our hair. The clouds of Thunder Peak moved fast, as if time sped up. Perhaps if we stayed like this long enough, us and the horses, we would end up in a different place.

'This train is fast!' I shouted.

'Where are we going, dear?' he shouted.

We looked down the other way, to the other hut.

'That train has stopped,' Sásho said.

Vasko was fixing the electric fence. He came for a cold Nescafé and to listen to the radio because his was broken. We sat in the porch, like on that first morning when I told them I wouldn't last long. I had lasted quite long.

Vasko was blue about Vanya and the boy. He didn't say why they left but felt it was because of him. Vanya was fired by The Privateer, that's why, Sásho told me. Sheep required a delicacy that cows didn't. Cows were wholesale, sheep were bespoke and Vanya was a cowgirl. She had put out 10 kilos of salt for 100 sheep, which was 8 kilos too many and killed some lambs. But Vanya later told me that she quit because The Privateer hadn't had her registered locally and she didn't want to live in the cracks of the system. I believed all of them.

On the national news, damage was reported after the storm. A woman was killed by a lightning bolt. Hikers were advised not to walk or camp alone in the mountains because of bears. Bears were plentiful this year and had come into contact with trekkers on alpine paths. There were even cases of campers' food being stolen by them.

We laughed and turned the radio off. Tourists' lunches are nationally important but when a shepherd is maimed or dies a lonely death, it makes the local news at the most.

There was no talk about why Vasko had put his lights out. He'd been too drunk to care, we all knew it, and why analyse the terrors of the night when you have the new day to face?

CIRCLES AND LINES

The wind left our valley some time in the night with a message: strewn jackets and towels. The aerial party was over. A bright and clean new day, a day for the lakes. I checked my face in the little porch mirror, the only thing still hanging on a nail.

'Nice, eh? I stole it from a lodge.' Sásho grinned next to me. We looked frantically alive. My face was skinny. His eye was still inflamed. I packed food and a flask of tea while he checked the sheep for wounds and dodgy legs. It was a miracle that not a single leg was broken or twisted, even wee Mouse was intact.

All the dogs came. Muna and Topi were due for an adventure after days in the hut. The dogs were more focused when they went on a proper outing. Hanging out in the valley all day made them sluggish.

'They're like us. They need to move,' Sásho agreed. 'Or they become lazy.'

Kito limped badly and had bleeding cuts from a fight, either with Kasho or with a wolf. There was nothing we could do. He would limp until he stopped limping.

Sásho packed 10 kilos of salt for the sheep that he carried to a sheltered area of flat-lying stones. The sheep were fed salt every few weeks, something to do with the mineral balance in their blood and reproductive health. We climbed through the dwarf-pine grove, upstream the waterfall that sang a morning song, stroked by tall rowans with red berries. Elecampane! A now rare, yellow-flowering plant of the sunflower family with medicinal roots that cure clogged chests and make you high – the ancestor of pseudoephedrine. Bog cotton with miniature white heads fluttering in the breeze immediately took me to Scotland. Sunshine and stillness. The blue world was impossibly pure, like an initiation.

The sheep fell on their favourite hellebore.

'They like hellebore and I like hemp,' Sásho grinned. 'But hemp doesn't grow this high.'

He picked it in the Orelek hills and the tea gave him awesome dreams in his cell. The earth is perfect. It has everything. Then the alpine world opened up. The air changed. The grass was chlorophyll-green. Sásho showed me two springs with the coldest water that only shepherds knew.

'Remember the location,' he said. 'If I'm not here.'

The springs were icy and hidden under spongy grass.

The older sheep rushed to the salt stones before Sásho had put the salt down. They remembered. We left them to it and went to look for signal on top of some stone ruins where we settled for a while. When I pulled away from my phone, I saw that there had been a settlement here. All the way to Etip's, which I was fated not to see.

'There are lots of stone ruins there,' Sásho said.

Remains from dairy houses, animal pens and sawmills. Probably from communist times, though the legendary Etip must have had stone buildings too. Plus, twenty sawmills had been in use between Black Water and Sinanitsa next door. The superior pine of Pirin was already exploited in late Ottoman times. At one point, this whole side of the mountain belonged to one local *bey* (feudal lord). Trees were taken to the gorge on the backs of men and bulls, then down the river on rafts. They passed through Prairie and the Tinder's house had rooms where loggers could recover from accidents and exhaustion. They were given sheep's milk and rakia.

The combination of manual tree felling and extensive grazing kept the mountain mosaic healthy. Those who stayed here the longest left the least trace and did the least damage to the mountain – none, in fact. They only used what they needed for the season. By next season, things regenerated.

The great pastoralists fed and clothed everyone and kept the mountain sane, and like their ruminants they left no footprint. No monuments, buildings or excavations. Not even graveyards. Just – these animals. A vast and vulnerable legacy. A bank vault with the gold of life itself.

Where did they bury their dead? I wondered. If we die here do you think Kámen would take our bodies down on Mimi's back or is that too much work?

We laughed.

'Too much work,' Sásho said. 'I'm happy to be buried here. So I can roam. Graveyards are crowded.'

Everything up here made you think of life and death. It was the thinness of the air. Piles of unmarked human bones have been found in places like these, probably from relatively recent nomad burials, but also executions from the time of the bandit revolutionaries even more recently. The fanatical one from Orelek with all the monuments brought up twelve of his co-villagers here to the lakes, including a woman, and had them executed for being 'traitors'. Read: they disagreed with him. Once, he personally cut the throat of a woman for having an affair with a Muslim. Why his band of cut-throats and shepherds gone bad forced their own neighbours to hike all this way just to kill them, I can't fathom, or what they did with their poor bodies.

'They wanted a ransom but killed them anyway,' Sásho said. 'And left the bodies to the wild animals. Then some shepherd found the bones. Some wretch like me.'

When a Karakachan died far from the towns, which is how most of them died, four men made a trellis and carried the body or mounted it onto a horse saddle with rugs and took it to the nearest Christian cemetery. Those who stayed in Turkey for the winter, where it was harder to find a Christian cemetery, buried their dead in the wild, which was the practice in earlier times anyway. It was less footwork and saved on money and trouble – in the Ottoman admin-istration, the dead had to be declared and tax paid. The Yuruks also preferred to bury their dead in the open, near a sacred tree, some-thing closer to their hearts than a mosque, since they were more animist than Abrahamic.

Dead shepherds were often placed under a sheltered rock and covered with rocks that mossed over and blended with the landscape. They were not marked.

'I haven't found any human bones yet,' Sásho said. 'But once in

Sleepy Field the colleague and I went to the border barracks at the top and the dogs dug up a human skull.'

'Where would you rather die: here or in a hospital?'

'Here,' Sásho said. 'I want to die the same place I live, somewhere beautiful.'

The Karakachans had a custom: when the dying suffered a lot, the family would load them onto a horse or cart and drive them around until they expired. They were buried in that spot. Movement brought relief, even in death. If they died at home in the hut, all the water was poured out of vessels, to ease the process, since Haros caused the invisible lifeblood of the dying to pour out of them. The outside and the inside had to resonate at all times. After the moment of death, a woman whose age matched that of the departed one immediately began to knead dough for bread because the soul had a long road ahead of it.

Wherever the body rested, relatives visited for forty days. For forty days, the soul revisited all the places the person had seen in this lifetime but returned each night and only left on the fortieth day, then it was finally free. The mourners did not eat meat for forty days because the animals were in mourning too.

On Etip's plateaux were scattered the cows, like a partially looted necropolis. Next year, the cows might not be here, and this year was the fourth in Kámen's five-year contract for summer pastures. We were towards the end of a cycle.

'That's me,' said Sásho. 'I learned this profession. And it's towards the end.'

'What's gonna happen to your legs if you give it up?'

'I'll become crippled like the old shepherds,' Sásho grinned.

En route to the lakes, Sásho showed me the clutch of dwarf-pine where he pitched the tent and I immediately went off the idea of camping. It was exposed and the only firewood was the dwarf-pine, which burns well but is prickly to chop and you need an axe. We'd stick to the luxury of the hut. We climbed in and out of stone piles that were like catacombs of an expired civilisation. You could just about see the tenth mountain from here. It blended with the sky.

The tenth mountain was pure anima.

It was cold in the open arena of the lakes and the wind had not left the mountain, only our valley. The spongy tussock was like a sodden carpet. The river springs basted the land constantly, but when they hit marble scree, it was sucked underground and became invisible. The whole of Black Water was the basin of a river, it's just that most of it was beneath the surface.

We stopped at each of the three big lakes, taking our cue from the sheep who sampled the grass like gourmets at a smorgasbord. We sampled topics and moods.

He told me how as a child, he went to see Vanga, the blind clairvoyant of his hometown. He was roaming the streets and met a woman sleeping on a bench. She had come from another part of the country to see Vanga. He brought her a blanket for the night and at dawn took her to Vanga, pretending to be her son.

'You're not her son, don't lie to me, Vanga said when we went in, her son is dead. But I know you, she goes, I've met you somewhere before. Your task is to help others. That'll keep you on the right path. Now leave the room.'

And so it is, Sásho said, I help others to stay on the right path.

The green lake at the top where we met a year ago was the most beautiful, patterned and shimmering like a kaleidoscope. The sheep feasted for two hours and we lay on the ground with our hats and hoods up against the wind. The shepherd's way is to recline sideways on the ground, leaning on one arm – when the weather is fine. And when the weather is poor, to lie face down and cover their back with what they have. That way, the wind buffets them from behind, not face-on. There was no shelter and the two-legged pegs on the ridge stopped and looked down at us but none made the descent. The thought of seeing a new face was exotic. Horse Plaza was empty. This is where the four phantom sheep were spotted. I could almost see phantom horses.

'And over that ridge is a lodge,' said Sásho. 'Just an hour's trek.'

We had some cash between us, forgotten in the covers of phones, and I fantasised about trekking there while Sásho stayed with the flock, and bringing back some stuffed pastry or meatballs. On the other side were the other lakes, Stamen's territory.

The crises of the previous days felt far behind us.

'What's ahead?' I wondered.

'This,' Sásho waved at the emptiness of the corrie. 'You can leave, but I have to stay to the end.'

'The drinking wrecks everything,' I said. 'It's not for me.'

'No it's not. It's not for me either but I'm trapped,' he said.

'Today is Black Tuesday,' I said. 'He'll be legless.'

'Aye. It's a closed circle,' Sásho said. 'We go round like sheep. *Beeee.* When one of us keels over, the other picks up the stock.'

If there was more of a community than two isolation shepherds, the death roulette would stop. Drunkards would be rejected or have to sober up.

It made sense now, that the nomads were so conservative. It was about survival. On summer pastures, men only visited their huts once a month, to change their clothes. It made sense that everyone had a fixed role according to gender and age. It is because life in the wilderness is full of the unexpected that nothing was left to chance. By arresting the clock of social evolution, they balanced out the constant dangers of mountain living. Continuity and change: for the pastoralists, it was a dance along the razor's edge.

Nomads were a vulnerable minority in a sea of peoples that they had to negotiate with. They were a stateless mini nation, made more vulnerable yet by the epic nature of their routes. When you married, you might join a different company with a different itinerary and not see your parents and siblings for years. You'd meet at crossroads and stopping places. Here at the lakes, I got it, why a bride left her home hut at night, like Persephone entering the underworld, and why Karakachan wedding songs are laments, like this:

> Farewell my highlands, farewell my parents.
> I leave you three medicine pots –
> the sweetest for the morning, the bitterer for lunch,
> the bitterest for the night.

Their pattern of movement was made up of concentric circles that span at different speeds. The greatest was the seasons. All pastoralists in the Balkans observed the same calendar: from May to October and

October to May. Shepherds, horsemen and drovers were hired in May and fired in October or vice versa. The inner circle was the company made up in spring and unmade in autumn, and inside that, the clan in the hut.

On a distaff, a thread was pulled from a ball of wool like a line from a circle. Round and round and round, then suddenly out-out-out. A map of patterns and colours was then drawn across the empty canvas of the loom.

There is a geographical map like no other: the map of nomad life. It is made of circles and lines. The circles are the winter camps. The lines take them to the summer camps that become circles. The clock of history ticks, the map of the nomad shrinks. The circles move closer and the lines are shorter. Black lines appear: borders that can't be crossed. And till the end, at the heart of the mandala remained the flock. When the heart was ripped out, the whole thing stopped spinning and died or almost died, because here we are, with our black revolving flock.

Three types of people are left in pastoralism. The first type are people like Kámen and Stamen; livestock is in their blood but it's also a personal choice. They are the big players.

Then there are the die-hard family shepherds with an inherited small flock who won't make it big and don't want to. It's the way of life they won't give up. I met a young guy in the mountain across, who had 200 sheep with his father. They were the local white, long-legged breed that isn't endangered. He was an outdoors nerd, ill at ease in mainstream society and resigned to bachelorhood.

'Ah, the Ladybirds!' Sásho said. He knew them after his years in that mountain. They'd fought over pasture grounds. 'That youngster's got a short fuse. The whole family are like that. They can't talk to you without a row.'

A row about territory. For them, this life was not a matter of choice but fate.

Sásho was the third type: the hired hands who came from marginal rural backgrounds and didn't mind hard labour. Vagabonds, eccentrics, former delinquents and Roma used to living on the fringes. Simultaneously denizens of our past and our future. That future is already here, most of us are not ready for it.

This is what industrialisation, hybridisation, sedentarisation, homogenisation and finally, globalisation have achieved. Those who fight
on the frontline of extinction to keep our oldest animals alive are an
underclass, nameless savages glimpsed in the distance surrounded by
dogs and sheep or is that goats?

The word Gypsy comes from Egyptian, which was how Romani
travellers were seen by Europeans in the Middle Ages. It's an exonym.
And the word Vlach comes from a Germanic word for 'other'. A
negative turning point for humanity was when wanderers began to
be seen as others by those who were static. And ostracised, perhaps
because they were in fact envied by the static ones, the way a flight-
less bird envies the real bird, dimly remembering the time when it
could fly.

'I don't know, am I lost in my own life or am I roaming a world
where everyone is lost?' Sásho said, rising from the ground where we
lay face down as if hiding from snipers.

'It might be the same thing,' I rose too. We were beginning to
freeze by the green lake.

'Do you think people will notice if these sheep disappeared off the
face of the earth and there's no more milk and cheese like theirs?' I
mused.

And all we have then is milk, yogurt and meat from stationary
animals that have never known freedom. Mostly cows. Like the
yogurt you buy in the shops that tastes more of starch than milk. Like
in Scotland, the land of sheep, where you can't buy sheep's milk or
cheese at all.

'No, of course they won't notice,' Sásho said. 'Because we are
already disappearing, dear. And already nobody is noticing.'

The blue lake was the deepest and today it was dark and choppy like
a small sea. The mood changed from major to minor at these lakes. We
were infected with existential grief. It emanated from the lakes.

'I'm between worlds,' I said. 'I don't know which to inhabit.'

'But at least you have a life in one of them,' he said. 'Me, I'm
already like bai Anton. He's gonna die with the livestock.'

'If you had to choose between staying up here and staying in the
lower world, which would you choose?' I asked.

'Here,' he said. 'And you, if the borders closed tomorrow, would you stay here or in Scotland?'

'Scotland,' I said and a chill went through the lake, and us.

By the time we reached the brown lake, the shallowest and warmest, a heavy melancholy had infused the scene. Clouds moved across the water like dreams. It was too windy to bathe. There was a fourth mini lake. These are four of the sixty lakes that drain into the great river. I rolled up my trousers and waded.

'Don't go further please!' Sásho called.

The lakes did not make us free. Everything felt remote. The sheep had that look in their mineral eyes that said we don't give a shit about your freedom.

In their eyes, I saw it: they are pastored by us but they don't need us. It's us that have chosen to herd them along trails and guard them from predators for thousands of years. This is our project, not theirs. They did not specifically ask to be saved.

There is a nomadic saying that is self-mocking in nature: the Bedouins are parasites living off the camel.

And another thing I saw: they would fight to the death for the survival of their species but they are not precious about extinction. They'd take it on the chin and move off the earth with their collective soul, to wherever the extinct roam. It must be a busy place.

The dogs lay in the high grass. They were all bloodied now after they bickered on the way up. Our little tribe going round in circles. It was the nature of it but I felt a need to pull a thread out, for a linear path to take me forwards and beyond Black Water or at least to show me a way forwards.

An animal-human sect living in the shadow of mass death, that's what we were. Not because of what we were doing but because we were so alone.

It would be different if there were more of us. There's got to be a better way forwards. Yes, the pastoralists are forgotten, dejected, the last of something but by pastoring the last flock, they might suddenly take a detour from humanity's reckless arrow and make an emergency landing somewhere like Black Water and save the day.

Sásho smoked and didn't eat anything all day. On the way down

the waterfalls, he carried Mouse for a bit, seeing the brave wee thing
was struggling:

'Mouse, you should go back to Orelek.'

Then we stopped by the ruins again to wait for the flock and he
said to me out of the blue:

'Do you know what circling the square means in jail?'

No idea.

'It means going round and round in your cell, trying not to go
mad.'

And he told me a much sadder story than the previous version he'd
told me.

Aged sixteen, he was arrested on trumped-up charges for robbery.
There were no witnesses and his track record was sparkly clean, but
there was no one to pay for a lawyer or bail out the street kid and the
1990s were a predatory time. The courts were criminal. The police
were criminal. The two worked together. Big criminals became busi-
nessmen and politicians. The robbery had been carried out by
someone else who was bailed out and a scapegoat was needed. A
vagrant kid was ideal. Once inside, he was forgotten.

He spent three years in and out of jail awaiting trial, then another
year while he was being found innocent. The prosecutor admitted
that they had made a mistake but there was no compensation and
nothing could get him those years back.

'The years and the stolen dignity,' he said. 'I've been trying to get
it back ever since. These animals have helped me more than anything
else.'

We watched the sheep graze like at a last supper.

'But it's not the lost time that's the worst. The worst is that my
time inside made me into the robber I wasn't before. You become the
thing you're branded with. Like B for Balkán, eh my boy! T for thief,
a mark of shame. It still burns my soul.'

He celebrated his twentieth birthday inside, with a rapist in his cell
that he beat up. He hated rapists – and got beaten in return. When he
was let out on probation, he worked in a foundry factory, then
because of his comedic talent he ended up doing stand-up comedy
for the wretched of this world: in prisons, correctional facilities,

cancerous factories. He made men laugh, for which they dubbed him The Smile and when he was finally freed and his record cleared, he turned to robbery in earnest. Back in his border town, he hit the streets again. He couldn't sleep indoors. He lay in bed and looked at the ceiling, wanting to blast it to hell, so he could see the sky.

It was to save himself from himself that he took refuge in the Gypsy 'hood.

'What did you do all day in the cell, dear? I'd go mad. I have claustrophobia.'

'I circled the square,' he grinned and in his clear eyes was the pain I saw a year ago, at the green lake. 'That's how I learned to wait.'

Waiting for injustice to end is a long-term project.

'I don't want to conjure up those years,' he said. 'But I had to tell you. Otherwise you won't really know me. And I want to be known by one person in this world.'

'Yes,' I said.

We moved downhill with the godmothers, us and the sorrow.

The dead ram was a white skeleton polished by canine jaws and wind. The dogs prowled the circular perimeter. The seasons rolled over. The earliest human calendars are round mandalas. Shepherds carved round animal shapes out of the heads of their crooks: a ram with a snake's tail but the tail ended with the snake's head. This is the shepherd's ouroboros, the alchemical snake that bites its tail in a cosmic cycle of rebirth. The cycle of life was unimaginable without the ram. The ram was unimaginable without the dog-wolf.

'How quickly things are forgotten.' I pushed the ram's skull with my foot and it came off the spine.

'Not just forgotten, dear. Erased,' Sásho said. 'Nine years now I've roamed these mountains. I see things but there's nobody to tell. You must write it all, just as it is.'

We were blue from wind, altitude and premonition or maybe that was just the past seeping into the present. The only difference between aftermath and premonition is time.

The hut was cold. I stoked the stove to reheat lentils and brew tea. Sásho homed the flock and fed the dogs. I lit a Chinese moxa stick. A

well-earned evening of rest and recovery, I thought, still reeling from
what I'd heard.

Then Vasko appeared, drunk and with stomach pain. Sásho made
him eat olives with the stones, for gastritis. Then he walked him
home and took a long time to come back. It was late when he returned
clutching a mug of rakia. A long monologue began.

'You're very kind and I'm happy like a child. Am I using you to be
happy? I might never see you again. It tears me apart. I want the borders to close now. I want to live with you in a cave. In the tenth
mountain. Are we there yet? No. We'll never ever get to the tenth
mountain.'

I wept. He wept. Dialogue with an avalanche is impossible. I
needed to sleep. He turned the radio up, then smashed it against the
hot stove and overloaded the stove with wood so it glowed red and I
feared it might explode. During the night, I was woken by noise.
Sásho crashed into things. He went out, headtorch on and opened the
pen gate. I went out too.

'What are you doing?'

'I dreamt they were suffocating in the pen. I'm their mother. I
can't let my children suffocate.'

But the sheep didn't budge and the dogs looked at him with pity. He
closed the gate. I glanced at the sky just in time to see a shooting star.

In the morning, I started packing before I got out of bed. This
time, everything. Sásho groaned and asked for a painkiller.

'Why did I drink that rubbish, dear? You're not leaving, you're
just trying to scare me so I sober up quickly.' Then he picked up the
pieces of the radio and put it back together – to show he was an electrician and not just a drunk shepherd.

'See the magnets,' he showed me two round magnets and turned
the radio on. 'The magnets can't be parted. They belong together.'

And now the weather forecast.

Packing was the easy part. The difficult part was getting from
Black Water to The Beeches alone, something that scared me, and
finding a lift to Orelek.

When Vasko turned up with the bottle, they set themselves at the
table. Sásho let the flock out of the pen. Their snotty illness was gone

but the pastors were still sick. Sásho saw that I was really leaving and poured himself a large drink.

'You're pathetic,' I said. 'You've completely abandoned me.'

'It's you that's abandoning me,' he said meekly.

I trekked across the white desert to Signal Rock and managed to get through to Kámen. I explained the situation, my voice unsteady. Kámen couldn't come up for me.

'Why don't you call one of your friends in the gorge?' he said. 'If not, call me back and we'll figure something out. In a couple of days.'

Fair enough, I thought, without anger. By stepping into the circle, I had threatened the balance between these men. They couldn't cope. I had to cope alone.

The Privateer had just been to The Beeches yesterday where he'd dropped off provisions, chiefly booze and where Vasko had trekked to pick them up, which is why I had to run away now. Thanks, Privateer.

Stamen was my last hope. He picked up.

'You're in luck,' he said. 'I'm taking luggage to my hut. Wait for me at the Beeches. I should be back there by three.'

At our hut, they had lit the fire. I begged Sásho to walk part of the way down with me. We all knew there was a bear.

'Can't leave the flock,' Sásho avoided my eyes. 'Wolves and so on.'

'Look me in the eye,' I said.

'I can't. I'm ashamed. Don't leave. I'll stop drinking.'

'It's my fault,' Vasko threw his full glass into the fire where it smashed. Then they threw their hats in the fire, looked for more things to throw in and Vasko reached for the bottle. 'Don't,' Sásho stopped him, 'you carried that on your back.'

I strapped on my rucksack. Vasko turned on the electric chainsaw and handed it to Sásho.

'Cut off my head, plague. This life's gone on too long.'

'Come Muna, it's just you and me now,' Sásho said. Muna put her head in his lap. He sat hunched, like a beaten dog.

Topi and a limping Kasho came to the bottom of the valley to see me off, then turned back. I stopped to take in Thunder Peak one last time.

The path to The Beeches was a straight arrow but a long one. I hummed the entire time, to let the bear know. Terrace after terrace multiplied, the mountain generated them just to spite me as if the line kept looping into a circle and I'd never arrive. The path was not marked. The national park rangers were no use to either hikers or shepherds and some meadows were partly covered with pine groves where you quickly became lost and where the bear liked to hang out. Little stone pyramids were made by tourists. Thank you, tourists. How many ruined huts there were! How many people had lived here.

I sang. My adrenaline was peaking. After weeks of living on the edge, I could no longer tell danger from non-danger. Pan, the god of the wild, likes to nap in caves and be left alone. When disturbed, he unleashes bad dreams like bad weather and a traveller caught up in it is seized with dread and runs senselessly in the wrong direction. This is called pan-ic. He could do this to entire armies. Pan's bad dreams followed me.

And to make it clear that the bear is not just a concept, there were paw prints the size of which I'd never seen before. Marina would be measuring them, but I sped up. The bear had walked along the trail, like a hiker. The prints were fresh. What did the shepherds of old do when pursued by wolves? They trailed a long piece of clothing behind them: the cords of their leather moccasins, a woman's headscarf or the long woollen band that men wound around their midriffs, but something told me this wouldn't work with the bear.

What did the Karakachans say when they were caught up in floods and storms? God, have mercy, give my soul a rest. Then, there were the river rapids below and somewhere in the gorge, dogs barking. They could only be Stamen's dogs but why were they so low down if the flock was up at his hut? His dogs were much more likely to attack me than a bear. I recognised the last stretch of the path where Kámen had thrown sheep around during the exodus and where I heard the growl. A lush green world, then the steep path down to The Beeches and Stamen's jeep! I threw my rucksack into the windowless back and splashed in the icy river, shouting with relief. Then, a boy startled me. He'd snuck noiselessly to the car to look for cigarette filters. I hadn't realised that there were people at the hut next to the empty pen. They were soundless, the horses too, as if they were wearing soft moccasins.

'We're here with the horses,' the boy said. I went up to see and there was Rocky, Stamen's shepherd, saddling two mares with luggage. The bear was an aggressive large male, Rocky told me, and lived here in The Beeches. There was another bear up at the hut and Stamen was taking reinforcements up, hence the barks.

'You waiting for the boss?' Rocky asked. He was a gloomy man.

'Do you like living here?' I asked the boy. He nodded, then shook his head.

'It's not so much that he likes it, but he's got no choice,' Rocky said.

Stamen and Kámen wanted their boys to be like this boy but the difference was that this boy survived as a necessity, and Stamen's and Kámen's boys survived as a hobby.

Then they were off with the loaded horses, just as quietly, and The Beeches assumed its naked atavism. With the sun gone by the mid-afternoon, the gorge began to squeeze shut. The roaring river was a presence but not a soothing one.

The hours passed and fear crept in again; the thought of spending the night in the windowless jeep was bleak. I prepared for it. Inside a ready-made stone circle by the river, I stacked a fire from pine branches that I chopped with the axe in the jeep. I had a lighter but no torch, and a half-bottle of Keratsuda wine under the seat. The key was in the ignition, the radio worked and I charged my phone, not that it served me except to see the time, which didn't really help.

So, my linear movement was interrupted. There was nothing I could do except enter a different circle, right here. In the middle of the old beech forest, which like a city began to draw its curtains at dusk when its denizens scuttled looking for shelter, I conjured its spirits as best as I knew how to. Male and female, human and animal, night and day, all of this flowed together through the great Beech city and I let it stream through me. I was not solid but morphing like plasma and I suddenly loved it that I was this creature without a home except the Beech city. The forest, the bear, the river, this was my home now.

Something shifted, like layers of forest floor. The fear fell away and an impersonal, ruthless force came through. When the cold and dark arrived, I was ready for them in the passenger seat, wrapped in a rough blanket with Radio Gaia on. I sipped from the wine bottle. Let the strange dreams begin. I don't know if wild and remote are the same thing but this place was both and you just had to become wild and remote like it and no longer wait for anyone. To just be a thread in the web. Anima was inside and out. Anima contained all the previous nights at The Beeches that had been survived. Anima is pantheistic. Pan's bad dream released its grip. Then there were voices, a torch. Stamen came down the path, a sheep draped over his neck and his two boys in tow. How he'd carried this sheep down these terraces I don't know but I wanted to hug him.

'We're late.' He dumped the sheep in the back of the jeep.

I put the bottle of wine back under the seat and threw out the rocks.

'You've done the right thing,' Stamen saw my preparations. 'Boys, this is exactly what you do when you're stranded in the wild. So you know, when I'm not here.'

The boys nodded. They were exhausted and the sheep had a broken leg. The jeep engine spluttered to life and we drew a zig-zag line down the darkening mountain. But the mountain is never as dark at night as you think, just as it's never fully light. The terraced amphitheatre was drenched in red, like the final act of a play when you count the survivors.

I told Stamen I'd been afraid of the bear.

'There *are* bears this year,' Stamen said. 'They're only an issue with the flock though. I don't know of anyone killed by a bear.'

But hikers died every year from the weather.

'Always men,' Stamen said. 'People have no business up here in winter. And sometimes in summer too.'

Then he told me a bear story for fun.

'There's a narrow squeeze on that trail, by the brook and the big rock.' Where I'd heard the growl. 'That spot is called Shaban's date.'

There was once a man in Orelek called Shaban who spat a lot.

Once, Shaban was coming down from Kamen klet from cowherding. Kamen klet had the poorest pasture – stony, like its name – and that's why the cows were kept there.

'He was coming down and in that spot he met a bear. He began to spit like mad. And the bear spat back. Spitting, they squeezed past each other and he arrived in The Beeches drenched in bear spit.'

It was good to laugh again.

'What was the story with the four missing sheep last week?' I asked.

'There's no missing sheep. None. A misunderstanding,' he said.

The boys argued in the back then fell asleep on top of the sheep. Stamen turned to me, unsmiling.

'This morning you didn't sound so good. What happened up there?'

Everything. But what happens in Black Water stays in Black Water.

'Nothing,' I said. 'Nothing happened up there.'

PART FOUR

THE WEB

MILK

In the dark kitchen, Kámen and I are eating a melon from a tray, morosely. Flies alight on the slices. He empties the full ashtray into the wood stove full of rubbish, to be lit in the cold months. The TV is on. The news is bad.

Bai Anton has gone to bed after his usual day: milking the goats, walking the goats, milking the goats, feeding the dogs and today, watering the wolves.

'I forgot about the two wolves,' I say to him when he sits in the kitchen to share some cold potatoes and red wine.

'You lived with more than two of them, up there,' Anton grins his lopsided grin. 'Is the colt alive?'

I tell him.

'That mare has been luckless,' he says.

We've taken to eating together. Kámen is always late for dinner even when dinner is late. Anton is the only person I see, first thing in the morning and last thing at night.

It's been three days since my escape from Black Water. I've been lying low in my high room, battered and relieved like after a short war. Anton has spread some herb out on a bed in my room while I've been away. It's a crinkled, tobacco-coloured leafy pocket, shaped like a coin. Anton makes a cough tea with it. It takes me a moment to realise this is the coin tree that tore my hair all those weeks ago, like years. The coins were golden then.

It's good to have small concerns again, like watching where you step on the stairs because of the pigeon shit and in the yard because of the dog shit, which dries quickly because of the extreme heat and can be scraped off like patties. The flies. I'd forgotten what it's like to have thousands of black flies biting your flesh or lying dead in trays of poison. 'Even the poison costs me hundreds,' Kámen mutters. But it's nice to have flies again.

The Loopies clingfilmed me in drool, panting with joy, especially Kalina-Malina and Bear short-ears who bai Anton says should be going out with the goats like a real guy instead of getting fat and also Gutsi who lies on the doorstep of the kitchen so you can't close the door without pinching his tail and Metsi who limps on three long legs. Glavcho punctures holes in my trousers. But Sunny, whom I've missed, is the most excited to see me, and I him. Have you missed me, Sunny? Sunny! You live in the dark recesses of the pen now. You are bored here, guarding sheep that don't need guarding after months of roaming with the pack but it was your choice to stay down with your girlfriend Karamana. You clamber up the pen door for a long cuddle. Thank you, your cuddle means a lot. The Loopies push me over with their weight and bare their teeth at Sunny. Love is a precious commodity. Karamana is in the pen with Sunny, and Griffy too, who is chained and barking on his own, as neurotic as ever but at least he has company here. Sunny's nose is still scarred from Kasho all that time ago. He returns to the dim recesses of the pen full of munching young sheep.

My first days are spent doing laundry and writing. I am also hobbled by a dog bite. It happened the night of my arrival. Not expecting visitors so late, Kámen had let Barut off his rock chain and he bit me behind the knee the moment I stepped out of Stamen's van. Seeing that there were no veins hanging out, just a bleeding puncture wound, Kámen passed me the antibiotic spray for dogs.

'It wouldn't be complete without a dog bite,' I joked, reeling from pain and fatigue, and Kámen was glad I didn't make a scene.

Now, at the table, Kámen is ashen faced. The price of everything is rising. There is a 2-litre plastic bottle of rakia on the cold stove, ready for him to take up on his next ascent.

'When I see this bottle, I feel sick,' I say. He scoffs.

'Now you know how I've felt for twenty years.'

'I'm trying to understand what's behind their drinking,' I say.

I'm slipping into the contemptuous 'they' speech that the family use for all hired workers, past and present. Kámen scoffs again.

'It's called alcoholism. There's nothing to understand.'

Maybe he's right. Maybe some things can't be understood, only endured. I am grateful to be in this low-ceilinged kitchen full of his crushing sobriety.

He is like the rock to which Barut is chained, and Sásho is like Barut. They are earth and fire, linked by a chain to each other and the mountain. Sometimes, the chain breaks and someone gets bitten.

'This is the only profession where these people can drink and not get fired,' he says. I can't argue.

'From tomorrow, I'll milk with you. To get close to the milk,' I say.

' 'Cos you mostly got close to the rakia, to date,' he quips.

I feel some of his pain. The whole of his pain is too deep for anyone to feel, that's what he broadcasts every day.

Kámen is glad that I have fallen out with Sásho. This way he won't be abandoned. We will all remain alone and bound to his circle. The flies are finishing off the melon.

'These people are possessed by the devil,' he goes on. 'You can't win against that.'

'Don't take up this rakia,' I say. 'When there isn't any, they don't drink.'

And I crack up and tell him about the accident with the horses a few weeks ago, just to show him what's at stake when he and The Privateer take up bottles. I hadn't told him out of loyalty to Sásho but that loyalty has crumbled. Kámen sighs but is not surprised.

'Sásho knows he has a problem,' I say. 'Help him by not pouring booze down his throat.'

'Help him? People don't change,' Kámen opens another pack of cigarettes and the kitchen fills with smoke. He throws the lighter on the table like dice. He didn't use to smoke. He would sit at the table and draw. Now, he just smokes.

'People do change,' I say with desperation. 'But they need support.'

We look at the National Geographic channel. Horses gallop across the Mongolian steppes. This is Kámen's dream – a world filled with animals, no people.

'In Mongolia, there is respect for horses and pastoralists,' he mutters.

But pastoral nomads in Mongolia are on the brink of disappearance too. Like the modern Karakachans, they live in apartments. Their horses have gone wild. They are the stuff of films. All that is left is a word that has travelled: *cherga*. Used throughout the Balkans for rug, tent or Gypsy camp, the word seems to have come from Mongolia. On horseback.

I rise from the table to go to bed. I can hear Anton's hacking cough upstairs. Being close to the animal people takes a toll. There is no middle way. There is no relenting. The ruminating animals churn thorns into milk. Everything turns into something else, if you stay long enough. You're not the same by the end of season. Already, I am not the same.

'Don't delude yourself about Sásho,' Kámen says.

'I'd rather delude myself than live without hope,' I say.

'Hope,' he snorts. 'I can't afford to live with hope.'

'What do you live with, Kámen?'

'Reality,' he says with gritted teeth.

The days begin with milk. There's always a pot of raw milk in the fridge, left to self-ferment and clot like sour cream. I tiptoe into the dark kitchen. Kámen is asleep on the narrow bed next to the second fridge where only the milk products are kept: yogurt, quark, clarified butter in jars, made by his mother when she is here or by him when she isn't, though I never catch him in the act. He must alchemise the milk after midnight.

I wonder if he too turns into something else, after midnight, to escape this human condition. To slip into one of his unfinished paintings. He sleeps in raw wool blankets. It's the way here. I used to think that he had a proper bed in the goat house, but this is his only bed. He sleeps here with the dogs by the door. From up here, he can survey his kingdom. A massive ram's bell hangs above his head and next to it, rusted shearing scissors, pointing down so they would maim him if they fell. His talismans. It is said that wealthy families had ram bells made of gold and silver and under threat of attack they'd bury them in the forest. Folk ballads tell of ram bells poured from 'three litres of gold'.

Before Stamen and his father left, the old shepherd slept on this bed and Stamen slept upstairs. Now Kámen slept in the old shepherd's bed, in the mould left by his body. And I sleep in Stamen's old bed, where the mother sleeps when she is here. I tiptoe out of the kitchen. The milk is creamy, its taste subtly different each time. Velin the gourmet is right, Kámen's goat yogurt is the best and that's because his milk is the best. The thickest, most thrilling goat milk this mountain produces, and the most unpredictable.

That is what the wild is. How can I walk away from it now that I've survived it? I need it like a drug.

The next evening, I limp down the white dust road, past Barut on his chain who looks on from his cave with his droopy face – nothing personal, I'll bite anyone who arrives unannounced in the dark – and past the creature-like rock stacks. I splash across the river, past the chained Mecho because of whom I can't do a day out with bai Anton and the goats. I will milk the goats without grazing them. I've been watching the milking since last year. The following evening, Kámen lets me in.

Anton and Kámen are crouched, their black and white heads lost in the black and white hair of the animals. They are filling plastic tubs with pristine milk. There are fifty goats to milk, down by half since last year. They are still too many and Kámen is trying to sell the kids at a half-decent price. Yesterday, he went downstream to a slaughterhouse to discuss a sale. But the bastard was playing hard to get, pretending he couldn't make up his mind just to beat my prices down, Kámen said.

Before the milking, the kids must be separated from the mothers, having had their fill. Kámen does this effortlessly. The mothers follow him outside and the kids return to the indoor pen, where they cough like disenchanted old men and cry: '*Neee, neee.*' They don't know if their mothers will be back.

The kids are adorable with their curly fringes and perfect heads. It is appalling to slaughter and eat a creature so exquisite. Yet, if the slaughterhouse deal goes through, this is what will happen. With the price of feed having doubled since the war in Ukraine, Kámen can't afford to keep them all. If bai Anton sickens, there is no replacement. Goatherds are even harder to find than shepherds. It is all hanging by a goat's hair. But how can you get rid of the goats? They have been here since the beginning.

'I can't do without these goats,' Stamen said. It has to be the long-haired ones. Kámen said nothing, but felt the same.

There is a stunning indoor pen with an impressive roof for them, every beam cut by hand, like something out of a pastoral painting. That was the thing, with this family of artists: everything was meticulously crafted and pulsed with a love that couldn't articulate itself in words. But it was here, and more beautiful than it needed to be.

In the outside pen, the females are ushered into a small enclosure by the dozen, to be milked. The bucks must be removed or they cause havoc. Chasing a buck, even in a small space, is hard and their crown of horns suddenly becomes a weapon. You can't force them, you must lure them.

Then, the milking begins. The two men move with a choreographed precision, taking hold and letting go, a ballet of udders and hands. When a bucket is filled to the brim with foamy milk you put it outside the pen, to be taken into the dairy room and processed.

Kámen pushes a suitable goat my way. She doesn't trust me, I am new. Kámen shows me how to get hold of her – by the udders from behind, firmly but without force then she can't move. Then another one. It takes me ages to half-fill a 5-litre tub. I am covered in sweat and the milk is covered in goat hairs. The hairs are long, sometimes caked with dust or shit. They stick to the udders. They reach the ground. The main skill with these long-haired goats is to separate the milk from its pollutants. The second skill is the milking itself. After a few sessions, I get better at the second, but not at the first.

You squeeze the udder from the base out, to move the milk through. A robust jet of milk well aimed into the tub is joy. You get into a rhythm: breathing, squeezing, head to butt to head, until you are part of the circle. Your hands ache and you use one hand at a time to rest the other, which slows you down. The animals know exactly what is happening. They are smart, you sense their thoughts as they chew the cud and inspect you. They express themselves well, through their milk, their eyes and their independence. You, the human, are suppressed, packed full of emotions you can't channel so they remain under the surface. Because 'the devil' is in you, but the devil goes quiet when you milk. Milk is an antidote.

When I stand on the little balcony at night, the village houses among the rock stacks are dark, except for one lit-up window: Kámen is in the dairy.

He disinfects tubs and cloths, pours the milk through a sieve and a linen folded four times, which is the tradition, pours it into the double-sided vat where a propeller churns in a sea of milk, washes the tubs again, cleans the floor with bleach, prepares everything for the morning, or the evening — the next time always comes too quickly, with pitiless monotony. There are no days off. There is no one except him and bai Anton.

'I'll find you a goatherd so good, he'll graze with the goats!' someone teased the family when Ugrin the Radio left. Of course, they never did.

The dairy room is not used to its full potential. The investment has not paid off, Kámen must do it all alone. Years of dedication have come to this: washing, endless, thankless washing. The dairy room is his laboratory but he has become a sad alchemist who no longer believes in his craft, like with the paintings.

People don't change.

Why labour day and night when nobody appreciates it?

Why do people still make cheese that sells at 7 euros a kilo?

But the milk still flows. When he lets the yogurt set, when he lines up jars in the fridge and writes 'quark' on the lids, when he opens the jar of clarified butter and puts a small knob on his toast, he is himself. I am myself. Milk is a lifeline.

Some days later, Kámen leaves me in charge of the dairy processing for a night, reluctantly but there is no one else. He is going up to Black Water. I knew he was going from the list on the kitchen table the day before:

Bread
Potatoes
Phone voucher
Cigarettes

'Wash everything five times,' he anxiously instructs me, 'I can't afford to sell dirty milk.'

The milk is kept in the vat at a permanent temperature of 14 degrees Celsius for up to four days, then Kámen takes it down to Andrea's dairy. Andrea then makes cheese for 7 euros a kilo.

Anton is alone when I enter the pen. The goats rush to the other side.

'Get the kids back!' he shouts as he takes the mothers through the big wooden gate, too low for me so that I hit my forehead on a badly placed latch every time I pass. It's almost like Kámen put it there to hurt you, because it's not hard enough already.

The kids stick with the mothers. They sense that Kámen is away and don't know my intentions. I run around the yard and can't separate them. Bai Anton gives me a stick to urge the kids back. It's a stampede. I have no control and the stick doesn't help. By the time the goats are separated, I am covered in sweat.

Outside, I get into position behind a goat with my bucket, part her matted hair like a curtain and feel the teats. Each goat has uniquely shaped teats. You get to know them and they get to trust your hands and your presence at their back. It takes time. Stamen told me: when you walk into the pen, the animals suss you out. If you're a good shepherd, they accept you, otherwise not. I really want to be accepted by them.

This one has one small and one large udder. That one has hard udders. I am still not able to get all the milk into the bucket. You must direct the teat with your hand so that the warm milk doesn't spurt at random, like in your face, crotch and hair. Everything is milk, fragrant, warm and sticky. I am drunk on milk. I'd never laugh if Kámen was here or he would think I was mocking his animals, but I laugh now.

'Just put your mouth there and get it straight from the horse's mouth, as it were,' bai Anton advises. We giggle over our tubs.

It suddenly goes well. I get into the dream-like pulse of milking, the teats are warm in my hands, all the goats study me close-up, the way the sheep never do.

'Thank you, dear,' I say to each goat that makes the job easy, and they *are* doing us a favour. Their milk is meant for their own kind. Not for us.

Sásho calls every other day to apologise again and again, and ask how I am, dear? 'I'm traumatised, and I am not your dear!'

But I can't sever the connection.

'I'm traumatised too,' he says. 'I lost what I love. I made a colossal mistake. I clamber up and down with the godmothers all day and ask myself: why, why did I hurt you and myself? You threw that drink in my face spontaneously but I got drunk deliberately. To hurt you. To pre-empt the hurt of your departure.'

'No, you got drunk because you're an alcoholic.'

'Please don't call me that, it sounds hopeless,' he says. 'I wake up in the night and can't believe you're gone.'

'Yeah, and you wouldn't even walk me halfway.'

'I went looking for you later, to Kamen klet. In case you'd changed your mind and wanted to come back. To walk you back.'

'A bit bloody late.'

Our conversation continues, even when he has no signal and no battery. I look at Thunder Peak many times a day and talk to him. He lies in the darkness of the hut and talks to me. What is to be done?

From my monastic bed, I gaze at the millions of little flies that have hatched on the walls, accepting that I can neither understand them, nor they me, we just have to live together. It's a few nights of mad spawning, a phenomenon called *calamitet*, Kámen tells me. A calamity of flies for us, and new life for them.

I change over to another goat and a third one butts me in the forehead, its horns hard like stone. I am momentarily stunned. Bai Anton is butted in the back, his goat kicks the bucket and half the milk spills in the dirt. They are rebelling. There is a stampede.

'You motherfuckers!' bai Anton shouts. His fury is sudden.

'Bloody Kámen!' I shout. 'Why is it so hard? There should be a milking cot! Like with the sheep.'

Blood drips into bai Anton's bucket, and it's not his. He has punished the kicking goat by damaging her teat. The heat beats down on us. I am furious but we must humble ourselves to get the job finished.

'You can't get angry at an animal,' Sásho told me. It's never their fault. When your fingernails fall off, you wait for new ones to grow. When the sheep udders are so small you can't get hold of them, you try again. I never saw him hit an animal, except that time above Black Water when the rams went on an orgy and he broke his stick against a horny ram's back but the ram deserved it.

'They don't deserve it, dear. They're wild mountain sheep.'

I appease myself, and head against rump, I work the milk down the udder. I like the smell of the goats, even the male ones. It's hair, sperm, grass, rain on dry earth, lust and death, hot breath and milk.

My skin is milk-sticky, my hands are numb. I haven't developed the muscles for it. To be a shepherd, you must be hard and gentle, like your hands. If you hurt the animal, you hurt yourself. I am drawn to the hands of manual workers, men and women alike, an atavistic recognition of a time when everybody's hands were more like the earth. As if a part of me never left the pre-historic mountain with other mountain souls and bodies. Sásho's hands and nails are misshapen with thickness and injuries, though his fingers were once thin and nimble, the fingers of a hungry child thief.

'If you put on all your rings, I'll steal them one by one and you won't notice,' he said once. 'To show you what my life was like.'

You took my trust and threw it to the dogs, you robbed me already! I shout in my head and look up at Thunder Peak. It's a crazy blue, like another planet. I wonder where they are today. Up by the lakes, up along the stone funnels to Etip's or stuck on the 'landing strip'. I wonder if he drinks during the day or only at night.

But what did I expect? I turn up, enter his life and demand that he clean up overnight. I clench my jaw and milk. To milk twice a day, every day, without a day off. It's like prayer. You sit on your prayer stool, contemplate the inscrutable rump of the goat god and out comes the milk.

You must be calm when you squirt into the bucket, calm when you step into the wellies at the door of the dairy room, calm when you wash the sieves, the straining cloth, the tubs, then line them up for the next day. Calm when you sweep droppings and straw from the goat pen every other day, when you pour feed for the kids into long wooden troughs, four big buckets every morning just for the kids who eat ravenously, their eyes mad with gluttony under the curly punk fringes.

'How can they always be ravenous?' I am alarmed.

'That's ruminants for you,' says Kámen, calmly.

One kid lies dead in the pen and flies already blacken its little face. It strangled itself at the trough, squeezed by the others.

'Killed by gluttony,' Kámen summarises. Greed in humans disgusts him but he forgives greedy animals. It will be appreciated by Vachka and the hybrid.

A few days later, Kámen sells the kids to a father and son from the central Rhodope Mountains. They will add them to their flock, they won't go to the slaughterhouse. I am relieved, Kámen must be too. The son is eighteen and has his father's big hands and weather-beaten face, and wears old-fashioned rubber galoshes and woollen socks. It's like seeing the young Stamen with his father.

They have the largest flock of sheep and goats in the Rhodope, over 2,000. Ten men are employed to do the milking. They're all Roma and come with the usual baggage: families that must be driven and fed and drunken dramas managed.

Father and son load the bleating kids into their van – *Neeee, neee* – and are off.

The mothers bleat too. I wonder when they will forget the loss, perhaps their bodies will forget as soon as they get pregnant again; some of them already are.

When you're calm, you hear the goats talk. Clearly. They talk with human voices, in syllables and words. There are dialogues, between mother and child, between adults and separately between kids. They look at you with reptilian yellow eyes with horizontal black pupils and you see someone halfway between human and dragon. They sneeze and mind their own business. They are wise and wicked, they measure you up. The bearded bucks are chasing the females just as Sásho had hilariously imitated them, with their tongues out, like old perverts offering oral sex that nobody wants. Their mating dance is more articulate than the rams'.

Now I see why there are goat people and sheep people, because they are so different. There are also goat-milk people and sheep-milk people. Velin is a goat consumer, only interested in goat milk, goat cheese and goat yogurt. Bai Anton is a goat person, a day out with the sheep and he's had enough.

'They lie down and three hours later they're still there. It drives me nuts.'

The goats drive him nuts too, they move too much. But this he can cope with. Sásho is a sheep person, he empathises with the sheep but finds the goats malicious and unrelenting. Gradually, you become like your animals.

One goat turns around while I milk her, sniffs me and sizes me up. They are individuals, then they become part of the herd, but not for long before the individual pops out from the herd again as if it was never part of it.

At sunrise, the mountain is a film that I watch from the balcony with my milky coffee. My faith rises with the sun. My faith is absolute like the sun.

Someone is calling animals from across the gully. It's Velin. 'He stands on his balcony in the morning and calls out like he's got livestock,' Sásho told me. 'Eehee! But it's the cats.'

I go over to his house to say 'hello' but he is only here for the day before he zooms back to the capital. 'I'm busy. You are busy, we're all busy,' he says, munching goat's cheese.

I don't want to be busy. I want to notice things like this: the willow tree that strokes the roof of the sheep pen has been snapped by the storm. There is a scorpion in the shower. At dusk, silence lies on the village like a blanket. The mountain is a painting. The light, the contours of Thunder Peak and Little Horse, the composition, it cannot be represented because the mountain makes its own art and represents itself.

When Orpheus went to the underworld, he knew the rules and broke them. Every time I leave this mountain, I look back. The object of my yearning vanishes. I cannot be reconciled and end up coming back. Each time with a different approach, through a different doorway. East, then west. Always making my pilgrim's way to the glacial lakes, where you can't stay long or you go kooky, melancholy or drunk.

'Sásho manages to drive everyone away in the end,' says Kámen at the table.

My initial relief at being in the house has been replaced by the sombre grind of Kámen's judgements. Sásho drinks but is very forgiving. Maybe some things are constitutional.

I sit by the sink downstairs while bai Anton feeds the dogs, my clothes covered in dog drool, goat hair and milk, then we eat the pastry I've made, stuffed with the leeks he has pilfered from some garden, the rice with the ceps he picked last season, the stew Kámen made days ago and we watch the terrible news, wash our tin plates and trudge up the steps, avoiding the pigeon droppings, to bed where I listen to him cough and the dogs bark through the night. The nights are full of animals and animals are full of milk. Sap moves through animals and animals move through the mountain.

They are shadows in the hills, in the empty pens, grazing in the forest of Coin trees, the ghostly animal city. There was once a clairvoyant in Orelek. She foresaw the fate of her village. They would disappear, in groups, in packs, in pairs, down the chasms of the river, in an end-of-days exodus, hunted, slaughtered, purged, industrialised, nationalised, sedentarised, corporatised, monetised, sanitised, extinct.

To be here is to fight against that. To leave the gorge now would be to quit and I am not quitting.

In the morning the sap rises, the dogs bite each other and I sip my milky coffee. But afternoons and evenings are sad, with the blanket of oblivion lying over the village and only the log trucks thundering up and down the dust road. There are two of them and they do several runs a day, undertakers carrying the corpses of the forest.

In the evening, the chime of bells announces the goats' return. For as long as the animals are here, milk runs in the veins of the world. Milk is everywhere. In the milk thistle that grows on the slopes, in the figs, sticky and sweet. People used to put fig sap in goat milk, to curdle it but the goats don't go for fig. They go for plums, wild pears, mushrooms and apples, and they love willow. The big willow tree in the square is still my office. I sit at the broken table to get phone signal. I have steadied myself since Black Water but now, when Shaban comes and puts his head against my chest, I nearly cry.

The fridge is full of yogurt jars and I eat out of the jar with a spoon. For a while, I bought yogurt in the shops not to be a burden on the family but then realised that this was an insult to Kámen with his homemade yogurt. That he preferred it when I ate his yogurt with a spoon out of the jar, even if he never invited me to do so.

It is late. I am sitting in the kitchen, eating yogurt out of the jar. I've stayed up to wait for Kámen who is back from Black Water.

'How are things on Golgotha?' I ask and he almost smiles. He won't allow himself a proper smile.

'I didn't see Sásho but the hut is reverting to its natural state. The bedding is in a pile. The pen is all mud. A mess.'

A week later, Sásho tells me the pen is so muddy that when the sheep lie down they can't walk in the morning. And anyway, they don't want to lie in the mud. Mountain sheep are like that. They'd rather sleep on the rocks so he keeps them by the river bed overnight, which leaves them exposed and makes the dogs howl all night. Sásho can't sleep because of that, from thinking about what happened, from thinking about his life.

'Ah,' he laughs when I tell him about the bite, 'Barut has punched you with his two staples!'

'If you keep losing your teeth, you'll become like Barut,' I tell him.

He laughs his good-natured laughter. We can't help it, we are affectionate again and he is ditching the drink, he tells me, because it's not for him.

'What's this milk doing here? It should be in the fridge!' Kámen says.

A tub of milk from this evening. I have managed the task in the dairy room but wasn't sure what to do with this tub.

'It'll be ruined now,' he says.

I clench my jaw. 'It's only been a couple of hours. I thought you wanted it at room temperature.'

He looks pained.

'Maybe we can make rice pudding with it,' I suggest.

'It'll go to the dogs,' he says.

'Goodnight,' I say.

The milk turns out fine. In the morning, I open the fridge and scoop up a mouthful with my tin, with relish. Relish feels like rebellion here.

Kámen is curled up on his side, blanket off, like a boy.

A boy who loves everything in the yard. Who beams when he holds a new-born lamb. Who adopts homeless dogs, cats and ravens and gives them names. Who is one with the web where milk runs through everything. Who senses that only some of that web is visible, the rest is underground, under the skin and the eyelids. The only way to express this is to draw a line on paper. Even the unvarnished wood frames of his unfinished paintings are carved with animals and leaves. I look more closely at them: the puzzle-like weave of creation. Dogs, hawks, owls, wolves, bears, bearded goats, giant rooted trees and somewhere inside the web, the outline of a pastor in a hooded cape, all locked together in an embrace or a fight. It is night-time in his paintings. The night of the living mountain where you need second sight to see all that is there. I turn them back to the wall. I don't know if he wants me to see them, these incomplete paintings that are the price he has paid to keep this going. He has given up art for animals. It is a sacrifice. To quit the animals after twenty years of not painting, he would never forgive himself. I almost reach out to pull the blanket over him, then tiptoe out of the kitchen with my hard-won spoonful of milk.

★

It's raining. Thunder Peak is invisible, as if it never existed. As soon as I come down the stairs, I know slaughtering is on the schedule. Bai Anton paces, smoking, his bootlaces undone. I'm used to the slaughtering now. It's the weekend before Assumption Day and people order lambs or goat kids for feasts like these. Bai Anton is the butcher on duty. Two days later, the feast over, he must do it again. An animal must be sacrificed for a man who gives Kámen pastures for the goats. This is their annual pay-off.

Kámen enters the pen with intent. The young sheep are in the back, with Sunny, Karamana and Griffy, even Griffy looks worried. Kámen paces slowly among the young sheep. At first, they come to him, relaxed, then they suddenly realise and huddle together. The mood changes. One of them must die. They all look at Kámen. The one who feeds them has betrayed them. This is the worst moment, worse than the knife across the throat. Kámen hates all of it.

'They have a collective mind,' Kámen told me. 'They know which one I've chosen. And they press together to protect it.'

Anton is at his post at the slaughtering stone basin. The knife rests on the edge. Kámen makes his choice and picks up a lamb. It protests feebly – *beeree* – then gives up. The rest of the animals remain huddled and silent. The dogs too. It is a small mercy that the sacrifice is out of sight for the surviving sheep.

'Don't watch,' Kámen said to me the first time but he doesn't say it anymore because here I am again, sitting on the steps. It is my duty to watch. I eat the delicious buttery flesh of the lambs and goat kids, I eat the yogurt made from their milk, I walk with them in the hills, I count them and worry when they eat psychotropic hellebore and foam at the mouth. When one of them is killed by one of us, I must watch. It's part of the deal.

Kámen looks away. He can't bear it. Twenty years on, it still causes him distress.

Sásho feels the same.

'You birth it in winter, you get it to suckle from its mother to survive, you cuddle it. Then you graze it in spring, you watch it grow from mouse to fat little thing, you carry it when it's hobbled, you worry about it, you talk to it, you get to know it. It trusts you. And then, one day you wake up and put it to the knife. No.'

Anton runs the knife across the lamb's throat, the blood comes out in a jet and pools in the stone basin. Like the milk in the bucket. Instead of the shock I used to feel, there's a sad acceptance that all flesh must die. That milk becomes blood and blood becomes milk. Nobody is exempt from this cycle.

Tenderly, like a midwife, Anton holds the agonised lamb in his hands until it stops twitching. The blood flows down the stone steps onto the white dust road and the rain washes it away. Anton cuts off the head. He cuts off the hooves from the back legs and makes incisions in the skin that will make it easy to hang it up on the hooks in the ceiling.

Kámen has driven off in his white van, his cloudy mood settled for the day, like the weather. Yet the weather will be sunny again tomorrow. Anton inserts a little metal straw into the incisions and blows hard under the skin. This makes the stripping of the skin easier. Some do it from the head end, Anton does it from the feet. The beautiful creature is a carcass: no head, no feet and soon, no skin. There's no getting away from the truth: it is simply wrong that our kind does this to another kind when we don't have to, to survive. This is an 'extra', as the shepherds say. The fact that Sásho rarely tastes the meat of his flock is not unusual. Shepherding people are not casual meat eaters. They are milk and cheese eaters. The Karakachans only slaughtered an animal on special occasions or when it was sick. They who walked the earth for their sheep knew what it took. They had too much respect. The whole animal was used of course. The skin was cured and used for the huts and even the ribs were used for divination, especially if a long migration or other dangerous event was imminent.

The innards go to the dogs.

The biggest meat eaters are those most removed from animals, whose reflex action is to reach for the cheap pack of lamb chops in the supermarket, brought by one of those lorries from another country.

Later, two fat men arrive in a van to pick up the lamb. They are too scared to get out of the van – ten dogs are barking at them. 'It's okay, they don't bite,' I shout from the balcony but they are taking no chances and wait until Kámen comes. They wait for a long time in the van and the carcass hangs on a hook in the kitchen, dripping blood into a tray. The lamb will be filling their bellies tomorrow. When they die, these men who eat too much, their bones will feed the earth ready for more pasture, for more milk. The thought is strangely satisfying. I am thinking like Kámen!

No, I am thinking like the earth. This is how milk travels. The best milk on earth is thousands of kilometres long. Its mileage is equal to that of bai Anton and Sásho. Milk travels from the centre of the earth into the soil, the grass, the trees and their fruit. It travels through the gut of the goats, their blood and lymph and their mammary glands. It travels into the mouths of their kids and into tubs and vats, then via funnels into bottles. It is packed into the backs of vans and Andrea turns it into cheese that travels to human mouths and guts. For milk to travel, everybody must digest. Now I understand why the goats chew constantly. The only time milk appears static is when it sits turning into yogurt but its molecules are moving. Milk is movement.

The village is empty in the rain, as if crying. The dogs are flopped on the flagstones with the Sunday blues. Gutsi is chewing the rest of the lamb's head. Kalina-Malina gets up to greet me with her pink snout and remind me that life is Yes, yes, yes.

I see again how Sásho throws his hat, his whole life into the fire and wants to turn the page and start afresh in the morning. He has plenty of hope but can't cope without drinking.

I see Kámen bent under white sacks, milking, straining, washing, carrying his burden up and down mountain terraces, waking up in a sweat from the nightmare of a lost flock, bargaining with drunkards, watching unclean men take his clean animals away, falling asleep in front of the TV and – it's time for the milking again. To cope with his sobriety, he has to cut out hope.

Kámen and I pass each other without eye contact. It's his way and I'm tired of being upbeat against a tide of gloom. It's easier to be like him; sullen, cross at the world.

When I lie on my bed, I hear someone coming, voices. But nobody is coming. Everybody is already here. The tok-tok tokachki. The dogs bark at the slightest noise, but really just to amuse themselves, to make music: first violin, bass guitar, solo, backing choir. Loopy Junior is chewing a log. Kalina-Malina is chewing the bottom step. Another one is chewing the hose with which I have tried to distract Glavcho but he just wants my trousers. Two of the others are in their sand pits, digging.

'Muna,' I hear Sásho, when Monkey was digging under the bed again. 'I'll give you a spade and make you an archaeologist!'

I miss them. I've been reading about the last Karakachan nomads in the work of an ethnographer who spent time with them from the 1930s to the very end in the 1950s, and I discover that they allowed their dogs in the huts, especially during the day when the men were out with the flock and the women were doing chores outside. Dogs and small children kept each other company. I'm also surprised to find out that in summer, the sheep were sometimes milked three times a day and to do that, these huge flocks were brought to the milking pens each time, then out to pasture again. And again. Yet meat remained a rare treat.

In the evening, bai Anton and I sit in the kitchen and chew. Anton drinks a mug of beer most evenings. Sásho eats cheap salami instead of lamb and bai Anton drinks cheap beer instead of goat's milk. The shepherd's diet: bread, cheese, onions and vegan stews.

These last three days, we've been sharing a large bottle of wine made from local Rubin grapes. It is sold in the big roadside shop that truckers frequent; the family who own the shop make it from their vineyard. Everybody here has a vineyard.

'Me and the goats, we slipped between the drops today. But up there . . .' he nods at the cloud that hides Thunder Peak. 'Sásho will be sodden and the livestock too.'

He knows Black Water. He stayed there one summer, when the flock was small.

'He is a good man,' he says. 'I don't know what it is with him and the drink.'

Bai Anton has his moments too. When he drinks, he marches on the spot, like a soldier and his sister gives him a row. When Sásho drinks, he hides it from Kámen by running short stretches and stopping, like a rabbit. Bai Anton marches without moving. One, one, one. Rebellion in the ranks. Then they hide, Anton upstairs with his herbs, Sásho in his room. I go into his room now, it is dirty. His clothes are piled on the spare beds. There is a sack of rubbish. There are full rubbish sacks all over the house because rubbish vans don't come up to Orelek, the road is too poor. I wipe crumbs from the table. A bit of rain comes through the taped-up window. 'I'd put on curtains if I knew I'd stay permanently,' Sásho said. But you've been here three years. 'That's not permanent,' he grinned. I just can't stay angry with him.

'I took the radio apart again,' says Sásho on the phone. 'I saw the other side of the magnets. I repelled you and I'll always regret it. I know I'm on probation now.'

'You are,' I say sternly.

And to bai Anton: 'I miss them.'

'Well, with this rain, they'll be coming down in a few weeks,' he offers gently.

Bai Anton never speaks of his own family. They have not visited him once.

'They're not keen on livestock,' is all he says.

During his years in the mine, Anton survived a fire that paralysed half of his face and left him half-deaf. And thirty years later, he was here when a fire broke out, the one that destroyed the old house and the goat pen. He was getting the goats back from the gully when the flames arrived.

'Everybody said, save yourself and run! But you can't run when you have livestock. No, you stay with the livestock.'

The others in the village ran, except for Velin. On the farm, everybody stayed: Anton, his sister, Ugrin the Radio, Kámen and Achilles and Moni the Mute. They stayed and faced the flames.

'The goats scattered and lived but the ones in the pen burned. And two dogs.'

'I'm leaving tomorrow,' I say to Anton. He flinches. 'I'll be down in the town.'

'These bloody fleas. I'll tell Kámen to spray the goats,' he offers quickly. The fleas have entered my clothes and my body is aflame. I can't sleep and the scratchy blankets make it worse. The only thing that helps is yogurt. I lie on my bed and cover my body in cold yogurt to stop the agony. Bai Anton is immune

'It's not the fleas,' I say. 'It's just I've stayed long enough.'

We sit in silence. Even mental contact is an indulgence in this house. The milk, the blood, the rain. All our lives we perform tasks while waiting for something to click into place. For somewhere to put our love.

In the morning, bai Anton picks up his rucksack. Kámen's white van is gone.

'I'll be stopping them soon,' Anton threatens. 'Whoever wants milk can get their own milk.'

But he'll continue milking them until October. Tonight, he will return, dusty and parched with his daily harvest of apples and unload them onto the table. He will reheat yesterday's stew.

'We won't say goodbye,' I say. He nods.

'More rain today,' he looks at the sky. 'Same old song. I don't know where to take them. Maybe Fat Oaks.'

Down the white dust road, a hermit with his stick. Before the bend, he stops and turns. We look at each other without waving.

CHEESE

Hotel Strymon give me an apartment with a view of Thunder Peak. I stare at it with my mixed feelings and it stares back with its whole body.

This time, there is no list to make. I brew some herbs, sleep in clean sheets and remain close to Pirin, but outside of its fortress. The road shakes with lorries. The figs are fat like udders and I almost reach out to milk them. The warm wind blows sand from Melo, making the whole scene slip into the past. Everything feels unstable. In heavy rains, pieces break off from Melo with a roar and slip down the back of the town.

I walk along the railway. Graffitied wagons pick up passengers from the platform overgrown with weeds. Things don't stop moving, yet they are the same as last time, like a film on a loop. There is activity but no change. It's completely predictable. Holidaymakers in squeaky white trainers get out of well-washed cars and sit down for lunch. But they are not hungry. It's just something to do. They take selfies. Sometimes they buy a jar of sheep's yogurt or goat cheese from roadside sellers.

'So many sheep,' I hear Sásho's voice, 'I must gather them! *Prrrr. Prrrr,*' and his forgiving laughter that never mocks, except himself. I forgive him, the trauma has moved through me and is turning to something else.

'SHEEP YOGURT. GOAT'S CHEESE. FIGS' say the hand-written roadside placards.

Do you know what goes into this jar of yogurt so thick you can cut it? I want to wrench the glazed travellers from their coma. Do you know that this is the cleanest, tastiest, most nutritious yogurt money can buy? No. And I'm afraid you wouldn't care even if you knew. Even climbing to the top of Thunder Peak won't be enough.

You must live with these animals to understand the way of real milk and cheese. I was like you. I had no idea. Now I do and I no longer mock Jehovah's Witnesses. I understand what it's like to have seen something so true and beautiful, you want everyone to be touched by it. Saved, even.

'Dear, we lost a sheep today. Coming down from Etip. Pushed by a ram and crushed by a stone. I tried to move her but the stone was bigger than me,' says Sásho on the crackling phone. 'I couldn't cut off her ear with the tag. I'm looking at the crows now. Kámen will be gutted.'

'How's your eye?'

'Ach, it's flared up,' he says, 'serves me right.'

And we get cut off. I buy the antibiotic drops that should have been applied ages ago, call The Privateer and by chance catch him en route to Black Water. He agrees to wait halfway up the hairpin-turn road. I drive past Warm Spout where Kámen found the mare, through an old native forest of Black pine that is one of the last in Europe, past a ridge that has been called Potter since antiquity because of its fine clay soil from which vessels were made, past grotty communist-era bungalows that sat on top of old Roman mines, to a turn in the road where only trucks and vans continue to The Beeches. The Privateer and Vasko have waited for an hour.

'You've got an ace Subaru, why do you drive like a geriatric?' The Privateer complains, then calls me later to ask if I'd sell him the Subaru.

I feel a bit sick at the sight of Vasko and Vasko looks shifty at the sight of me but he always looks shifty. They take the drops and some canvas sneakers and crackers for Sásho and drive away in the camouflage-coloured van. For the first time, I notice that The Privateer treats Vasko softly, like a damaged son, and it'll be Vasko who carries the luggage up that bear path, without complaint.

I cross railway, river, road and hear a cacophony. Frequencies, trails, veins, mammary channels. The milky web is everywhere, like the Struma with her tributaries out of sight in the head of the mountain. I vibrate inside this web like a note inside the song of milk and juices. I need that song. Pomegranate trees and grape vines line the streets. Marigolds bloom red and orange through cracks in the pavement. Every bit of land neglected by humans is thriving.

The 'book of wild men and animals' is how a French historian in the early twentieth century described our pre-industrial planet. The book of wild men and animals once had innumerable volumes. Innumerable like the herds that crossed the land. A gorge like this is a volume in itself. A few pages are still left in the plundered green library of the earth. They are the only reading that feels urgent to me.

The river is brown after the rain. Black herons perch on stones and remain motionless for so long that they look like carvings by Kámen's father. I munch Keratsuda grapes. This gorge is so abundant, it's freaky. The peaks look snowy but it's marble scree. I still have the bruises from that scree.

'The river hasn't hidden itself yet,' Sásho reports. 'It's been too wet.'

After a couple of days, I am acclimatised and a bit lost. No milking. No dogs to greet you in the morning. No hills to climb, no bag to pack, no moving horizon. How do I follow the weave of the web? I know it doesn't end when you come down the mountain, it's here somewhere. A young man from Sásho's 'hood pushes a converted pram full of some plant with small yellow flowers. 'What is it?' 'I dunno,' he says, 'some herb I pick for a plant buyer.' A Roma couple on a horse cart are taking bags of manure somewhere. Manure is precious currency when you need the land. The Karakachans paid the owners of pastures they used in sheep manure. Shovelling manure in the pens is a hard job that gives you tendonitis.

'Moni fills up bags from the goats and sells them for a couple of lev to people with gardens,' says Andrea the cheese maker. 'He is a hard grafter.' She never calls him 'the mute'.

Moni was the longest serving of Kámen's shepherds and Kámen speaks of him with nostalgia. Moni the Mute would get up at five in the morning and sweep the sheep pen, Sásho would never do that, but now Moni works for Andrea and Boyko who have 140 long-haired goats.

Andrea and I are having coffee and bowls of couscous boiled with goat milk and sugar. Today is cheese-making day and it starts at nine.

We have met a few times now. I have sat in their garden and chatted over coffee. There is something solid about Andrea and Boyko. Their teenaged children are serious and their boy who travels standing in the back of the pick-up truck helps with the farm work. Their daughter complains that it ruins her designer nails but helps in every other way and both children are enthused by the family enterprise. 'Because it's something different from what everybody else is doing', sums up their daughter.

Boyko is in the dairy rooms doing 'the great wash'. In a dairy, everything begins and ends with the great wash.

'Cheese requires squeaky cleanliness,' says Andrea.

Once, a dairy had three people in it: a master cheesemaker, an assistant and an apprentice. Andrea boils the straining cloth in a pot outside. They don't use bleach or detergents, only organic soaps. They respect the dairy too much to desecrate it with chemicals, they say. Andrea's dairy is one of five or six in the Kresna Gorge. They used to do it in the basement but her mother put her foot down and said: 'you will build a dairy away from the house. You will dig and I will pay.' Three generations live in the three storey-house. Andrea's family come from a pastoral lineage. They are all small, resilient and pragmatic. Her father sometimes sits at the covered table outside. He is eighty.

'Goat cheese is good for the bones,' he said the first time. 'I took the goats out for fifty years and when I stopped, my legs seized up. The doctors said I needed a knee operation. I said no way and took the goats out for a few weeks, and that fixed it.' He still does that when Moni takes a break.

I thought that people who lived in the mountain had perfect health but that wasn't true. Nomads fared worse than lifelong shepherds like this man, especially the women who took the brunt of everything, suffered from stomach ailments and often died in childbirth. Older women were crippled by arthritis, worn out after decades of merciless walking, cold draughts, lifting heavy loads and pregnancies. Doctors were difficult to access and people helped themselves with fish oil and analgesic herbs.

Andrea and I are in the dairy. One hundred and eighty litres of milk are heating up. Kámen's milk is mixed with theirs. Different herds, different pastures, same goats. Andrea and Boyko started with long-haired goats from Kámen, now they just borrow a choice buck from him for a few months in breeding season to strengthen the breed. They are Kámen's only friends in the gorge.

Andrea's milk vat doesn't have a propeller, which means she must stir it from time to time with a long metal spoon that has holes in it. It must reach a temperature of 69 degrees, plus 1 degree when left to rest. The heating takes over two hours and Andrea uses the time to make some quark in the garden. A pot of self-fermented milk is strained through a cloth. The raw whey is kept aside for people with stomach problems or just those who like it, like me. A couple from another town arrive to buy 2 litres. The man is obese and can barely eat. Dietitians have told him to drink raw whey from goats. Looking at the non-descript whey in the tub, I remember the story of how a Karakachan cooperative between two headmen had fallen apart one summer in the early twentieth century: they fought over the divvying up of the whey. Nothing has changed; joint ventures rarely work when two alpha males are involved.

The strained lumpy milk is slowly heated on the stove until it's too hot on the skin.

'It has to have just the right consistency,' Andrea says. 'You must have a flair for the quark, feel it on your skin. And every time, it's different. Because the milk is different.'

The taste depends on what the goats are eating. Now, it's sour plums. Later it will be wild pear and apple, then acorns.

'You leave it to cool overnight and the next day you strain it again. And you have quark.'

We eat small bowls of it, still warm. It is light and fluffy in your mouth with the mild nuttiness of goat milk. The liquid that comes from this second, cooked curd is *matenitsa*: buttermilk, sold in 1.5 litre plastic bottles for 2 euros, the same price as the milk.

Andrea learned to make cheese by watching others. They were all secretive about their methods but she is a quick learner. She is self-effacing and measured, a foil to her loud man. They are perpetually busy. The only time they sit down is when they eat at the big table outside.

'Do you have a title for your book yet?' Boyko shouts from the pick-up truck outside. He is off to the farm. He is goatherd today because Moni and his wife are off for a few days. 'How about *The Wheel*. Because that's our life. A wheel that never stops.'

He waves us goodbye.

'My father's family had one prized possession,' Andrea stirs the milk in the double-walled vat. 'Their copper cauldron. Copper was expensive. It was either wood or copper. People ate in wooden bowls but cooking, washing, boiling milk, that was done in the cauldron. It was so precious, they buried it every single day after they finished using it. In case someone stole it.'

Displaced twice by war across the border, their children were born on either side and given either Greek or Bulgarian names, and everywhere, the family carried their copper cauldron with them. One day, back in their Strymonian village, the tax inspector came while the family were out with the flock. For once, they'd left the cauldron out in the open. He fined them by taking the cauldron.

'They were devastated.' Running from armies hadn't been as bad. They went to the market and sold their second most-prized possession, their two oxen. This is how much a new cauldron cost.

'Sixty-five degrees. Almost there.'

People come through the gate for cheese, all pre-orders. Occasionally, a drop-in:

'Got any left?' The word cheese is implied.

'None left,' Andrea would say. But if they plead with her, she'll relent: 'I might have a small lump somewhere.'

This is as fresh as cheese gets. It's easier to digest than ripened cheese, and less fatty.

'Sixty-nine degrees. Now we leave it to rest. By the way, my great-grandmother was Turkish.'

This is a surprise to me. The Muslims of Struma either left in waves of refugees or were dispersed in pogroms during the reign of terror whose leader is memorialised in Orelek. Many had fled to Turkey earlier, including the Yuruks but Yuruks had already mingled with settled Muslims and were simply called Turks. The upper Struma where Andrea's maternal family came from had a high concentration of Yuruk settlements up until the nineteenth century.

During the Muslim exodus in the early twentieth century, five girls stayed behind in a house. One of them was Andrea's great-grandmother. It's like that with exoduses. Someone always stays behind. Those who want to purge the land are never entirely successful.

People moved into the empty properties left in the wake of the exodus. It was a bonanza of free land, herds, houses and barns – and one of the five girls went off with an incomer from another village. The couple had eight daughters and remained poor. The men were always away in wars or working in Greece's cotton and tobacco fields. One autumn, the eight daughters were sent down the Kresna Gorge on horseback to pick grapes in a vineyard owned by an Orelek family. The girls' daily wage was a basket of grapes and a jug of goat milk. They brought no money home. This job was a way to send them away from a home that couldn't feed them. One of the girls fancied the son of the family in Orelek and simply stayed with him. That was common and saved on travel through this tough terrain. That couple became Andrea's grandparents and they lived in a house whose ruins I saw every day in Orelek.

'What my grandmother had left from her mother was the Turkish language and a pair of gold-coin earrings.'

Like the ones that nomad women wore in their hair and sewed into their clothes, inside and outside, their mobile wealth of coins and animals.

'Now we let the milk into the bath.'

She opens the tap at the bottom of the vat and the milk rushes through the taps like the waterfalls of Black Water. She has lined the bath with a cloth and a plastic sheet, like a metal cot with low walls, and the bath begins to fill. The milk is a white not seen anywhere else. Everything takes time and you can't rush it. As soon as it's in the bath, the milk changes in a subtle way.

'Everything moves, constantly,' Andrea confirms. 'This is the magic of cheese.'

While the bath fills, she shakes up a pot of probiotic yogurt and adds it in. Then she puts live liquid rennet in a bit of water. It has to be one part to 55,000. It can't survive outside the fridge for more than twenty minutes.

What did dairymakers do before fridges?

'They took a yeasty curd substance from the stomach of a slaughtered lamb or goat kid. But it had to be a suckling.'

Or raided an ant heap for ant's acid. And if you lived near figs the milk from the leaves and stalks of fig trees.

When the bath is full, she stirs in the rennet and leaves it for an hour. It smells of milky baths and babies' heads, like a nursing room. It makes me sleepy.

Lunch is roast rabbit with cabbage. I thought it was her mother who did the cooking but the family employ a cook because Andrea's mother is occupied elsewhere. Andrea's mother never leaves the house, though she is out of view. I visited several times before I discovered that down some tiled steps, in a small basement apartment, in a room full of icons like a rock church sat a child-sized woman with a disfigured back and a lined face: Andrea's mother. There is something of a caged bird about her, but also the hidden power of the witch because Andrea's mother is a folk healer. She does not perform rituals after midday, though. 'It's got to be in the morning, dear,' she says, 'otherwise it's no good.' But we can chat. She pats the bed beside her. I sit down. There is something eerie about her. She is both here and not here.

Dessert is rice pudding with goat milk and cinnamon. Afterwards, Andrea begins to strain the milky baby through the cloth and the water separates from the milk. The water runs through a tap in the bath into a bucket. The straining is done by gently lifting the four corners of the cloth, one corner after another and more brine comes out. Buckets of it.

This baby is hefty. We laugh.

'See, cheese is not complicated,' she says. 'But it needs someone to be here all the time.'

With milk and cheese, there are no holidays. 'Holidays are when you sell your animals,' Andrea says. 'Then you have a holiday. But your life is empty. You are bereaved. So you buy a couple of goats and start all over again. It's an addiction.'

Yes. I dread the moment when my life will have no warm milk. We are still straining the baby until the surface becomes smooth.

'Otherwise the inside becomes lumpy. And we don't want lumpy cheese,' says Andrea. When no more brine comes out, she wraps up the baby by folding up the four corners of the cloth and presses it down firmly with especially crafted well-fitting wooden planks and weighs it down further with buckets of water.

'Now we leave the baby to rest for four hours.'

The buckets of brine, which she calls 'the mother' are covered up.

'When we cut the cheese, we pour the mother over it. It's a whole other thing, to be with the mother.'

In the large dairies, they put salted water in with the packaged cheese. Large dairies use milk from large stationary farms where animals don't roam extensive pastures like here and where more productive breeds of goat are used. They use citric acid too, to make the cheese last longer. No mother. Commercial cheese is orphaned cheese.

'Nothing can replace the mother!' Andrea says.

And anyway, when you deal with animal milk or meat close-up like this, everything must be used. Nothing is discarded. It's respect for the animal.

'Count the things you can make from milk,' she says. 'Yogurt, cheese, many kinds of it, quark and cottage cheese, ice cream.' She and Velin the Grape made goat-cheese pesto with almonds from her own almond grove.

We pass the time at the long table crumbling bunches of dried summer sage for when they make sausages in winter from their pigs and goats.

'I was telling you about my grandmother. She and my grandfather raised animals in the hills of Orelek that you're now familiar with. Then, the communists took away their flock and they came down here and built a house. They were not well off after they lost their flock.'

The grandfather was an invalid and worked as a baker. While they lived in Orelek, her grandmother became an apprentice of the village healer-seer, the one who saw the disappearance of her village, and took her skills down the hill with her. And her own copper cauldron. Years later, their daughter fell into a ditch and broke her back. That's Andrea's mother. She spent half a year in plaster without moving but the guy she was seeing didn't give up on her and they got married. How she then gave birth to four children, I don't know.

'Come,' she pats the bed.

The gold-coin earrings on her bloodless earlobes catch the morning light. There are two single beds in the room. She sits on one, I sit on the other. On the table is a bowl of raw eggs for divining and her other tools: spools of red wool, a knife, a bowl of water; staples of the everyday witch.

As a young woman, she began to have dreams in which three female 'saints' appeared and had dialogues:

'We'll take her with us,' said one.

'No, we can't leave her children orphans,' said the second one.

And the third one said: 'We'll take one of her children instead. And in return, we'll give her second sight. To help people.'

Soon after, one of her daughters sickened and died.

A man came to her door the day after she buried her. His child had been missing for days. She saw three men bringing back a boy by the end of the day. That man was from Sásho's border town. I think of Sásho as a boy, running away from home time after time and three cops bringing him back.

'I was left with two girls. Andrea was the last born and that made three girls.'

Her husband brings three figs on a plate for me.

The three fates appeared in her dreams again with their frightening dialogues. They told her about her daughters. One said:

'Your eldest, all the men in her in-law family will die young.' And so it was.

'Your little girl that we took is fine, don't you worry about her,' said the second one and showed her the girl in the company of a woman made of light.

'And the last born will give to people,' said the third one.

'Sometimes I wonder,' Andrea said, 'if this whole thing with the cheese is less about business and more about giving. I'm always handing something to people. A piece of cheese. A bottle of milk. A goat kid. And I'm still not making serious money.'

People started coming to the newly minted healer, for lost animals, for lost health. She made special belts for women who couldn't conceive. Did she treat addiction?

'Bring me the largest padlock you can find,' she instructed, 'and a thread the length of his bed.' I think of the plank in the hut. I have no idea how long it is. I return with a heavy padlock and Sásho's peaked hat that he left in my car. I know that an object does the trick too. 'For example,' said the mother, 'if you have small children in the home with no supervision, leave your broom with them.' The broom stands for the woman. The cauldron stands for life: fire, water, milk, herbs, the witch's brew. The padlock stands for fate. Not that I believed in it, but you never know, and I wanted to see her methods.

She takes the padlock and opens it. It's heavy. She unspools some red thread and measures the length of the hat three times, then cuts the thread in three.

'What's his name? Okay, Alexander.'

She stuffs the thread into the hole of the padlock, mumbles a spell and locks it shut, then wraps it and the little keys in a piece of pre-cut sheet of newspaper – a pile of them sits on the table – and gives it to me.

'His addiction is inside it. Keep it and bring it back from time to time to refresh the spell.'

When you can't fight it, lock it. Maybe the soul responds to spells.

'Dear,' she says in her placid way, 'everything is down to the soul. Just as the body travels to and fro on its petty tasks, so the soul travels at night. That's why the dead appear to us then. It's not them that come to us, it's the soul that visits them. Where there are no bodies.'

It is not a place, it's a realm. Don't startle the sleeping awake or their soul might never return from its wandering.

She speaks matter of factly, like Andrea. The gold-coin earrings of her grandmother ripen with the late morning sun, the only part of her that looks warm.

It smells like a bakery in the dairy room. Andrea unwraps the baby. It is perfectly set, with a silky wobble on the surface. A loaf of milky bread. Three-hundred goats have given up their milk for this. I have milked some of them.

'Now we must cut the baby,' she says.

Each piece of the body is placed in a clean white tub. She bastes them with 'the mother' and seals the lids shut.

'This is the magic of cheese,' she takes off her wellies. 'You see, it's simple.'

It is six o'clock. I walk away with a small tub and a sense of satisfaction. I will sit on my balcony and eat slices of fresh cheese with tomatoes while the sun sets over Black Water. Sásho will be bringing down the godmothers and re-heating yesterday's beans and lentils.

'The wheel is turning,' shouts Boyko from the truck. He is picking up Andrea. Their son stands in the back, upright like a soldier although he is a weedy, pale boy, not at all macho like his father and you don't have to be macho to be an animal soldier. You just have to turn up on time, and it's time for the evening milking.

GOATWALKING

Ugrin the Radio spent five years as goatherd for Kámen and in that time he increased the herd from 100 to 250.

'Then I came down from Orelek and started with ten of my own.'

Now he had one hundred, and another twenty he grazed for others for a small fee. Today, I was goatwalking with him. He was one of several livestock breeders in the little town. All of them were children of Orelek who remained plugged into the pastoral web: Andrea and Boyko, a young gravestone mason with sheep, Ugrin and some others.

Ugrin was my neighbour, here in my rented house-flat just below the pens overlooking the little town. I couldn't stay in Hotel Strymon anymore. I was scanning Thunder Peak all the time. They say: to quit an addiction, change your environment.

Now I looked to the other mountain with its milder body forms, and I had a kitchen of my own. I drank raw sheep's milk from glass bottles sold in a roadside café and made my comfort foods: fried courgettes topped with sheep's yogurt from the same family, tomatoes with Andrea's cheese and rice pudding with milk from Ugrin's goats. His family couldn't afford to invest in dairy rooms so their milk was given to another family with a dairy who turned it into quark, cheese and clarified butter for Ugrin to sell.

Every few days I entered their courtyard and bought a bottle of milk or a ball of quark from his mother or his wife. I learned how to tell raw milk from the homogenised milk in the shops: when you boil raw milk, some water separates from it, you see it evaporate in the pan. With homogenised milk, it doesn't. Ugrin sold his products even cheaper than Andrea.

All the animal people here had set itineraries that were mutually agreed and a neighbourly ethos prevailed. There were no territorial face-offs in these lower floors of the mountain. The wars were waged higher up, between the big herds and the big egos of Kámen and Stamen. Breeders down here were more modest, there was space for everyone. Although everybody knew that once, there were lots of people who had just a few animals living in their yard and now there were few breeders with larger flocks. The reason was that by the time you had a few, you had to have a hundred. And then, 250. Otherwise you couldn't sustain it, financially and logistically. Everybody who understood pastoralism regretted this. It was a monopoly, like supermarkets pushing out small shops, and it was the fault of the subsidy culture, the corrupt state that held livestock breeders in contempt and a European Union run by urban technocrats, who can be found in the pool of the pampered people. They issued the squeamish regulations that strangled pastoral produce, which is why the freshest organic products like these weren't in the shops. Pastoralists had to rely on local custom at rock-bottom prices.

But Ugrin was not a complainer. He was hopeful for the future. Appetite for organic goat products had shot up in recent years and he could barely keep up with the demand.

Ugrin walked with his goats from his pen, over Melo and the rolling hills beyond, to Warm Spout where I first saw his goats last summer. Then, back down the steep sandy beds of tributaries, now dry. It was a long way and I was surprised that Ugrin was chubby despite clocking up a huge mileage every day. His brother died from obesity and goatwalking kept Ugrin from a similar fate, he said. He was fifty-something and hoped to be on his feet with his animals for the next fifty years.

'After us, there's nobody,' he said, matter of factly. 'My son helps with the milk but he won't goatwalk and no one from his generation is interested. My daughter won't touch the animals. And she's off to university soon.'

He didn't blame them. It's how it was. This must be the first time in the history of goatwalking that we face the end of it because we have grown too lazy, too vain and too busy to walk with animals.

The mountain goat was the second grazing animal humans domesticated after the sheep. The first breed, a European wild goat called

Capra prisca, is extinct in its original form. For Ugrin, though, it was about living with goats full stop. He liked all the breeds.

'You've gotta love these animals, otherwise don't do it.'

We climbed the Melo. He batted apples and pears from trees for the goats. The flock formed a pretty patchwork of black, white and rust-red. There were three breeds: long-haired, curly-horned and a local breed with short smooth hair that were milkier. The long-haired ones were cropped like youthful punks to stop their hair dragging on the ground and make milking easier. Ugrin got the lowest subsidy, 15 euros per head each year. That's 1,500 euros a year, plus what he made from the milk products.

'But goats are more economic than mountain sheep,' he said.

They didn't require a seasonal exodus and were much easier to milk. At this number of non-special-breed goats and no other source of income, you couldn't afford to hire a goatherd.

'But I'm pleased with my animals. And with myself.'

So am I, this is fantastic, I thought at the start of the day when the sun climbed over us and we climbed over the hills and the hills were full of wild fruit, and from the top of the Melo a golden music of highs and lows unrolled at our feet. I saw why Velin fought the new motorway for twenty-five years. It's because there was no good place for it to go. On this side of the river, it would wreck pastures, mineral springs, the Roman road that traced the river, the cathedral canyons and the whole web of western Pirin. On the other side of the river, it would kill the community of millennial sycamores, the most beautiful tributary of the river, the whole web of eastern Maleshevo. And there was a road already. Why was it imperative to build a bigger one?

'It's the lorries,' said Ugrin who stood to lose from the new motorway because his pastures would disappear. 'There are lots of accidents.'

The people of Kresna suffered pollution and sudden death from heavy traffic. That's why many of them wanted the new motorway. It would bypass their little town but their little town was here because their grandparents were forced down. Their little town was a village a generation ago and before that, just riverside inns. As life came down from the highlands to the lowlands, the new motorways wanted to climb into the mountains. Once the web was broken, it was easier to break it further.

'Who is the goatherd now?' Ugrin asked about Orelek. 'And the shepherd?'

He shouted at the goats when they lingered, looking at him from the corner of their eye and when we skirted a dell that was a wolf haunt, he threw firecrackers that startled the three dogs but that's how Ugrin was, a gregarious extrovert. Plus, he'd had goat kids killed by wolves in daylight, in this dell.

Goats are different grazers from sheep. They make individual choices. Willow, acacia, wild pear and little shrubs. They don't follow on from each other, it's just that they move companionably as a loose gang. They are more like guardian dogs than sheep.

Ugrin had a little notebook and wrote in it every time a buck mounted a she-goat: today's date and which goat. That way, he planned for the birthing season. In January, he moved to the little hut next to his pen to keep an eye on the expectant mothers. He had a stove and a bed and what luxury to be so close to town and the shops, to have internet and someone bring you a hot meal.

Goats and sheep are pregnant for 150 days.

'You don't want them to give birth out in the open because they hide and you might not find them for days, then foxes and wolves gobble the kid.'

At Warm Spout, the goats drank from a small reservoir and he put out salt for them. Here was a shooting range for hunters and a large wild boar was imprisoned in an enclosure, the poor thing served as a practice target. I shared my lunch with him. He had long white eyelashes and a friendly, smart expression.

'Why are we so horrible to animals?' I said. We rested in the shade next to the pig enclosure, long enough to eat lunch. He was a hunter himself and quite the meat eater.

'If you kill an animal, you've got to eat it,' he said. 'That's fair. Otherwise it's not.'

On the way back, the heat doubled. I was parched and in need of a nap. I kept sitting under trees to close my eyes but when I opened them, I found one goat peering at me in a sort of ruminant critique. The flock had moved on and Ugrin was shouting at the goats who were beginning their afternoon tricks. Knowing we were going back, they slowed down, scattered and pissed you off. Not only do they not let your soul rest all day, then they scatter in a gully so wide we have to use our last bit of energy to round them up. Ugrin unleashed streams of obscenity at a special pitch. He channelled the voice of the angry shepherd that I'd heard come out of Kámen's mouth, and Sásho's and Anton's.

'Motherfucking wily goats! Now you decide to eat pears. Now you're pear grazing. Didn't you have all day? See this stick you mother-fucking pear eaters.'

It could go on for a good few minutes and the goats didn't give a shit about his verbiage, it's the high-pitched intonation they respond to, as to a discordant music, and as soon as the offending individuals moved on, unfazed, smug, having had the last chew but without wasting precious energy unlike their demented pastor, his anger evaporated as if throwing the off-switch. He grinned at me. It was just role playing. He was an actor and the goats were his chorus with their ruminant refrain, day after day. It was their dance.

The thought of doing this again first thing in the morning, and then the next morning, and so without respite, staggered me, even if they were your own animals. To keep up with the goats required sur-render and a suspension of self, at least self in the modern sense, the self that demands to be at the centre of things and not a companion to a bunch of other animals.

But maybe the modern self is not quite real. Maybe its understand-ing of centre and periphery is an illusion. Maybe it wouldn't be that difficult to give it up. It might be a relief.

Ugrin was not after ecstasy, pedigree or even recognition. He was not after saving breeds. He was not proud, except when it came to his milk: Is my cheese as good as Andrea's? He was ordinary, yet to run with the goats all your life was extraordinary. But that's only because the club of the goatherd had lost almost all of its members in the last couple of generations.

This is an ancient club. The order of the goat is one of the oldest heraldic stamps of the human-animal bond. Goats were depicted on ancient coins, and ritual gold drinking vessels used by Thracian and Greek aristocracy had carved goat heads, which symbolically 'purified' the liquid. A local told me that years ago he was poking around the Roman fort when he found a bronze statuette of a kneeling goat. He sold it to the National History Museum for a small sum and was gutted when he saw it later in a catalogue, dated 14,000 years. He could have asked for much more money!

People only came into contact with goats through their skins, now. Bulgaria and Macedonia still have an active relationship with goats because of the fertility games played since antiquity, known as *kukeri*. Kukeri are masked men who dress in long-haired goat skins and belt themselves with bunches of goat bells and perform comical and sinister dances in January, which is lambing and kidding season. It's a shamanic leftover, you don the body of the buck and become the buck and the buck's innermost qualities are: priapic vitality, tricksterish cleverness and endurance in harsh terrain. The mountain goat outlasts cold, heights and predators. It's an all-round miraculous animal. These games are enacted in public spaces and along the Struma, kukeri are taken very seriously. It's competitive. There is an industry in kukeri costumes which means dealing in animal skins but most people have no idea where those skins come from. They buy them from dealers or straight from the breeders at great expense and they *have* to be long-haired. You cannot be a kuker without the skin of a mountain goat or sheep, and thousands are paid for them, Ugrin told me. Prices were higher twenty years ago when the long-haired breed was in danger of disappearing.

I met a man who was a skin dealer. He toured animal expos in the Alps looking for rare goat breeds but every time he offered Swiss and Italian farmers large sums for the skins of beautiful bucks, they came to blows because the farmers were affronted by the dealer's savage proposition. Shamanism *is* savage, you ingest the spirit of the goat and are in turn ingested by his body, a mutual devourment. Real shamans are initiated through dangerous death-and-rebirth psycho-tripping with spirit animals which involves dismemberment in the spirit world but modern kukeri bypass the spirit bit. They bag the skins, the fur, the horns and the bells and spend the year crafting their next season's costume.

In the 1970s, East German biologists studied the population of the Kalofer goat, which happened to be concentrated in this very region, and concluded that this valuable autochthonous animal was being pushed out by more productive imported breeds. They bought a flock and took them to Thuringia's zoo, to safeguard the genetic stock. Thirty years later, having successfully bred their flock without signs of inbreeding and the genetic stability proving that this genus was very ancient, they came to Orelek to buy a few bucks to boost their flock. By then, the breed had been restored to healthy numbers here in its homeland, thanks to Kámen, Stamen, Marina and Achilles.

Now, there are quite a few long-haired mountain goat enthusiasts, and most breeders along the Struma still breed them for their skins, even if the price of skins has gone down as their numbers have gone up. The bucks of this breed have the longest hair of any goats in Europe – up to a metre – and that's why more males are kept than are otherwise needed. Milking and grazing is hard work, but skinning a goat is quick and lucrative. Having bucks in your flock is like having pentacles on four legs. All the people with goats deal in skins but don't talk about it because it causes them pain. Yet there is no choice. Under the current laws, you could not survive on milk and cheese alone, and there is no appetite for goat meat. People go for pork which is cheapest, lamb which is traditional, and rarely, the more expensive beef, for special occasions.

'Kukeri fanatics get off on dressing up as goats,' Stamen said earlier. 'It's a sort of madness. Me, I get off on taking the goats out to pasture and watching them climb and graze to their hearts' content.'

Every goat lover needs his goats alive. Fetishists deal in the dead, lovers deal in the living.

I remembered this every time I drove up to Orelek, past the waterfalls that make rock cathedrals and where Stamen liked to take the goats in winter, back in his Orelek days, because here was warmer and less icy. The goats entered the cathedral and he was in heaven.

This is why, when he left Orelek and came down to the gorge, the goats returned to the cathedral.

There was something fanatical about these goats or maybe it was the people who loved them. Stamen had split from the association dedicated to the protection of this goat and joined an alternative association. It was his way – schismatic but it's also that he had strong views on this goat's defining characteristics, something to do with whether all or some of them had curly horns. Stamen and Kámen both told me the following: when they have an important decision to make, they sleep in the pen. Kámen with the sheep, Stamen with the goats.

Ugrin's mother and wife were sitting on an old sofa outside the pen, smoking. His wife was just back from the sewing sweatshop where she worked for 300 euros a month. They set to milking in the pen. I walked down the steep lanes, past the bundles of oak branches collected by livestock owners as winter food, in the deep, deep beauty of the sunset. The street was fragrant with figs and animal droppings. God, what an abundant earth. I can't fathom it. I can't explain it.

To goatwalk is to be loyal not just to the free-grazing goat, but to the very idea of the goat. Like a Don Quixote, you set out each day with a song in your heart and affection for the goats. Each day, you get over yourself and become more like your animals. You shadow the goat and the goat shadows you, and today I goatwalked with Ugrin to shadow Sásho and our flock. Because I missed them. I missed their skin, their fur, their faces, their voices and their inalienable goodness.

I could almost recall a time, in some faraway galaxy of the soul, when I was dressed in goat and bear skins and my teeth had fallen out though I was still young, and my children and my man were killed when the Roman colonist bastards invaded our gorge and enslaved everyone and requisitioned our animals. I escaped to Black Water with a few goats I had tucked away and my dogs. And I watched the deep, deep beauty of the sunrise, amazed to be alive in my hut surrounded by wolves in sheep's clothing and my surviving tribe in bear skins. We kept the hut fires warm in the midst of devastation.

Through our history as a species, animals have kept us company when all else has failed.

All human–animal communes dressed in each other's skin and took on each other's spirit until they were robbed of spirit and skin. Extinction can come quickly. At the beginning of the twentieth century, Bulgaria had 1.5 million goats of indigenous breeds. At the end of the century, the most ancient and culturally significant of those – the long-haired mountain goat – was endangered. Another mountain breed, from Rila Mountain, had been bred with a more productive type in the 1970s, then the breeders lost interest and slaughtered the lot.

A hundred years ago, there were thirty-seven autochthonous breeds of domesticated grazing animals, endemic to Bulgaria or the Balkans. In just a few decades, six breeds were extinct, twelve reached the brink of disappearance, sixteen came under threat of disappearance and three were threatened.

Without the people in this story, the long-haired goat would have only survived as a costume to put on once a year and pretend.

After a day of goatwalking, I looked at people's faces and saw goats and that was without any magic mushrooms.

Sásho was on the phone today. I could hear the bell chimes of our flock.

'How's your eye?'

'Fine. What are you doing, who are you seeing? I'm jealous.'

'Goatwalking with Ugrin,' I said.

'Ah, the Radio! Not jealous of him. But anything you tell him is between you, him and the whole gorge.'

They knew of each other but their territories didn't overlap.

'Is it hot down there? It's cold at night. Thank God for your stuff or I'd freeze my balls off.'

I'd sent him a thermal top and waterproof jacket via The Privateer.

'Have you spoken to Kámen?' I asked.

'No, have you? If you do, tell him to call me.'

Kámen hadn't been to Black Water for ten days because of a broken-down van but I was doubtful about everything now.

'The sheep have mouth ulcers. I don't know what to do,' Sásho said.

He had run out of bread and was eating Vasko's bread.

'I'm goatwalking with Moni next.'

'Say hi to goat man from sheep man.'

Then he told me how yesterday, when he took the flock up to the lakes and put out their salt, a wild chamois joined them. It wasn't afraid of Sásho, the dogs didn't bother it and for a moment, he thought about picking up a rock and bludgeoning it to death – a once-in-a-lifetime chance to taste chamois. Then he looked at it again. A beautiful animal, and he wanted to rob it of its life.

'Humans are sick, dear. That's why I don't mind becoming more like a dog. Or a sheep.'

Moni was seated on a milking stool. Andrea let the goats through a little pen door. There were sixty animals for him to milk, sixty were milked by Boyko. That was nothing after the 400 sheep he'd milked for Kámen.

I nodded hello at Moni and he nodded a curt smile. After all I'd heard about him, I was surprised by his boyish looks. Maria's bleached hair was piled up in a bun. She was from a different part of the country and different Roma stock. They met through a dating website. Moni was divorced and Maria was younger and from a better-off family.

'It beats me,' Kámen said once at the kitchen table, 'how an illiterate deaf person can have this much success with women.'

When Maria wanted to come and live with him, the workers' room in Orelek became too small but when Moni asked for one of the rooms upstairs in the house, preferably the one with the double bed, it was 'no'.

Kámen: 'It was just sex. He was fine with me then she scrambled his brains.'

It's not that Kámen didn't want women in the house, he didn't want relationships. This is how Kámen lost his shepherd of thirteen years. Andrea and Boyko wanted to hire Moni on the spot but worried about falling out with Kámen and they were dependent on his choice bucks for the strength of their herd, and for his milk which boosted their cheese production. The only other person with long-haired goats in the gorge was Stamen and they didn't get on with Stamen. At first, Moni went to work for another breeder who did what Sásho's former employer had done – after two months' work, no pay. There was no contract in place and no honour to keep.

Moni and Maria lived on Andrea and Boyko's farm above town, perched among orchards and allotments and which the family had built on the grounds of an antique dwelling. They had realised this when they hit on a huge ceramic amphora, used for wine or grain 2,000 years ago, which was quite a common occurrence here. They reburied it, intact.

Maria made coffee on the patio and we waited for Moni. They lived in a comfortable bungalow beside the goat pens, with a view over the fertile river plain, the greenhouses and the abandoned factor-ies where storks nested. Every day, Andrea brought them cooked dinner, with pudding and a 2-litre bottle of beer for Moni who drained it after the evening milking. 'It's not cheap to have hired shepherds', Boyko said. 'By the time you've covered food, transport and addictions, you're out of pocket.'

It was a tense dance between hired shepherds and livestock owners. Both sides lived on the brink of subterfuge to get what they needed. Both were vulnerable in a world oblivious to their struggle to pre-serve something valuable for all. The stakes were high, the gains were low and these last pastoral warriors needed each other desperately.

The tubs with snow-white milk were taken down to Andrea's dairy in the pick-up truck. Moni let the goats out. Maria and I were joining him today. Maria was not a shepherd and only went with the herd when boredom got to her, and she was very bored. No work and no friends, because it isn't easy to meet people when you are deaf. All she had was the internet and the town beautician.

The goats filed up the path – full-coated, curly-horned celebrants in full regalia setting off on a grazing parade.

Three dogs from Kámen's lot led the way. Andrea wished us a nice day and Boyko waved to us from the pick-up truck. It was a very dif-ferent scene from Orelek.

Maria, Moni and I hit it off at once. I picked up a bit of sign language and they read my lips. Maria was sociable and Moni was bright, with an easy smile. It's true what they say, most communication is done through the body.

Moni had a light touch and his experience was obvious. No effort to control the animals, he observed them as they scattered in the orchards. *I'll go ahead, don't worry, the stragglers will catch up*, he told us soundlessly. Maria and I rounded them up at the back. She'd brought her pet Chihuahua. The little dog and the three big dogs trotted along together. Then lay down in the shade together.

It was a horizontal itinerary with a few climbs and obstacles, like the eroded river banks. We followed the water: first, the tributaries of Orelek River, then under a road pass where the rapids rise suddenly and in the old days before the road, you got stranded and had to wait for the river to recede. The main goatwalk was along the Struma. Here, the river is wide and majestic with its flowing green hair. The goats were curious. Sheep are interested in pasture but goats are interested in geography. They like places and faces. When they lingered under some old sycamores, we sat down for a conversation. The goats wanted conversation too. A few of them sniffed my hands, intrigued by the novelty with a notebook, their eyes covered by curly fringes.

How do they see with these fringes? I asked Moni. He laughed.

They see, don't worry, he gestured.

Sásho sends greetings from Black Water, I said. *Shepherd* is a fist under your chin. *Goatherd* is that, plus horns.

Black Water is *hut* with my hands, and I pointed up.

Wow! How long did you stay?

Maria's jaw dropped.

Me, I'd never go there, she said. *If Moni goes up, I'd wait here.*

Moni showed me photos of the lakes and the tent he pitched at the lakes, the summer before Sásho was hired.

Wow. You were alone there.

Quite happy, Moni smiled. *Flying like a bird.*

How many people do I know who would be happy to spend three months in Black Water with several hundred sheep and no internet? Or even without sheep and with internet. I honestly don't know.

Sásho and I were buddies, Moni showed me.

Moni and Sásho lived together in the workers' room perched on the precipice. Moni introduced Sásho to the flock and the geography. They shared the bed in Black Water. Sásho, who is highly literate, helped illiterate Moni on the dating sites and wrote sweet messages to Maria on Moni's behalf.

But now they didn't cross each other. It's the way of shepherd friendships. They belonged to the flock. It's not personal, it's territorial. Like guardian dogs or wolf cubs who leave the family by age two, and never meet except from a distance, when they call out and recognise a familiar voice. *Awwwww*.

Biologists say that the dog is the only animal who has a double or even triple identity – one for its canid family, one for its human family and for the guardian dog, the flock. But biologists should include another creature in this anthro-zoological category: the shepherd.

Is Sásho alone up there? Moni asked me.

I showed him that Sásho drinks and that's why he was alone now. He laughed. His many missing teeth made him look like a boy and an old man at once.

Me, I don't drink, Moni showed me his serious look. *Only from time to time*.

Not true, Maria countered.

Always criticising, Moni mock despaired.

Get out of here! she berated him.

He laughed soundlessly and slid off to see what the dogs were doing. He had a way of moving soundlessly too. He spotted a change even before the dogs barked, with the corner of his eye. He sensed the goats' intention to move on. Moni was plugged into the web at all times. He only unplugged when he drank, and he had no intention of quitting. Just as Maria had no intention of cooking, cleaning or getting a job. She was happy to let others do everything for her. They accepted each other's severe limitations. Silence was a peacemaker.

Maria showed me that he drinks, that she wants to leave him but that she loves him.

We walked on in the white dust. Her little dog kept up. We passed under a bridge, passed the open roadside dump made by rubbish thrown by drivers, the poplars whispered. A holiday from words. How restful, to express the things that pass through you with your face, your hands, your hair and with the long willow branches, the long hair of the goats, the long flow of the river. Everything expressed you and you expressed it back.

The afternoon was a warm pool and we crawled at the bottom of it. Some old memory was unlocked, of some old life when I was always on the move across oceans and mountains, with armies, caravans, shepherds, itinerant plant buyers, pilgrims, bards, dervishes, zealots and troublemakers. The memory was in my cells: how to walk with ease across the pages of the book of wild men and animals. My cells remembered being on four legs and galloping with the wind in my mane or having no legs and crossing a pond, breathing with my powerful gills.

Movement is the part of us that is free, and it's hard-wired. Walking across the land connects me with the wild self just as the Karakachan sheep, the Karakachan horse and the long-haired goat are now domesticated but carry the imprint of their wild selves. Biologists call it a 'genetic bank'. Its currency is life itself. This whole place is a giant bank.

Once, the river pulsed with traffic. The Strymonians made large rafts and loaded them with goods. Some of the goods were trees brought down by loggers all the way from the lakes. On the rafts, the drovers tied up a sheep or goat and a mule. That way, they had fresh milk to last them the journey downstream to the Gulf of Salonika, then they sold the milking animal and returned home on muleback. These men were called *shabani*, ploughers. They ploughed the river. Bridges were rare and roads were narrow. Brigands were everywhere, ravaging the land with their self-enriching enterprises, like now. Back then, they were extortionists. Now they are extractors. That's why they need bigger roads.

When we emerged briefly onto the road, by the rubbish dump and the abandoned bus stop, we looked outlandish to the speeding drivers, with our goats and sticks, like figures from the past or the future. We moved at a speed that the cars couldn't register. We didn't aim to get anywhere or achieve anything, to be first, second or even last. Our task was millennial. Coated in fine sand, sweaty and silent, we walked with a dogged devotion.

God, what a long road it's been and there is no sign of the paths running out. I love these paths too much for words. The only meaningful thing left is to retrace them like a lover's body. Staff in hand, to wade through garbage and flowers and find the words for it.

At the abandoned bus stop was a man selling vegetables from his van. He was a friend of Andrea and Boyko's through the pastoral web. After twenty years as a builder in Italy, he had returned to his river and bought 1,000 long-haired goats. Unable to cope with drunken goatherds, he took up the staff for a while then sold the lot. Now he had black buffalo that didn't require herding, just chasing like wild horses.

'Come and chase them with me,' he invited me and gave us a bag of pink tomatoes called 'buffalo heart'.

The breeze ran its hands through the silvery poplars and our hair. The goats brushed past Moni who counted them and wrote in the sand with his stick: 140. All here. Seeing that a buck struggled with a heavy bell, Moni unfastened the bell and put it on another buck; both goats were pleased with the arrangement.

Maria was tired, fed up and dragged her feet. Goatwalking is not for everyone. Back at the farm, Andrea waited for us with roast chicken and potatoes. Maria and I ate on the patio and enjoyed the sunset, while Moni milked for an hour then joined us with the same easy smile he'd had in the morning, untouched by fatigue, as if he hadn't spent the last fifteen years goatwalking the earth.

Hired shepherds and their employers are different breeds. The farmers are empire builders. They count pentacles and worry about pedigree, legacy and what their enemies are plotting. Hired shepherds count stars and empty bottles. Both work relentlessly and neither get rich.

When Pan challenged Apollo to a flute-playing contest, everybody knew that proud Apollo would win, not because he was better but because he had privileges on Olympus. But Pan's pan-flute remained the most popular. In the forest, all living things loved to listen to Pan's music: nymphs and satyrs, beasts and plants, rocks and humans. Apollo the golden boy was frankly a bit dull.

Hired shepherds are what's left of the nomads, that is why many of them are Gypsies or Gypsy-like, because they can walk with just the clothes on their back and leave no trace. They are equally at home in myth and in manure. They can goatwalk like it's a religion, like there's nothing else to be done.

Even having no name adds to your power, by being the goatherd you become all goatherds. The lineage is in your crook, so the well-dressed townspeople had better be nice to you who wear the margins like an invisible cloak as the animals follow you out of town to the ends of the world.

EXODUS FROM BLACK WATER

This long August is ending. The hot wind blows from the south and brings news of something fragrant. The two mountains talk across the river and send each other seeds on the wind. I send up a phone voucher and another charging battery for Sásho's phone via The Privateer, who lives down the street from my house and because Kámen is not picking up his phone.

'Are you still taking up booze for them?' I ask The Privateer. He frowns.

'If I don't, they'll get it anyway.'

'Sásho told me he doesn't drink anymore.'

He scoffs. 'They drink like skunks. It's the nature of the beast.'

But The Privateer cares, in his own way. He understands addiction and he understands relationships. 'Did Sásho tell you he now smokes the thin Karelias? Did you tell him you included a voucher in your package?' he calls me later when he returns from the huts. ''Cos I forgot to tell him and it might have slipped out. And tell Kámen he needs to take up bread to his shepherd, at least.'

The Privateer thinks I'm still on Kámen's team, but Kámen, who comes down to the Gorge every day on errands, does not answer his phone. He is like that with everyone. If you want to speak to him, you must drive up to Orelek and sit in the empty house until he turns up. I visit Andrea on the day he delivers his milk. He sits at the couple's outside table scrolling through his phone and ignoring his hosts. 'I tried to call you,' I say, and he shrugs. I know from Sásho that he hasn't taken the charging battery up. I can't believe he'd do it out of meanness. Maybe he has forgotten, he has more important things on his mind, but this has cut Sásho off from the world completely.

'It's easier to communicate with the deaf than with you!' I said to Kámen and he smirked.

He enjoyed it. You were meant to be grateful for scraps, a classic display of power through withholding. I didn't think that communication with Orelek could get worse but Kámen cut himself off like he was drawing up the moat bridge. In our lone mountain terraces, I strived to connect us and Kámen to disconnect us; me in the gorge, Kámen in Orelek, Sásho in Black Water. I wondered if I'd made some mistake that had pushed Kámen back into his shell, but I hadn't. He simply could not let those inside his circle have any sovereignty. Bai Anton had surrendered all of his and Sásho had surrendered some but I hadn't and by leaving his circle, I had somehow betrayed him.

People who love livestock are difficult.

The exodus was on everybody's mind and in the absence of information, you had to read the signs. Sásho on the phone: 'This is the homeland of Vanga, dear. We specialise in divination. But I know my livestock.' He meant Kámen. Sásho divined that it was a short season this year because of the late move and the wet weather. By law, they had to stay at Black Water for a minimum of two months. That was mid-September.

'I'll wait,' I said. But I had other work and couldn't stay indefinitely.

'Kámen came up today and left me Johnny,' Sásho said. 'I found him in the hut, trying to light the stove. Nice guy. Doesn't drink.'

Johnny was a young guy from the 'hood and the new helper. I wondered how long he would last. He'd worked as a pen cleaner in Orelek but Black Water was something else.

Sásho was pleased because they got on well, he learned the ropes quickly and at night, they drank tea and went to bed, Sásho reported primly. Now that he had a colleague, he didn't see Vasko much but Johnny was afraid of the wild and couldn't be left alone at all.

I went to see buffalo man in his low-lying mountain downstream that was so ancient, the land was discoloured from too much use or maybe it was the southern light. There was a village here called Sklavé since the Romans. Local people were bought and sold at slave auctions here and like Spartacus were sent off to bleed and die for the pleasure of the pampered people. We roamed in search of the twenty black buffalo and buffalo man played a little flute for me, like a real shepherd.

'You know this one?'

Of course I knew it. It was a famous tune, but I didn't know it was called 'The Lost Flock'. It's a masterpiece of tonal subtlety that changes from major to minor key every few seconds, like sped-up weather passing over the hills and emotions passing through the human body. The hills *are* the body.

Without words, it tells the story of a shepherd who falls asleep and loses his flock. He goes in search of it, playing his kaval flute, until he sees them scattered over a hill and rejoices, but no, they're stones and he is plunged into sorrow. Then he sees them and is overjoyed, but no, it's someone else's flock, double sorrow. The melody ends in a major key theme that makes you want to dance, like him, when he finally finds his flock.

Hurray! The buffalo emerged from a pine forest; gentle, intelligent, and something in them touched a nerve, perhaps the knowledge of what had befallen buffalo in the early years of Communism and then again in the years after it: wholesale slaughter.

Buffalo man's parents were caught up in the maelstrom of collectivisation, when every family was forced to gather stones to the tune of 1 cubic metre for the state co-operatives. This meant dismantling ancient chapels and forts in which the Struma abounded, just as the herds of buffalo and sheep had been dismantled. Buffalo man was trying to salvage something in the wake of that. Buffalo of various Mediterranean breeds roamed the Struma basin in large numbers in the 1930s. They were used as beasts of burden and for their milk, long valued for its health properties, but the arrival of mechanisation spelt doom for the indigenous buffalo. In the 1970s, agronomists noticed the decline and decided to boost their numbers *and* the milk productivity of those that remained. Black Murrah buffaloes were imported from India and mixed with the indigenous ones, to produce this breed, Bulgarian Murrah. Now, there were 10,000 individuals and their subsidised status encouraged breeders but not lovers, the same as with the other grazing animals. Buffalo man was a lover, but not specifically of buffalo. He was more into places. His dogs roamed with the buffalo and he didn't feed them except on visits like this. They too were free grazers, of the buffalo excrement, which he deemed nutritious, and whatever else they found in the hills. Definitely not a dog lover!

'What made you come back from Italy?'

'A dream,' he said.

We stood on a hillside with a view to three mountains and a chapel dedicated to St Elijah, who is our old friend Perun in light disguise.

In the dream, a woman instructed me: go there, see that and do this, he said. She showed me this chapel and its empty bell tower. I was to come back and have a bell made for it.

This is what he did. And he stayed, back in his homeland of rolling vineyards and ancient buried towns. He made proper money from the buffalo subsidies. He owned a lot of land which he sold to developers, plus grazing pastures and farm buildings, so when he showed me where he lived, I was taken aback. It was a shambolic hilltop bungalow, stuffed with old glass bottles and Roman and Thracian fragments, the worthless mixed with the priceless. He was treasure hunter, hoarder, shepherd, entrepreneur and wanderer, a child of this land. He didn't mind whether it was long-haired goats or black Murrah buffalo, as long as he continued to live inside the mountain.

To live inside the mountain rather than on top of it, you need a mission that involves gods or animals.

'What will happen when people like you are gone?' I said.

'There will be no more people like us and no more animals like us,' he said. 'The two are one.'

His grown-up children had no interest in the mountain. 'But I planted a grove of walnut trees for them,' he said. 'They can harvest them and make a living from it, if all else fails.'

Every evening, I stood on the bridge. The hot wind caressed my skin. The hot wind never reached Black Water but Black Water transmitted images and I caught them like radio frequencies, and I was transmitting my own to it. When I fled Black Water, I was sure I'd never reconnect with Sásho but this certainty had shifted, like everything. I had gone up with the flock, I had to come down with it. It wasn't Sásho, it was the flock I was waiting for. But it was the same thing.

'You inspire me to free myself of the drinking chains,' said Sásho on the phone.

He is on Horse Plaza. The godmothers are feasting. The wind is howling.

'It's not the wind, dear, it's several winds. I'm getting "Welcome to North Macedonia" and "Welcome to Greece" messages on my phone but I don't want to go to Greece or Macedonia. I just want to come down to you.'

Horse Plaza is another country and he is the only inhabitant, him and the ghost horses. He inspires me too. To face the void, again and again. The next day, he was on Etip's.

'I'm amusing myself writing our names with big stones but I've run out of stones to finish my name. Yours is more important anyway.'

The peaks glow and our valley is in shadow. I can see it as if I'm still there. I *am* still there. I left a shirt in the hut and he wears it at night. I'm smoking after years without it. I can't let go of the world we shared, this fairground of the mountain where you swing from terrifying heights over the abyss – and once you learn the ropes, you can't stop swinging.

I thought of all the other addicts I know, and they are many: those who have a bottle of wine every night, those with social media addictions who don't feel real unless they post something every day, those with food addictions, with addictions to social status, those addicted to criticising and complaining, those in co-dependent relationships and those who buy more stuff than they can use. They would be lost if you took it away from them. The way I am lost when I imagine spending the rest of my life in lower earth.

Velin looked like a wizened child in his large jeep.

'Ah, you're still here. It's that inebriation,' he said. 'Twenty-five years now I'm in love with the same mountain. I almost said the same woman.'

Not a happy story but a passionate one. He zoomed off, he was busy, we were all busy.

The dogs have lost weight, except Muna who is pregnant, Sásho reports the next day. 'I'll give them more food from now on. I have fourteen bags left. I hope Kámen doesn't bring up more bags 'cos he'll drive me mad.'

One thing that'll make it impossible to bring up more dog food is to get rid of Mimi and the saddle.

The other mare and the stallion went down, he reported. He tied Mimi to a pine tree to stop her, 'cos Kámen said to keep her but she pulled up the pine tree and went after them, tree and all. And he cut the rope and said: 'Go Mimi! That'll be me soon. If Kámen keeps me up here.'

Can a pine tree be uprooted by a horse? But I believed him.

Give the dogs less food, Kámen instructed him last time. He gave them more.

'Dear, I've got a blue eye. Yesterday, we were hacking pine kindling and a piece of it smacked me in the eye. Not lucky with eyes this year, but I have your drops.'

Then Johnny left Black Water. He'd lasted ten days. Once again, Sásho was alone.

'What are you doing here?' Kámen said. I'd driven up to Orelek to drop off a phone battery and socks for Sásho. I put the bag on the table.

'That blue eye Sásho's got. It's not from a splinter. He got a thrashing,' he said.

'What?' I said.

'A proper beating,' he said with relish. 'They were in the other hut. The Privateer's friend was there, the retired copper. He said something about you. Sásho punched him, there was a fight. That's why Johnny left.'

I felt sick. I didn't know what to believe. I left the smoky kitchen and drove past the lit-up centre where the kids sat around a fire, supervised by a limping Marina who was at breaking point from overwork and shouted at the kids for no reason. They looked at her the way the lambs looked at Balkán that nervy morning when he bit them on the necks.

It's hard to be a pastor of an unruly flock, exhausting to bend everything to your will. And it was harsh, being part of this circle, like a cult where taking leave or showing weakness makes you officially unfit.

At the waterfall, I burst a tyre on a sharp stone. I had no jack, only a spare tyre. I'd be damned if I called Kámen for help. There was Marina or else I abandoned the car and walked down to town in the darkness, past a hunting lodge with mean dogs, which would take an hour and the thought of which scared me.

And there with its uncanny timing came the windowless jeep. Stamen with his two boys and a sheep in the back, returning from Prairie. He pulled over. He looked like he hadn't slept lately. Like me, he didn't have a jack. We called Marina and she came down in her jeep like a limping knight in shining armour, leaving 'her kids' and 'her wolves' behind. They greeted each other curtly and she changed my tyre in no time. Next to Marina even Stamen looked helpless but his boys helped.

'You were an Amazon in another life,' I said. She smiled through her exhaustion.

'And in this one,' Stamen said.

(How many nights they'd climbed under the stars, looking for lost goat kids among the rocks and wolves – Stamen and Marina. How many rivers they'd crossed to look for dogs, sheep, wolves, over nine mountains to the tenth.

'I loved them,' Stamen said of the family. 'Do you know how it is to love someone and have them turn their back on you?'

Yeah. It makes you crazy.)

Marina, Kámen, Achilles and Stamen had this in common: their contract in life was not with humans but with animals. They needed challenges to feel alive and inside the living web challenge is guaranteed. Yet the force that had brought them together and made them perform miracles had also pushed them apart, like the other side of magnets. Now, each of them buckled under the weight of their messiah complex, injured and separate.

'I owe you one,' I said to Marina.

'You've given already,' she said. I'd volunteered at the centre for a couple of days because her colleagues were all sick. To her relief, the children were leaving tomorrow. 'But get yourself a jack. You've got to be self-sufficient, especially the way you're lucky with bears.'

Quick grins, then the three of us went our separate ways.

What did I learn? That I too have a saviour complex. They save animals and I save places and people. And sooner or later, you become bankrupt. Can't they see you are saving them? Can't they see how selfless you are? Ungrateful sods.

Every few days, I walk the long flat line of road and railway to the restaurant that sells sheep's milk and yogurt. The road to Orelek and Thunder Peak is deserted. I sit by the railway, stuck in a limbo. I can neither go up nor leave the gorge.

It is raining with Sásho, mud everywhere.

'How do you feel?' I ask.

'Like a dick in the wrong hands,' he sums up. 'Like the loopy lamb, number 1677.'

'I thought it was dead!'

'Nope, still here. And still spaced out. Goes off and doesn't come back to the pen and doesn't give a shit about the wolves.'

The 'loopy sheep' syndrome was well known to the Karakachans. At around one year of age in summer, a sheep can lose its mind and behave exactly like number 1677. They successfully treated this with trepanning, piercing a hole in the skull with a hot knife and 'draining the madness' or by pouring a salty yeasty sourdough kvass into the patient's mouth.

The pressure in my head is so great at times, trepanning isn't such a bad idea.

'Dear, I had a dream,' said Sásho on the phone. 'I had this medallion that shone like the sun and shadows chased me for it. I ran up some stairs to a flat where you waited for me. I grabbed you and we ran together to the roof of the building. The shadows came after us. We stood on the edge of the roof and there was nothing to be done, we jumped. And the medallion was magical because we sprouted wings and flew over Black Water.'

'What's that thundering noise with you, like the mountain's falling in?'

It's Black Water, so swollen from the rain that stones are flying down it and it's dangerous to get close. In the pen it's so muddy the sheep won't go in. They hate mud. The mud mixed with manure corrodes their hooves and causes 'crooked' sheep so they sleep next to the river and now, they have split on two sides of the river. How to get them back together?

'I'll wait for the river to go down again. There's no other way.'

The rain stopped and after dark the river decreased and he herded them to a place where it was easier to cross, and where the family of wolves prowled. But it wasn't the wolves that showed up that night. It was the bear. The bear came out of the pines. Sásho shone the torch on it. The dogs barked, then growled but the only ones who approached were Kito and Kasho. The flock, terrified, ran down the hill and straight to the pen. Karakachan dogs jump on the bear's back to avoid being clawed to death. Karakachan dogs fight to the death to protect their flock.

Kito and Kasho did not attack though, and neither did the bear. The dogs and the flock were agitated all night and Sásho expected another attack in the pen, but the bear didn't return.

And the eyeless ram? All that's left is his curly horns. Sásho took them to the hut and fixed them above the door. Every season leaves its souvenir in the hut, for the next ones to decipher. Our flag from the mountain rescue has been shredded away to nothing by the wind.

A lamb has lost sight in one eye and Sásho has run out of antibiotics. Kámen is not picking up his phone.

With all the rain, he is running out of dry wood. There is enough in Black Water for another two weeks. There's also no petrol left in the chainsaw and Kámen's van is broken, again. Because of the renewed zealous checks by park rangers, the flock can't be taken up so Sásho takes it down to Kamen klet. The thought of crossing and recrossing that eroded riverbank with all the animals appals me. He is sheltering from the wind in a ruined hut.

'There's an eagle that lives here,' he says. 'Keeps me company.'

I know the one. It flew out of that ruin when I fled.

A few hours later, he calls me again. I've been to the town market, talked to people, visited Andrea and he is back in our hut. A young sheep is missing. He is afraid it wandered down to The Beeches where it was nicked by Rocky, Stamen's shepherd. 'Cos it's a nice one and they're no strangers to nicking a sheep or five.

Why is Rocky down at The Beeches?

Because they've moved the whole flock from the huts to The Beeches. It is not clear whether they are taking the flock down for good or giving it a break from the lakes. That wouldn't make sense, it's too much work. Either way, the sheep is our loss and their gain.

'I'm giving the dogs a bag a day. We're down to fourteen bags. That's fourteen days.'

The lambs were really beefing out. 'They're like wrestlers,' Sásho said, 'short and wide, they can barely walk, that's how I amuse myself. Kámen will be pleased!'

The lamb that's gone blind in one eye now only goes to the left. ''Cos everything is left, left, left. Just like with Balkán it's out, out, out. It's a closed circle here.'

Wee Mouse was taken down on Kámen's back and Sásho was happy.

The other day, two hikers shouted after Sásho as he came down from Horse Plaza. 'There's a sheep and a dog! The dog'll hurt the sheep!'

We laughed. Topi had stayed behind with the loopy sheep. Sásho waited with the flock at the brown lake and the stoner came running to rejoin the flock, with proud Topi behind.

This is how September went, clinging to our floors of the mountain in suspense. I had a hunch that Kámen was deliberately holding things up and that I'd leave without seeing the flock come down, but maybe I was becoming paranoid. It was infectious. I look at giant Melo. It wouldn't take much for pieces of it to crash down. Chimney smoke rose over the rooftops. The trees whispered with September wind even as the August sun still heated the gorge. I envied the birds, the only ones that travelled between the lower and upper realms. In a single hour, a raven could peck the grapes in the gorge and the eyes of a dead sheep in Black Water. A raven could see the human sheep down here and the ovine people up there. I tried to see through the raven's eyes.

Cold morning in Black Water. A shepherd wakes up. 'Was that you snoring or me?' he says to the dog at his feet. He doesn't light the stove. He puts on his sheepskin coat and steps outside. The sheep are motionless. He checks up on the three lambs with diarrhoea, they seem better. He counts the bags of dog food. Ten. What a long life it's been. What a long summer, he'll never forget it. All he wants is to get them down safely and count them.

A few days later, Kámen called me from town. It was dark. I drove to Hotel Strymon, pleased that he wanted contact at last. We sat under the linden trees.

'What are you and Sásho plotting?' He threw his lighter on the table.

'Excuse me?' I said.

'Why is Sásho talking about mid-September? Who planted that idea?'

'He said Johnny wanted to come down in mid-month and that seemed a good time to bring them down,' I started explaining, but Johnny was gone.

'Stop talking on the phone, you're scrambling his brain!' Kámen said.

'We want a few days together in a normal environment,' I said.

'And what if you can't?'

I was stumped.

'Then that's life,' I said, not meaning it. Why did I appease Kámen when it was really him that was out of order?

Because I saw what he was up against and in this battle, I was on his side. But I also saw what I was up against: a battle of wills. In a regime of divide and rule, you need stamina and I had no intention of stepping down from the ring. Yes, Kámen, I could be *inat* too, stubborn to the point of self-harm. I'd come with a mission and I'd see it to the end.

'I know it's hard for you,' I said. 'But it's hard for him too.'

'I'm not saying it's easy for him. You wonder why I don't believe stories of inflamed eyes anymore but too many times he's cried wolf. It's like he does it for fun. You haven't known him long enough.'

The boy who cried wolf is as old as Aesop the fable-maker. There was once a young shepherd in the hills. Once, he cried wolf and the villagers went up to help but there was no wolf. Twice, he cried wolf and again – false alarm. Then one day, he cried wolf and nobody came. The wolf ate him and the flock.

Kámen's second worst fear after losing his flock was losing his shepherd.

'Isn't he due for a break when you bring them down?' I said.

I could've added: last time he came down for a break, he returned to you the same day and you never thanked him for it, or me.

'Why are *you* telling *me* when to bring my flock down and when my shepherd should rest?' Kámen said abruptly.

He stormed off to his van and put the headlights on. I was shaken, and his face too was on the brink of uncontrollable emotion, tears, even.

'Don't call me anymore,' he said and I didn't.

The nomads knew it: the freedom to move comes at a price: you cannot stay forever. Come end of season, you must load up your horses and take the road.

I walk in the golden light of Pirin, as if for the last time. Nothing I do can fill the emptiness. The date of the exodus slips back. I wake up in the middle of the night and hear an owl. Is it the end of season yet?

With Kámen, I keep hitting stone and with Sásho, there is no ground at all. Stamen is friendly but his agenda is inscrutable. Breeders and hired shepherds alike walk on moving sands. Trying to retain balance in a tug of loyalties, I've lost my peace of mind. The milky web is a web of complicated relationships that turn to intrigue. It's not for me.

'This is the south,' Sásho said. 'We specialise in intrigue.'

Then, Anton takes a break and goes home to Steelworks Limited. He calls and I go up to Orelek to fetch him because Kámen is busy. We have a coffee in the square and he treats himself to a newspaper. There can be no exodus until he comes back, because now Kámen will have to be goatherd. On the forecast, there is snow above 2,000 metres in the next ten days.

Down in Orelek, pasture is abundant because of the rain. It makes sense to have the flock back at Orelek soon and put an end to the hardship.

'If Kámen brings me more dog food, I'll chuck it in the river,' Sásho said. 'The dogs are all butched out. You won't recognise Topi. He's become like Balkán.'

And something else he told me later: he was giving some of the dog food to the sheep, to finish the bags sooner. The sheep enjoyed it.

I told Sásho about my run-in with Kámen.

'He's afraid,' Sásho said. 'That I'll run away with you. I won't.'

He never complained but there was a dreariness about being in Black Water now. It was wet, cold, comfortless and he was kept in the dark.

'I said to Kámen, if you don't come up in the next week, just leave it for next year won't you! Me and the godmothers will still be here. Just dig us out of the avalanche.'

We laughed.

'I could bolt like Mimi, pine tree and all, but I can't leave the kindergarten. They need me, dear. They're all my children.'

The wind nearly took the roof off the hut last night. Yesterday, he called Kámen. 'Can I come down just for a day?'

'No,' Kámen said. Sásho hung up, smashed his stick on a rock and screamed at the green lake. He was at Horse Plaza again. There was nothing but wind and tourists wrapped up and wearing wind glasses. They stopped and looked down at him. He screamed at them and they moved on.

To join the exodus, I must find out the date in advance, drive up to Orelek before dawn to catch Kámen and Achilles when they go up and suffer Kámen's bad blood again.

It is 1 degree at Black Water and minus 13 at Thunder Peak at night.

'Kámen is pissed off 'cos he has to be goatherd,' Sásho says. 'I know my livestock.'

I want to pack my stuff and go, end the heartache, the suspense, the power games and the stranglehold of the web. I have too many towels and pillows, plates and mugs and no one to share them with. Life is like that, either too much or not enough.

I can't tell anyone except Andrea that I'm waiting for Kámen's flock to come down, in case it gets him in trouble for being short of his three-month contract with the park. You can't hide the movement of 600 sheep, of course, but I am loyal to Kámen to the end, and when I run into Stamen in town again, and he casually says: 'I guess Kámen will be bringing them down,' I shrug. Because I don't trust Stamen the park ranger not to slap a fine on Kámen for falling short of his three months. When I ask 'When are you bringing yours down?' Stamen says 'We're staying to the end.'

But I know from the shepherds' grapevine that they are bringing them down to Prairie soon. You can't hide the movement of 600 sheep but this is part of the repertoire. It's like that when you have livestock. You can't trust anyone, not even yourself. Everything shifts, like the floors of the mountain. Sand blows from the Melo and makes the town turbid like a ruined kasbah. It wasn't just Crooked Yanko the horseman, all the animal people are crooked heroes. They take their animals over nine mountains to the tenth and cover up their tracks, like Hermes the messenger who delivers you to the underworld wearing his shoes backwards.

Shepherds used to have contests – outdancing, outplaying, out-singing and outlying each other, men and women alike. Who will tell the tallest tale. Sásho would win that one but Stamen would be a contender, while Kámen would get gold in the loaded-silence contest.

'People who love livestock are dangerous,' I said to Stamen under the linden trees. 'Cold to the touch, but underneath there's a furnace.'

He smiled darkly. He couldn't smile any other way.

'You've got us. The hearth is cold, you think the fire is gone. Then someone blows on the ashes. A spark flies and the fire looms. The passion, the mission, the fight to the end.'

In the cave church of Andrea's mother, I eat three figs on a plate and with her bloodless lips she utters:

'The sand ate up the body, dear. And set the soul free.'

She never speaks in the future tense. Everything has already happened on the material plane, as far as she is concerned. What we call events are variations on a couple of themes: birth and death. The important things happen between death and rebirth, among the stars.

But I want my soul to be free before the sand eats up my body. That's why I am here, a hostage to this metamorphic mountain. Can the soul be addicted?

That anything can happen any time, this is the vitality of the web. A fight breaks out over a choice ram, the goats have human faces, there's a rush of blood to the heart. You turn your life around for a dog, walk the earth for a horse, sleep with the flock for omens and fall in love with a sheep, but it's about the mountain.

The mountain is a god, and I believe in it.

'The humans are the animals and the animals are the humans, dear,' Sásho sums up.

One weekend, he calls, elated: they are coming down on Monday or Tuesday. I am desperate to join the exodus after six weeks of waiting but in the end I don't go. I know I have been excommunicated from Kámen's animal church, and I too have my pride.

A few nights before the exodus, I dream that I am with the flock, Sásho and the dogs. We are trying to get them down but there is fog. We are looking for a way across the river but it's wide and without banks. A river of fog. We must keep everyone together. The forest is grey, we are lost in time.

'Over here, dearest,' Sásho calls.

But not once do I see him. I only hear his voice, and some sheep bells. I have three dogs with me, then just one. It's Sunny or Topi, a young male with a head like the sun, but something bad can happen to him. He is protecting me and I am protecting him. I cannot make it across the river. The dog knows how I feel. He stands for Sásho.

The exodus happens on Monday. Kámen and Achilles drive up to The Beeches early in the morning. Sásho meets them halfway down at Kamet klet with the flock and as much luggage as he can carry; kitchen things will have to be left in the hut. Sásho and Achilles get

the flock safely to Orelek in eight hours. Achilles records the event
with his camera and Sásho herds them home where Kámen anxiously
awaits. It's another seasonal rite of passage.

The evening before the exodus, it rained heavily in Black Water. A
group of German hikers got stranded and pitched tents across from
our hut. Sásho watched them fail to light a fire with wet wood and
waded across the risen river to take kindling to them. Then he gave
the last of the lentil stew to Muna, packed his stuff and my remaining
things and lay in bed, listening to the rain drum on the roof. The
sheep were in the pen and he worried about mud getting into their
hooves just before the exodus, about fog, about how much time we'd
have together, about everything. Now that the exodus was imminent
and after weeks of suspense, it all felt daunting. Facing lower earth
after two months in Black Water is like leaving the army and finding
yourself in civvy street. You are a war veteran and nobody cares.

In the morning, the last fire of the season had gone out in the
stove. Who would rekindle it next July? He picked up his stick and
opened the pen.

'Come on darlings, we're going home.'

Vasko was staying to the end, another three weeks. Alone. He
never complained about the snow that started falling two days later.

'I woke up this morning and – pines and snowflakes!' he said to
Sásho on the phone later. 'Father Christmas is coming to town!'
Read: The Privateer was bringing up provisions.

Sásho and I had a week together in a village near his border town,
called Katuntsi, rug people, because people and animals of the rug
had lived there since the Middle Ages. Katunari. Chergari. Gypsies.
A horse fair was held here once. When the thing is gone, the name
remains.

'It'll be like that with the shepherd one day,' Sásho said.

In the mornings he wanted to 'let them out' and check the sky for
rainclouds. I saw hills, he saw grazing itineraries. A small flock of
white sheep passed through the sleepy village every day and he
couldn't watch them without getting involved.

'*Brrrr. Shhht.* Why are they so skinny? Those ones are lagging.'

Post-traumatic shepherd's disorder. The English owners of the

Anima

guesthouse had rescued dogs, including a Karakachan, and this eased the change from the animal to the human world. We watched a reality TV show called *The Farm*: people with manicures and designer goatees had breakdowns trying to milk a cow. It was not the milking that caused their mental collapse but the need for self-reliance. We managed to share wine in a controlled way, cooked, played ping-pong, gathered walnuts and drove over the bleached Strymonian country that Sásho had escaped as a child, only to end up in prison. It was a silent land wrapped in the vapours of hot springs, criss-crossed by the hooves of wanderers, tattooed with messages in a forgotten language. The winds of fortune still met at these crossroads and we are their children.

On the day of the exodus, the flock arrived in Orelek at six in the evening, in one piece. Then, it was straight into the Orelek routine for Sásho: check the flock for injuries, feed the dogs, dump his rucksack in a dirty room where the rubbish hadn't been thrown out for two months.

Scenes from Stamen's family came to me: at the end of September, his young grandparents load a horse with a tin of stuffed pastry and a jug of wine and trek to the huts. The shepherds feast before the return exodus. It is still the old ways, before collectivisation smashed them. When they bring the flock down, his grandmother hands each of them a pile of socks and undershirts she has knitted from the finest-spun wool and his grandfather hands them their wages. The shepherds take the road back to their villages. They'd become attached to the flock and the dogs and life in a small male commune; some of them cry when they leave, not knowing what kind of winter lay ahead and whether they would be back next May.

Kámen had made an effort. He had cooked a stew to welcome Sásho back, and rice pudding. After all, the casualties were not big this summer: out of 600, we'd lost the ram, the sheep crushed during the storm, two others who died from illness and the nice one that was lost at Kamen klet.

Then, just before midnight, when he ran out of more important things to do, he took Sásho down.

'There's a delivery of fodder on Friday,' Kámen said in the car. 'Will you be back by then?'

'I might be,' Sásho lied. Then to me on the phone: 'I'm down.'

I walked through the empty streets of Kresna, followed by owl hoots. It was six weeks since I had said goodbye to Black Water.

He stood under the linden trees in the empty square, reduced by hardship, with a faded bruise under his eye that could have been from an accident or a fight. It was odd to see him without the flock and the dogs. He had no bag.

'I'm late,' Sásho stepped out of the darkness, the gap in his smile.

There was a formal moment before we hugged so tightly that nothing could have prised us apart. Just as it should be at the end of a successful end-of-season exodus from Black Water.

ORELEK, WINTER.
SCOTLAND, WINTER

The trees lose their leaves first in Orelek, then in my Scottish river-side village.

After three months away, my spaniel Bella is surprised to see me – Oh, it's you! – but the forgiveness is instant. She was a puppy when I left her in the care of my closest friend. Now she is a toddler with long legs and remembers the layout of the house and our routines as if there's never been a break. Thank you, Bella. You blunt the shock of losing the dogs of Orelek.

In Orelek, it's business as usual. Sásho takes the godmothers out – all 500 of them pregnant – checks for injuries and pulls his hood up against the cold drizzle.

'Come on girls, it's another lovely day! You're a pain in the ass, all of you.'

The dogs are so happy to see him after a week away that all of them follow him into the hills, not just the regular workers but the Loopies too, who have never been out with the flock, plus Baguer the Digger and Kalina-Malina. That's sixteen dogs! It's a festival.

'Never seen anything like it!' bai Anton mutters. Kámen is banging doors.

Sásho sends me clips of Topi, Kito and Kasho who have all beefed up, Sunny who is a man now but is attacked by the other males who don't consider him part of the pack anymore, Karamana who looks serene after giving birth to four fluffy ones, two of whom are black and white like her and two blond, like Sunny. Kámen sells two of them. They come with pedigree certificates, and these ones are from the lineage of the Karakitans.

Kalina-Malina becomes so attached to Sásho she bites the other dogs when they approach and is jealous even when he is on the phone.

When the lambs are born, she climbs onto Sásho's back to stop him handling them.

Loopy Junior has come out, fat and short-eared and excited to be roaming the hills like a real dog. He is so pleased with his new job that he sleeps in the open pen now and growls at anyone who approaches him as if he is a pet, like Kámen's mother who is here for the winter. She is put out by the dog's transformation. Because in this household, people don't change.

Mama Metsi on her three legs is going with the flock too. How will she keep up? 'With breaks,' Sásho says. They just don't want to be in the house.

'They want love,' Sásho says. 'Like everybody.'

The autumn light of Orelek is poignant. On the phone, I see all the places where I went with him. He is walking inside a memory, trying to combine being there and not being there.

'I'm wandering in a lost world,' he says. 'Who's gonna take up the crook from me? I can't do this forever, dear. Nearly ten years. I've become unfit for human society.'

The only dog that is missing is Muna the Monkey. She has given birth somewhere and nobody tells him anything. Sásho feels more isolated than ever on the island of Orelek. Phone signal is poor. Our rhythms are out of sync and we live in different time zones. In a moment of despair, he smashes his phone on a rock and cuts off contact with the world for a week. It's the longest we haven't spoken and not knowing what's wrong, I get an anxiety attack and he has a hypertension attack and ends up in the cardiology department of the nearest hospital.

Later, we learn that on that day Muna the Monkey died.

'Ah yes, your beloved is gone,' the mother breaks it to him. 'Swelled up and died.'

Post-partum complications, we guess. Her two puppies also died. Balkán will only ever be a father to the sheep. Muna's death is not discussed in the house and initially, Sásho takes it in his stride, but later becomes stricken.

It takes months for both of us to accept it.

'She understood me.'

'And me.'

'There was not another like her.'

'She was always with you. She had three voices.'

'She was a useless guard dog.'

'And a great person.'

'I remember when she was born. She was always different.'

'She was right not to want to get pregnant.'

'I kept her from it for three years.'

'She should have stayed down.'

'Some things can't be stopped, dear.'

How quickly a world becomes lost.

'Kalina is the new Monkey, eh Kalinka-Malinka?' he consoles himself and she covers his face in kisses. Soon, the other orphan comes up with him too, Malina-Kalina, who was a fluffball in July. She is a toddler now. She and Kalina-Malina are stepsisters, but the older girl doesn't let the younger one get close to Sásho.

'Monkey was mellow,' Sásho said. 'Kalina is aggressive. They're unique.'

'Like people.'

'Not like, dear. They *are* people. And people are the animals.'

Then he goes on a week-long bender, sobering up just enough in the mornings to take the flock out. He spins into chaos, wolves attack the flock and kill sheep in broad daylight despite the dogs, Sunny is poisoned by evil hunters but survives, Barut nearly strangles himself on a wire trap hung on a tree by the same hunters, Kámen has it out with Sásho about the wolf attacks, Sásho decides to leave but stays, sobers up forever, then a month later the cycle is repeated. He ages before my eyes. Distraught, I walk away from the phone, only to come back when he sobers up and vows to change. He finally admits that he is an addict and needs help.

'Last night, I dreamt that you reached out your hand to me across a river. I'm trying to catch it but can't. These shadows are at my back. And you move on without me.'

'And I dreamt that I came to the ghetto with Kámen to look for you. We drove up this dead-end road lined with Gypsy women and mountains of colourful stuff. They were once chergari and now they're in this rubbish dump selling their rugs. I knew you'd left and taken the road, but Kámen was still looking for you 'cos people don't change, and we argued in the car until we reached the dead end and turned back.'

'Your dream is spot on, I must break the circle open and make a new path out of it. And you have to write this book.'

In Scotland, it is all snow and dogs on leads. In Orelek, it's rain and wolves. Like in that winter before the schism. They shadow the flock at Fat Oaks, they lurk by the river, they keep attacking sheep at the reservoir and Kito, Kasho and Readhead push them back, but the wolves turn up again above the pen, where Vachka and the hybrid are still loving each other across a fence.

The lambing starts in November and doesn't let up for two months. It's like a calamitet. Hundreds of sheep are giving birth, sometimes ten at a time, out in the hills and in the pen at night. Sásho pulls out lambs, makes sure the mother doesn't reject the baby or crush it, ties sisal string to a clump of hair to mark them as postpartum, then paints mother and child with a unique symbol – two dots, three dots, so they can keep track of them, and carries lambs in his pockets to keep them warm. Sometimes, a ram comes to the birthing sheep and lies down next to her. The newborns are blind for the first few hours and follow the mother by voice and smell. They are tough things, on their legs immediately, resistant to cold and suckling with gusto. This instant resilience sets them apart from other breeds.

'In two months, these wee mice will be so strong, when they butt the tit the mothers jump up from the impact.'

Baaa, beeereee. Voices fill the hills. The Model gives birth to twins and rejects them, but they attach themselves to surrogate mothers. The rams are separated from the sheep and placed in their open pen across from the house, with Spintop on his chain. 'They'll eat without fucking,' Sásho sums up, 'that's the way here.' Newborns who are too small are collected in the hills by Kámen, who drives up when Sásho calls him with fingers covered in afterbirth.

In the clips he sends me, I get it, how pastoral communes worked. When an animal gives birth, there's no yours and mine, you must bring that lamb to light and get it to suckle. I also see how easy it is for lambs to move from one sheep to another. It suckles where it can, and stays on, and this is how you can shift quite a few lambs over to your flock.

When a sheep gives birth in the hills, the dogs come and lie beside her and when the newborns take their first steps, the dogs look proud like parents, then they eat the placenta. Sásho is proud too. Even frozen, wet and sapped by sleep deprivation, he beams each time he pulls out a little black lamb the size of a kitten, head folded to its legs, then strokes the mother.

'Look at my babies! Look at my brave girl. This morning I've had fifteen.'

They are quiet but occasionally they groan with human voices. A sheep of this breed normally gives birth to one lamb but there are freakish numbers of twins. There are over 600 newborns, a madhouse.

'What did you do with them up there!' Kámen mutters.

In the summer, Kámen was worried about lambs dying at birth. Now he is worried about too many healthy ones. The twins are a strain on the mothers. There is no space in the pen and by March it's a stampede, 600 lambs run around going '*Beeeee*' in their sweet and comical voices. Before Christmas, Kámen manages to sell 100 pregnant sheep to another stockbreeder downstream.

Everyone is exhausted and comes down with colds but not a single day can be taken off. A helper is brought in, a Roma man who spent years on a horse farm in Germany until he was kicked and maimed by a horse. He is a recovering alcoholic who wrecked his life. He and Sásho share a room, duties and life stories, he helps Sásho go teetotal and they are together with the flock in Dragon hill when a massive bear comes out of the bushes and walks just metres away from them. Sásho sends me a close-up photograph worthy of *National Geographic*. But the helper leaves in the spring and once again Sásho is alone. The flock has never been stronger, larger or more spectacular. The future has never been more uncertain. Kámen has raised Sásho's pay to 600 euros a month and tries to support him in quitting the drink.

I walk with Bella past enclosures where sheep graze all year round. I recognise the brown Hebridean sheep with horns and black ragged sheep I've not noticed before that look like the Karakachan ones and have the same wild look in their eye. They are from the western isles of Scotland. I send a photo to Stamen who writes back: 'Gorgeous. Let's steal some.'

But the white Cheviot sheep rules over Scotland in a case of mass import that was deemed more productive in meat and wool than the native ones. Enclosed sheep behave differently to their free-grazing cousins, I notice. They are always scattered, there is no need to herd them, they only move them from paddock to paddock. Their lives are safe and dull.

I miss the goat's milk and sheep's yogurt. I examine the packaging of the plant beverage I drink, made from oats. I drink this 'milk' because I can't digest cow's milk or even the goat milk I buy in cartons from a stationary goat farm in England (but milk from long-haired free-grazing goats agreed with me). The packaging is covered in hipsterish chat: 'What cow does oat milk come from?' or 'Don't read this bit if you are bored'. There is nothing particularly ethical or cool about drinking almond, soya, oat and hazelnut 'milk' from single-crop groves far away from me that are sometimes planted where forests were felled or where free-grazing animals roamed. Those crops are harvested by people I'll never meet and carried by trucks along motorways that wreck the Kresna Gorge, so that I can sip my vegan latte.

Yet here are the sheep and cows within strolling distance of my house, whose milk would be the most ethical, healthy, economical and ecological milk for my village. I look up the sheep breeds of Europe and Central Asia and it's clear at once: in Central Asia, sheep and goat milk is still going strong, a reflection of preserved pastoral practices. In Europe, the sheep kept for milk rather than for meat alone are found in the extreme south. That's the entire Balkans up to Croatia, plus Italy, Spain and the French Pyrenees. This map overlaps with the map of the earliest pastoralists. It is a map of a Europe industrialised much later or not at all. There is a crofting family with goats near me, but they are not legally allowed to sell me the milk because they lack the proper health or trading certificate. This is all wrong.

The lambing season in Scotland starts in April and I wait for the little ones to appear in the fields. By then, the wee mice of Orelek will be fat, about 150 of them will go into ovens for Easter, and the milking of the ewes will start at the same time. The Scottish hills are snowy and when I look at Ben Wyvis, I also see Little Horse. I am between pastures, overwintering until next season when I must load up and go on the road again or suffer the madness of limbo.

In January, a mountain drone spots a frozen body by the green lake, in the place where the four of us sat that first time: Kámen, me, Sásho and Vasko. The rescue team, which includes Stamen, retrieve a second body: seasoned climbers who had gone up alone. One had died in an attempt to save the other.

Vasko continues to herd The Privateer's cows. They will keep taking them somewhere high, laws or no laws. Come spring, long before the grass burns, the cows bolt up the mountain like wild horses. You can't stop them.

Vanya returned to her old job as a cowgirl and Constantin went back to school, 'but here too we have unsavoury characters.'

Andrea continues to make the best fresh cheese in the gorge.

Ugrin the Radio was delighted with the new generation of goat kids. He might have to grow the herd after all. He couldn't bear to sell them for their skins.

Velin the Grape moved back to the capital with his mother. Sásho and I fantasised about buying his house together, he would go with the flock and bring me sheep's milk and I'd write and make yogurt. Then he lost his phone again.

Marina received a bag from an anonymous local and inside it was the severed head of a wolf. A gift that was both a message from the hunters – you can't stop us – and an offering – since we've killed the wolf, you might as well memorialise it and put it up in your 'hotel'. And that's what she did: she had it mounted by a taxidermist for the centre. It's not every day you come across a perfect wolf's head.

Stamen is building a large base with dairy rooms above the gorge.

'But we need women, men, children. Like-minded people who are into mountain breeds. Sheep, goats, dogs.' He now employed Bimo, Kámen's old shepherd, who was fresh out of prison for drunk driving.

'Doesn't he howl at night?'

'Nobody's perfect,' Stamen said. A few months later, Bimo took some money from the house and vanished.

Stamen would even swallow his pride and work with Kámen again, he said, to rebuild something from the ashes of their first commune. There was a détente with Achilles and Marina. When she came to Orelek, they'd go in search of the horses together, like in the old days.

'When we start climbing she smiles. And when Marina smiles, it's like the sun comes out again,' Stamen said.

But Kámen kept a cold eye on Stamen's manoeuvres. Stamen's empire was outsized now. What's more, in the spring he made a big breakthrough with his colleagues across the border, to coincide with the opening of a new border checkpoint: they would work together for the restoration of the Karakachan sheep and dogs. There was now a third official nucleus flock in Macedonia and rams were already being exchanged, this time without smuggling manoeuvres, and bypassing Kámen in Orelek. Like a territorial dragon, Stamen blew his fire-and-ice breath over two mountains now: Pirin and Maleshevo. He didn't want his name carved in stone, no, but he wanted these animals to roam these mountains forever.

Meanwhile, with a heavy heart, Kámen decided to halve his goats, down to fifty. The rest were sold. Bai Anton was stricken, even if it meant less work for him. To compensate for the loss, and egged on by Sásho who wants to lead the largest flock in the gorge, Kámen decided to double the number of sheep. Again. Just for the hell of having 1,200 of the world's oldest sheep.

Last night, coming down from Prairie, Stamen crossed Kámen in Orelek. They stopped. The only two people under the January moon.

'Nobody but you and I go round this mountain at night,' said Stamen.

'Just you and I at the finishing line,' said Kámen.

'Aye. It's endgame,' said Stamen.

Kámen lit a cigarette and smiled to himself. Stamen drove down in his windowless jeep, his jaw set.

When Sásho and I speak, my location on Google maps doesn't show at all because I walk an overgrown river path. The river where I live birthed one of Scotland's great glens. Sásho's location is shown as 'Road with No Name'. I know where he is, above the river that birthed Spartacus and the oldest sheep in the world. Some places are indelible from the inner map.

It came as a surprise to all when reconstruction work began on the road to Orelek. The first dig was done at Warm Spout, at the fork in the road. By next season, the road would be good for the first time in living memory and it would change Orelek's fortunes. 'For the worse,' Velin muttered. 'The new-rich will buy up the place and move in with their hunting parties and the logging mafia will carry out the forest faster.' True, the road opened up the whole side of the mountain. The new road would lift the old curse of Orelek but might bring a new one. I had found this place at the end of an era.

All winter and spring, Sásho performed the twelve labours of Orelek. Cleaning Kámen's stables, tracking the wolves that stalked the flock, delivering 'uncounted' lambs, keeping the dog of Kámen's depression at bay – but the hardest was slaying the hydra of the bottle. Every few weeks, he'd take a short break and spiral into chaos. Other people used his phone and I'd get distressing calls, he rode river, road and train in a fugue leaving wreckage behind, then returned to his cell in Orelek and the bargaining and explaining began on the phone. With a coil of sisal rope in his hand, to hang himself if I gave up on him. From his river to mine, the wheel came off the Gypsy cart and crashed through my days. I had left Black Water but it hadn't left me.

'You told me you were in one place and you were in another. Drunk. You lied!'

'It wasn't a lie, it's how I wanted it to be. See, you're the writer and I'm the shepherd who cried wolf. We're like twins.'

'And the wolf will get you in the end. I fell out with Kámen to defend you but you drive everyone away.'

'It's you that's driving me away. Watch out or I'll get hitched with Kámen. He doesn't like women and you are far away. We might as well.'

'I think you're a perfect match. You're the only person that can put up with him. And he wants to spend the rest of his life with you.'

One day in winter, he began therapy for addiction. He found a psychiatrist in his border town and in the frozen hills of Orelek he walked and talked to the psychiatrist, newborns inside his jacket.

'Lie down and relax, he tells me. But I can't lie down, there's snow on the ground and the godmothers are giving birth!'

'But this psychiatrist isn't registered anywhere. Have you made him up?'

'No dear, it's that he isn't completely real himself. All psychiatrists are like that.'

'I dreamt that three zombie dogs chased Bella to kill her,' I said. 'I think that's post-traumatic stress.'

'Last night, I dreamt I went to Black Water again. You were calling me from the dwarf-pines. Sáshooo! The flock heard you and went up the waterfalls and split in two. They re-joined but I couldn't find you. You'd given up on me. Don't give up on me.'

But I had to. Giving up my hope of his miraculous redemption was like letting go of the drink for him. Unless you are Jesus, you cannot redeem another, only yourself. The world is not yours to save, it has its own destiny. A sobering potion.

Sásho said he couldn't face another season in Black Water. He was afraid of relapsing into the drink but neither could he leave Kámen before a replacement was found. There was no replacement for him, and he couldn't imagine life without the dogs.

'When I leave, I want to take Muna the Monkey with me,' he said.

That's what he called one of Karamana and Sunny's puppies. Like the original Muna, she had a face full of premonition. I miss them.

During that hard-earned week of rest in the village of the rug people, we dropped into Sásho's family house in his border town. It was a handsome three-storey house, each floor an apartment. We jumped the fence like thieves. He had no key and there was no need, the doors were missing. Dogs and cats squatted inside and family albums and chess manuals lay chewed on the ground. The furniture was piled up in the corners.

'I'll fix it,' Sásho saw my shock. 'I'll build you a balcony with a mountain view!'

But he wouldn't even put doors in the hinges. Why would he? A rug, at most, to stop snowdrifts. He was a soul of the rug, he was born that way. We are all born that way but only a few are left, to walk for the rest, so we don't completely forget what we are.

Black fugitives. Walkers. Citizens of the earth with its moving rugs of animals, seasons, waters and feelings.

The ground would never stop moving under Sásho's feet. He would follow the rainbow to the edge of the cliff each time. All my life, I have wandered some hinterland looking for the sore delinquents, the lunatic bards, those caught out by genocide, the wanderers with the last of the rugs. My old, dangerous family. I too hate this about the road, dear: you just get used to something and then you have to go.

Last night, I dreamt I went to Black Water again. Me, Sásho and Constantin sit inside the hut by the lit stove. The dog-wolves are silent outside, the flock breathes. The boy is in the middle and he is not a boy anymore. I look over at Sásho. He is asleep with his head on Constantin's shoulder. Let him sleep, he is tired. We are all safe in this moving picture.

We will meet again in the spiral clock of the stars. Till then, like in that song, we are left with three medicine pots, the bitterest one for the night when ghosts lie next to us and the wind howls. Like the settled nomads, I will visit the old haunts from time to time, glimpse Emin's horses in the distance, Kámen's black sheep under the white peak and their mirror flock on Stamen's side of the ridge, the sixteen dogs that loved Sásho, I'll drink from the spring that only shepherds know and listen out for Marina's wolves.

Those who know this mountain like a person will always look back.

And when the sand eats up the body and sets the soul free, we won't be separate and injured anymore. I look forward to it.

ACKNOWLEDGEMENTS

Human protagonists and some places appear with pseudonyms or in translation. Among others, Thunder Peak is Vihren, Little Horse is Koncheto, and Prairie is Polena. Some biographical details have been omitted for discretion. All experiences are true to life and unadorned.

I thank all of the people who helped to make this book by letting me into their lives and sharing their knowledge and passion. Many thanks also to the brilliant team at Jonathan Cape, and my agent Sarah Chalfant.

For the record, the Kalofer goat is long-haired and the Vitorog goat is curly-horned; when they are both long-haired and curly-horned, they are Kalofer goats.

The original titles of some of the songs quoted are as follows: 'The Lost Flock' is Izgubenoto stado (Изгубеното стадо), 'The Mountain Has Overturned' is Prituri se planinata (Притури се планината). I have quoted from some of the following works. They all contributed to my grasp of pastoralism, nomadic movements, mountain ecology, indigenous animals and people and local history. Other works quoted are by ancient authors and include *The Geography of Strabo* (transl. by Duane W. Roller) and Herodotus's *The Histories* (transl. by Aubrey de Sélincourt).

Пътуване по долините на Струма, Места и Брегалница (*A Journey of the Struma, Mesta, and Bregalnitsa Rivers*) by Vassil Kanchov

Местните породи кози в България (*Autochthonous Goat Breeds of Bulgaria*) by Atanas Vachkov

Биоразнообразие на Кресненския пролом (*Biodiversity of Kresna Gorge*) ed. by Petar Beron

Brave and Loyal by Cat Urbigkit

Goatwalking by Jim Corbett

In Defence of Dogs by John Bradshaw

Каракачаните в България (*The Karakachans of Bulgaria*) by Jenya Pimpireva

'*Каракачанското куче*' ('The Karakachan Dog') articles by Venelin Dinchev, Sider and Atila Sedefchev

Where the Souls Rest (*Къде душите си почиват*), a film by Boyan Papazov

По пътя (*On the Road*) by Krasimira Krastanova, Meglena Zlatkova, Maria Kisikova, Elitsa Stoilova

Принос към изучаването на произхода, бита и културата на Каракачаните в България (*Study of the Origins, Lifestyle and Culture of the Karakachans of Bulgaria*) by Vassil Marinov

The Caravan Moves On by Irfan Orga

'The Preservation of Autochthonous Breeds of Domestic Animals in Bulgaria' by Jordan Danchev

'Study on the Current State of the Karakachan Sheep Breed in Bulgaria, in Order to Assess the Risk in Conservation as a Genetic Resource' ('*Съвременно състояние на породата Каракачанска овца в България, и оценка на риска при съхранението*') by Atanas Vuchkov, Boyko Stoyanov, Sider Sedefchev, Atila Sedefchev and Todor Georgiev

Влахи (*Vlahi*) by Todor Drachov

Βλάχοι (*Vlahi*) by Nikolay Yankov and Elena Shtereva

'*Устна традиция, митове, легенди, празници, музика и танци*' ('Culture and Nature: The European Heritage of Sheep Farming and Pastoral Life') by Georg Kraev, Natalia Rashkova, Leonora Boneva and Svetla Rakshieva

Юруците (*The Yuruks*) by Alexei Kalyonski

KAPKA KASSABOVA is a poet and prose writer and most recently the author of *Elixir* (2023), *To the Lake* (2020), and *Border* (2017). *Border* won a British Academy Prize, the Scottish Book of the Year, Stanford-Dolman Travel Book of the Year, the Highland Book Prize and the Prix Nicholas Bouvier. It was also a finalist for the National Book Critics Circle Award. The French edition of *To the Lake* won the Prix du Meilleur Livre Etranger (nonfiction). Kassabova grew up in Sofia, Bulgaria, and studied in New Zealand. Today she lives by a river in the Scottish Highlands. *Anima* is the final book in her Balkan quartet exploring the relationship between humans and their environment, following *Border*, *To the Lake*, and *Elixir*.

The text of *Anima* is set in Bembo Book MT Pro.
Book design and composition by Jouve (UK), Milton Keynes.
Manufactured by Versa Press on acid-free,
30 percent postconsumer wastepaper.